# Dark Green

# Reimagining Ireland

**Volume 114**

Edited by Dr Eamon Maher,
Technological University Dublin – Tallaght Campus

PETER LANG
Oxford • Bern • Berlin • Bruxelles • New York • Wien

# Dark Green
## Irish Crime Fiction 1665–2000

**David Clark**

Oxford • Bern • Berlin • Bruxelles • New York • Wien

Bibliographic information published by Die Deutsche Nationalbibliothek. Die Deutsche Nationalbibliothek lists this publication in the Deutsche Nationalbibliografie; detailed bibliographic data is available on the Internet at http://dnb.d-nb.de.

A catalogue record for this book is available from the British Library.

Library of Congress Cataloging-in-Publication Data

Names: Clark, David, 1956 May 31- author.
Title: Dark green : Irish crime fiction 1665-2000 / David Clark.
Description: Oxford ; New York : Peter Lang, [2022] | Series: Reimagining
   Ireland, 1662-9094 ; vol no.114 | Includes bibliographical references
   and index.
Identifiers: LCCN 2022016555 (print) | LCCN 2022016556 (ebook) | ISBN
   9781800798267 (paperback) | ISBN 9781800798274 (ebook) | ISBN
   9781800798281 (epub)
Subjects: LCSH: English fiction--Irish authors--History and criticism. |
   Crime in literature. | Detective and mystery stories, Irish
   (English)--History and criticism. | Spy stories, English--History and
   criticism. | LCGFT: Literary criticism. Classification: LCC PR8807.C74 C58 2022
(print) | LCC PR8807.C74 (ebook)
   | DDC 823/.0872099415--dc23/eng/20220604
LC record available at https://lccn.loc.gov/2022016555
LC ebook record available at https://lccn.loc.gov/2022016556

Cover image: Silvia Vázquez Lorenzo.
Cover design by Peter Lang Ltd.

ISSN 1662-9094
ISBN 978-1-80079-826-7 (print)
ISBN 978-1-78997-893-3 (ePDF)
ISBN 978-1-80079-828-1 (ePub)

© Peter Lang Group AG 2022

Published by Peter Lang Ltd, International Academic Publishers,
Oxford, United Kingdom
oxford@peterlang.com, www.peterlang.com

This publication has been peer reviewed.

*For Aila and Erea*

# Contents

# Acknowledgements

I'd like to thank my colleagues from the "Amergin" Institute for Irish Studies at the University of Coruña and from the Faculty of Philology who have encouraged me and given me technical and moral support during the long years of gestation of this project. Heartfelt thanks, therefore, to Antonio de Toro, Eduardo Barros, J. Miguel A. Giráldez, José Manuel Estévez Saá, María Jesus Lorenzo and Teresa Seoane. Thanks also to the postgraduate students who have helped me, including, but not only, Clara Rodríguez, Rocío Moreno, Yarizán Pan, Paula García and Silvia Vázquez. And special thanks to Ciarán Mac Dáibhí, my Irish-language advisor.

Working on Irish literature from Galicia, culturally and emotionally close to Ireland in so many ways, but still a long and costly geographical distance away, especially in times of pandemic, I have bought a large number of books, and recall with particular affection tracking down hard-to-find copies of works by J. B. O'Sullivan and Sheila Pim. I would, however, have been lost had it not been for the excellent work of the librarians at my university, both in the central and in the faculty libraries who have helped me to obtain numerous inter-library loans. My thanks also to the helpful staff at the National Library of Ireland, Trinity College Library, the National Library of Scotland, the British Library and the Biblioteca Nacional de España in Madrid.

Grateful thanks to the great team at Peter Lang who have been most helpful in every moment.

Thanks also to my friends and colleagues in the Spanish Association for Irish Studies (AEDEI), the Spanish James Joyce Society, the European Federation for Centres and Institutes of Irish Studies (EFACIS) and the International Association for Studies in Irish Literature (IASIL). And thanks to Galicia, for giving me a home away from home.

Ba mhaith liom mo leithscéal a ghabháil freisin, mar fhoghlaimeoir Gaeilge, gur foinsí tánaisteacha den chuid is mó iad mo chuid foinsí do shaothair Ghaeilge. De réir mar a thagann feabhas ar mo chuid Ghaelige, tá súil agam níos mó leabhar a léamh sa teanga seo.

This work is part of the activities being carried out in the context of the research project "NEMICATID: Aesthetics, Ethics and Strategics of the New Migratory Cartographies and Transcultural Identities in Twenty-First-Century Literature(s) in English (2007–2019)" (PID2019-109582GB-100), funded by the Spanish Ministry of Science and Innovation (MCI/AEI/FEDER, UE)

# Introduction

Cain killed Abel, Prometheus stole the divine fire, and Daedalus was wrongfully imprisoned. Cú Chulainn killed Connla, Queen Medb tried to steal the stud bull Donn Cúailnge, and Diarmuid and Gráinne were subjected to a ferocious manhunt. Crime narratives have existed for as long as humankind has told stories. Irish crime writing has existed for almost as long as has the genre itself, and indeed has provided the English language with many of the great specialists in the field. Until recently, however, Irish exponents of the genre have generally been included within an English or British tradition of crime writing, and this status has not been repudiated by the large number of Irish writers who have set their fiction within a markedly English context, translating their criminal narratives to English geographical and social settings. Thus writers such as Eilís Dillon and Nigel Fitzgerald, both working in the middle of the twentieth century and both of whom purposely set their novels in Ireland, are in a minority when compared with all the writers who located their works in England. In this study, Irish crime writing is widely considered to be that which is produced by writers born on, or who are or have been resident in, the island, regardless of the setting of such works. As for Elizabeth Mannion, an Irish setting will be "an option rather than a criterion for defining".[1] An American writer such as Bartholomew Gill is included both for his long term residence in Ireland but also for the relevance his works had at the time of their production, their popularity in Ireland and the influence they had on subsequent Irish crime writers. Dicey Deere or Anne C. Fallon will not be included, despite the latter's surprising appearance in an anthology of Irish crime fiction. Just as an Irish setting is an option, it is not the only criterion for inclusion in this study. Some writers of doubtful "Irishness", such as L. A. G. Strong, have

---

1    Elizabeth Mannion (ed.), *The Contemporary Irish Detective Novel* (London: Palgrave Macmillan, 2016), 2.

been included for motives which are generally made clear in the sections dedicated to them, and other non-Irish writers have been included for a variety of reasons. Lionel Shriver and Chris Petit, for example, made a significant contribution to the Troubles thriller, which this work wishes to acknowledge.

The linguistic question is also of great importance, as Irish crime fiction has generally been written in English, while attempts at writing in the Irish language "have generally floundered".[2] Caitlín Nic Íomhair admits that crime writing in Irish was scarce during the period covered by this volume, and only started "to gain traction" at the start of the new millennium.[3] Nevertheless, she stresses the case of Cathal Ó Sándair who published 160 books, mostly for children, a pioneer in the genre in Irish, or that of Ruaidhrí Ó Báille's novella *Dúnmharú ar an Dart* (1989), which gained such popularity that it was the subject of multiple reprints. Ian Campbell Ross makes reference to the writers in the Irish language who published crime fiction in magazines such as *An Squab* in the early years of the Free State where the state-funded publishing company, *An Gúm*, a branch of the Department of Education, produced intermittent works of crime narratives, mostly directed towards younger readers. Ross wryly notes the apparently contradictory attitude of the Irish authorities who, while encouraging the production of Irish crime fiction for children, effectively banned true crime magazines for over three decades.[4]

Irish writers have been remarkably, and for some, perhaps, surprisingly, influential within the genre. The early appropriation of the picaresque, the merging of the gothic with the process of detection, the introduction of occult detective, the medical detective, the female master-criminal and

2    Ian Campbell Ross, "Introduction" in *Down These Green Streets: Irish Crime Writing in the 21st Century*, ed. Declan Burke (Dublin: Liberties, 2011), 20–21.

3    Caitlín Nic Íomhair, "'A land of shame, a land of murder and a land of strange, sacrificial women': Representations of Wealth, Gender and Race in Modern Irish Language Crime Fiction" in *Guilt Rules All: Mystery, Detective, and Crime Fiction*, ed. Brian Cliff and Elizabeth Mannion (Syracuse, NY: Syracuse University Press, 2020), 234.

4    Ian Campbell Ross, "Irish Crime Fiction" in *The Oxford Handbook of Modern Irish Fiction*, ed. Liam Harte (Oxford: Oxford University Press), 357.

the international spy thriller: all have been part of the Irish contribution to crime fiction. Although the political and economic situation of Ireland meant that the "Irish novelistic tradition" often presents a discourse which "is directed at an 'encoded English reader'",[5] the recent growth in both the quality and quantity of Irish crime writing perhaps requires a more extensive survey of the genre in the years prior to the boom in Irish crime writing over the last twenty-five years. Cliff and Mannion have noted that crime writing has had a "fragmented history in Irish literature", and that the notable practitioners have worked "for the most part, isolated from each other".[6] Perhaps because of this, until relatively recently few critical studies of Irish crime writing have appeared. Declan Burke, a journalist and novelist whose defence and encouragement of Irish crime writers has been constant through his blog and newspaper reviews, edited what can be seen as the first book-length study of the genre, *Down These Green Streets: Irish Crime Writing in the Twenty-First Century* (2011). This study includes articles by many noted contemporary crime writers, and, of special interest, an important historical overview of the genre in Ireland by Ian Campbell Ross. Ross briefly discusses the importance of works by Le Fanu, Meade, Dowling, Wills Crofts and other important precursors, stressing the relevance of these writers, despite the fact that Ireland and Irish writers "have rarely featured prominently in accounts of early crime fiction".[7] Ross proposes a number of reasons for such neglect. These include "the ways in which the critical codification of the genre took place in Britain and Ireland", thus subordinating "many elements of crime writing's pre-history, not least its links with the gothic, in order to privilege the rational and scientific deduction that the 'Golden Age' writers valued above all else".[8] Ross also proposes that the disregard for Irish crime writing can be partly attributed to a widespread rejection of the Anglo-Irish literary tradition, predominant in the field of crime writing, coinciding with the

5  Gerry Smyth, *The Novel and the Nation: Studies in the New Irish Fiction* (London: Pluto, 1997), 44.

6  Brian Cliff and Elizabeth Mannion, *Guilt Rules All: Irish Mystery, Detective, and Crime Fiction*. (Syracuse, NY: Syracuse University Press, 2020), i.

7  Ross, "Introduction", 19.

8  Ibid., 19.

attempt to create and develop a nationalist literary system. Finally, and not of least importance, Ross notes the fact that many Irish writers were forced to publish in Britain, leading to their perceived need to cater for a British reading public. Ross has recently expanded on this introduction in his chapter on Irish crime fiction in Liam Harte's *The Oxford Handbook of Modern Irish Fiction*.

Elizabeth Mannion's *The Contemporary Detective Novel* (2016) provides another important contribution to studies within the field, even though, as the title suggests, its scope is limited to recent detective fiction. Nevertheless, in her introduction, Mannion does consider the relevance of earlier formats such as the gothic and sensation fiction and their influence on recent detective writing. The first book-length monograph on Irish crime writing is Brian Cliff's *Irish Crime Fiction* (2018). Although Cliff concentrates mainly on recent writers and their works, he, like Mannion, uses his introduction to discuss the historical condition of the genre in Ireland. He notes, for example, the historical tendency of Irish crime fiction to deal with "varieties of clientelism and corruption".[9] Cliff collaborated with Mannion to edit a collection of essays by various authors under the title *Guilt Rules All* (2020). Once again the introduction looks at the "fragmented history" of Irish crime writing, stressing the editors' belief that it is the task of scholars "less to recover an overlooked tradition" but more "to trace the emergence of a diverse but cohesive body of Irish crime writing in recent decades".[10] The focus, therefore, is on contemporary writers, with chapters dedicated to recent authors such as Claire McGowan, Arlene Hunt, Colin Bateman, Liz Nugent, Adrian McKinty and Gene Kerrigan. Despite the emphasis on contemporary writers, the volume also contains interesting essays on Freeman Wills Crofts, by Shane Mawe, and on Bartholomew Gill, by co-editor Elizabeth Mannion. *Guilt Rules All* is also notable for its inclusion of the essay, mentioned above, by Caitlín Ní Íomhair, which deals with the often sadly overlooked topic of crime writing in Irish. Like Cliff's *Irish Crime Fiction*, *Guilt Rules All* accentuates the transnational nature of much

9    Brian Cliff, *Irish Crime Fiction* (London: Palgrave Macmillan, 2018), 6.
10   Mannion and Cliff, *Guilt Rules All*, i.

recent crime fiction, and the extent to which this has influenced and been present in crime writing from Ireland.

Early criticism on crime writing was almost unanimously dedicated to the various facets of detective fiction. Traditional accounts of the genre would trace a historical lineage leading from Poe to Holmes, from Christie to Chandler, embracing early detective tales, schematic clue-puzzle mysteries and hard-boiled pulp, accepting the police procedural as a recent addition to a limited corpus. More recent critics, however, have expanded the admittedly protean boundaries of crime writing to include the earliest crime-centred narratives, including tales of the picaresque, of prison accounts, of ballads and cautionary tales. Leading commentators like Priestman, Knight and Horsley have realised the importance of using the term "crime fiction" to include "detective-less" writing.[11] This has led to the incorporation of criminal-centred narratives, but also spy thrillers, in which the espionage agent takes on a role akin to that of the detective figure. For Cawelti and Rosenberg, Conan Doyle's Sherlock Holmes fiction had shown how the spy theme "could be synthesised with the structures of mystery and detection".[12] Clive Bloom believes that the spy thriller has its origins in "the amalgamation of the imperial detective tale and the detective novel",[13] sharing the key element of secrecy.[14] Like the detective story, the "fundamental principle of the mystery story is the investigation and discovery of hidden secrets", and this discovery generally leads "to some benefit for the character(s) with whom the reader identifies".[15]

When talking of "Irish" crime fiction it is, perhaps, worth noting the difficult and often contradictory relationship that exists between crime fiction and the concept of "nation" or "state". Since Ernest Mandel's

---

11   Lee Horsley, *Twentieth-Century Crime Fiction* (Oxford: Oxford University Press, 2005), 3.

12   John Cawelti and Bruce A. Rosenberg, *The Spy Story* (Chicago: Chicago University Press, 1987), 40.

13   Clive Bloom, "Introduction: The Spy Thriller: A Genre under Cover?" in *Spy Thrillers: From Buchan to Carré*, ed. Clive Bloom (London: Macmillan, 1990), 1.

14   Ibid., 3.

15   John Cawelti, *Adventure, Mystery, and Romance* (Chicago: Chicago University Press, 1976), 42.

ground-breaking *Delightful Murder: A Social History of the Crime Story* (1984), many critics have highlighted the close relationship between this popular genre and a wide variety of contemporary social issues. As Haut states, "to examine a culture one need only examine its crimes".[16] The essentially "realist" infrastructure of most crime fiction gives it a particularly clear mandate to fulfil the early Marxist criteria for social fiction, providing, as it were, an accurate picture of society and its inherent contradictions. This tendency towards realism has been exploited by crime writers as a means of revealing, both explicitly and implicitly, the tensions of issues such as social class, gender, race and the relationship between the individual and society, or the authority which represents said society. It is for this reason that, while many studies have been written on class, gender and crime, for example, until relatively recently the "national" status of crime fiction has been largely ignored. The hegemony of crime fiction from major nation states with linguistic, economic and political dominance was a truism throughout the early years of the genre right up until the second half of the twentieth century. Thus American, English and French models provided the dominant examples of the genre throughout its formative and evolutionary periods. The importance and relative stability of the state as institution within these countries helped to create the different sub-divisions of the genre, with France, the UK and the USA providing the clearest examples of early etective, Golden Age, hard-boiled and police procedural fiction, to use the sub-divisions proposed by critics such as Martin Priestman and John Scaggs.[17]

As Mandel notes, during the nineteenth century, and coinciding with the bourgeois revolution, "a stronger state and more powerful police force were needed to keep a watchful eye on the lower orders, on the classes that were ever restive, periodically rebellious, and therefore criminal in

16    W. Haut, *Neon Noir: Contemporary American Crime Fiction* (London: Serpent's Tail, 1999), 3.

17    Martin Priestman (ed.), *The Cambridge Companion to Crime Fiction* (Cambridge: Cambridge University Press, 2003). John Scaggs, *Crime Fiction* (London: Routledge, 2005).

bourgeois eyes".[18] With the reification of the concepts of law and order, of crime and punishment, the bourgeoisie became steadily more implicated in the maintenance of the status quo. Such a status quo assumed the "stability of bourgeois society and the self-confidence of the ruling class", which "assumed that this stability was a fact of life",[19] and, as such, any revolt against social order was immediately assimilated into criminal activity, and the proletariat became identified with the criminal classes. Crime fiction, for Mandel, takes root in a society only "when bourgeois ideology in its purest sense becomes all-pervasive".[20] From the early nineteenth century up until the middle of the twentieth, the large, industrially advanced nation states were, therefore, not surprisingly, the prime producers of crime fiction. Irish crime fiction suffered from the peculiar status of Ireland as a colony and then as a nation, with its subjugation to British standards and demands. It also, however, was able to reach markets far wider than that afforded by the island, thanks to the use of the English language attracting potential readers in the USA and in the nations of the British Commonwealth. Irish crime fiction was, so to speak, caught between the devil and the deep blue sea. On one hand it was potentially denied its peculiar "Irishness" by a large section of its readership, which, on the other hand, accepted works by Irish writers as part of a wider field of English-language crime writing.

As this book seeks to demonstrate, Irish crime writing has an extremely rich and varied history. This is the first in a two-book project dealing diachronically with Irish crime fiction, from the picaresque of the seventeenth century up to the late 1990s when the "Emerald Noir" boom began. My aim is to show that there is a real and thriving history of this type of literature, and that Irish writers, often without due recognition, have been instrumental in the development of the genre on an international level. The peculiar relationship with Irish writers and crime is, of course, influenced by the complex association with crime and its detection in Ireland,

---

18   Ernest Mandel, *Delightful Murder: A Social History of the Crime Story* (Minneapolis, MN: Minnesota University Press, 1984), 13.
19   Ibid., 44.
20   Ibid., 45.

itself directly related to the difficult relationship between the Irish and the forces of law and order.

It is not, perhaps, surprising, that the picaresque should be so fruitfully adopted by Irish writers. The colonial situation experienced in the island during the mid-seventeenth century lent itself to the precarious economic conditions, the distorted concept of self and the disputed sense of belonging or nationality. Richard Head, born in Ireland, but whose father was a soldier in the English army, must surely have felt the sense of displacement and liminality which finds particular resonance in the Iberian format of the picaresque tale, whose hero, using only wit and imagination, is engaged in a constant struggle to survive against the apparently unsurmountable challenges set by a hostile social system. Head's *The English Rogue* was immensely popular, a best-seller in its time, widely translated and adapted, and a victim of literary piracy. The picaresque model would later be used by William Chaigneau, Thomas Amory and Charles Johnstone, and, in the nineteenth century, by Charles Lever. Even today, abundant traces of this literary mode can be found in works as diverse as John Banville's *The Book of Evidence*, Patrick McCabe's *The Butcher Boy* or Liz Nugent's *Unravelling Oliver*. The broadsheet ballads and Newgate Calendars, now considered to have played a fundamental role in the development of crime writing, were prolifically produced in Ireland, often differing from their counterparts from England and Scotland with specifically Irish nuances. The ballads are of great interest in that they merge politics and crime, and reached such a level of notoriety that they were effectively prohibited by the authorities of Dublin Castle in 1832. The Newgate Calendars provided early examples of criminal-centred narratives, a mode of crime writing which would remain highly popular in Ireland.

The Act of Union of 1800, which brought about the UK of Great Britain and Ireland in January 1801, would have a profound effect on Irish writing and publishing. The Irish publishing industry, which had flourished before the Union, would collapse under a barrage of restrictions and the competition from London and Edinburgh. Maria Edgeworth's story "The Limerick Gloves" would attempt to spread the author's support for the Union, an early example of crime writing being used to express a determined political agenda. The early nineteenth century also saw the first police forces operating on an island-wide level in Ireland, under Robert Peel's Peace Preservation Act (1814) and the Irish Constabulary Act in 1822. Unlike their British counterparts, the Irish police were armed, billeted in barracks and were almost universally hated by the local population, who saw the police as an army of occupation. The Irish Constabulary would play a large part in the suppression of agrarian unrest and the secret societies which had arisen, and this would be reflected in works which contain many features of crime writing by authors such as the Banim brothers, Charlotte E. Tunna, Anna Marie Hall, Thomas Moore and William Carleton. Carleton particularly emphasised the importance of the past on present events, a theme which would see continual reiteration in Irish crime writing. Carleton's criminals are moved by the necessity created by their harsh living conditions, but also by greed and avarice, encouraged by the existing political situation. Gerald Griffin also anticipated future crime writing by his recreation of events of true crime as basis for his fiction.

Much has been written about the importance of the gothic within Irish fiction. One of the primary representatives of Irish gothic, Charles Robert Maturin, examined the relationship between crime and the supernatural, and his work is of particular note for its profound psychological insights. Melmoth is a detective, a quirky ancestor of later detective figures. Joseph Thomas Sheridan Le Fanu is widely considered to be one of the founders of the modern crime narrative, one of the first writers to introduce the "locked room" mystery and the occult detective. Le Fanu was also one of the primary influences on Arthur Conan Doyle, Georges Simenon and other later writers, due to his skilful introduction of strategies and techniques such as the delayed denouement. His later work, bearing many characteristics of the then-fashionable sensation fiction transferred features of the gothic into a modern, middle-class context, featuring questions of inheritance, domestic crime, bigamy and murder, substituting the castles, towers and graveyards of the gothic for the drawing rooms and parlours of the contemporary bourgeoisie. The growth of sensation fiction – an early version in many respects of the modern crime thriller – in the second half of the nineteenth century, meant that other Irish writers such as Charlotte Riddell, Annie French Hector and Frances Hoey would obtain great popularity among Irish and English readers.

The last quarter of the century also saw "true" narratives of policing in
Ireland by writers such as Robert Curtis and Henry Robert Addison, taking
advantage, perhaps, of the renewed interest in crime in Ireland, largely provoked by the activities carried out by Fenians, including bomb attacks in
Britain. The period also saw a marked growth in Irish crime fiction, with
the mystery novels by Richard Dowling achieving high sales in the Irish,
British and American markets. Dowling's works – mainly "triple-decker"
crime romances provide a fascinating link between mid-century sensation
fiction and the detective narratives from the end of the century. Although
many of his novels were set in England, it is perhaps the works with an
Irish setting which reveal Dowling's mastery at its best. *The Mystery of
Killard* (1879) and *Sweet Inisfail* (1882) both provide fascinating glimpses
of the Royal Irish Constabulary at work. *A Baffling Quest* (1891), set in
England, contains many traits of the modern detective mystery, with a
private detective, plans of the mansion where the crime is committed and
numerous elements heralding modernity, such as telephones, telegrams,
electricity and forensics.

The other great figure of the late nineteenth and early twentieth century is that of Elizabeth Thomasina (L. T.) Meade who published over 300
novels and collections of short stories, and who shared the front cover of
*The Strand* magazine with Arthur Conan Doyle, as her stories and those
of Sherlock Holmes shared space within the publication. Meade has been
credited with being the first writer to use a doctor as detective, the first
to develop plots involving "impossible" crime, the first to create a series
featuring a female murderer and one of the first writers to use a female detective. Bram Stoker, whose *Dracula* (1897) contained many rudiments
of the detective novel, also wrote crime narratives, as did Oscar Wilde
("Lord Arthur Saville's Crime", 1897) and Somerville and Ross. Matthias
McDonnell Bodkin introduced Paul Beck, his "plain man" detective, who
would appear in a series of works in the early years of the new century.
Bodkin was also responsible for the creation of Dora Myrtl, a female private investigator with all the characteristics of the "New Woman". While
the individual works featuring Beck and Myrtl are excellent, the convoluted coupling of the detectives in a romantic relationship in *The Capture*

*of Paul Beck* (1909) is frankly unconvincing, as is the appearance of their offspring *Young Beck* in the homonymous novel (1911).

The prolific Belfast clergyman Robert Owen Hanny, writing as George A. Birmingham, produced a number of crime-based narratives, the best of which are still readable today, and Dorothy Conyers reflected the hunting and shooting manners of the Ascendancy Anglo-Irish in a number of works which often centred around the investigation of a crime. Erskine Childers, who would be executed in 1922 for revolutionary activity by the new Free State government, published *The Riddle of the Sands* in 1903, widely regarded as one of the first ever espionage thrillers.

The years between the end of the First World War and the beginning of the Second World War saw the advent of what has become known as the Golden Age of crime fiction. Represented by authors such as Agatha Christie, Dorothy L. Sayers, Margery Allingham, Michael Innes and Ngaio Marsh, Golden Age detective narratives are often considered to be quintessentially English, and the setting is often, in fact, the heartland of the English Home Counties. The Irish influence on and contribution to this influential period is wide and varied. The "locked room" mystery, so often employed in Golden Age fiction, was introduced by Le Fanu before being famously used by Poe in his "The Murders of the Rue Morgue" (1841) and many of the tropes first tapped by L. T. Meade are used in interwar mysteries. Also of importance is the model of the Irish "Big House" novel. "Big House" fiction had captured the anxieties of a specific social grouping – the Anglo-Irish upper-middle class and minor gentry – which was cut off from the outside world through a lack of communication with the local community, generally perceived as being hostile. The closed community of the Big House is often replicated in the Golden Age detective novel, with a large house in the south of England taking the place of its Irish equivalent. The residents and their guests are markedly disassociated from the local community, and the sense of claustrophobic endogamy resembles that of the Irish Ascendancy novel. Irish writers were also prominent among those associated with the Golden Age. Dubliner Freeman Wills Crofts, who published his first novel in the same year as Agatha Christie published hers, was extremely popular during the 1920s and 1930s. His no-nonsense police officers, most particularly Inspector French, figured in a large number of

novels and short stories in which the careful study of factual information –
train timetables, shipping statistics, chemical formulae – usually leads to
the successful resolution of cases of an increasing complexity. The intensely
factual nature of many of Wills Crofts' works differed from much of the
fiction produced in the Golden Age which, although strictly adhering to
the "rules" of the genre, concentrated more on psychological factors than
on an analysis of dry objective information.

The works of C. Day-Lewis, writing as Nicholas Blake, represent a
highpoint within the field of Golden Age detective fiction. Blake's novels
concentrate on the human and emotional aspects of murder, and although
the setting often replicates that of other writers working within the genre –
the closed community, the house, school or institutional building – his
sensitivity to social issues lends a sense of relevance to his works, often
missing in the seemingly apolitical normality of most of the great Golden
Age authors. Blake's detective is Nigel Strangeways, an intellectual detective, initially modelled on Lewis's friend W. H. Auden, but who develops in stature and density in the thirty years in which he featured in
the novels. Another Irish writer was also a member of the Detection Club,
the unofficial academy for Golden Age writers. Mrs Victor Rickard (Jessie
Louise Moore) produced a number of highly readable novels during the
interwar period, but her work has been sadly neglected in most analyses
of the Golden Age phenomenon.

The Golden Age was, of course, as already stated, considered to be
a highly "English" period of writing, and despite the important contribution of the Irish writers mentioned above, or Scots such as Josephine
Tey or Michael Innes, and the New Zealander Ngaio Marsh, the central
image of the Golden Age novel is that of the country house in the Home
Counties. While in Britain the "clue puzzle" narrative triumphed, the political and social conditions in Ireland meant that the concerns of most Irish
writers lay elsewhere. Wills Crofts was a Dublin-born Protestant, whose
education and employment took him first to Belfast and then to southern
England. C. Day-Lewis was a member of the Anglo-Irish Ascendancy whose
focus was always more directed towards London than Dublin, while Mrs
Victor Rickard was the widow of an English army officer. Their interests
and concerns were distant from an Ireland immersed during this period

between the World Wars in a revolutionary process of war, independence, partition and civil war. Interestingly three of the most relevant writers of crime fiction working in Ireland during this epoch had participated actively in revolutionary activities. While Eimar O'Duffy wrote his crime works for purely financial reasons, Robert Brennan is notable for his use of a detective working within a contemporary Irish setting, while Liam O'Flaherty produced a number of remarkable studies of crime located in the early years of the Free State.

The popularity of American hard-boiled crime fiction would also see a reflection in Ireland. From the mid-1940s, J. B. O'Sullivan published a large number of "pulp" novels, and throughout the late 1940s, 1950s and early 1960s his works developed from his stereotypical American detectives to an innovative use of Irish police officers detecting Irish crime in an Irish setting. Brian Moore, then living in Canada, also climbed aboard the pulp bandwagon, producing a number of works under different aliases which, thanks to the paperback boom of the early 1950s, allowed the author to make some money before embarking on his "serious" writing career. Moore's pulp works used international settings, as did many of the novels by John Welcome and Manning O'Brine. Sheila Pim and Eilís Dillon, on the other hand, adapted the Golden Age style to an Irish context. Both provide interesting portraits of the Gardaí, the former using comfortable Anglo-Irish settings, while the latter's novels centred around the native Catholic bourgeoisie. Patricia Moyes, whose long career started in the late 1950s, would also adapt the Golden Age style to her murder mysteries which featured the English detective Henry Tibbett and which often used exotic settings. Also starting his career in the late 1950s, Nigel Fitzgerald used both Irish and international settings for his novels. Although Fitzgerald was attracted to the mid-century vogue for exotic locations, his best works are those set in his native land, which include interesting details of Garda investigations, treating the Irish poice force as a competent, modern service.

Throughout the 1960s there was a marked rise in the number of spy and international thrillers published, and a number of Irish writers excelled in this field. Brian Cleeve and Shaun Herron, for example, achieved great popularity, while Jack Higgins, born in England, but brought up by his Irish mother in Belfast, became an international best-selling author. Not surprisingly, perhaps, the "Troubles" in Northern Ireland would become the subject of much of Higgins' fiction, as he joined the ranks of international thriller writers who would take an opportunistic interest in the state of affairs in Northern Ireland. While Higgins had actually experienced the mood in Belfast, his Troubles-based novels would rarely be anything other than formulaic. Many works, however, by writers from both Northern Ireland and the Republic, reflected the conditions in the North in excellent examples of crime fiction, or of fiction in which crime played an important part. Blair McMahon's *Nights in Armour*, for example, provides a fascinating view from the perspective of a serving police officer, while Eugene McEldowney's Cecil Megarry novels are especially interesting in the way they examine the relationship between the Northern and Southern police forces. Works by Maurice Leitch, Benedict Kiely, Terence De Vere White, Danny Morrison, David Park and Glenn Patterson, among others, have contributed texts which, to some degree or other, deal with crime within the context of Northern Ireland and its Troubles.

Meanwhile, the 1970s would see the introduction of one of Ireland's most famous and popular detective figures. The Miss Flanagan stories from *Ireland's Own* magazine appeared on a weekly basis, and the mysteries which featured this spinster and former schoolteacher reached amazing popularity. Despite, or perhaps because of, their contrived homeliness, their explicit Catholic message and their use of outmoded and well-worn techniques, Miss Flanagan became a household name and, perhaps, the first Irish detective to be widely embraced by the general population. During the same decade the first Peter McGarr novels were published, written by the American author Mark C. McGarrity under the pseudonym Bartholomew Gill. Gill's McGarr works also achieved great popularity, suggesting, perhaps, that Ireland was ready and willing to accept popular crime fiction set in Ireland and which, although written by an American, highlighted Irish police solving crimes committed by Irish criminals.

Both McGarr and Miss Flanagan would continue to be popular during the 1980s and early 1990s, a period in which real crime in Ireland was increasing at an unprecedented rate. The mass use of narcotics, the easy access to arms, related to the Troubles in the North, and the growth and dominance of efficient inner-city gangs with charismatic, if often brutal, leaders, saw a change both in the methodology used by lawbreakers and in the sheer amount of criminal activity. Such change demanded a new way of looking at crime, both in a fictional and in a real context. As the Irish read accounts of the new gangs and their flamboyant leaders, of risky heists, kidnappings and murders in their Sunday newspapers, the number of "true crime" books would also grow. Fictional works on contemporary Irish criminal activity grew in popularity, and authors such as Joe Joyce and Vincent O'Donnell incorporated drug trafficking and gang activity in their novels; the short-lived Glendale imprint would produce a number of highly readable novels which reflected the situation. The 1990s would also witness a resurgence of the thriller. While native writers such as Sarah Michaels and Richard Crawford replicated the extraneous Troubles thriller with all its clichés and platitudes, other Irish novelists such as Daniel Easterman, Glenn Meade, Victor O'Reilly, Con Cregan and Tom Phelan would produce international thrillers written from a particularly Irish standpoint. In the same period, Brian Gallagher, Jim Lusby, John Brady and Jim Galvin with their police-based thrillers, and Rory McCormack with his novels featuring a veterinary surgeon as detective, helped to cement the existence of a growing tradition in home-grown Irish crime writing.

There were, it can be argued, three factors which strongly affected the growth of Irish crime fiction in the 1990s. The first of these was the cataclysmic economic change that came to be known as the Celtic Tiger and which rocked the foundations of the Irish economy in the middle of the decade. Between 1995 and 2000 the growth of the gross domestic product (GDP) reached a high of 11.5 per cent and the country reached a level of prosperity hitherto unknown. The second factor was the IRA ceasefire of 1994, renewed in 1997 and which lead to the peace process that would terminate in the Good Friday Agreement, bringing a period of relative stability to both the Republic of Ireland and Northern Ireland. The other factor was the murder of investigative journalist Veronica Guerin by members of a leading Dublin drug gang in June 1996. This murder brought about a huge public outcry at precisely the moment when Ireland, recently entered into the dynamics of the Tiger economy, was at its highest level of self-esteem. Guerin, whose newspaper articles had resolutely condemned the drugs gangs which operated with apparent impunity throughout the Republic, was a popular public figure whose murder caused the country to call into question its own status as an advanced nation. The result was the passing of a package of anti-crime legislation which led to the creation of the Criminal Assets Bureau (CAB), a multidisciplinary agency with powers to seize any assets ordained to have proceeded from illegal activity, and the design of which has since been adopted by many other countries including the UK.

The creation of the CAB and the growth of the Celtic Tiger economy saw a change in the habits of crime in Ireland. The new economic self-confidence was enshrined in effective new legislation which ensured that the gangsters of the 1980s and early-to-mid-1990s found life and criminal activity in the new Tiger Ireland much more difficult. The focus of crime in the late 1990s and in the first decade of the twenty-first century moved away from the old gang-based robbery and kidnappings towards the more lucrative and initially less perilous area of white-collar crime. The Celtic Tiger period was characterised by an enormous growth in the property market, and the quick profits that could be gained from this prompted a whole new level of criminal activity. This activity would be documented by many Irish crime writers who started writing in the 1990s, and others whose first works would appear at the beginning of the new millennium.

A large number of writers who would later achieve prominence started their activity in the 1990s. Some, like Gene Kerrigan or Liz Allen, would start as newspaper reporters who would later produce volumes of a "true crime" nature, before turning to fiction in the next decade. Others would publish their first novels in the 1990s before becoming appreciated as major figures in the buoyant world of Irish crime fiction in the 2000s and 2010s. These latter include Colin Bateman, whose comic crime thrillers would become hugely successful, Ken Bruen, whose early works contained many of the features that would bring fame to his later Jack Taylor novels, or Paul Charles, like Bruen living in London at the time. English writer Peter Tremayne inaugurated his Sister Fidelma series which would become highly influential in the sub-genre of historical crime fiction, while Eoin McNamee's first works appeared, as did John Connolly's first Charlie Parker thriller.

This book has been written as an introduction to the vast field of Irish crime and mystery writing since the seventeenth century until the end of the twentieth century. Although some excellent articles and chapters have appeared, this is, I believe, the first book-length study of the area. I realise that many people have become interested in the phenomenon of Irish crime fiction thanks to the flourishing state it enjoys in the first quarter of the third millennium. In this volume I hope readers will come to realise that the Irish contribution to this genre has been, although somewhat overlooked, also fruitful and influential. Realising that many of the works covered here are difficult to obtain, I have attempted to provide short, coherent summaries of their contents. For those few who have read the works, I apologise in advance, but the advantage of providing such summaries does, I believe, far outweigh the disadvantage.

The epigraphs contained within the chapter titles are quotations taken from one of the books discussed within that chapter.

# "that my Thefts might pafs undifcovered." Picaresque, Rogue Tales, Broadsheets and Newgate Calendars

Recent critical studies on crime fiction have come to question the canonical and pro-Enlightenment focus through which the history of the genre has been approached by the majority of critics. Crime fiction, it was often claimed, was "rooted in pre-modern enigma stories, implying that rationality was the guiding light of the genre".[1] Such a perspective privileged the objective and empirical methods of detection which would be shaped into a convenient narrative of continuity leading from Poe to Holmes, to Christie and Sayers, to Hammett and Chandler. Championed by early critics, few voices differed from this model. Only, perhaps, F. W. Chandler, who in *The Literature of Roguery* (1907) sought models in the various types of early modern rogue literature from both domestic and continental sources, escaped from the orthodox classification of crime writing which has been dominant in most of the critical writing on the genre. Recently the unique status of the Poe/Holmes tradition has been contested, especially on considering that aspects of crime narratives from the late twentieth and early twenty-first centuries rely on topics such as the materiality of the body, the importance of bodily fluids and the predominance of physical violence – all of which have their roots in an alternative lineage, one rooted in the popular narratives of the seventeenth, eighteenth and nineteenth centuries, in the picaresque, rogue tales, broadsheets and Newgate Calendars, in the gothic and sensation fiction.[2] Early Irish crime writing was heavily influenced by all of these forms, and indeed, in the adaptation of the continental picaresque narrative into the

---

1     Maurizio Ascari, *A Counter-History of Crime Fiction: Supernatural, Gothic, Sensational* (London: Palgrave Macmillan, 2007), xiii.

2     Ibid., 1.

English-language rogue tale, Irish writers can be considered to be in the vanguard.

Garrido Ardila identifies three distinct but converging types of "crime" or "rogue" narrative which were being produced in the English language in the seventeenth century. These included the presumably indigenous "cony-catching" pamphlets which had started to appear in the late sixteenth century, the ever-popular criminal biographies which would later develop into the enormously successful Newgate Calendars, and the picaresque narratives influenced by the popularity of translations into English of the great Spanish picaresque novels. The anonymous *Lazarillo de Tormes* (1554) saw its first English-language translation in 1576, while Mateo Alemán's *Guzmán de Alfarache* (1599–1604) was first translated by James Mabbe as *The Rogue* in 1622. Francisco de Quevedo's *El Buscón* was written around 1604 and published, without the author's permission, in 1626, with a first English translation appearing in 1657.[3] The lack of copyright legislation meant that these and other key Spanish picaresque works were the object of numerous translations, adaptations and abridgements and the first English language copy of the picaresque tale is generally considered to be Thomas Nashe's *The Unfortunate Traveller: or, the Life of Jack Wilton* (1594) which contains many of the characteristics of its Spanish models.

It is, however, with the Irish writer *Richard Head's The English Rogue* (1665) that the picaresque narrative in English starts to take shape. What little is known about Head we learn through the short biography of the writer in William Winstanley's *The Lives of the Most Famous English Poets* (1687). A personal friend and acquaintance of the author, Winstanley relates that Head was born in Ireland to an English clergyman father who was killed during the Irish Rebellion of 1641. Being taken by his mother to live in England, Head was a student at Oxford where his father had studied although, it would seem, the writer did not graduate, as Winstansley tells us that he was bound as an apprentice to a Latin bookseller in London before marrying and setting up his own bookselling business. Being, however,

---

3   J. A. Garrido Ardila, *The Picaresque Novel in Western Literature* (Cambridge: Cambridge University Press, 2015), 123.

"addicted to play",[4] he lost his savings and returned to Ireland where he wrote a play, *Hic et Ubique*, which, according to Deena Rankin, shows some of the features of the picaresque in a work which raised "compelling methodological questions concerning the ways in which we might legitimately decipher the influence of his accident of birth".[5] This play provided Head with the public respect and financial wherewithal to return to London where he had the work printed and which, dedicated to Lord Monmouth, he hoped would have some success on the burgeoning London theatre scene. The play was not, however, as successful as Head had hoped and, once again, he opened a bookselling business. Again losing large amounts of money on gambling, Head started to write the first part of *The English Rogue* which "being too much smutty, would not be Licensed, so that he was fain to refine it, and then it passed stamp".[6]

First published in 1664 or 1665, and censored for obscenity, *The English Rogue* was republished in 1665 by London publisher Henry Marsh. The narrative is told in first person by Meriton Latroon, the "rogue" of the title who, by birth at least, is, in fact, Irish rather than English. For Garrido Ardila, this is the first of "a prolific string of Guzmanian imitations published in the last years of the seventeenth century".[7] The same critic looks to the Spanish picaresque model for the protagonist's name, as Latroon is obviously a transposition of the Spanish *ladrón* (thief) and Meriton could come from the Spanish *mérito* (merit), so Meriton Latroon would be the Meritorious (or worthy) Thief.

Latroon, like Head himself, is the son of a Protestant clergyman who, like Head's father, is killed in the 1641 Rebellion. Taken, again like Head, by his mother to England, Meriton, as a child, starts on a life of criminal

---

4    William Winstanley, *The Lives of the Most Famous English Poets, or, The Honour of Parnassus in a Brief Essay of the Works and Writings of Above Two Hundred of Them, from the Time of K. William the Conqueror to the Reign of His Present Majesty, King James II* (London: Samuel Mansip, 1687), 208.

5    Deana Rankin, "Kinds of Irishness: Henry Burnell and Richard Head" in *A Companion to Irish Literature*, ed. Julia Wright (Chichester: Wiley-Blackwell, 2010), 117.

6    Winstanley, *English Poets*, 209.

7    Garrido Ardila, *Picaresque Novel*, 124.

activity by stealing and torturing geese, before being sent to boarding school where he indulges in extortion and continues to develop his cruelty towards animals. Running away from school, the protagonist joins a band of wandering gipsies with whom he learns how to beg and steal. The narrative breaks at times while the narrator provides lists, most significantly a glossary of "canting vocabulary" he has picked up from the gipsies and thieves with whom he associates.

Moving to London, Latroon is employed by a merchant as an apprentice. He joins a group of fellow apprentices in the city who make an illicit living from defrauding their masters and eventually gains fame and infamy as a skilled professional thief, forger and confidence trickster. Apart from his illegal activities, Meriton also has an active if immoral sex-life, which Head describes in ribald detail. He makes a maidservant pregnant and tricks her into believing he is willing to accompany her and the unborn child on a voyage to Virginia where, he convinces her, they will settle. On the morning they are to elope, the rogue accompanies the girl to the ship but disembarks before it sets sail, leaving the hapless maid alone to face a new life in the colonies. Even as the ship is sailing out of the port Meriton seduces and robs another woman he meets on the shore.

Latroon becomes a highwayman, a professional armed criminal, and working alone or in groups he terrorizes the passengers he comes across on the highways around London before being captured and sentenced to hang. The death penalty is never executed, however, and the final part of the novel takes the rogue on travels as he is sold as a slave and later freed when he is shipwrecked off the Indian coast. At the end of the work he marries an Indian woman and, amidst promises of repentance and reform, apparently settles down to a happily married life with his exotic bride.

*The English Rogue* was an immensely popular work. Leah Orr recognizes at least three rewritten versions, three prose abridgements and no fewer than eight imitations published within eighty years of the appearance of Head's text, while twelve unrelated works mention the book by its title.[8] We must add to this an immensely successful short verse abridgement and

---

8    Leah Orr, "The English Rogue: Afterlives and Imitations, 1665–1741", *Journal for Eighteenth-Century Studies* 38, no. 3 (2015), 361.

the fact that *The English Rogue* was the first English-language prose fiction to be translated into any continental language – a German translation was published in 1672. Such was the popularity that Henry Marsh's successor at his London publishing house, Francis Kirkman, requested that Head write a sequel to the work. Head refused, apparently because, as Kirkman states in his introduction to the second edition, so many readers thought the story autobiographical that the Irish writer did not want his name to be associated with any further adventures of his anti-hero. Whether this was indeed the case or rather, as Orr suggests, this was a tactic used by the publisher to add controversy must remain a matter of conjecture, but three further parts of *The English Rogue* were subsequently published and, despite speculation, their authorship remains doubtful.[9] While critics agree that Head was not solely responsible for the sequels to the narrative, there is some doubt as to whether the Irish writer collaborated with Kirkman, or with the hired scriveners employed by the publisher. Part Two is almost universally accredited to Kirkman or his hired hack, while Parts Three and Four cast doubts, with many critics suggesting a joint authorship with at least minimal involvement of Head. The attribution of the first part to Head is based on the corresponding entry in the Stationer's Registry, while there appears to be no independent corroboration of the authorship of the other parts, and both Head and Kirkman are credited with their authorship.[10]

What critics do tend to agree on is the superiority of the original instalment of *The English Rogue* over its sequels, *The English Rogue: Continued in the Life of Meriton Latroon, and Other Extravagants: The Second Part* (1668), *The English Rogue: Continued in the Life of Meriton Latroon, And other Extravagants, Comprehending the most Eminent Cheats of Both Sexes: The Third Part* (1674) and *The English Rogue: Continued in the Life of Meriton Latroon, and Other Extravagants: The Fourth Part* (1680). F. W. Chandler calls Head's original narrative "the first and best part" and believes that if the work had been completed (in its subsequent parts) as Head had intended "it might not have been deserving of unqualified blame".[11] Leah

9    Ibid., 362.
10   Ibid.
11   F. W. Chandler, *The Literature of Roguery* (Boston: Mifflin & Co., 1907), 81.

Orr believes that Head's single-volume edition "has a complete narrative arc" with "no indication that a sequel was planned",[12] while C. W. R. D. Moseley criticizes Part Two for its lack of narrative resources by having the rogue narrator, instead of relating his own adventures, meeting the "simple expedient of meeting talkative strangers".[13] For Moseley also Parts Three and Four, despite the presumed collaboration of Head, are more repetitive than the original narrative.[14]

Head's narrative is, however, for the modern reader of crime fiction, an interesting link in the pre-history of the genre. It follows only loosely the Spanish models on which it was partially based. Like these models, *The English Rogue* has the episodic plot typical of southern European picaresque, with the focus on a single main character, while the narrative is based on the events in the life of this rogue character who "commits more or less petty crimes rather than pursuing a grand adventure or ambition".[15] Usually told in the first person, these fictions generally aim towards complying with the basic rules of realism while frequently introducing satire – towards the authorities, towards the masters, towards the Church and the dominant social classes. They share an almost organic unity between form and content and the narrative is generally "shaped by the actions of the main character".[16] Significantly, in the Spanish picaresque, the *pícaro* or rogue is often immoral, regularly sacrilegious and refuses to bow down before the injustice of ill-used authority, but his crimes are usually minor ones based on petty theft, fraud, confidence tricking and other stratagems aimed at ensuring the rogue's very survival. In these original Iberian examples of the genre, the *pícaro* rarely commits serious crimes. Garrido Ardila argues that Head's novel is not fully picaresque because Meriton "is not a rogue because he is never forced to become one".[17] The English-language rogue

---

12   Orr, "English Rogue", 363.
13   C. W. R. D. Moseley, "Richard Head's *The English Rogue*: A Modern Mandeville?" *The Yearbook of English Studies* 1 (1971), 103.
14   Ibid., 103.
15   Leah Orr "From Pícaro to Pirate: Afterlives of the Picaresque in Early Eighteenth-Century Fiction" in *The Afterlives of Eighteenth-Century Fiction*, ed. D. Cook and N. Seager (Cambridge: Cambridge University Press, 2015), 72.
16   Ibid., 73.
17   Garrido Ardila, *Picaresque Novel*, 124.

narratives, from Head onward, would seem to combine the features of the Spanish model with the domestically popular criminal biographies, which involved real criminals and which generally ended in repentance before the execution of the protagonist.

Significantly, perhaps, and possibly because of the title, few critics dwell on, or even acknowledge, the "Irishness" of both author and protagonist. John Wilson Foster, who gives Head's birthplace as Carrickfergus, sees Meriton's illegitimacy as "a memorable metaphor for the unrootedness of the British in Ireland" and observes in Head's sprawling episodic narrative the roots of future Irish works such as *Tristram Shandy* or *Ulysses*.[18] Garrido Ardila detects a possible significance in the trauma which Meriton has endured as a result of the Irish Rebellion of 1641 and his father's death in this uprising and hence that society or the circumstances of history are responsible for the rogue's anti-social behaviour, but goes on to demolish this hypothesis because, he claims, "the fact that the setting of his roguish adventures is England, where he is no outsider, renders the satire much less patent".[19] Here the critic ignores the fact that the protagonist Meriton Latroon is Irish, and as such does not, perhaps, understand the complex nature of the rogue's relationship to the two countries, England and Ireland.

The sense of displacement the protagonist experiences could easily be seen to point to the liminal status of this character, who is neither Irish in Ireland nor English in England. Deana Rankin recognizes the significance of Head's Irish birth and how this is mirrored in that of his protagonist. She suggests that the author "can be figured as a writer between England and Ireland" whose "fascination with origins and wanderings – that by now familiar cocktail of birth, blood and dislocation – not only drives his fiction, but also goes some way to explaining the autobiographical tension of his writings".[20] More recently Derek Hand has noted the unresolved sense of identity apparent in the work, stressing how Meriton "at some level, is

---

18    John Wilson Foster, *The Cambridge Companion to the Irish Novel* (Cambridge: Cambridge University Press, 2006), 7.

19    Garrido Ardila, *Picaresque Novel*, 124.

20    Rankin, "Kinds of Irishness", 117.

either Irish or English or, rather, is both Irish and English simultaneously"
thus undermining any feasible notion of stable national characteristics.[21]

Despite the success of *The English Rogue*, which ran to twelve editions
by the end of the century, and despite Head's apparent involvement with
Kirkman's Parts Three and Four of the saga, Head did not himself dupli-
cate the successful formula implied in his rogue narrative. *The Complaisant
Companion, or New Jests; Witty Reparties; Rhodomontados and Pleasant
Novels* (1674) was, as the title suggests, a multi-genre potpourri, which
contains several short one to two-page tales of tricksters and cheats of the
type that could be found in chapbooks and pamphlets, and which would
later be used in periodicals and which might be regarded as an ancestor
of the short crime fiction that would appear in the nineteenth century.[22]
Also of interest is Head's *The Miss Display'd* (1675), a fascinating example
of early female picaresque. The heroine, Cornelia, had an Irish mother and
an English father. After an affair with the knight who is her master while
in service, she moves to Dublin where she sets up a successful brothel.
Containing some excellent descriptions of the low-life of seventeenth-
century Dublin, the use of a third-person narrator would seem to deprive
it of the sense of reckless urgency found in *The English Rogue*, and, after
moving to London, being arrested and sent to Newgate prison to await execution, the ubiquitous acquittal of the heroine strikes the reader as merely
formulaic: Cornelia ends up a rich woman living in Paris.

While Head did not profit from the rich vein he had discovered in *The
English Rogue*, other writers were quick to take up the challenge. Starting
with Francis Kirkman, a large number of European writers would shame-
lessly copy the formula used in Head's narrative. The use of the formulaic
title reveals, according to Leah Orr, the fact that, although all subsequent
rogue tales were, like Head's model, related to Spanish picaresque models,
the primary influence on these works was that of the Irish writer.[23] The

---

21    Derek Hand, *A History of the Irish Novel* (Cambridge: Cambridge University Press,
      2011), 25.
22    Calhoun Winton, "Richard Head and the Origins of the Picaresque in England"
      in *The Picaresque: A Symposium on the Rogue's Tale*, ed. Carmen Benito-Vessels and
      Michael O. Zappala (Newark, NJ: University of Delaware Press, 1990).
23    Orr, "English Rogue", 368.

last quarter of the seventeenth and the first half of the eighteenth century saw the appearance of a large number of rogue narratives, often published anonymously. Among these were *The German Rogue*, *The French Rogue*, *The Scottish Rogue* and *The Highland Rogue*. Suggestively, there was also *The Irish Rogue*, an anonymous work, presumably written by an English writer, first published in 1690, which is narrated in the first person by its protagonist, Teague O'Divelly. The work, replete with anti-Catholic and anti-Irish sentiment was republished in 1740 with the name of the protagonist changed to Darby o Broghan.[24]

In the eighteenth century, features of the picaresque can be found in the "fortune hunter" or "ramble" novels, featuring Irish characters who seek a good match to revive family fortunes. Examples of the "fortune hunter" novel include: the anonymous *The Adventures of Shelim O'Blunder, Esq., The Irish Beau* (1751); William Chaigneau's *The Adventures of Dick Hazard* (1754); Edward Kimber's *The Juvenile Adventures of David Ranger* (1756); the anonymous *The Fortune Hunter; or History of Jack Fitzpatrick* (1762); and John Oakman's *The Life and Adventures of Benjamin Brass: An Irish Fortune Hunter* (1765). While these novels continued to use the picaresque mode, they also made use of a stereotype of the Irish gentleman looking for a wealthy woman to marry as "a figure of contempt due to his status as much as his nationality".[25]

The maturity of the Irish picaresque can be found in *William Chaigneau's The History of Jack Connor* (1752). Chaigneau (1709–81) was born in Dublin of Huguenot descent and published the novel anonymously in both Dublin and London. A second edition, with numerous revisions, was published the following year. *The History of Jack Connor* has a contemporary setting – the narrative starts around 1720 – and, according to Aileen Douglas, exudes a "mood of Enlightenment optimism" which has more in common with Tobias Smollett's *Roderick Random* than with Fielding's *Tom Jones*, despite the "elaborate complements" paid to the latter.[26] Certainly,

24   Ibid., 368.
25   Joe Lines, "Contesting Masculinities in Thomas Amory's *The Life of John Buncle, Esq.* (1756–66)", *Journal for Eighteenth-Century Studies* 41, no. 3 (2018), 449.
26   Aileen Douglas, "The Novel before 1800" in *The Cambridge Companion to the Irish Novel*, ed. John Wilson Foster (Cambridge: Cambridge University Press, 2006), 28.

in common with Smollett, Chaigneau is interested in the liminal status of his protagonist and, like the Scottish writer, explores questions of national identity in both overt and covert fashion.

The eponymous hero Jack Connor is born in Ireland, the illegitimate son (as we discover towards the end of the work) of a Protestant landowner and a Catholic peasant mother, the tellingly named Dolly Bright. Dolly has worked as a servant for Sir Roger Thornton who, on discovering the girl's pregnancy, marries her off to Jeremiah Connor, a Williamite soldier who has remained in Ireland after the wars and who Jack regards as his father. Wounded after an altercation with his wife, Jeremiah is obliged to undergo surgery, during which he is blinded by an inept surgeon. Blindness in the main wage earner in eighteenth-century Ireland meant almost inevitable poverty, and the family is forced to turn to begging in order to survive. After the blind man's death when Jack is six, his mother abandons him and cohabits with a lustful priest, leaving Jack outside the home of the Truegood family in County Meath. The names of the characters, like that of the mother, reflect the characteristics of their bearers, and Jack is raised by the well-meaning steward at Truegood's household, Mr Kindly. Jack is on good terms with the members of the family, becoming a friend and schoolmate to Truegood's heir, Harry, but is forced to leave after being discovered in bed with the schoolmaster's niece.

After leaving the Meath home, Jack wanders through Ireland, England, France, the Low Countries and Spain before eventually returning to Ireland. Meeting and being employed by such characters as Mr Champignon, Mr Sangfroid, Sir Peter Shallow and Sir John Curious, Jack, who changes his surname to Conyers, is involved in numerous petty crimes and sexual escapades and becomes, like his predecessor Meriton Latroon, a highway robber and is sentenced to death only to be reprieved at the last minute. On his travels across Europe, becoming an accidental soldier and companion to the Wild Geese – exiled Irish soldiers enlisted in foreign armies – he encounters in the various armed forces, Jack develops both materially and spiritually. Being informed of the true nature of his birth in Cádiz, Jack returns to Ireland where, discovering also that he is a blood relation to the Truegoods, he marries Harry's sister, Lady Harriot. Bernard Escarbelt compares Jack's real and spiritual journey through life as "a sort of pilgrim's progress, an onward march towards a form of salvation which allows little room for divinity except when Providence and God's grace manifest themselves by affording social advancement".[27] Certainly, Jack's social elevation is in stark contrast to the rough living conditions of the Irish peasantry depicted in the opening scenes of the novel and, as was often the case with Anglo-Irish fictions, and with the wholehearted acceptance by the protagonist of Protestant values and social manners perceived as being English.

Ian Campbell Ross accepts that the work can be loosely classified within the picaresque tradition despite "significant variation",[28] and the novel makes overt reference to Le Sage's *Gil Blas*, itself a French adaptation of the Iberian picaresque model. Much more, however, than Richard Head, William Chaigneau examines the Irish background of his protagonist and how this affects and conditions his behaviour. Jack's changing of his name from Connor to Conyers reveals a symbolic rejection of his birth-right, and this rejection is further emphasised by his attempts to develop an English accent and, in continental Europe, to pass himself off as an Englishman. Although Ross detects the anti-clericalism typical of most picaresque or rogue narratives in the novel, the work also shows a distinctively anti-Catholic side, as it constantly privileges the values and codes of Protestantism against those of the Roman church.[29] Both Ross and Escarbelt recognise the importance of Jack Connor as a work of Irish prose fiction. While the former laments the neglected status of Jack Connor and other eighteenth-century novels by Irish writers, he concludes that the work is "an authentically Irish novel" which is "among the best examples of eighteenth-century Irish fiction".[30] Escarbelt tentatively agrees with those critics who have called the work "the first Irish novel worthy of the name" while stressing that it was written at a time when both literature and publishing "essentially belonged to England and targeted English readers,

27    Bernard Escarbelt, "William Chaigneau's *Jack Connor*: A Literary Image of the Irish Peasant" in *Rural Ireland, Real Ireland*, ed. J Jacqueline Genet (Gerard's Cross: Colin Smythe, 1996), 57.

28    Ian Campbell Ross, "An Irish Picaresque Novel: William Chaigneau's *The History of Jack Connor*", *Studies: An Irish Quarterly Review* 71, no. 283 (1982), 270.

29    Ibid., 273.

30    Ibid., 278.

for whom the indigenous Irish world was remote, little known and well-nigh incomprehensible".[31]

*Jack Connor* contains numerous descriptions of Irish rural life. This alone makes the work exceptional in terms of eighteenth-century fiction,[32] and the first part of the narrative ranges across the country portraying Counties Meath, Limerick and Tipperary, as well as the city of Dublin. The harshness of life in the Irish countryside is conveyed at times with great realism, and Chaigneau criticises the economic conditions of the peasantry and how "the Transition from an Irish Cottager to a Beggar, is very natural and common in the Country".[33] Although Jack aspires towards Englishness – by changing his surname and adopting an English accent and English manners – he constantly reveals his sympathy towards the Irish and the injustices they suffer both in their own country and overseas. Chaigneau observes "the wretched Condition of the poor Inhabitants" and expresses his belief that "their Idleness and Sloth, with the Swarms of ignorant Priests, and the Treatment of some Landlords, kept them in a constant miserable Situation, and even depriv'd them of sufficient Spirits to wish a Change of Condition".[34] The ill social conditions undergone by the Irish peasantry is, for the writer, caused by the peasants' own laziness, the depravity of Catholic priests and the negligence of the landlords.

Chaigneau's underlying Protestant ideological leanings constantly come to the fore. The model schools that Lord Truegood has established on his estate are a sign of Protestant enlightenment, and this is reflected in Jack's decision when, now a moneyed gentleman, he returns to visit the hovel in which he was raised and comes to the decision to donate a large sum of money to set up Protestant schools in the Irish countryside. Despite the symbolic significance of Jack reclaiming his Irish surname,[35] the rogue has mellowed into a defender and stalwart of English values and, according to Douglas, "the abandoned barefoot boy has so successfully taken on the

31    Escarbelt, "Jack Connor", 51.
32    Ross, "Irish Picaresque", 276.
33    William Chaigneau, *The History of Jack Connor. Second Edition*, 2 vols. (London: W. Johnston, 1753), vol. 1, 11.
34    Ibid., 52.
35    Ross, "Irish Picaresque", 277.

characteristics of a Protestant English gentleman that he can be invited to colonise his native land".[36] Nevertheless, in his travels through Ireland and Europe, Jack is the protagonist of a sadly neglected narrative which, like Head's earlier work, can be situated at the centre of the neo-picaresque tradition, an important ancestor of later models of crime fiction.

An interesting variation on the picaresque narrative can be found in *The Life of John Buncle, Esq., Containing Various Observations and Reflections Made in Several Parts of the World; and Many Extraordinary Relations* by *Thomas Amory* (c. 1691–1788). Superficially related to the "fortune hunter" model, *The Life of John Buncle* openly challenges many of the conventions of the format. Although the work has the "basic narrative frame of a disinherited Irishman leaving home and wandering across England, seeking both friends and a wife",[37] Buncle, educated, devout and ingenious, differs from the stereotype, and although his character changes in the second part of the novel, published a decade after the first, his story constitutes what can be seen as a reverse picaresque mode. This anti-picaresque can also be found in the three volumes of *The Adventures of Anthony Varnish; or, a Peep at the Manners of Society* (1786) by *Charles Johnstone* (1719–1800). Varnish, an orphan, is, like the traditional rogue, forced to adapt to a number of situations, using only his cunning and dexterity to survive. While the *pícaro* always manages to get the upper hand, however, Anthony Varnish is constantly tricked, exploited and mistreated by a series of unscrupulous masters, employers, travelling companions and supposed friends.

In Ireland, as in England, Scotland and Wales, criminal biographies, very often of a highly fictional nature, were popular. From the "black-letter" (Gothic type) broadside ballads circulated in the sixteenth and seventeenth centuries to the Newgate Calendars of the eighteenth and nineteenth centuries, the populace had a seemingly insatiable desire for narratives about crime and criminals, be these in an oral or written format.[38] The Newgate Calendars originated in the late seventeenth century as a bulletin of executions compiled by the Keeper of London's Newgate Prison and was soon

---

36    Douglas, "The Novel before 1800", 29.
37    Lines, "Contesting Masculinities", 448.
38    Victor   E.   Neuberg,   *Popular   Literature:   A   History   and   Guide* (Harmondsworth: Penguin, 1977), 103.

made into broadsheets and chapbooks sold by pedlars at executions, fairs and markets. These gave dramatic details of the life of the criminal, the crime, the trial, the confession of the convicted party and, usually, of his or her execution. *The Newgate Calendar* was first published in collected book format in 1773, and would be reprinted and updated with great regularity in subsequent years. The individual "accounts" were written by the "ordinaries" – the Anglican prison chaplains – whose purported aim was to secure the repentance of the convict and attempt to steer the readers away from a life of crime. For Ascari, these "accounts" still retain the "divine detection"[39] of middle-age and early modern crime narratives such as, for example, the revenge tragedy, producing "an ambivalent relation with reality".[40] The "detective apparatus of providence"[41] is still of greater importance than anything even remotely similar to later detection, and the criminal biographies from both calendars and broadsides can still, he suggests, be considered to be "providential fictions", even though the crime and its subsequent castigation appears to be "less pervaded by God's gaze and presence".[42]

In her study of 247 "accounts" from the period 1680–1770, Barbara White finds seventy-nine pertaining to Irish convicts who, she states, constituted 16 per cent of prisoners hanged at Tyburn in the second half of the eighteenth century.[43] These Irish prisoners, more often than not Roman Catholics, often refused to cooperate with the Anglican chaplains, and in the years 1730–55 White notes an increase in the number of Irish Catholics who refused to give their confessions to a Church of England chaplain.[44] *The Newgate Calendar*, which contained the biographies from criminals imprisoned not only in Newgate but also in other prisons throughout Britain and Ireland, contained numerous "accounts" of Irish criminals, most of which contain a mixture of factual and fictional material. Typical of

---

39    Ascari, *Counter-History*, 19.
40    Ibid., 34.
41    Ibid., 30.
42    Ibid., 34.
43    Barbara White, "'The Inferior Sort of the Kingdom of Ireland': Irishmen and the Tyburn Tree", *Irish Studies Review* 6, no. 1 (1998), 17.
44    Ibid., 22.

these is the case of John M'Naughton, son of a prosperous Derry merchant who woos a 15-year-old girl and tricks her into a bogus marriage ceremony. He is successfully contested in court by the girl's rich father and, owing to massive debts, M'Naughton flees to England. He returns to Ireland and murders the girl, is put on trial and sentenced to death. Without repenting for his crime he is taken to be hanged but, when the rope breaks, the process has to be repeated. Despite the public wanting to help the convict to escape, the second attempt at hanging is successful and M'Naughton dies. Another "account" is that of the Irishwoman Mary Young, who becomes an expert pickpocket and gang leader. In the "accounts", as in the broadside murder ballads, the culprit is arrested either by an admission of guilt, or by a series of random events which lead to their capture. For Stephen Knight, this confirms the sense of an organically controlled society, with the belief that "just as society can sometimes suffer from disorderly elements, so it can deal with them by its own integral means".[45]

Broadside ballads also enjoyed great popularity in Ireland. The earliest recorded example dates from 1626, and ballads were still published in the broadside format until as late as the 1920s.[46] At least sixty-eight printers operated in Ireland producing these, and some two thousand to three thousand copies exist in British and Irish libraries.[47] Although Irish broadsides continued to enjoy wide popularity after their decline in England and Scotland, and like their British counterparts were generally sold by pedlars and ballad singers, there is evidence that many Irish broadsides were more overtly political, so much so that the Dublin Castle administration saw fit to ban their sale in 1832 because of their alleged seditious content.[48] Irish pedlars allegedly overcame this prohibition by selling straws and giving away the broadsheet with the straw.[49]

45  Stephen Knight, *Form and Ideology in Crime Fiction* (London: Macmillan, 1980), 11.

46  Colin Neilands, "Irish Broadside Ballads: Performers and Performances", *Folk Music Journal* 6, no. 2 (1991), 209.

47  Ibid., 210.

48  Ibid., 210–211.

49  Ibid., 212.

Existing Irish broadside ballads are often of a political nature, such as "A New Song: Billy Pitt & the Union" (1798) and "The Blackbird of Avondale: or the Arrest of Parnell" (1882), or comment on trials and allegedly criminal activity of a political nature, as in "Condemned Men for the Phoenix Park Murders" (1882) or "A New Song On the Attempt of the Life of the Very Reverend Father Ryan" (1860). Broadsides based on the trial, confession and execution of criminals are not nearly as abundant in Ireland as in England and Scotland, but those that exist are often fascinating. A number of the broadside ballads published in Dublin provide good examples of the basic tendencies of the format; the sensational details of the crime, and the repentance and execution of the criminal. "A Sorrowful Lamentation on the Hollywood Tragedy where Two Sisters Have Been Brutally Murdered" (1867) appeals to the reader's sense of mystery as, although it relates the discovery of the bodies of the two sisters and the acquittal of their brother, the murderer is still at large. The descriptions are sensationalistic and blood-thirsty:

> It was on a monday [*sic*] evening Richard Murphy did come home
>
> When he beheld a dreadful sight – caus'd him to sigh and moan.
>
> His sister Ellen near the door lay bleeding in her gore,
>
> Two awful wounds in her fair neck her scull [*sic*] was batter'd sore.[50]

The writer appeals to the reader or listener's sense of justice in a pious ending which evokes divine justice on the perceived failure of its secular equivalent:

> Alas no bloodyer [*sic*] murder was done in the most cruel times,
>
> Two fine young women murdered for neither stain or [*sic*] crimes,
>
> We hope all freinds [*sic*] & neighbours, will devoutly for them pray,

---

50   "A Sorrowful Lamentation on the Hollywood Tragedy where Two Sisters Have Been Brutally Murdered", Broadside BPP 1001-274, <https://rbsc-prod.library.nd.edu/collections/ead_xml/images/BPP_1001/BPP_1001-274.jpg>, accessed 23 March 2018.

Vengeance ist [*sic*] mine said the Lord upon the judgment day.

God help their dear relations they now are pained in grief,

By this most cruel murder for them there's no relief,

As these two sisters were beloved by all the neighbours round,

We hope to hear before it's long of the murderer been [*sic*] found.[51]

Both the "The Sorrowful Lamentation of Andrew Carr Who Was Executed on the 28 of July at Richmond Jail for the Murder of Margret Murphy" (undated) and "A Sorrowful Lamentation on the Execution of Patrick Power Who Suffered at the Front of Wexford Jail on the 4th of April for the Unnatural Murder of his Father" (1860) provide fine examples of the broadside equivalent of the Newgate Calendar model, containing the biography, crime, repentance and execution of the criminal. In the first of these, Andrew Carr laments joining the army and killing Margret Murphy with his "army arzor" [*sic*].[52] He repents after seeing the blood on his hands in a public house, and hands himself over to the authorities, recognising that his crimes were instigated by "night walking, drink and company" and urging "each pious Christian" to pray for his soul.[53] In a similar vein, Patrick Power regrets the "base and fearful murder" of his father, brought about, he claims, by "Satan's curse'd temptation".[54] Power, a Catholic, has confessed to "the good Preist [*sic*]" and on the gallows issues a warning to other young men who might feel tempted to follow his path:[55]

---

51    Ibid.
52    "The Sorrowful Lamentation of Andrew Carr Who was Executed on the 28 of July at Richmond Jail for the Murder of Margret Murphy", Broadside BPP 1001-272 c1, c2, c3, <https://rbsc-prod.library.nd.edu/collections/ead_xml/images/BPP_1 001/BPP_1001-272-c1.jpg>, accessed 23 March 2018.
53    Ibid.
54    "A Sorrowful Lamentation on the Execution of Patrick Power who Suffered at the Front of Wexford Jail on the 4th of April for the Unnatural Murder of his Father", Broadside BPP 1001-273, <https://rbsc-prod.library.nd.edu/collections/ead_xml/images/BPP_1001/BPP_1001-273.jpg>, accessed 23 March 2018.
55    Ibid.

Farewell to Newtonbarry & my neighbours one and all

O watch & pray both night and day or you will surely fall

Let each wild & wicked youth a warning take by me

Be guided by your parents & avoid bad company.[56]

In the picaresque narratives, in the Newgate Calendars, and in the crime broadsheets, the central figure is that of the criminal. Justice is seen as stern and, its representatives, the judges and magistrates, are distanced from ordinary society. The criminal is viewed with pity, but also with scorn, someone who must pay for their misdeeds, firstly before the secular authorities and then before divine authority. Detection, in the modern sense, is virtually inexistent, and early controlling authorities, such as the watchmen and constables, and the Baronial Policing Service, the "Barnies", were often figures of fun – the thief-takers and the contractor-gaolers inspiring hatred and fear rather than respect. Rogue tales were written to amuse and entertain, and the convict biographies and broadside ballads, although ostensibly aimed at the spiritual redemption of the reader, were presumably read more for titillation than for moral edification. The line between the factual and fictional was never easy to trace, as the problems that Richard Head encountered when readers took his fiction biography too literally demonstrate. The "true" stories of the "calendars" and the broadsides are as steeped in fiction as they are in fact, but crime writing was developing a market and a public willing to consume all types of criminal narratives.

56    Ibid.

# "The peasantry of Ireland have, for centuries, been at war with the laws by which they are governed." The Early Nineteenth Century

The Irish Rebellion of 1798 and the subsequent parliamentary Union of 1801 heralded the start of a century of enormous transcendence for Ireland. The defeat of the Rebellion and the resentment towards the Union felt by many conditioned the early years of the century, which would see growth in the movement towards Catholic emancipation and the rising activities of secret societies such as the Ribbonmen, the Whiteboys and the Rockites. The activity of these societies was witnessed by Sir Robert Peel, Chief Secretary for Ireland from 1812, who saw the need to combat the perceived disorder of Ireland which, he believed, had been aggravated by the withdrawal of military garrisons during the Napoleonic Wars.[1] Peel was responsible for the foundation of the Police Preservation Force which, according to Liam McNiffe, "provided an important link between the traditional idea of the old constabulary and the modern concept of a civil police force".[2] Peel's plan was to create a unique force for a unique situation, taking the administration of the system away from the existing situation controlled by local magistrates, many of whom were believed to be corrupt and uncooperative towards the new system.[3] Although some initial detachments were established, the scheme did not become fully operative until after 1822, when the Westminster parliament passed the Irish Constables Act, which created four provincial police forces.[4]

---

1   Conor Brady, *Guardians of the Peace* (Dublin: Gill & Macmillan, 1974), 4.
2   Liam McNiffe, *A History of the Garda Síochána: A Social History of the Force 1922–1952, with an Overview of the Years 1952–1997* (Dublin: Wolfhound Press, 1997), 3.
3   Brady, *Guardians*, 6.
4   McNiffe, *Garda Síochána*, 4.

From the very beginning, the Irish police, the first officially constituted force in Great Britain and Ireland, was designed as a well-armed paramilitary force, and would remain so, unlike the later English, Scottish and Welsh forces, for its entire history.[5] This fact would help to distance the police from a large part of the population and, for many, the police, which became the Irish Constabulary under the 1836 Constabulary (Ireland) Act and later the Royal Irish Constabulary (RIC), was seen as being both partisan and as the defender of the interests of a specific point of view. If the development of the police in western Europe during the early years of the nineteenth century was "an inevitable result of eighteenth-century post-Enlightenment thought",[6] in Ireland it appeared to represent a regression to earlier years of repression. The RIC acted on behalf of the Dublin Castle administration in all of the significant social conflicts of the century, even as a fully fledged military force during the Fenian risings of 1848 and 1867, and the unique position of the Irish police is an important factor to bear in mind when contemplating the history of crime fiction from the island of Ireland. If, for a substantial proportion of Irish men and women, the police were seen as agents of a repressive force, how, it must be asked, would this affect the fictional representations of the police? The tendency, for many years, to situate Irish crime fiction outside Ireland must be seen as intimately related to the unpopularity of the Irish forces of law and order, and the Irish police would be represented in a largely negative way in Irish fiction for many years.

The Union also had a considerable impact on the Irish publishing industry and the production of books. The Act of Union meant that the British copyright laws of 1709 were extended to Ireland,[7] but Margaret Kelleher points out that, despite this apparent advantage, the Irish publishing trade collapsed after the Union.[8] James H. Murphy notes that this decline was

5    Ibid.
6    John Scaggs, *Crime Fiction* (London: Routledge, 2005), 18.
7    Siobhán Kilfeather, "The Gothic Novel" in *The Cambridge Companion to the Irish Novel*, ed. John Wilson Foster (Cambridge: Cambridge University Press, 2006), 79.
8    Margaret Kelleher, "Prose Writing and Drama in English, 1830–1890: From Catholic Emancipation to the Fall of Parnell" in *The Cambridge History of Irish Literature: Volume I. To 1890*, ed. Margaret Kelleher and Philip O'Leary (Cambridge: Cambridge University Press, 2006), 451.

due in no small measure to the end of "the lucrative eighteenth-century Dublin trade in pirated English fiction" which was later sold in Ireland, England and the USA.[9] In the years following 1801, most Irish writers published their novels in London and not until William Carleton did any Irish novelist publish primarily in Ireland.[10] One such writer was *Maria Edgeworth* (1768–1849), whose *Castle Rackrent* has often been seen as one of the pivotal works of Irish fiction. In "The Limerick Gloves" Edgeworth produced a curious narrative which provides one of the first studies of the myth of Irish criminality from the perspective of the English. Published in the collection *Popular Tales* (1804), but written in 1799 and so "composed in the uneasy interim between the rebellion and the Union",[11] "The Limerick Gloves" is set in the English city of Hereford and tells of an Irish glover, Brian O'Neill, who gives a gift of a pair of gloves to Phoebe Hill, a local beauty with whom he has fallen in love. The girl's parents are less than pleased that their daughter is being courted by an Irish immigrant and Mr Hill, the local tanner, suspects O'Neill of all sorts of possible crimes against the community, from the theft of a dog or the destruction of a rick of bark, to a plot to blow up the cathedral. Phoebe's father's investigation into the supposed criminal activities being carried out by an Irishman in the peaceful English market town finds resonance amongst the town folks who readily support the tanner's flimsily based assertions and O'Neill is charged with the crimes.

A benevolent and enlightened magistrate is eventually able to unravel the mystery, which reveals that the theft of the dog has in fact been the work of an unscrupulous gipsy fortune-teller in league with a Jewish pawnbroker, transferring the guilt, conveniently, perhaps, to two other representatives of suspect minorities. The destruction of the rig had been carried out by a group of Irish labourers, incensed by the ill-treatment of their countryman, while the most scurrilous crime, the attempted attack on the cathedral was made by a rat burrowing under the building's foundations. The Irish

---

9    James H. Murphy, *Irish Novelists and the Victorian Age* (Oxford: Oxford University Press, 2011), 21.

10   Ibid., 451.

11   Brian Hollingworth, *Maria Edgeworth's Irish Writing: Language, History, Politics* (Houndmills: Macmillan, 1997), 109.

artisan is therefore innocent. Edgeworth's intentions, given the political climate and the writer's avowed support of the Union, seem obvious, as it is shown that the Englishman and the Irishman can easily live together in harmony – a tanner needs a glover and a glover a tanner – and that peaceful and harmonious co-existence is of both economic and social convenience. The theft had been carried out by outsiders, while the vandalism to the oak bark rig was carried out by an ill-advised and over-enthusiastic rabble who lacked the values of equity and moderation shared by the English and Irish artisans. Social class overrules the strictly national in terms of adherence to social norms. The attempted destruction of the religious edifice by a rat – a rat which also happens to be a child's pet – makes light of the importance of religious differences where the Union is concerned.

Edgeworth's "The Limerick Gloves" simultaneously builds up and destroys the myth of Irish criminality, by revealing and implicitly criticising the implantation and growth of prejudice and showing how this can give rise to the establishment of stereotypes, which ultimately damage not just those against whom they are directed, but the entire community. The stereotypes that the English directed towards the Irish were also in the mind of *Gerald Griffin* (1803–40) when he wrote *The Collegians* (1929) after spending three years in London. Before this he had published two collections of shorter fictions. *Holland-Tide; or Munster Popular Tales* (1827) contained the novella *The Aylmers of Bally-Aylmer*, which sees the hero accuse his guardian, Cahill Fitzmaurice, of murdering his father during a smuggling expedition. The apparition of what seems to be his father's ghost and the resulting court case produce a surprising result, which leads to a satisfying conclusion. A court case is also used as the climax for another of Griffin's novellas, *The Rivals*, published in the Third Series of *Tales of the Munster Festival* in 1829. Darker in many respects than *The Aylmers of Bally-Aylmer*, *The Rivals* portrays the rivalry between two suitors, one of whom, Richard Lacy, is a magistrate charged with upholding the law, while the other, Frances Riordan, is a rebel who is involved in "outrages" against the crown. Both are in love with Esther who, after swearing love and loyalty to Riordan before he goes into enforced exile, becomes betrothed to the insistent Lacy, but she, apparently, dies before being able to marry. On his return, Riordan, driven to near madness by Esther's death, digs up her coffin and takes it to his house where the girl, apparently miraculously, returns to life. Her death has been like that of Cahill in *The Aylmers of Bally-Aylmer*, a type of catatonic unconsciousness, and Riordan and Esther marry. The feud between Lacy and Riordan continues, however, and Lacy is seen to use his legal authority and the abuse of his power against his rival. The climax in the local court reveals how the magistrate has acted and how he has used his "peelers" against the interests of Francis and the country people, and also reveals the hatred of these people towards the forces of order in general and towards Lacy in particular. While the court scene in the earlier novel had been of a light-hearted nature, in *The Rivals* it is obscure and ominous, revealing how the representatives of public order are able to freely manipulate the court system, which never ceases to operate in their interests and how, even in the case of Lacy who, clearly seen to be guilty of the abuse of power, is allowed to walk free.

Griffin's time in London "had impressed upon him the sad and seemingly perennial fact that the English, when they bothered to think about Ireland at all, saw the neighbouring island as a morass of potential trouble-makers",[12] and as such, he worked to dispel this stereotype. Although Griffin's novel can be seen as an attempt to justify the validity and stability of the emerging Catholic middle class, the attraction of *The Collegians* for the student of the crime novel lies in the skilful handling of primary materials and their conversion into a gripping and exhilarating narrative of suspense, tension and mystery.

*The Collegians* is based on a true case, popularly known as the "Colleen Bawn" murder, which had occurred in Ireland in 1819. The body of a young girl was washed ashore on the banks of the River Shannon and her identity revealed through dental evidence. The girl was discovered to have been seduced by John Scanlan, the scion of a notable local family, and a lieutenant in the Royal Marines, who was subsequently tried and executed for the girl's murder. Furthermore, a boatman whom the executed marine officer had originally accused of the murder admitted to being an accomplice, while claiming that the murder had been planned solely by Scanlan. This boatman

12   John Cronin, *The Anglo-Irish Novel, Volume One: The Nineteenth Century* (Belfast: Appletree Press, 1980), 66.

was also accused and executed for a crime which captured the interest of the entire country at the time, an interest which was exacerbated by the fact that Scanlan had been defended by Daniel O'Connell who, apparently, and despite The Liberator's scepticism about the lieutenant's innocence, came close to securing a verdict of not guilty for his client.[13] Griffin may have been present at the trial as a reporter for a Limerick newspaper, but it is certain that the case caught the writer's imagination and was used as the raw material for his first novel.[14]

Griffin opted for transferring the events further back into the past, presenting these as occurring in the 1770s, but he retained many of the features of the case in the novel, which starts with a tranquil picture of middle-class Irish life in the then-fashionable Limerick suburb of Garryowen. *The Collegians* treats the crime as the result of a fatal misunderstanding between Hardress Cregan, passionate and impetuous son of a Protestant gentleman, and his hunchback servant Danny Mann. Cregan has married a young peasant girl, Eily O'Connor, the daughter of a rope maker but, owing to the differences of social class that exist between him and his bride and the reticence he feels towards revealing the match to his family, he has hidden her in the cottage belonging to Danny's sister and maintains the wedding in secret. The figure of Hardress is contrasted with that of Kyrle Daly, his friend and ex-college companion, the member of a rising Catholic middle-class family. Kyrle is in love with Cregan's cousin, Ann Chute, who has herself been selected by Hardress's mother as a future desirable bride. The gradual realisation that he has made a mistake in marrying Ely is exacerbated by the young gentleman's apparent realisation that he is in love with his cousin, a match which, despite the blood relationship, would be more socially acceptable and more economically beneficial, as well as complying with the wishes of his overbearing mother.

After a fierce argument with Eily, Hardress confides his scruples to his hunchback servant, who offers to kill the girl for his master. Although he refuses, Cregan later entrusts his servant with removing the girl from the vicinity and ensuring her passage to Canada. The hunchback gets the wrong

13    Ibid., 65.
14    Ibid.

idea about his master's scheme, however, and murders Eily. Hardress, despite feeling guilty about the murder, continues with his plans to marry Ann, but the discovery of the girl's body leads to the arrest of his servant who is taken into custody. Although Hardress helps Danny to escape, the hunchback refuses to leave the area, provoking Cregan to giving him a brutal beating. Bruised both physically and morally, Danny goes to the authorities and confesses to the murder while, at the same time, implicating his master in the events. The servant is sentenced to death and hanged, while Cregan is deported but meets his death before reaching his destination. The happy ending is provided by the "national marriage" of the Catholic, middle-class Daly to Ann, a representative of the Protestant gentry.[15] The ending, as Derek Hand indicates, shows justice to be done within the realms of an almost providential nature as "more transcendent laws come into play".[16]

Griffin's novel is remarkable for the suspense the author creates in a story which, one imagines, would be well known, at least to his Irish readers. The growing tensions between Cregan and his peasant wife, his realisation of the folly of having married below his social station, and the seemingly overwhelming pressures to which the young man is subjected create an atmosphere of confusion and strain which is skilfully manipulated to allow the reader to feel a certain sympathy towards Hardress, to all effects a distinctly unsympathetic character. Seamus Deane points out that Griffin deliberately "espouses the cause of the respectable and civilized Daly family against that of the hard-drinking, duelling, rapscallion Cregans and Connollys of the small gentry".[17] Although deserving of more empathy, Kyrle is to all extents a less congenial character, lacking the impulsive dashing arrogance of his friend.

Cregan is, one feels, capable of development and provokes a degree of compassion when he admits his moral guilt to his mother in an impassioned speech which in some way exonerates his heartlessness:

---

15 James H. Murphy, "Catholics and Fiction during the Union, 1801–1922" in Wilson (ed.), *Irish Novel*, 100.

16 Hand, *History of the Irish Novel*, 87.

17 Seamus Deane, *A Short History of Irish Literature* (Notre Dame, IN: University of Notre Dame Press, 1986), 102.

I am the murderer of Eily! It matters not that my finger has not gripped her throat, nor my hand has been reddened by her blood. My heart, my will has murdered her. My soul was even before-hand with the butcher who has sealed our common ruin by his bloody disobedience. I am the murderer of Eily. No, not in act as you have said, nor even in word! I breathed my bloody thoughts into no living ear. The dark and hell-born flame was smouldered where it rose, within my own lonely breast. Not through a single chink or cleft in all my conduct, could that unnatural rage be evident.[18]

The novel is also notable in its often explicit criticism of the legal system in force in Ireland at the time. Griffin makes it clear that there existed one law for the ruling class and its defenders and another for the poor. The magistrate who interrogates the witnesses after Mann's detention ridicules the linguistic differences between himself and the locals and cuts short one witness for using the Irish language in his declaration. The author also emphasises the difficult relationship that the Irish peasantry has with the prevailing legal system, a peasantry which has "for centuries been at war with the laws by which they are governed, and watch their operations in every instance with a jealous eye"[19] and which "obtains a mere spirit of commiseration in their regard from the mere spirit of opposition to a system of government which they consider as unfriendly".[20] The Collegians, apart from its other values, is a remarkable chronicle of crime, society, investigation, punishment and guilt which stands as a worthy precursor to later Irish crime fiction. A sign of its relevance can be seen in the huge popularity of the work and its subsequent development into stage plays and even opera. One stage version was that adapted by Irish actor, producer and dramatist Dion Boucicault as The Colleen Bawn, which was the outstanding success on the London stage in the season of 1860 and which, according to some critics, gave rise to the first considered usage of the word "sensation" as it would be later applied to "sensation fiction".[21]

18    Gerald Griffin, The Collegians (1829, Belfast: Appletree Press, 1992), 233.
19    Ibid., 318.
20    Ibid., 253.
21    Nicholas Daly, "Fiction, Theatre and Early Cinema" in The Cambridge Companion to Popular Fiction, ed. D. Glover and S. McCracken (Cambridge: Cambridge University Press, 2012), 38.

*William Carleton* (1794–1869) also incorporated criminal activity into much of his best fiction. This can be seen, for example, in his narratives regarding the secret societies of the first half of the nineteenth century, most notably "Wildgoose Lodge" (1833) but also in many other fictions such as "Phelim O'Toole's Courtship" (1830) or *Rody the Rover or the Ribbonman* (1845). Before this, in an early story "The Broken Oath" (1828), Carleton had broached the subject when the protagonist, who has been encouraged to return to the consumption of alcohol by a priest, is evicted after his illegal still is discovered. He joins the Whiteboys, a secret agrarian association, and is involved in the murder of a revenue officer. "Wildgoose Lodge", originally published as "Confessions of a Reformed Ribbonman" in the Dublin Literary Gazette in January 1830 in is a remarkably mature story which, like Griffin's *The Collegians*, uses a true event to create the tense narrative of the raid of the lodge in the title and the brutal murders of its inhabitants in revenge for the alleged passing on of information about the secret society. The highly atmospheric story is noteworthy for the detailed characterisation of the leaders of the Ribbonmen, particularly Paddy Devaun, whose body the young Carleton had seen hanging from a gibbet, thus inspiring the story.

*Fardorougha, The Miser* (1839), Carleton's first novel-length narrative, also has crime and a secret society at its centre. The miser's kind son Connor helps local youth Bartle Flanagan, whose family are in financial difficulties largely due to the exorbitant interest rates charged by Connor's father. Connor is in love with the daughter of a local well-to-do family, Oona O'Brien, but the miser refuses to provide any money to his son, thus incurring disapproval of the match from Oona's father. Meanwhile, Bartle, apparently from gratitude for Connor's generosity towards him, warns him of an impending attack on the O'Brien's farm by the Ribbonmen. Connor is, however, discovered near the farm and accused of leading the attack on it and setting it on fire. The main accusation is led by Bartle, who has given Connor false information with which to incriminate him and, as such, exact revenge on the miser. Connor is tried and sentenced to hang, but his sentence is commuted to transportation and he is sent to New South Wales where his parents later join him. At the end of the novel, the truth is discovered and Bartle stands trial for his crime. He is consequently hanged and Connor is free to return to Ireland and marry Oona.

The apparent simplicity of the story is given depth by Carleton's profound analysis of the motives and consequences of sectarian killing and the moral dissolution of the secret societies who, the writer suggests, have forfeited any right they might have had at one time to claim that they were acting in the name of justice. He suggests that the supposedly altruistic aims of these groups have been so deformed that questions of revenge are commonly deflected from political adversaries to questions of personal revenge against personal enemies and "the private bickerings and petty jealousies that must necessarily occur in a combination of ignorant and bigoted men, whose passions are guided by no principle but one of practical cruelty".[22] This moral corruption which Carleton identifies in the secret societies is central to the narratives which have the Ribbonmen as protagonists – Carleton himself had been initiated into the society at the age of nineteen – and these investigations of the warping of innocent idealism into uncontrolled personal interests would be used by later Irish writers who were to use as the subject of their writing other "secret" groups of the future, in periods ranging from the period of the Civil War, of the Troubles or of the post-Troubles North, where the ideals of paramilitary groupings would often degenerate into common criminality.

*The Black Prophet* (1847) is generally regarded, if guardedly and with important reservations, as the most outstanding of Carleton's works. Declan Kiberd notes that the novel "has been castigated for its melodramatic plot, which is accused of undermining rather than embodying its central theme".[23] Written and published at the time of the Great Famine, Carleton distances his narrative in time, setting his events during an earlier famine which, nevertheless evokes the horrors of the contemporary crisis. An unsolved double murder of some twenty years before the main events of the story forms the backbone of the often melodramatic narrative, which centres on the haunting figure of Donnal Dhu McGowan, the Prophet of the title

22   William Carleton, *Fardorougha, The Miser* (1839, Belfast: Appletree Press, 1993), 267.
23   Declan Kiberd, *Irish Classics* (London: Granta, 2000), 286.

and his fiery daughter Sally. The memory of the two previous murders is revived when Sally finds human bones which are believed to be those of a carman and a man named Sullivan who had been robbed and killed at the time of the 1798 Rising. Corny Dalton, who had previously been arrested under suspicion of the murders, is once again captured and put on trial. The dramatic appearance of Sullivan, supposedly one of the victims, alive and well adds mystery to the case. The final revelations show how there had in fact been only one murder, that of Peter Magennis, the carman, who it is discovered had been the Black Prophet's brother-in-law. Donnal Dhu is accused, found guilty and hanged. Wayne Hall criticises the novel's closure and the artificial nature of the ending, seeing Donnal's guilt as a "violation of our sense of fair play" as the Black Prophet "has behaved like a murder suspect since our first encounter with him".[24] Although few readers could have doubted Donnal's guilt, Carleton still manages to create a sensation of suspense and uncertainty throughout the novel which belies the simplicity of the plot. The depiction of a land blighted by famine, the bogs, the moors and the hovels, creates an atmosphere which helps to convert an unsolved murder mystery into an example of how the past can return and affect the present, just like the famine itself, creating, as Hand says, the view that in Ireland "nothing ever really changes, nothing is ever really gotten over".[25]

In *The Emigrants of Ahadarra* (1848) Carleton again shows how corruption seems to arise whenever questions of land ownership come into play. Hycy Burke craves after M'Mahon's land, but also covets his wife, and his greed leads him to seek to incriminate the farmer by paying tinkers to build a still on M'Mahon's land. The farmer is arrested and is saved from transportation by Nanny Peety, a beggar girl, who supplies evidence proving that Hycy was responsible and had paid the tinkers. Once again, political circumstances are used to cover up personal greed and avarice; political corruption gives rise to a wider corruption at a personal level which permeates

24 Wayne Hall, "A Tory Periodical in a Time of Famine: *The Dublin University Magazine*, 1845–1850" in *The Great Famine and the Irish Diaspora in America*, ed. A. Gribben (Boston, MA: University of Massachusetts Press, 1999), 5.

25 Hand, *History of the Irish Novel*, 96.

"the internecine disputes of a desperate local community.[26] Crime, for Carleton, is a reflection of man's basic desire to better his condition, even if this is at the expense of his peers. Carleton's villains use adverse social and economic conditions to their own advantage, shielding their actions under the shelter of secret organisations or agreements which have long lost any intrinsic moral compass and which can be cynically manipulated to the advantage of the baser of human instincts.

Several other writers used the subject of agrarian unrest in their novels. *John and Michael Banim* included "Crohoore of the Billhook" in the first series of their *Tales of the O'Hara Family* (1825); *Charlotte Elizabeth Tonna's The Rockite* was published in 1829; while *Anna Marie Hall's The Whiteboy: A Story of Ireland* already looked on the phenomenon as being one of historical interest when issued in 1845. Carleton himself would return to portray secret societies in *The Tithe Proctor* (1849), but perhaps the most fascinating book to deal with the topic is the poet *Thomas Moore's* highly entertaining *Memoirs of Captain Rock: The Irish Chieftain with Some Account of His Ancestors* (1824). In *Captain Rock*, Moore has an English missionary meet the infamous (and, of course, fictional) Captain Rock, the name used by agrarian agitators as an alias with which to credit their actions. Rock entrusts the hapless Englishman with his memoirs, consisting of a potted history of Irish grievances against the English and of his "family" – his father, we learn, had been a Whiteboy, an Oak-Boy, a Heart-of-Steel Boy and a member of "all other fraternities of Boys then existing".[27] The tone is humorous, and Rock is first encountered disguised in "green spectacles and a flaxen wig",[28] but Moore's purpose is most serious. While ironically claiming that his "unlucky countrymen have always had a taste for justice",[29] his fictional Captain reminds the reader of the historical injustices from which such countrymen have suffered.

---

26   James H. Murphy, *Irish Novelists and the Victorian Age* (Oxford: Oxford University Press, 2011), 56.

27   Thomas Moore, *Memoirs of Captain Rock: The Irish Chieftain with Some Account of His Ancestors*, ed. Emer Nolan (Dublin: Field Day, 2008), 84.

28   Ibid., 2.

29   Ibid., 19.

*Marguerite Gardiner, Countess of Blessington* (1789–1849), a famed society hostess, born Margaret "Sally" Power near Clonmel, County Tipperary, is best remembered for her "silver fork" fiction and her narratives recounting events within the European aristocracy as it moved from one continental watering hole to another. *Meredith* (1843) contains elements of the "silver fork" school, and a healthy presence of leisured aristocrats, but also contains a plot involving kidnapping and usurpation of identity, which would not be out of place in a work published in the 1890s. Although parting from a typical tale of "desperation to match financial power with entry into fashionable society, of adulterous longings, vicious scandal and heartless unpleasantness", Murphy notes how Meredith takes up and develops a wide series of styles, "from adventure, to something close to Gothic, to proto-detective and finally back to the silver fork style".[30]

*Charles Lever* (1806–72) used a variation on the earlier picaresque in his early novels. In his first work, *The Confessions of Harry Lorrequer* (1839), "the emphasis is on light entertainment within the conventions of the picaresque mode",[31] and this emphasis can also be seen in his light, early military novels *Charles O'Malley, The Irish Dragoon* (1841), *Our Mess: Jack Hinton, the Guardsman* (1842) and *Tom Burke of "Ours"* (1844). Traces of the mode can also be found in more mature works such as *Roland Cashel* (1850) and *The Daltons: Or, Three Roads in Life* (1850), while *Davenport Dunn, A Man of Our Day* (1859), *The Martins of Cro' Martin* (1856) and *Lord Kilgobbin* (1872) introduce criminal activity, and in *Barrington* (1863) and *Luttrell of Arran* (1865) James Murphy recognises signs of experimentation with then-fashionable sensation novel.[32] It is, however, in *Confessions of Con Cregan: An Irish Gil Blas* (1849) that Lever develops a dialogue with the continental and insular picaresque of the past and firmly places the mode within an overtly and recognisable Irish context, commenting, as it does, on the problematic nature of the concept of "Irishness". The overt reference to Le Sage's eponymous hero in the subtitle places the work firmly within the neo-picaresque, and Lever's hero provides a witty and often

---

30    Murphy, *Irish Novelists*, 34.
31    Hand, *History of the Irish Novel*, 88–89.
32    Murphy, *Irish Novelists*, 91.

ironic version of the established rogue figure. The novel starts with Con's early life in Ireland, learning the first tricks of roguery from his father, who works as judge's flunkey, writ-giver and general hanger-on on the edge of the precarious Irish legal system who makes his living through an exhaustive and self-taught knowledge of the intricacies of the legal system. Con himself learns law by making copies of Sessions papers, and effectively "cons" his father by handing over incriminating papers to an enemy of his father's – the attorney Mr Morrisy – and subsequently ensures his father's prosecution and ensuing sentence of transportation for life. Con's betrayal of his father is emotionless and seemingly unmotivated. Young Con also loses out by his father's exile, as the elder Cregan's property is confiscated by the Crown and his son is left penniless. Rejected by his neighbours, who tag him with the unwanted epithet of informer, Con is forced to fend for himself. His coincidental meeting with the young Trinity student Henry Lindsay leads him to Dublin where, after seeing – but being unable to participate in – the life of students from rich families, Con is introduced to the seamier side of life in Ireland's capital. Working as a "horse-holder", the young rogue is arrested for using one of the horses with which he has been entrusted to ride in a race for gentlemen riders. Using his knowledge of the law to escape punishment, Con is taken under the wing of the disreputable Sir Dudley Broughton with whom he undertakes a sea voyage which will eventually take him to Quebec.

After a long and eventful stay in Canada, Con accompanies a group to the southern states of the USA before crossing the border from Texas into Mexico. There, he meets the beautiful Donna María but he is forced to flee the country and return to Europe. After numerous adventures, involving deception, theft, confidence tricking and not a little debauchery, Con moves from France to Spain, then in the middle of the Carlist Wars. In Spain he is imprisoned but, after escaping to Italy, he once again meets up with the ex-Trinity student Lyndsay. Through his adventures, Con has seen a constant rise in his social status and the closing stages see him as possessing a French countship and holding a position of importance in the French military in Algiers. His return to Ireland is triumphant and the romantic ending seemingly required of the Irish and British variants of the genre sees him reunited with his Mexican love Donna María in Dublin.

Like Head's Meriton Latroon, and Chaigneau's Jack Connor, Con Cregan undergoes social and economic progress despite behaving on the wrong side of the law. The cruel circumstances under which all three characters live are mitigated by the ingenuity and seemingly intuitive savoir-faire of the protagonists.

# CHAPTER 3

# "Wherever reserve exists there is mystery, and wherever mystery – guilt." Le Fanu and the Gothic Crime Mystery

A number of recent critics have stressed the important influence that gothic fiction has had on later crime narratives. The gothic, arguably succeeded by the phenomenon of sensation literature, contained many of the elements which would give form to the genre and which would feature in works pertaining to the various sub-genres of crime fiction. Catherine Spooner defines gothic fiction as being a category in which the sins of fathers are revisited on their own children, where the victims of crime are usually members of the perpetrator's own family and in which crime is usually committed by influential male characters, has particular significance within the family unit, and takes place in a past which is connected to and has "continuing and visceral effects" on the present.[1] For John Scaggs, the gothic in fiction is "characterised by the disruptive return of the past into the present", emphasising the reliance on the discovery of hidden family secrets.[2] The presence of a crime which has to be investigated so that order may be restored places gothic fiction close to the crime novel, despite the reliance of the former on supernatural factors and the latter's apparent proximity to realism. Gothic novels usually contain an unstable criminal character who is subject to feelings of guilt, or who is obsessive or paranoid in his behaviour. The restoration of order is central to both the gothic and the crime narrative, as is the existence of a mystery which has to be solved. Despite the use of the supernatural, of an obligatory setting in the past, the use of stock characters and the obvious

1    Catherine Spooner, "Crime and the Gothic" in *A Companion to Crime Fiction*, ed. Charles J. Rzepka and Lee Horsley (Chichester: Wiley-Blackwell, 2019), 245.
2    John Scaggs, *Crime Fiction* (London: Routledge, 2005), 15.

divergence from the realist mode, the gothic can be seen as one of the many literary models from which crime fiction would take its shape.

The relationship between Ireland and the gothic goes back to the early days of the genre, when the Sublime, as identified by the Irish philosopher Edmund Burke, became central to the aesthetic concepts which would abound in the articulation of the gothic as a literary form. The perception of Ireland which was held by the English reading public in the late eighteenth century was readily adaptable for the use of the island as a kind of pre-Enlightenment wilderness which, when combined with its linguistic, religious and cultural "otherness", provided a fertile territory for the growth of a literature which favoured the supernatural, the uncanny and the numerous features which unite to make up the genre or mode. Jareth Killeen has identified two Irish works, the anonymous *The Adventures of Miss Sophia Berkley* (1760) and the historian Thomas Leland's only work of fiction, *Longsword: The Earl of Salisbury* (1762), which contain notable gothic features and both of which pre-date Horace Walpole's *The Castle of Otranto* (1764), considered by many to be the founding text of the gothic.[3] Published in 1771, Elizabeth Griffin's *The History of Lady Barton* (a novel which Killeen cites as a possible source for parts of Mary Shelley's *Frankenstein*) also contains elements of the gothic.[4] Numerous Irish gothic novels were published in the late eighteenth century, including Mrs Kelly's *Ruins of Avondale Priory* (1796), and Mrs F. C. Patrick's *The Irish Heiress* (1797), while the huge popularity of Waterford-born Regina Maria Roche's *The Children of the Abbey* (1796) gave a definitive boost to the genre as interpreted by Irish writers. The success of Sydney Owenson's *The Wild Irish Girl* and that of Charles Robert Maturin with *The Milesian Chief* and *Melmoth the Wanderer* helped foster a tradition which would be continued throughout the nineteenth century by writers such as Joseph Sheridan Le Fanu, L. T. Meade and Bram Stoker.

It is, however, in the late gothic of *Charles Robert Maturin* and, especially, in the works of Joseph Sheridan Le Fanu that the connection

---

3    Jareth Killeen, *The Emergence of Irish Gothic Fiction: History, Origins, Theories* (Edinburgh: Edinburgh University Press, 2014), 116–122, 174.
4    Ibid., 61.

between the gothic and crime fiction can most fruitfully be traced. Maturin (1782–1824) produced in his *Melmoth the Wanderer* (1820) a vast narrative of crime and retribution, and this can be considered to be the work which best epitomises the so-called Protestant gothic. Maturin's novel was a late arrival in the field of the gothic, generally considered as flourishing primarily between 1787 and 1807, and differs from many earlier gothic narratives in its reliance more on psychological effects than on the mainstay of earlier works within the genre which tended to rely on lurid atmospheres, natural disasters, madness or the special effects of ghosts, demons, witches and other supernatural beings. The novel does not totally disregard the uncanny, but *Melmoth* is principally a work of psychological investigation. Its complex narrative structure – a series of chronicles nested one within the other – adds complexity to the novel, which replicates the wandering travel narrative of Head and Chaigneau's rogue fiction. John Melmoth's investigation into the actions and fate of his ancestor provides a fascinating precursor to the detective model.

*Joseph Sheridan Le Fanu* (1814–73) is commonly classified as being a writer of gothic fiction, as being a leading author in the fashionable field of 1860s sensation fiction and as being the creator of an output of supernatural and occult fiction. It is also worthy of mention that he is one of the very few Irish writers – and often the only one – to be regularly mentioned in mainstream histories of crime fiction. Kate Flint sees his early short story "The Murdered Cousin" as a work which "helped to inaugurate the sub-genre of the locked room mystery",[5] while Julian Symon wrote that Le Fanu "produced a dozen novels mostly concerned with crime, of which four are worth remembering and one is a brilliant mystery puzzle".[6] Peter Penzoldt sees the influence of the occult detective "editor" of the stories contained in *In a Glass Darkly* (1872), Dr Martin Hesselius, on other later

---

5    Kate Flint, "Sensation" in *The Cambridge History of Victorian Literature*, ed. Kate Flint (Cambridge: Cambridge University Press, 2012), 239.

6    Julian Symons, *Bloody Murder: From the Detective Story to the Crime Novel*, 2nd edn (Harmondsworth: Penguin, 1985), 85.

detective figures, including Sherlock Holmes,[7] while V. S. Pritchett called the Dublin-born writer "the Simenon of the peculiar".[8] The early stories which appeared in *The Dublin Magazine* between 1838 and 1840, and which were posthumously collected in *The Purcell Papers* (1880), show a heavy leaning towards the gothic, with stories like "The Fortunes of Sir Robert Ardagh" (1838) and "Schalken the Painter" (1839) echoing the atmosphere of Maturin's *Melmoth* with decaying Big Houses and Faustian bargains, with nightmare visions of hellish demons or, in the case of the latter, the devil himself, who comes to drag the characters down to Hell. Demons also claim the drunkard in "The Drunkard's Dream" (1838), a madwoman is resurrected in "A Chapter in the History of a Tyrone Family" (1839) while, anticipating, perhaps, Wilde's *The Picture of Dorian Gray* (1891), a portrait comes to life in the humorous gothic tale "The Ghost and the Bone Setter" (1838). One of the most interesting of these early tales is "Passage in the Secret Life of an Irish Countess" (1838), which would later become "The Murdered Cousin" in the collection *Ghost Stories and Tales of Mystery* (1851) before being developed into the novel *Uncle Silas* (1864).

"Passage in the Secret Life of an Irish Countess" starts with a body being found in a locked room with no sign of the murderer and for which the only suspect is a family member. The story then moves forward in time to focus on the countess of the title, Margaret, from the next generation of the same family, who is sent to live with her Uncle Arthur who, despite his avuncular façade starts to act suspiciously. The tension increases as Margaret begins to suspect her uncle's guilt. Le Fanu in this early tale uses all the resources the in his power to create an accomplished tale of mystery and suspense and despite the numerous gothic features, the story is a fine example of mystery fiction by an Irish author using an Irish setting.

Le Fanu's first novels are broadly works of historical fiction, which show the influence of Scott as well as that of gothic predecessors like Radcliffe, Roche or Maturin. In his 1980 monograph, *Sheridan le Fanu*, W. J. McCormack accredited *Spalatro* (1843) to Le Fanu, although the work

7    Peter Penzoldt "The Supernatural in Fiction" in *Reflections in a Glass Darkly: Essays on J. Sheridan Le Fanu*, ed. Gary William Crawford and Brian J. Showers (New York: Hippocampus Press, 2011), 111.

8    V. S. Pritchett, "An Irish Ghost" in Crawford and Showers (eds) *Reflections*, 128.

was originally published anonymously in *The Dublin University Magazine*.[9] This would, therefore, be the writer's first novel, a tale divided into two parts and telling the tale of an Italian highwayman who relates his life story to a monk as he awaits his execution. The narrative is "told" by the monk, Frai Giacomo, supposedly using the highwayman's own words and relating the events which led him into his profession. The structure of this first part is, therefore, similar to that of *The Newgate Calendar* criminal-makes-confession-before-execution narratives – still popular in the first half of the nineteenth century – with the repentant prisoner telling how he had been forced to witness a murder and had thenceforth commenced a life of criminal activity with neither scruples nor fear of the consequences. The second part of the novel, however, anticipates the paranoia and claustrophobia of later works such as the tales collected within *In a Glass Darkly*, with Spalatro tormented by hellish nightmares, demonic possession and the vision of a female vampire as he slips into apparent madness.

*The Cock and Anchor* (1845) is set in the time of the Wharton administration in the early eighteenth century – the Lord Lieutenant himself is a minor character in the novel – while the events narrated in *The Fortunes of Colonel Torlough O'Brien* (1847) take place in the late seventeenth century in the time of Richard Talbot, Earl of Tyrconnel, also a minor character in the novel. In *The Cock and Anchor* Edmond O'Connor, the son of a famous Jacobite soldier, returns from exile and is reunited, now a rich man, with Mary Ashwoode, the daughter of Sir Richard, a Protestant landlord. Their relationship is opposed by Mary's brother, the dissolute Sir Harry Ashwoode who is heavily in debt to Nicholas Barton. Ashwoode tries to kill Barton but fails, and the latter demands Mary's hand in marriage, threatening to bankrupt the landowner if he refuses. Edmond learns of the conspiracy through an Italian servant and, after a trial and attempted reprieve is finally sentenced to death. The tragic death of Mary, which thwarts the couple's happy ending, is juxtaposed with the peaceful death of the villain, Barnet, who dies on a feather bed.

In *The Fortunes of Torlough O'Brien*, Sir Hugh Willoughby, an old Whig peer from County limerick is accused of false charges of treason

---

9     W. J. McCormack, *Sheridan Le Fanu* (Oxford: Oxford University Press, 1980), 58.

brought about by his cousin Miles Garrett who is an apostate who has
changed from Protestantism to Catholicism to benefit from the favourable
climate for followers of the latter religion under the Lord Lieutenancy of
Tyrconnel. Garrett covets his cousin's land and wants to marry his daughter
Grace, against Willoughby's wishes. Because Sir Hugh's wife, suffering semi-
imprisonment in Dublin, had had an affair with Tyrconnel, Garrett has the
means of blackmailing the peer, whom he manages to trick into insulting
the king. When King James enters into Dublin, Sir Hugh is brought to
trial and his castle taken by a gang of Garrett's "rapparees", armed bandits
and veterans of James's military campaigns. Grace, who was in the castle
when it was captured, is rescued by Torlough O'Brien, a descendant of the
castle's true owners, whose return had been foretold in local legend. O'Brien
falls in love with Grace and unsuccessfully tries to argue her father's case
before the king. Despite Torlough's intervention, however, Sir Hugh is sentenced to death. Luckily O'Brien discovers that Sir Hugh's estate cannot be
taken over by the king as it will not revert to the state on his death, and as
such he is safe while the deed is being searched for. O'Brien returns to the
wars, fighting at the battles of the Boyne and Augharim before returning
defeated and wounded. On his return, he discovers that Garrett has once
again turned coat and is now a Williamite and Protestant. Nevertheless,
O'Brien is able to marry Grace and return to Sir Hugh's estate, with the
old man still alive and pardoned under the new king. Garrett, meanwhile,
is killed in a skirmish with neighbouring "rapparee" Ned Ryan.

Both *The Cock and Anchor* and *Torlough O'Brien* show the struggles of
moderate men trapped by the circumstances of wild violent times, perhaps
reflecting Le Fanu's perception of his situation in the mid-nineteenth-century milieu of Catholic Emancipation and Parnellism. Interestingly, the
preferred heroes of Le Fanu, himself a Protestant, are both Catholics who,
despite having fought for their religion, are shown as moderate, reasonable
men. The most interesting characters in both novels are arguably the villains.
Both Barton and Garrett are strong-willed evil characters, who place their
ambitions before any moral scruples. The former is directly compared to
the devil and shares many of the characteristics of the gothic tempter, while
the latter's constant change of stance depending on the political climate
creates a memorable figure of criminal greed and expediency.

In 1851, Le Fanu published the collection of short fiction *Ghost Stories and Tales of Mystery*, which contained two stories from the 1830s, "The Murdered Cousin" and "Schalken the Painter", and two new tales "The Evil Guest" and "The Watcher" (also known as "The Familiar"). He would not publish a new novel until *The House by the Churchyard* (1863). By this time, he had purchased *The Dublin University Magazine*, which he would subsequently edit, and in which most of his ensuing fiction would be published. The death of his wife in 1858 had produced a profound depression in the author, but the reclusion he sought and his almost complete withdrawal from society would coincide with a decade of great productivity. Like the previous novels, *The House by the Churchyard* was historical in scope, but unlike these was much more rooted in the field of mystery and intrigue. Amidst a mass of subplots and divergences, including a full short story "An Authentic Narrative of the Ghost of a Hand", *The House by the Churchyard* presents a convincing and complex murder mystery in which, in true gothic fashion, a murder committed in the past affects the events of the present. Narrated by the elderly Charles de Cresson, the novel starts with a prologue related a century after the period in which the story is set in Chapelizod, Dublin, in 1767. De Cresson tells of the discovery of a skull in the local churchyard with marks from blows to the head and a small hole, apparently the result of the prefrontal leucotomy, or trepanning. The narrator then moves the story into the past, starting with the burial of a mysterious coffin identified only by a plaque bearing the initials "R. D.". It is later discovered that the body in the casket is that of Lord Dunoran, who had been found guilty of the murder of a gambler named Beauclerc to whom Dunoran had lost a large amount of money at cards. Dunoran had been surreptitiously buried after committing suicide while imprisoned for the murder.

A newcomer arrives in Chapelizod, a Mr Mervyn, who takes up residence in the Tiled House, which is reputed to be haunted. Mervyn falls in love with Gertrude Chatsworth – the daughter of the commander of the local army barracks, General Chattesworth – who is also being courted by Mr Dangerfield, the manager of the English estates of landowner Lord Castlemallard who is visiting Ireland at the time. The military doctor, Sturk, recognises Dangerfield as being, in fact, Charles Archer, the real murderer of Beauclerc, and attempts to blackmail him. As a result, Sturk is attacked in Phoenix Park and left for dead. He is, however, left in a coma, and Dangerfield realises that he will have to kill him to ensure his silence. Winning his way into the confidence of Sturk's wife, Dangerfield decides to have Sturk trepanned, a process, he has been told, which would inevitably lead to the military doctor's death. The drunken and apparently inept doctor employed for the trepanning is, however, unusually successful and Sturk regains consciousness at least for enough time to confess the whole story about how he had been attacked by Dangerfield and how this latter had murdered Beauclerc. Dangerfield is arrested as a result of Sturk's confession and found guilty of the murder, thus allowing Mervyn's father to be posthumously declared innocent. Before suffocating himself to death in his cell, Dangerfield – or Charles Archer – confesses all to Mervyn who is reinstated as the rightful Lord Dunoran.

The novel, which uses a vast number of legal and medical strategies to delay the denouement and increase suspense, offers far more to the reader in terms of complexity and incident than the earlier works. Although Mervyn shares many of the features of Le Fanu's earlier heroes like Edmond O'Connor or Torlough O'Brien, a moderate revenant who is forced to reclaim his rightful place in society, the most interesting character is arguably Dangerfield/Archer, a classic villain who returns to the community in which he has committed a crime and in which he will continue to live unsuspected, much in the same way as Yelland Mace/Walter Longcluse in the later *Checkmate* (1871). Indeed, Dangerfield is in many ways an improved version of the prototypes of Le Fanu's earlier villains Barton and Garrett, as well as providing a model for the later criminal characters created by the autor – evil and highly motivated by social as well as financial impulses. The evil of Dangerfield echoes that of the classic gothic villain, with the difference that although he is monstrous he is not a monster; he is a human being with no supernatural traits and, as such, ultimately inspires in the reader greater fear.

*The House by the Churchyard* was to be Le Fanu's final historical novel. *Wylder's Hand* (1864) was set in contemporary times and eschewed an Irish setting for an English one, apparently on the insistence of the writer's English publisher Richard Bentley who believed Le Fanu would sell more books if he were to cater for the ostensible wishes of the English reading public, influenced by the rise of the "sensation" novel of the 1860s.[10] The necessity of complying with Bentley's wishes revealed, according to McCormack, "the absence of a native publishing industry in Ireland" which "placed the writer at the mercy of the British market".[11] This British market had surrendered in the early 1860s to the phenomenon of sensation literature, spearheaded by the enormous popular success of Wilkie Collins's *The Woman in White* (1859), Ellen Wood's *East Lynne* (1861) and Mary Elizabeth Braddon's *Lady Audley's Secret* (1862). Interestingly, the term "sensation" as applied to this new literary mode, had, according to some critics, been first used in reference to the production, inundated with spectacular special effects, of *The Colleen Bawn* (1860), an adaptation of Gerald Griffin's *The Collegians* by the Irish stage manager and actor Dion Boucicault,[12] although Allan identifies an earlier use of the term in the American press in 1858.[13]

Sensationalism was, according to Ascari, "rooted in a wide range of discourses, both literary and non-literary, including the gothic, melodrama, Newgate novels, the street literature of broadsides and the nascent mass medium of journalism".[14] Although Anne-Marie Beller sees the emergence of many of the features of the genre in the 1850s, it was in the next decade, coinciding with Le Fanu's commercial relationship with Bentley, that sensation fiction dominated the literary marketplace.[15] Beller recognises "sensational techniques" in Le Fanu's short fiction of the 1850s, and the debt which the new genre owed to the gothic is generally acknowledged.[16] The sensation novel was, for Lyn Pykett, "a journalistic construct, a label attached

10    Ibid., 140.

11    Ibid., 238.

12    David Amigoni, *Victorian Literature* (Edinburgh: Edinburgh University Press, 2011), 86.

13    Janice M. Allan, "The Contemporary Response to Sensation Fiction" in *The Cambridge Companion to Sensation Fiction*, ed. Andrew Mangham (Cambridge: Cambridge University Press, 2013), 88.

14    Maurizio Ascari, *A Counter-History of Crime Fiction: Supernatural, Gothic, Sensational* (London: Palgrave Macmillan, 2007), 111.

15    Anne-Marie Beller, "Sensation Fiction in the 1850s" in Mangham (ed.), *Sensation Fiction*, 7.

16    Ibid., 15.

by reviewers to novels whose plots centred on criminal deeds, social trans-gressions or illicit passions",[17] but although these features were all present in gothic fiction, sensation fiction favoured contemporary domestic set-tings instead of the exoticism and bygone settings of its predecessor. In the sensation novel, secrets and mysteries are central to the plot, but the genre "re-adapts Gothic conventions to a secular and materialistic modern world, using multiple identities, fake death and science to re-animate the dead".[18] Sensation fiction "exchanged medieval castles for well-appointed London apartments and the maidens of yore for heroines who use the telegraph and travel by train"[19] and contrasted the horrors found in the old gothic romances with the new horrors hidden in ordinary middle-class reality.

Sensation novels were usually centred on aspects such as inheritance and domestic crime, murder, bigamy, adultery, class transgression, female criminality, mistaken or deliberately falsified identity. Mid-nineteenth-century fears about the position of women, the disintegration of class and gender barriers, the appearance and potential danger of foreigners or other "outsiders", coupled with apprehensions concerning the perceived growth in criminal activity and growth of policing techniques and their implementation throughout society were all codified within the new genre. Although Le Fanu himself repudiated any connection with sensation fic-tion,[20] his works after and including *Wylder's Hand* (1864) can be safely included in any study of the genre. The movement from an Irish to an English setting fools few readers – Elizabeth Bowen in her introduction to *Uncle Silas* called the work "an Irish story transposed to an English set-ting"[21] and Michael H. Begnal argues that Le Fanu's "London is Dublin,

17    Lyn Pykett, "The Newgate Novel and Sensation Fiction, 1830–1868", in *The Cambridge Companion to Crime Fiction*, ed. Martin Priestman (Cambridge: Cambridge University Press), 33.
18    Laurence Talairach-Vielmas, "Sensation Fiction and the Gothic" in Mangham (ed.), *Sensation Fiction*, 21.
19    Tatiana Kontou, "Sensation Fiction, Spiritualism and the Supernatural" in Mangham (ed.), *Sensation Fiction*, 141–142.
20    Ibid., 143.
21    Introduction to Sheridan Le Fanu, *Uncle Silas*, ed. Elizabeth Bowen (1864, London: Cresset Press, 1947).

and his English mansions are in actuality Irish 'big houses'".[22] It is also true that much of the work within the sensational field by Le Fanu is in fact composed of skilful re-workings of some of the earlier Irish short stories. Nevertheless, these novels provide an important page in the history of Irish crime writing, and Le Fanu's work would afford an enormous influence on the genre.

One of Le Fanu's biographers, Nelson Browne, described *Wylder's Hand* as "a masterpiece of mystery-story writing",[23] and crime writer and critic Julian Symons classified it as a "brilliant mystery puzzle" which he rates as "Le Fanu's chief contribution to the field of detection".[24] The novel has a complex and somewhat convoluted plot, a common feature of sensation novels, in which the planned marriage of convenience between Mark Wylder and the orphan Dorcas Brandon, a union which would end the age-old rivalry between the two families, is thwarted by the mysterious disappearance of the future groom. Brandon Hall has been visited by a cousin of the Wylders and Brandons, Captain Stanley Lake and his sister Rachel. While Stanley has pretensions towards Dorcas, Mark would appear to be more enamoured of the poor but attractive Rachel than of his betrothed. The appearance of Lake and his sister at the house creates a degree of tension in the atmosphere as it becomes clear through the narrator, Wylder's friend, the inauspicious lawyer Charles De Cresseron, that Lake holds some sort of power over Mark, and that this latter fears some information which Lake has and which could be used to his prejudice. Amidst this unmentioned threat of blackmail, Mark's disappearance leads to the naval cousin making claims on both Dorcas and on Mark's inheritance, apparently due to him on the absence of his cousin according to the complicated clauses of the legal deeds surrounding the properties of the two fathers.

While De Cresson suspects Mark to have been killed, several letters sent from overseas would seem to suggest that he is still alive. Mark's disappearance also has negative consequences for his brother, the impoverished vicar William Wylder who has foolishly accrued slight debts and has

22    Michael H. Begnal, *Joseph Sheridan Le Fanu* (Cranbury, NJ: Associated Universities Press, 1971), 14.

23    Nelson Browne, *Sheridan Le Fanu* (London: Arthur Barker, 1951), 42.

24    Symons, *Bloody Murder*, 58.

fallen into the clutches of the unscrupulous lawyer Josiah Larkin. Despite the contemporary setting, *Wylder's Hand* is full of references to the past and the influence of past deeds on the present. Both Mark and Stanley can be seen as victims of their family's past, whose draconian terms of inheritance have created an unsustainable situation for the modern generations of the family. The novel also features numerous gothic touches in atmosphere and the imagination of the characters. Brandon Hall is apparently haunted by the ghost of old Uncle Lorne, while from his arrival in the hose De Cressens is constantly regaled with tales of old family murders, crimes and hatreds. The supernatural is easily explained away by the natural – the ghost of Uncle Lorne is, in fact, the family's mad relative, Uncle Julius. The mystery is soon solved – the handwriting on the missives purportedly sent by Mark is found to have been falsified, and the physical hand of the doomed groom is discovered preserved in the earth in which he has been buried by his killer, Stanley Lake. While Lake, the murderer, is an unattractive character, his villainy is easily duplicated by the unscrupulous lawyer who, while goading William Wylder, has attempted to use his knowledge of Mark's disappearance to his advantage.

The English setting of *Wylder's Hand* is repeated in Le Fanu's next novel, *Uncle Silas: A Tale of Bartram-Haugh* (1864), a re-writing of the story he had already placed in an Irish setting "A Passage in the Secret History of an Irish Countess" (1839) and which itself was later reprinted as "The Murdered Cousin" (1851). Set in Derbyshire, Maud, the young narrator tells of her lonely childhood with her reclusive father Austin, a widower and disciple of the theories of Swedenborg. Some years before her birth, an unexplained murder took place at the house when a guest, Mr Charke, had been found dead with signs of violence, but inside a locked chamber. Although initial suspicion had fallen on Austin's dissolute brother, Silas Ruthyn, who had incurred outstanding gambling debts with the dead man, lack of proof and the passing of time led the incident to lay almost dormant in the collective memory. Schooled by a sinister French governess, Madame de la Rougierre, Maud inadvertently brings about the woman's dismissal after discovering the governess attempting to steal from her father's bureau. Foreseeing his death, Austin proposes an "ordeal" to his daughter – to corroborate her father's faith in his brother's innocence, she is to go and live with him at his home Bartram-Haugh. Austin subsequently adds a co-dicil to his will requiring the girl to remain with her uncle until she comes of age. Should she die before her twenty-first birthday, the estate would automatically pass into the hands of Silas's menacing son, Dudley who, the reader is aware, is in close and ominous contact with the now unemployed Madame de la Rougierre. Although aided by her father's friend and fellow Swedenborgian, the lawyer Mr Bryerly, and her cousin, the worldly lady Monica and the kind Milly, daughter of Silas's unfriendly servant Dickon Hawkes, Maud bears witness to her uncle's increasingly more regular drug-induced fits and starts to suspect that he has sinister plans for her.

Under the pretence of being employed to take Maud to a boarding school in France, Madame de la Rougiere returns, employed now by Silas. While the girl believes she is en route to the continent, the Frenchwoman actually takes her on a trip around London and back to Bartram-Haugh where she is locked in a bedroom. That night in Maud's bedroom the gov-erness unwittingly drinks the drugged claret that Silas had prepared for his niece. When, later in the night, Dudley comes to Maud's room and drives a spike through the head of the inert figure on the bed, he kills Madame de la Rougiere instead of his intended target, his cousin Maud. Maud es-capes with the help of Milly, and the next morning Silas is discovered to have died of an overdose of opium, while Dudley escapes and is believed to be in hiding in Australia.

*Uncle Silas* is a novel which skilfully combines the density of atmos-phere of the gothic with the major concerns of the new sensation fiction of the 1860s. While the character of Maud is largely passive, more in keeping with the heroine of the gothic than with the new female protagonist of the sensation novel,[25] the narrative also introduces features which would help provide the link between sensation fiction and the detective fiction of the 1890s. *Uncle Silas* is a novel which contains a central mystery, that of the murder of Charke in the locked room, and although this is not solved by a detective per se, the eventual resolution of the enigma by the mild-mannered lawyer Bryerly provides, along with the works of Poe, one of the first blueprints for modern crime fiction. The secret of the seemingly

---

25   Kontou, "Sensation Fiction" 145.

impenetrable room in which "[so] far as they could make out, Mr Charke had hermetically sealed himself into the room, and then cut his throat with his own razor"[26] is solved when Bryerly discovers a window of the room had been "provided with powerful steel hinges, very craftily sunk and concealed in the timber of the window-frame, which was concealed by an iron pin outside, and swung open upon its removal".[27] The happy ending – Maud marries the rich and handsome Lord Ilbury – is accompanied by a remarkably perceptive statement attributed to Maud, in which she muses that the "world is a parable – the habitation of symbols – the phantoms of spiritual things immortal shown in material shape".[28]

In 1865, Le Fanu published two novels, *The Prelude* and *Guy Deverell*. The latter, like *Wylder's Hand* and *Uncle Silas*, is centred around the disputes arising from a contested will and the questions of rightful heirship, which were also central to the author's earlier historical fiction. Like *Uncle Silas*, a mysterious chamber is crucial to the plot, in this case, the "Green Room", which is replete with secret doors and passages and which had been built to facilitate the comings and goings of lovers and was still used for such purposes. This room had a reputation for being haunted. Set in the confined space of the Marlowe mansion, *Guy Deverell* anticipates the Golden Age murder mystery in using almost exclusively the closed circle of the house party held there, reminiscent also, in many aspects, of the Irish Big House. The "Green Room" had been the site for the supposed robbery by Sir Jekyl of some deeds belonging to the heir apparent to the Mallory estate Guy Deverell, who Sir Jekyl subsequently killed in a duel. Among the guests at the house party are the enigmatic Monsieur Varbarriere and a young stranger who seems familiar to Sir Jekyl, Guy Strangways. The reader soon becomes aware of the plans harboured by Varbarriere, who is really Herbert Strangways, to regain the estate for his nephew, Guy – in fact, the real heir to the property and a direct descendant of the murdered Guy Deverell, who he resembles physically as suspected by Sir Jekyl and acknowledged by the baronet's mother-in-law and grandmother of the young

26   Introduction to Sheridan Le Fanu, *Uncle Silas*, ed. Elizabeth Bowen, 155.
27   Ibid., 435.
28   Ibid., 456.

Guy, Lady Alice, Sir Jekyl's chief critic in the novel. The novel ends with Sir Jekyl's death – killed, perhaps fittingly, by the elderly husband of his lover Lady Jane Lennox – and the young Guy recognised as heir and marrying the girl with whom he has fallen in love, Sir Jekyl's daughter Beatrix.

*After the Dark* (1866) revives the theme of spiritualism touched on in both *Uncle Silas* and *Guy Deverell*, but this slight romance is generally considered to be one of Le Fanu's weaker works. *The Tenants of Malory* (1867), set in the imaginary Welsh town of Cardyllian, once again uses a disputed bequest as the starting point for a contemporary romance in which the heir apparent, Cleve Verney, finds his inheritance, supposedly guaranteed after the death of his uncle in Constantinople, threatened by the demands made by the only witness to this death, without whose testimony it would have no legal standing. The re-introduction of the wily lawyer Larkin, from *Wylder's Hand*, helps to animate this minor fiction, a device which would also be used in Le Fanu's next novel, *Haunted Lives* (1868). The story focusses on the beautiful rich Laura Challys Gray who, despite her wealth, lives in semi-seclusion with an elderly companion in a suburban house in Old Brompton. Laura has it in her power to free from debts a decadent relative, Guy de Beumirail, incarcerated in the Fleet Prison for outstanding liberties. De Beaumirail, who Laura has not met personally, is at first aided in his attempts to relieve his debt by the lawyer Larkin, the Scottish banker Gillespie and the Jewish money-lender Levi. The mysterious, romantic Alfred Dacre appears on the scene apparently to help Laura, who has been the recipient of anonymous letters, each of which contains an item of her personal jewellery. Feeling herself under such harassment, Laura asks both Dacre and her distant cousin, the insipid Charles Mannering, to act as "detectives" and investigate the missives and their source. Dacre, of course, as the reader has surmised, is, in fact, de Beaumirail incognito, and the sender of the anonymous letters, a fact which Laura will not discover until after his death. Despite his initial intentions of revenging himself on Laura, he falls in love with her and, unable to free himself from his other creditors dies an honourable death in prison, thus avoiding any public humiliation for Laura, who marries Charles, this latter inheriting a peerage.

*A Lost Name* (1868) was a re-writing of "Some Account of the Latter Days of the Hon. Richard Marston of Doran" (1848), which itself had been re-published as "The Evil Guest" (1851) and would find posthumous publication as a novel also entitled *The Evil Guest* (1895). In *A Lost Name*, Mark Shadwell (Richard Marston in the other two versions) is paid a visit by his wealthy cousin Sir Roke Wycherley (Sir Wynston Berkley). In a fit of anger, Shadwell kills his cousin, but is unaware that the deed has been witnessed by the French governess Miss Marlyn (Madamoiselle de Barras), who blackmails him into marrying him. Coincidentally, however, one of Shadwell's servants, Carmel Sherlock (Merton) has been seen in the murdered man's room and is wrongly accused of the crime. While Sherlock dies in prison, Shadwell kills himself, presumably in remorse. The differences between these works are basically those of changed names and perspective, as both novel versions are narrated in the third person, while the short stories are narrated in the first. While Marston goes insane before killing himself, Shadwell appears to be fully in his senses before committing suicide, placing more emphasis on the question of guilt. A fine murder mystery, *A Lost Name* / *The Evil Guest* has perhaps suffered from the number of versions it has been subjected to and can possibly be judged inferior to the sharper, more concise short story versions.

*The Wyvern Mystery* (1869) also shares its main plot features with an earlier short story, "A Chapter in the History of a Tyrone Family" (1839). The orphan Alice, brought up by her father's enemy Squire Wyvern, is set to become his bride, but instead elopes with his son Charles Fairfield. Fairfield, who is deeply in debt, takes Alice to his secluded home where the fascinating, aged, rustic character Mildred Tarnley rules the roost. The gothic atmosphere is intensified by the suspicion that "the old soldier", the apparently insane Dutchwoman Bertha Velderkaust is, in fact, Fairfield's real wife and that his marriage to Alice is bigamous. Although this theory is finally disproved, with the help of Charles's brother Harry, the reference to Charlotte Brontë's *Jane Eyre* (1847) is obvious, with, according to Victor Sage, the Dublin writer "reclaiming" the character of Bertha from Brontë, who had been influenced by Le Fanu's short fiction.[29]

---

29   Victor Sage, *Le Fanu's Gothic: The Rhetoric of Darkness* (London: Palgrave Macmillan, 2004), 20.

*Checkmate* (1871) was a rewriting of *The Cock and Anchor*, with the events of the historical novel transposed to contemporary England, and the villain shed of his earlier incarnation's political motivation. Indeed, the strong point of this novel is the ambiguous and damaged villain, arguably one of Le Fanu's finest creations. Posing as the rich stranger Walter Longcluse, Yelland Mace has undergone plastic surgery to avoid identification and has, by befriending Richard Arden, cajoled his way into the Arden's luxurious London mansion, Mortlake Hall, and attempted to win the favour of Arden's beautiful sister, Alice. The murder of Monsieur Lebas, after a meeting with Walter/Yelland at a gambling establishment, leads, possibly for the first time in an Irish novel, to a detailed description of the activity of police officers, both in uniform and in plain clothes. As in the earlier novels, there is an open condemnation of foreigners who, as we have seen, in Le Fanu's writing, are rarely to be trusted. In *Checkmate* the police investigating the case are forthright about their suspicions regarding and subsequent arrest of foreign citizens after Lebas's murder.

*The Rose and the Key* (1871) is a remarkably modern novel with a heroine who surprises for her independent-mindedness and candour, especially bearing in mind the passive female protagonists with whom Le Fanu has us accustomed. Maud Vernon is "no insipid heroine"[30] and at the beginning of the novel, when she playfully conceals both her identity and her true social status from her unwitting would-be suitor Charles Marston, her infectious vivacity comes into stark contrast with her cold, calculating mother, Lady Barbara Vernon. Maud, on a walking tour with her ageing cousin and confidante Miss Max, finds herself being followed by a one-eyed man who would appear to be a spy sent by Lady Vernon. The tension between Maud and her mother at first seems inexplicable to the reader. The appearance at the Vernons' country house, Royston Hall, of the weak and sickly Captain Vernon leads to speculation that Lady Barbara is in love with this much younger man. Her obsession with Vernon leads to her trying to oblige her daughter to sign a document renouncing the Captain and, eventually, to having Maud interned in Glarewoods, a terrifying lunatic asylum run by the sinister Italian mesmerist Dr Antomarchi.

---

30   Browne, *Sheridan Le Fanu*, 66.

As with the majority of Le Fanu's works, a disputed will is central to the plot, and the threat to Maud's inheritance of the estate comes not from the insipid Mr Tintern, who hopes to inherit Royston himself, as the hints provided seem to suggest but from Maud's mother herself, who arranges for Maud's internment in the asylum to facilitate the inheritance passing to a secret son from her clandestine first marriage, who, it is finally revealed, is Captain Vivian. The cruel Lady Barbara is one of Le Fanu's most notable acts of characterisation, although the novel abounds in memorable minor characters such as the one-eyed spy Elihu Lizard, the mysterious lawyer Mr Dawe, the aptly named Darkdale, Lady Barbara's sinister factotum, the affable Irish curate Mr Doody, the menacing lady's maid Mercy Creswell and the strange inhabitants of the asylum. The doctors who appear in the novel are all fear-provoking, especially the selfish and financially oriented mesmerist Antomarchi, who guards the Malayan dagger which had belonged to his father and which this progenitor had used to kill a renegade priest after a row in Egypt.

The novel contains several notable scenes, including the carriage ride which shares certain similarities with the aborted journey to the French boarding-school imposed upon this novel's near-namesake, Maud Ruthyn, in *Uncle Silas*, or with the frightening shower-bath scene in which Maud watches fellow inmate Mrs Fish suffer a type of nineteenth-century water-boarding while tied to an iron chair. A casual meeting with Mr Doody allows Maud to smuggle out a letter to Charles who goes to see the asylum owner, the dour physician Dr Damian. Charles manages to convince this doctor that Maud has been confined because of her mother's selfish plans and the avaricious Italian mesmerist's greed, and he frees the girl and withdraws his financial support for Antomarchi's quasi-medical activities. The death of Lady Barbara beneath a painting of Cleopatra clutching the asp is brought about by the shock of the news of her son Vivian's elopement with Esther, Tintern's daughter, and Maud and Charles are free to marry, with the former acceding to her legitimate inheritance, thus ending on a happy note this "fully-fledged, gothic madhouse mystery".[31]

---

31    Sage, *Le Fanu's Gothic*, 157.

Amidst these novels of the 1860s and 1870s, Victorian romances, which can be classified within the mode of sensation fiction, the publication of *In a Glass Darkly* in 1872 was perhaps something of a surprise. Looking back towards his earlier fictions with historical settings and the influence of the supernatural, but at the same time forward to the rational detection of Sherlock Holmes and his counterparts, *In a Glass Darkly* is widely considered to be Le Fanu's masterwork. Although consisting of a collection of five stories (two of which are of the length of novellas), the book is held together by an intricate narrative structure in which an unnamed narrator acts as curator and editor of the papers left by the mysterious Dr Martin Hesselius. Hesselius is a doctor whose "case studies" provide a model for later detective figures such as Holmes,[32] and who Nelson Browne sees as "a projection of the author himself".[33] The fact that the "detective" is a medical practitioner and not a member of the police or detective force is seen by Martin Kayman as being symptomatic of the status of Ireland at the time,[34] but the mixture of psychiatry, physiology, mysticism and pure detection creates what Srjdan Smajic calls "the first occult detective in history",[35] whose task, like that of Poe's Dupin and Conan Doyle's Holmes "is to make inferences and conjectures, link effects to causes".[36] Smajic goes on to state that, while the methodology employed by Hesselius is similar to that used by the traditional detective he starts from a different premise, namely the belief in spirits, ghosts and the existence of the supernatural.[37] Despite this, however, the cases Hesselius solves, investigations into the illnesses of the human mind, are open to both rational and supernatural exploitations.[38]

32  Penzoldt, "Supernatural in Fiction", 111.
33  Browne, *Sheridan Le Fanu*, 78.
34  Martin Kayman, *From Baker Street to Bow Street: Mystery, Detection and Narrative* (London: Macmillan,2003), 45.
35  Srdjan Smajic, *Ghost-Seers, Detectives and Spiritualists: Theories of Vision in Victorian Literature and Science* (Cambridge: Cambridge University Press, 2010), 150.
36  Ibid., 155.
37  Ibid.
38  Browne, *Sheridan Le Fanu*, 78.

The first three stories presented in the collection, "Green Tea", "The Familiar" and "Mr Justice Harbottle", all deal with cases of haunting, but a haunting which appears to be rooted in the mind of the afflicted. In "Green Tea" an English vicar, the Reverend Jennings, tells Hesselius that he is being haunted by a weird monkey which is visible to him alone, and which encourages the clergyman to commit crimes and to cause harm to himself. The doctor approaches the case with an open mind, willing to accept the supernatural supposition of an actual haunting or the natural explanation of hallucinatory obsession, and finally comes to the conclusion that the tea the reverend is consuming is responsible for the visions. Far from providing a natural solution, however, Hesselius insists that the green tea is opening the vicar's "inner eye", giving rise to the vision of the monkey. The doctor's speculations are ineffectual in any case, as Jennings is eventually driven to suicide by the persistence of the monkey's presence. "The Familiar" is a re-writing of an earlier story, "The Watcher" (1851), in which Barton, a sea captain, returns to Dublin to discover he is being followed by a shadowy figure who takes the form of a strange dwarf. These visions are accompanied by accusatory voices, which seem to refer to some secrets hidden in the captain's past related to the mistreatment of a seaman whose subsequent death may have sparked the feelings of guilt which accompany the hapless Barton to his death. Hesselius distances himself, however, from a simply materialistic explanation and the story ends by the narrator opining that "whatever the truth may be as to the origins and motives of this mysterious persecution, there can be no doubt that, with respect to the agencies by which it was accomplished, absolute and impenetrable mystery is likely to prevail until the day of doom".[39]

Guilt and its effect on the human conscience is, once more, the subject matter of "Mr Justice Harbottle", again a revision of an earlier story, "An Account of Some Strange Disturbances in Aungier Street" (1853). The judge of the title, living in the mid-eighteenth century, is haunted by the spirits of those he has condemned to death in his assizes. In a dream-vision, the judge is himself tried by his mirror image and, at the end of the story,

39  Sheridan Le Fanu, *In a Glass Darkly* (1872, Ware, Herts: Wordsworth Classics, 1995), 68.

is found hanging by the neck in what appears to be a case of guilt-related suicide. "The Room in the Dragon Volant" (1872) is a historical mystery detailing the adventures of the young English narrator in post-Napoleonic France. Set in 1815, Richard falls in love with a mysterious French countess who tells the young Englishman her story of oppression at the hands of a brutal husband and convinces him to help her rid herself of her spouse. Despite the use of gothic conventions, like a haunted inn and a case of burying alive, the novella is primarily a "superb story of crime" which pits an innocent Englishman abroad against the wiles of a devious French fraudster whose motives are strictly of an economic sort.[40]

"Carmilla" is undoubtedly the best-known story contained within *In a Glass Darkly* and probably the author's most famous work. Regarded as a major influence on Bram Stoker's *Dracula* (1897), "Carmilla" is narrated by Laura who is living with her father, a wealthy English diplomat and widower, in a lonely castle in the forests of Styria in south-eastern Austria. Laura relates how as a child she had dreamt that she had been visited by a strange girl who had bitten her on the chest and now, aged eighteen, she and her father await the arrival of Bertha Rheinfeldt, the niece of an acquaintance of the father, General Spielsdorf. Informed of the girl's death before her arrival, Laura and her father take in another girl who has suffered a strange carriage accident close to their castle. Laura recognises the girl from her childhood dream, and this recognition seems to be replicated by the girl, Carmilla, who has been forbidden from revealing any information about her background or family. Despite the friendship which grows between the two girls, Laura is baffled by Carmilla's secrecy, by her periods of near-catatonic sleep and by her constant mood swings. Laura sees in a portrait of a Countess Mircalla Karnstein the exact likeness of her friend but, when her health deteriorates after a series of nightmares, her father takes Laura to the village of Karnstein where they meet Bertha's uncle who tells them that his niece before her death had met and befriended a mysterious young girl called Millarca before falling ill with symptoms similar to those of Laura. The fact that Bertha had died from these symptoms worries both Laura and her father who begin to suspect that Mircalla, Carmilla and Millarca,

40  Browne, *Sheridan Le Fanu*, 82.

all anagrams, are versions of the same vampire, Countess Karnstein, whose body is eventually exhumed and destroyed.

*Willing to Die* (1873) was the last novel published by Le Fanu in his lifetime. Serialised, like *The Rose and the Key*, in Dickens's *All the Year Round* in 1872, it was published in three volumes the following year after Le Fanu's death. The first-person narrator, Ethel Ware, is introduced to a mysterious stranger who proceeds to court her. This stranger, later revealed to be the dissolute Richard Marston, a name already used twice in the past by the author for characters, becomes engaged to Ethel but the disappearance of a will means that she loses her potential inheritance and is unable to marry Marston, who confesses that he is already married to an unsuitable wife who has been committed to an asylum. This confession is later discovered to be false as Laura Grey, a governess, reveals to Esther that Marston, a close relation of Sir Harry Rokestone had discovered that his relative intended to leave his money to Esther and wooed her as a means of obtaining her money. The involvement of the scheming Jesuit Carmel and his accomplice, the sinister Dr Droqville, gives the plot something of an anti-Catholic flavour, as the latter tries to convert Esther to Catholicism, knowing that such a conversion would annul her inheritance. *Willing to Die* is perhaps a minor work, but it is replete with dark atmospheres and sensational events, including a bloody duel in the Welsh forests, suicide, bigamy, scheming Jesuits and a shipwreck.

# "Reader, you have seen the singular and extraordinary circumstances connected with the handkerchief, the sledge, and the sack." Sensation and Mystery Fiction

Le Fanu provided an important early influence for *Fitz-James O'Brien* (1826–62). O'Brien was born in Cork but, after a spell in England, made his name in New York after emigrating in early 1852. There he befriended the Irish actor John Brougham who founded the magazine *The Lantern*, providing O'Brien with a steady income from his contributions. O'Brien would later contribute to important American publishing ventures such as *Harper's Magazine*, *The Atlantic Review* and *The New York Times* before his untimely death from complications to a wound he received fighting for the Union army during the Civil War. His literary output consisted largely of poetry and short stories, including several fine mystery tales. "A Dead Secret" (1853), published anonymously in *Harper's Magazine* shows the influence of Le Fanu, although his later mystery tales, such as "The Pot of Tulips" (1855), "The Golden Ingot" and "The Lost Room" (both 1858) and, most especially, "The Diamond Lens" (also 1858), show very clearly the influence of Edgar Allan Poe. "The Diamond Lens" is generally considered to be O'Brien's most successful story and has been reprinted and anthologised on numerous occasions. For Francis Wolle, it "shows very plainly the use that O'Brien made of the Poe technique – what he learned from Poe and made use of, what he added, and in what points he was incapable of following Poe's example".[1] The narrator, Linley, obsessed with microscopes, moves from his native New England to New York City, where he visits a medium who puts him in contact with the spirit of the Dutch scientist Antonie van Leeuwenhoek, who tells him

---

1    Francis Wolle, *Fitz-James O'Brien: A Literary Bohemian of the Eighteen-Fifties* (Boulder, CO: University of Colorado Press, 1944), 152.

how to construct the perfect microscope using a lens crafted from a 140-carat diamond. Linley kills his friend Jules Simon who possessed such a diamond, having stolen it from some Brazilian slaves he had been supervising. He fashions the microscope and, through the magnificent lens, is able to see, in a drop of water, the most perfect and beautiful of women. Linley falls in love with this apparition, who he calls Animula, but is frustrated as his relationship with such perfection is only realised through the lens of his microscope. Trying to rationally justify his reactions, he goes to the theatre in an attempt to cure himself by seeing a beautiful dancer, but he soon realises that she is dim in comparison to his perfect Animula. As the water on the lens starts to evaporate, Animula fades away, until she eventually disappears, and the hapless Linley is driven to insanity through his grief. "The Diamond Lens" is a magnificent study of monomania, and how the narrator's obsession leads him towards murder and madness. Like Poe, O'Brien at his best anticipates narrative tendencies which would not become fully developed until half a century later, and it is tempting to wonder what work the Cork-born author might have produced had he lived longer.

Apart from Le Fanu, the Irish contribution to the mode of sensation fiction was limited, and although elements of sensation novels are to be found in Irish writers over the next three decades, only *Charlotte Riddell* and Frances Cashel Hoey are generally categorised among the writers of the sensation boom of the 1860s. Riddell wrote under the assumed name of F. G. Trafford, and her three-volume *George Geith of Fen Court* was published in 1864. The work combines typical sensation features such as bigamy, bankruptcy, blackmail, the pernicious influence of wildcat capitalism and the usurpation of identity. The mystery, first posed at the very beginning of the novel, as to why George leaves the Church to attempt to make his life in the City, is not revealed until the end of the work, and creates a satisfactory mood of suspense which lasts throughout the novel. Riddell describes *George Geith* as the "commonplace story of modern men and modern doings",[2] featuring a protagonist who is "too commonplace

---

2    Charlotte Riddell (as F. G. Trafford), *George Geith of Fen Court*, 3 vols. (London: Tinsley, 1864), vol. 1, 3.

to be the hero of a novel".[3] The novel, however, also rigorously examines a society which, although legally permitting the concept of divorce, makes such a step prohibitive for all but the most affluent.

*Frances Cashel Hoey* (born Frances Sarah Johnson, 1830–1908) also turned a court case dealing with divorce into the central theme of her *Out of Court* (1874). First married at the age of sixteen, the author converted to Catholicism on marrying her second husband John Cashel Hoey, assistant editor of the *Nation* magazine in 1858. Her first published work was the novella *Buried in the Deep* (1865), which was serialised in *Chambers's Magazine*. Her first full-length novel, *A House of Cards* (1868), also takes divorce as a topic, when a young man, Henry Hurst, commits murder because his wife, who is also his foster-sister, refuses to grant him a divorce to allow him to marry his new love. Henry is unaware of the fact that his biological father had himself been a convicted murderer, although the stress on the influence of hereditary traits would not have been lost on the reader. For P. D. Edwards *A House of Cards* is "[s]lapdash in both style and structure" and "a fairly routine, nondescript sensation story", which lays emphasis on "such stock themes as the irresistible power of retributive fate, the ineluctability of hereditary evil, and the desultoriness of man's (or more specifically woman's) belief that early misdeeds or mistakes can be permanently lived down and concealed".[4] In other words, the perfect ingredients for any sensation novel that fancies itself as such. *A House of Cards* was first serialised in the immensely popular *Tinsley's Magazine*, edited by the journalist and novelist Edmund Yates. A controversy would arise in which William Tinsley, the great Victorian publisher and owner of the magazine, claimed that Hoey had been author, or at least co-author, of some of the works published by Yates in his own name.[5]

Hoey's prolific output of sensation fiction lasted beyond the period during which the format was blooming, and her eleven published novels, which include *A Golden Sorrow* (1872), *Griffith's Double* (1876), *All or*

---

3   Ibid., 13.
4   P. D. Edwards, "Frances Cashel Hoey", *Victorian Fiction Research Guides* no. 8, <https://victorianfictionresearchguides.org/frances-cashel-hoey/>, accessed 24 September 2019.
5   Ibid.

*Nothing* (1879) and *The Question of Cain* (1882), all bear the hallmark of sensation fiction, and many the embryonic themes of future crime fiction. In *All or Nothing* a thieving continental servant attempts a murder, and the failed assassination attempt precipitates the death of one of the heroines, but the central themes of the novel are those of marriage, the family, inheritance and fate, while the level of coincidence is high, with at least three characters in the novel referring to the sensation they have of "there being only half a dozen people in the world".[6]

Features of the sensation novel would also appear in the writings of Dubliner *Annie French Hector* (1825–1902) who wrote under the pseudonym of Mrs. Alexander and published at least forty-two novels in her lifetime, most of which centred around young women and their problems with family, love and their financial situation. *Her Dearest Foe* (1976) is an early detective novel in which the detection is largely undertaken by the heroine Kate Travers and her friend, the journalist Tom Reed, who endeavour to discover the truth of an apparently legitimate second will, which effectively disinherits Kate from her late husband's estate. Convinced that this will is false, they attempt to uncover the operation behind its signing and, although matters are complicated by the testament's new beneficiary, Sir Hugh Galbraith, falling in love with Kate, the case is resolved by solid amateur detective work before the conventional happy ending. Kate's investigation into the fraudulent document brings a refreshing note of agency to Kate's life, and the predictably romantic ending does little to spoil the exhilaration the reader shares with the protagonist during her brief period as a detective. Interestingly, the police have little to do in the way of detection in this novel. When Sir Hugh calls on officers of Scotland Yard to try to recover Kate's stolen pocket-book, they ignominiously fail in their task.

*False Scent* (1889) would reveal a more participatory role for the police, when a Russian aristocrat, accused of being a nihilist responsible for the murder of a government minister, is exonerated by the fittingly named Inspector Sharp and the police spy Lisle. Hope Farrant, an orphan, is travelling by train when a man, obviously in disguise, enters her carriage. This man, a foreigner, tells Hope that he is being pursued for a crime he did not

---

6    Mrs Frances Cashel Hoey, *All or Nothing* (London: Hurst and Blackett, 1879), 158.

commit, and that he will later contact her to prove his innocence. Hope suspects that he is a Russian anarchist, and becomes involved in the case being investigated by Inspector Sharp of Scotland Yard and the mysterious Lisle. The man is revealed to be, indeed, a Russian, but rather than an anarchist he is a rich aristocrat who, in the disappointing ending, marries Hope.

The 1860s also saw the publication of two semi-fictional accounts which provide fascinating insights into the process of criminal justice in nineteenth-century Ireland. *Robert Curtis's The Irish Police Officer: Comprising the Identification and Other Tales* (1861) is a series of short stories which, according to the author, were "originally compiled from memoranda, in my private journal, of interesting cases which occurred during my early experience in the Irish Constabulary".[7] While largely anecdotic, these tales deal with the variety of criminal activity carried out in rural Ireland from the 1830s, including theft, murder, land-related disputes and secret society activity. Most cases are solved by a combination of pure coincidence and suspicion, and little real police work is documented, although the unnamed narrator does make reference to identity parades and the systematic interrogation of witnesses, and states that the Constabulary "even at that early moment, of which I speak, had become well-organised and efficient".[8] Curtis also published *The History of the Royal Irish Constabulary* in 1871. Similar in many respects to *The Irish Police Officer* is *Henry Robert Addison's Recollections of an Irish Police Magistrate and Other Reminiscences of the South of Ireland* (1862). Based on the accounts of his father-in-law, Thomas Phillip Vokes, Addison's work is based on a time "when the horrors of agrarian outrage, and those of base assassination, threaten to fill the South of Ireland with just terror".[9] Addison praises the work of the former Police Magistrates, while voicing "doubts regarding the efficiency of the present police system".[10] The problem, he believes, lies in the tendency to try to make police officers too much like soldiers, along with an excessive reliance on

---

7   Robert Curtis, *The Irish Police Officer: Comprising the Identification and Other Tales* (London: Ward, Lock & Co., 1861), v.

8   Ibid., 90.

9   Henry Robert Addison, *Recollections of an Irish Police Magistrate and Other Reminiscences of the South of Ireland* (London: Ward, Lock & Co., 1862), vii.

10   Ibid., vii.

centralisation, so incidents are first reported to Dublin Castle and, as such, this "destroys every hope which would arise in the locality, of instant aid in the detection of the crime".[11] The cases which Addison evokes are often those which lie within the Irish collective imagination, including that of Captain Rock and that of The Colleen Bawn, and contain such unlikely events as the magistrate fooling peasants into believing he was a member of Captain Rock's gang "by his thorough knowledge of Irish".[12]

In *John Orlebar, Clk.* (1878), *James Franklin Fuller* (1835–1924), a Kerry-born actor, architect and novelist, tells a tale of an evil stepmother and step-brother who attempt to deprive Winifred Arderne of her inheritance on the death of her father, Sir Robert. The novel, like Fuller's earlier *Culmshire Folk* (1873), is largely set in the fictional English county of Culmshire, where a young curate, Orlebar, in love with Winifred, his half-cousin, enlists the aid of his friend, the local doctor Packenham, to find information concerning her mother, the first Lady Arderne. Packenham travels to Ireland, where he discovers that Winifred's stepbrother, Twinch, was really the son of an Irish rebel who had shot a policeman and escaped the country, and her stepmother was in fact Lady Arderne's paid companion, Mrs Twinch. *John Orlebar, Clk.* is notable for Packenham's detective efforts in a topical version of Ireland where he discovers "the apparent absence of all hurry in the movements of Irish trains and Irish officials and railway porters", and where "time is chape; and thanks be to God, we have lashings of it".[13] The ubiquitous happy ending in this novel, as neatly designed as Kylemore Abbey in Connemara, the best-known of Fuller's architectural works, sees Winifred inherit and marry Orlebar, who gives up the ministry to dedicate his time to improving the life of the tenants on their estate.

*Richard Dowling* (1846–98) enjoyed considerable popularity in the 1880s and 1890s, with a number of his works being reprinted on several occasions in both Britain and the USA. Born in Clonmel, Tipperary into a devout Catholic family, after attending the Jesuit school in Limerick he

11    Ibid., viii.
12    Ibid., 6.
13    James Franklin Fuller, *John Orlebar, Clk.* (London: Smith, Elder and Co., 1878), 233.

started working in the shipping office belonging to an uncle in Waterford.[14] He soon left to move into the world of journalism in Dublin where he worked on various newspapers and magazines before publishing a volume of essays *On Babies and Ladders: Essays on Things in General* (1873). In 1874 he moved to London where, working first for the *Illustrated Sporting and Dramatic News* and later *Tinsley's Magazine*, he started his first novel, written between 1875 and 1876 and published three years after its completion. *The Mystery of Killard* (1879) is set in County Clare at the time of the Famine, in "times thick with sombre horror in Ireland".[15] Much speculation is being made into the fortune of the Lane family, with many believing that the Lanes have discovered how to convert iron into gold. The current father of the family, David Lane, had sought a wife who was mute like his mother, and who was hence unable to reveal the secret of the family's gold. When David discovers that his son John is not dumb, as he had believed, the boy is forced into exile, travelling to China and Australia before returning to Ireland. The mystery of the story, the existence and provenance of the gold, leads to a number of adventurers arriving at the remote Bishop's Island to uncover the secret of the gold. The outsider, Edward Martin, who had arrived at the remote spot after his brother's death by drowning in the area, and with whose daughter, Mary, John Lane will fall in love with, eventually discovers the secret of the gold and its connection with a vessel which had been wrecked while carrying gold from Southampton. Although *The Mystery of Killard* is in many respects a typical three-volume romance, Dowling shows some early skill with his depictions of the wild coastal landscapes of Clare, and with the confusion between factual accounts and local legends, he maintains the element of mystery throughout the work.

The novel was followed by a volume of short stories, *The Sport of Fate* (1880). The best of these stories are well-crafted crime mysteries, all set in England, which bring into play the quirks of chance alluded to in the title. In "Red Hands", Charles Mallard, a poverty-stricken artist, deserts Agnes, the girl he is in love with, to take up with Louise de Beauvoir, an actress

---

14    M. Russell (as MR), "Sketches in Irish Biography. The Late Richard Dowling, the Novelist" *The Irish Monthly* 27, no. 30 (January 1899), 13.

15    Richard Dowling, *The Mystery of Killard*, 3 vols. (London: Tinsley Brothers, 1879), vol. 1, 113.

who, Dowling tells us ominously, has African blood. When Louise discovers Charles's locket, which contains a photograph of Agnes, she determines to kill her rival, but Agnes has died, presumably from the sorrow derived from Mallard's desertion. This death affects Charles in such a way that he believes he sees red stains on his hands, and he tries to leave the country after Agnes's funeral, only to be followed by the relentless Louise. "The Partners of Leather Lane" sees a market trader falling in love with a beautiful Italian customer, only to be murdered by his partner, while "The Marine Binocular" is an enjoyable murder mystery involving an urbane narrator who discovers a double murder after hearing screams from a neighbouring apartment. He seeks police help, and the officer he contacts, Detective Bracken, enlists the narrator's aid to capture the killer, a neighbour, through the ingenious use of the field glasses of the title.

Dowling's second novel, *The Weird Sisters* (1880), is set in the imaginary English town of Danesford, where Charles Walter Grey is a banker who has taken to cheating his customers. After deliberately bringing about the death of his alcoholic wife, whose body he conceals in a rooftop water tank, Grey tries to marry Maud, a young heiress and daughter of wealthy baronet Sir Alexander Midharst, the owner of a castle complex called the "Weird Sisters" and one of the victims of the banker's financial duplicity. Maud, however, is in love with her cousin, the Egyptologist and heir apparent to the baronetcy Sir William, who mistrusts Grey and suspects his motivation. Her father, on the other hand, trusts the banker implicitly, and asks him to be the executor of his will and to act as his daughter's economic guardian. On Sir Alexander's death, Grey, who is himself being blackmailed by a small-time burglar who has accidentally come across the secret of Grey's wife's death, takes on his role as Maud's guardian, with the hope of winning her love. The youthful Sir William, frequently absent from the country because of his professional activity, returns in time to save the girl from the clutches of the banker. The novel ends with a fire in Grey's house which destroys his wife's body, the only evidence of the murder, but also kills the banker, leaving Maud free to marry her cousin.

In 1881 Dowling published two new "triple-decker" romances, *The Husband's Secret* and *The Duke's Sweetheart*. This latter is set again in England, with a colourful protagonist named Charles Augustus Cheyne, a poor journalist and novelist, known to his acquaintances as the "Duke of Long Acre". Despite his poverty, Charles is, in fact, the heir to the rich aristocrat Reginald Cheyne, the Duke of Shropshire. He is in love with the beautiful Marion Durrant, but she is unaware of his background, and when Charles discovers that he is to become the next Duke she panics and runs away. Desperate to track her down, Cheyne finds Marion in a building on fire. Although he rescues her he is badly injured and, on his deathbed marries her before passing away. Similar melodramatic devices are also found in Dowling's next novel, *Sweet Inisfail* (1882). The events take place, as in *The Mystery of Killard*, in the author's native Ireland, and the novel is notable for its interesting depiction of the RIC and for the enigma which is central to the plot. Fitzgerald has inherited some land in Clonmore, County Tipperary and, after visiting his friends George Martin and his wife in Chelsea, Mrs Martin suggests that her husband, who fears a nervous breakdown, should accompany his friend to Ireland in order to take some rest. George is the possessor of a secret, the knowledge that years before while working with his brother Frederick as a telegraph clerk, he had been wrongfully accused of the robbery of money actually taken by Frederick who had used illicit information to enable him to falsely collect the winnings from horse races. While George had eventually been cleared of all blame, his awareness of his brother's duplicity has severely undermined his health.

On arriving in Ireland, Fitzgerald and George enter a telegraph office where the clerk, Pryce, who is really Frederick in disguise, recognises his brother. Fitzgerald, in love with his Irish sweetheart Agnes, the "sweet Inisfail" of the title, makes a land deal with the local farmer O'Grady, who hands over a large amount of cash to him. Frederick attacks Fitzgerald and, stealing the money, leaves him for dead, but on discovering that he is in fact still alive, hides him in a remote cottage where he attempts to nurse him back to health to avoid being hanged for his murder. Meanwhile, George, who himself has severe financial problems after being tricked by the Jewish money-lender Isaacs, is accused of the robbery and murder of the missing Fitzgerald. The police are called in, and the reader is rewarded with a fascinating portrayal of the RIC, in the persons of the Head Inspector and the Head Constable, Curran. This latter is offered a promotion if he is able to track down Frederick, who has now been identified and recognised as the assailant on Fitzgerald. With the help of Agnes and George's wife, Helen, who has arrived in Ireland to help clear her husband's name, Curran finds Frederick, who has tried to escape "to the wild west coast, where there were islands and villages in which policemen were unknown".[16] After an exciting finale in which Frederick Martin goes mad and tries to jump to his death in a quarry, taking the hapless Curran with him, Agnes and Fitzgerald are married and George and Helen are free to return to England.

Sweet Inisfail is one of Dowling's most satisfactory novels. The topical use of telegraph information as a motive for crime links the novel both to the sensation fiction of the 1860s and to the detective stories that would appear in the 1890s, while an interesting array of secondary characters add depth to the narrative. The anti-Semitism in the portrayal of Isaacs, a Jewish money-lender who is also a dwarf, a card-cheat and a swindler, is unfortunately typical of the age, while both female characters, Helen and Agnes, despite originally seeming to conform to the respective stereotypes of English rose and Irish colleen, actually assume an untypically active role in the release of Fitzgerald from his evil captive. Frederick Marton is an excellent example of the implacable Victorian villain, using new technologies to help his criminal enterprises as well as employing such "ungentlemanly" actions as cheating at billiards and cards and drugging his victim – in this case Isaacs – before robbing him. The police have an unusually central role in the investigation, although the author is critical of the efficiency of the constabulary, stating that the Irish police "are a poor breed of bullies" and that "the sub-constable is an accomplished cavalier compared to that dummy creature of respectability – the sub-inspector".[17]

The year 1882 also saw the publication of Dowling's second collection of short stories, A Sapphire Ring and Other Stories. The title story is, in fact, not short at all, occupying as it does over one volume of the three-volume set. Starting with an escape from prison, "A Sapphire Ring" is an interesting crime romance involving a wealthy ship-owner and the supposed attempted

16  Richard Dowling, Sweet Inisfail, 3 vols. (London: Tinsley Brothers, 1882), vol. 3, 209.
17  Dowling, Sweet Inisfail, vol. 3, 273.

murder of him and his son by his nephew and ward, Walter Langley. The fact that both cousins are in love with the same girl, the rich heiress Evelyn, seems to confirm Langley's guilt. Evelyn, however, helps Walter to escape from the harsh Cornish jail in which he is imprisoned, aided, surprisingly, by her other suitor, Walter's cousin, rival and, supposedly, one of his in-tended victims. Walter successfully escapes and his uncle admits to having falsely incriminated his nephew because he had wrongly believed himself to be facing bankruptcy. *The Sapphire Ring* is notable for two reasons. The first of these is the magnificent opening scene, in which the escape from prison is realised with panoptic techniques from a variety of perspectives, both physical and emotional. The second is the ending which, despite the proof of Langley's innocence, opens a pertinent question regarding the ambiguity of the legal system. Langley is innocent of the attempted murder of his uncle and his cousin, and his innocence has been corrobor-ated by a statement signed by his uncle before his death. However, Walter was imprisoned for the crime, and, by escaping from prison, despite his innocence, has committed another criminal offence. Although his uncle's written confession will secure his pardon, he cannot be exonerated for the crime he has in fact committed, his breakout from prison. Justice, at the end of the story, cannot be fully applied, and Walter is forced to flee the country where he is advised to stay for a period of years, being told, that, should he return to England after this period, the police would not inter-fere with him on his return. This imperfect solution is fascinating within the context of a world which saw its legal system as, if not perfect, having, at least, an answer to every ambiguity of this kind.

The open ending of "A Sapphire Ring", in which the indissoluble ri-gidity of the law is denied, would be repeated in Dowling's last novel *The Fate of Luke Ormond* (1905). The other stories in the volume do not meet the standards of the title tale, but "The Castle on the Cliff" is an eloquent tale of a newly rich industrialist's attempts to gain acceptance into high so-ciety by marrying the beautiful daughter of a degenerate aristocrat, using his seemingly dissolute son to help his plan, while "The Mystery of Lankhorne Place" is a slight mystery in a suburban setting, and "The White Lady of the Snow" and "Bertram's Cottage" are crime romances in historical settings, the former in Ireland and the latter in England. In "Through the Foam" the phobia against foreigners typical of much fiction of the period, and apparent throughout Dowling's work, appears once again in the figure of a roguish immigrant who tries by foul means to steal the wife of an Irish seaman.

In *The Last Call* (1884) the action moves from Ireland to England, from the imaginary seaport of Rathclare to Dublin and thence to London. Centred on the rivalry between two singers, the Irishman Eugene O'Donnell and the Frenchman Dominique Lavirotte, it encompasses not only the professional and artistic aspects of their relationship but also their conflicting romantic interests. *The Last Call* contains several melodramatic scenes, including the threat of bankruptcy faced by Eugene's father after the failure of a bank, the attempted suicide of Dora, Dominique's fiancée and governess to Vernon, the bank owner, a frenetic treasure hunt in St Prisca's Tower in London and criminal arson coupled with the kidnapping of Eugene's young son.

*The Hidden Flame* (1885) is a murder mystery involving the stock devices of conspiracy, false and mistaken identity, confidence tricks, and disputed inheritance, but which is of particular interest in the history of Irish crime fiction for its introduction of an efficient professional private detective. The confidence trickster Frederick Berl has taken the name John Lyster to ingratiate himself into the confidence of the elderly Richard Lyster and, together with the debauched Edward Rolt, conspires to murder the old man in what is made to look like a boating accident at a weir. The two conspirators fall out, and Berl, who wishes to marry Muriel, one of Richard's orphan granddaughters, and hence receive a substantial part of his inheritance, attempts to kill Rolt, who is only saved by the timely intervention of the young lawyer, Allen Prior, in love himself with Lyster's other granddaughter, Florence. Allen, a good example of the dynamic rising professional of the period, is aided by the "investigator" Mr Winter, who discovers that "John Lyster is, in fact, the fraudster Frederick Berl, who had previously been accused of theft from the bank at which he worked. Mistrusted by both sides – Allen sees him as looking more like the poor relative of an alderman than anything else",[18] and Berl calls him a "hireling

---

18    Richard Dowling, *The Hidden Flame: A Romance*, 3 vols. (London: Tinsley Brothers, 1885), vol. 3, 39.

spy",[19] – Winter is highly competent and resourceful. He discovers the carcass of a rat, killed by poison, and primitive forensic science is taken into account as the detective sends the dead rodent to a chemist for its analysis. It is not, however, Winter's intervention which brings the plotters to justice, as both villains die struggling together at the old mill under the light of the lamp which gives the work its title, and under the agonised gaze of Muriel who is driven mad by the horrific sight as the conspirators fall to their death amidst the swirling waters.

The year 1886 was a productive one for Dowling, who published the one-volume novella *The Skeleton Key* and two three-volume romances, *Fatal Bonds* and *Tempest-Driven*. This latter is again set between England and the south of Ireland, and features a murder which is at first believed to be a suicide. After happening upon the body of the elderly Irishman Davenport, Alfred Paulton enlists the aid of his Irish friend Jerry O'Brien who tells him the details of the past of the murdered man's young wife, Marion Butler. Discovering that Marion had left her lover Tom Blake to marry Davenport on her father's insistence, suspicion falls on Marion and her jilted lover who, it is discovered, had been blackmailing her husband. During a visit to Ireland, where Jerry has land, the two friends discover that Fahey, Davenport's partner who had been supposed dead, was still alive and "haunting" a remote cave. Alfred and Jerry find out that Davenport and Fahey had been involved in an international forgery scheme, and Fahey becomes the main suspect. *Tempest-Driven* lacks the happy ending typical of Dowling's earlier romances. Alfred proposes to Marion, but she refuses him before going mad, suggesting that she was involved in her husband's death.

*Miracle Gold* (1888), *An Isle of Surrey* (1889) and *A Baffling Quest* (1891) are all three-volume romances set in south-eastern England. *Miracle Gold* returns to the theme of Dowling's first novel, with the apparently alchemistic creation of gold being finally accredited to criminal activity and not the supernatural. Oscar Leigh, a hunchback, is a "hideous deformed monstrous dwarf"[20] who "looked like a wild beast, like some savage creature

19    Ibid., 59.
20    Richard Dowling, *Miracle Gold*, 3 vols. (London: Ward and Downey, 1888), vol. 1, 13.

that would crouch, and spring, and seize, and rend"[21] who, working from his workshop, claims to have discovered miracle gold using the legendary Philosopher's Stone. Oscar employs a poor but genteel young woman, Edith Grace, to look after his mother, and the politician John Hanbury, who is in Oscar's power, falls in love with Edith, initially because of her startling resemblance to his then-fiancée. The attempted murder of Oscar by Stamer, a hardened criminal, is thwarted, but the dwarf's workshop is destroyed, along with all his elaborate mechanical contraptions including an automaton which was mistaken for the dwarf himself, and the huge clock with thousands of historical figures, which Oscar claimed was more important to him than his soul. John and Edith marry at the end of the novel, and the gold which Oscar claimed had been created out of phosphorous is discovered to have been stolen by Stamer and a confederate, the hunchback being responsible only for its illegal distribution.

*Miracle Gold* cleverly juxtaposes modern mechanical invention with superstition in a tale which, despite its fantastic premise, creates a remarkable portrayal of the London of the 1880s. Dowling had a keen eye for the modernity and bustle of the streets of London, as he had demonstrated in his slight romances of city life – *Under St Paul's* (1880), *London Town* (1880) and the later *While London Sleeps* (1895) – and in numerous short stories. Memorable characters abound, including William Sampson, the "Negro and Street Entertainer", John, the politician, who faints at the sight of the negro's blood, and the criminal Stamer. Another excellent villain is presented in *An Isle of Surrey* in the figure of the unscrupulous Crawford, the assumed name of the gambler and fraudster John Ainsworth, whose nemesis, Frank Mellor is also living on the island on the Thames under the identity of Francis Bramwell.

*A Baffling Quest* is a complex murder mystery, of particular interest in this study in that it introduces two private detectives. Arthur Longton is an art teacher in the small town of Eyworth in the south-east of England who has fallen in love with the daughter of the eccentric vivisectionist millionaire recluse, Sir Andrew Brinfield. The dead body of Sir Andrew is found by two men, Purkiss and Meese, but as they go to report their finding the

21    Ibid., 27.

body disappears, along with Sir Andrew's will. All that is left at the scene of the crime is a hat, which is found to belong to Arthur's infamous uncle, the fisherman Jimmy Ware, who is immediately suspected of the murder and theft. Arthur himself, who would have benefitted from the missing will should he marry Miss Brinfield is also suspected of having aided and abetted his uncle. Arthur believes in his uncle's innocence, believing the situation to be part of a plot to discredit him. He consults Mr Granby, an elderly and reliable lawyer, who suggests that a private detective, Dunkley, be called to investigate the case. Dunkley examines reports of a strange dog which is reported to have been appearing on the fenland area in which the supposed murder has taken place, a dog which is eventually discovered to be a leopard, and which carries information regarding the missing will. A mysterious letter, from a man who calls himself "John Smith", offers to give Arthur the will. This "Smith" is in fact another private enquiry agent called Tufnell. Arthur is also contacted by a mysterious "uncle" newly arrived from Australia, who asks him to paint his portrait, before admitting that he is really Sir Andrew, and that he had used narcotics to fake his death.

*A Baffling Quest* contains many features of what would become common traits in later crime fiction, including the use of detailed plans of Barmead Hall, where the murder ostensibly takes place, the confusion of an exotic, wild beast with both a domestic animal and a supernatural being, a missing will, attacks by anonymous assailants on leading characters, a mysterious stranger returning from the colonies, the use of drugs to disguise a murder, and the involvement of efficient private investigators, one of whom, Dunkley, follows one of the supposed witnesses to New York to disprove his testimony. *The Crimson Chair and Other Stories* (1891) once again revealed Dowling's skill with the short story format, a genre which was once again to reach high levels of popularity in the 1890s. This collection, consisting mostly of tales published before in magazines, is especially notable for the story which gives the volume its title, an imaginative narrative concerning a mind-reader who has invented an electric chair which allows people to forget certain aspects of their lives, and several of the crime-related stories. In "A Midnight Walk" the well-to-do young narrator is imprisoned by gipsies and forced to consider the differences between polite middle-class society and the world of outsiders. In "Negative Evidence" photography is used to solve a crime; in "A Three-H Pencil" the criminal gives himself away by using a pencil which carries through the page on which he has written at a jeweller's; and in "In the Nick of Time" a photograph which the protagonist has seen at the Black Museum at Scotland Yard helps him to discover the true identity of the man who is courting his sister. These excellent tales of crime would not be out of place in an anthology of crime writing from the period, including works by Conan Doyle and L. T. Meade, but unfortunately, they were to be Dowling's final offering in the genre.

The decline in the expensive "triple-decker" three-volume novels, thus named in analogy with Nelson's battleships,[22] meant that the author would only write one more work in this format, *Below Bridge* (1895), which was published in the year of his death. The three-volume novel had been introduced with enormous success earlier in the century, riding on the success of Scott's highly popular historical fiction, and had been championed by Charles Mudie in his Lending and Subscription Libraries, but by the 1890s was in decline, and by 1897 almost inexistent.[23] It is, perhaps, however, unfair to suggest, as James H. Murphy does, that Dowling's decline in popularity was related to the decline of the format.[24] The author's untimely death in 1898 cut short a career which, in the one- and two-volume works published in the 1890s and the posthumous publication of *Old Corcoran's Money* in 1897 and *The Fate of Luke Ormond* in 1905, could have easily adapted to the more manageable editions of the new century. *Catmur's Caves or The Quality of Mercy* (1892) is a competent romance set once again in London and featuring a lion-tamer, a clairvoyant and a sad tale of a smuggling ring which operates between London and the Netherlands.

*A Dark Intruder* (1895) is a sprawling mystery, published in the unusual two-volume format, which once again features a non-existent homicide and introduces the common device of two almost identical brothers. Charles Ashmore, who has been behaving strangely, shaving off his beard

---

22    Amigoni, *Victorian Literature*, 41.

23    David Glover, "Publishing, History, Genre" in *The Cambridge Companion to Popular Fiction*, ed. David Glover and Scott McCracken (Cambridge: Cambridge University Press, 2012), 24.

24    James H. Murphy, *Irish Novelists and the Victorian Age* (Oxford: Oxford University Press, 2011), 248.

and buying a gun, is recognised by Herbert, the prodigal cousin of Charles's fiancée, Lil, who has just returned from the Americas. Herbert claims that he recognises Charles as a gambling scoundrel he had met in Mexico some months before, a claim which Charles steadfastly denies. A family friend, Dr Sylvester, hires a private detective to find out the truth. This private eye, Vereker, disguises himself as a carter to find information, and manages to hear a conversation in which Charles talks about the murder of one John Kimber near Wythburn some three years earlier. Vereker, keen to outdo New Scotland Yard because he believes that the regular police despise private investigators, attempts to bring Charles to justice. He learns, however, as Lil already knows, that Charles's mentally handicapped brother Edward had apparently killed a man, and that their father had entrusted Charles with helping his brother to escape to America. Anticipating the denouement of later Golden Age narratives, the wise Dr Silvester gathers all the protagonists together to reveal the truth, which he had discovered through Vereker. The man Herbert had seen in Mexico was Edward, Charles's mad brother, and the homicide of which he had been accused did not exist, as Edward had used the accidental drowning of Kimber in order to extort money from his father and brother. The novel ends with Edward being taken to the country to be looked after and Charles and Lil marrying, and subsequently, having a boy whom they name Silvester.

The first of Dowling's two posthumous novels, *Old Corcoran's Money* (1897), is set in the imaginary Irish town of Ballymore. The plot is possibly the most complex in all of Dowling's novels, involving a miserly hunchback, a bank teller who has been entrusted with the hunchback's finances, a cousin who has just returned from the Australian goldmines and two rival businessmen connected by marriage. When a large amount of money is stolen from the miser's escritoire, the guilty party is initially believed to be James McDonnell, the bank teller, who is in love with Mary Butler, the daughter of one of the town's most important men of business who is undergoing a period of financial difficulty. Mr Butler had promised his daughter's hand to the miser if he were to help him out with his debts, but the theft means that the hunchback is unable to do this, thus casting more suspicion on James. A host of further suspects, including the returned Australian adventurer O'Gorman, the town fool O'Hooligan, and the madman Dumb

Slattery complicate the case, which is placed in the hands of the local constabulary. The portrayal of the RIC, once again, is of special interest. The Head Constable, Cassidy, is a serious and concerned officer, who is eventually able to piece together all the strands of the complicated puzzle and assert the nature of the robbery and the innocence of the bank teller. Faced with the pressures of the two local businessmen, the financial power of the miser, and the demands of his Chief Inspector, the circumspect Cassidy retains a position of quiet authority and competence throughout the narrative, separating him from the bungling antics of officers from the RIC in other narratives. Indeed, his underling, Constable Meagher, although at first mocked for his broad speech, is also surprisingly competent and, as his superior admits, "a credit to the force".[25]

While *Old Corcoran's Money* is a creditable mystery set in Ireland, Dowling's last published novel returns to an English setting and to the world of strange mechanical devices so endearing to the author. Mr Allerton is a "mechanician" who invents and constructs automatons such as his latest invention, the "Automaton Reciter" which is currently reciting poetry at a fair in Piccadilly. Allerton is being blackmailed by the evil Luke Ormerod, who had persuaded the inventor to burn an unfavourable will belonging to his father, and who wants to marry Allerton's daughter Maud. When Ormerod is killed, apparently by one of the automatons in Allerton's workshop, the inventor is accused of his murder. The truth, that Maud's young brother Rob had been inside the figure, and had accidentally killed Luke, complicates the situation. Luckily, Maud has another pretender, the gallant sea captain Frank Morland, who contrives a false suicide for Rob before taking him overseas to New Zealand, from whence he can travel to Argentina, and freedom. On his return from New Zealand, Frank marries Maud, and with her father, they all go off to live a reclusive life in Devon. Luke Ormerod is similar to some extent to Dowling's earlier story "A Sapphire Ring", highlighting the inability of the law to bring true justice.

Richard Dowling was criticised in 1891 by the Irish writer Rosa Mulholland (Lady Gilbert), who accused him of bowing down to the requirements of English publishers, and urged him and other writers of

---

25    Richard Dowling, *Old Corcoran's Money* (London: Chatto & Windus, 1897), 139.

the period to settle in Ireland and to concentrate on Irish topics in their work. His fiction, however, provides a fascinating link between sensation fiction and the end-of-century detective tales and, at his best, he is capable of producing entertaining works which introduce aspects of modernity such as telephones, telegrams, electricity and forensics, while exploring issues related to imperialism, chauvinism and race, which reflected the concerns of the age.

# CHAPTER 5

# "A history of crime seemed to be written on both their faces." L. T. Meade and End of Century Detection

The two final decades of the nineteenth century constituted a particularly fruitful period for Irish writers dealing with topics of mystery and criminal behaviour, although these works were still largely directed towards the London literary marketplace. *Deborah Alcock's* (1835–1913) *The Czar: A Tale of the Time of Napoleon* (1882) and *The Spanish Brothers: A Tale of the Sixteenth Century* (1888) are historical novels which contain features of mystery basically designed to lend interest to what are, in fundamental terms, works of Protestant religious propaganda. There was a growing interest in Irish affairs in England during the 1880s, with the rise of Parnell and the electoral victories of the Irish Parliamentary Party, the growth of the Land League and the start of boycotting, The Phoenix Park Murders, the Fenian bombing attacks in London and the introduction of Gladstone's first Home Rule Bill – all ensuring that Ireland and Irish themes were highly topical and of interest to both Irish and non-Irish readers. This concern about Irish affairs was reflected in a number of novels including Mary Francis Cusack's *Who Fired the First Shot?, or, Ned Rusheen: An Irish Story* (1883), William Mackay's *Pro Patria: The Autobiography of an Irish Conspirator* (1883), Emily Lawless's *Hurrish: A Study* (1886) and James Murphy's *Luke Talbot; or, The Cliffs of Mullawn-Mor* (1890). Although Lawless's work was first published by Blackwood in Edinburgh, and that of Mackay in London, both Cusack and Murphy's novels were first issued by Dublin publishing houses.

*Who Fired the First Shot?* by *Mary Francis Cusack* (Margaret Anna Cusack, 1829–99), is a fascinating piece of early Irish detective fiction set in Ireland, and worthy of greater acknowledgement. Lord Elmsdale, proprietor of Elmsdale castle, "a cold, castellated building"[1] just south of Dublin is English, "or at least he liked to be thought of that nation. It was fashionable".[2] When Elmsdale is murdered, suspicion immediately falls upon Ned Rusheen, the under-keeper at the Castle and foster-brother to Edward, Lord Elmsdale's dissolute son and heir. Cusack, a nun who converted from Anglicanism to Catholicism, immediately distances Ned from the Irish characters with whom she assumes her readers to be accustomed:

> [He] was a handsome fellow, a true type of Irishman – not the stereotyped Irishman of modern writers, who says "yez" and "yarrah" at every other word; who curses "by gorra," or by "the holy poker;" who is lazy and won't work; who is dirty and won't be clean; who has the imperishable gifts of fortune showered on him by a benevolent landlord, and won't accept them. Such an Irishman exists only in the imagination of those who take their ideas of the nation from purely mythical description. [3]

The police investigation is carried out by two local officers and by the English official Captain Everard, who hates the Irish and who "regretted that the law, as administered in India, could not be put into execution in Ireland under present circumstances".[4] The indigenous officers, Egan and O'Brien, provide a surprisingly sympathetic and positive example of the Irish police, something which was highly unusual and would remain to be so, with a few notable examples, during much of the following century. Egan discovers a small piece of wool at the site of the murder and, after intricate detective work, traces it to a comforter pertaining to a local shop, and which had been sold to Ned. Egan's skill is recognised by Cusack:

> With a little early training, and a little experience of London life, he would have made a first-rate detective. In Ireland, his talents in that line were simply thrown away. There were no mysterious robberies of plate, garrotting was simply unheard of. The Irish were too far behind the age for that kind of thing.[5]

---

1    Mary Francis Cusack, *Who Fired the First Shot?, or, Ned Rusheen: An Irish Story* (Dublin: M. H. Gill & Son, 1883), 1.
2    Ibid., 18.
3    Ibid., 23.
4    Ibid., 104.
5    Ibid., 108.

Ned is subsequently accused and remanded for trial, while the house-maid, Ellie, with whom Edward is in love, entreats the heir to tell the truth about his father's murder and thus secure Ned's release. He agrees to do so on condition that she marry him, but she refuses and goes to court her-self to reveal the true events leading to Lord Elmsdale's murder and thus bring about Ned's acquittal. *Who Fired the First Shot*, in its attempt to compare British and Irish attitudes towards justice, the law and the nature of policing denotes an important landmark in the history of Irish crime writing. The author dwells upon "instinctive opposition to the law which is so often commented on, and so thoroughly misunderstood, in the Irish character"[6] and speculates that the "Celtic character is peculiarly alive to disgrace, none the less so because its code of honour and its ideas of crime differ in some measure from the code and ideas of other people's".[7] Ned's pragmatic concept of the law is contrasted positively with the rigid inter-pretation offered by Everard, and the young Irishman's innocence would seem to vindicate Cusack's hypothesis.

Belfast-born *William Mackay's* (1846–?) *Pro Patria: The Autobiography of an Irish Conspirator* has been seen as "a satire against its maladroit first-person narrator, who moves from aspirations to the status of a gentleman to involvement with a Fenian-type organization".[8] The conspirator of the novel's subtitle, Ptolemy Daly, does not share his father's staunch anti-English sentiments but, after an encounter with a local Protestant landlord and Justice of the Peace, he moves to Dublin to join a group of nationalist agitators. The novel is full of comical scenes: especially memorable is when Ptolemy dresses as a castle flunkey to obtain information, is arrested but then released because he is taken for a drunken footman, or when the judge wants to sentence him to three days' confinement while his own lawyer argues for a tougher sentence in order to convert his client into a martyr.

*Hurrish: A Study* was the fourth book published by *Emily Lawless* (1845–1913), daughter of a landowning baronet from County Kildare. *Hurrish* has been described as "a study of the darker side of personal

6    Ibid., 144–145.
7    Ibid., 206.
8    James H. Murphy, *Irish Novelists and the Victorian Age* (Oxford: Oxford University Press, 2011), 176.

motivation in the midst of land conflict".⁹ The widower, Horatio "Hurrish" O'Brien, living with his mother, his three children and an adopted niece-in-law, Ally, is in conflict over disputed land with Mat Brady. When Brady shoots at Hurrish from a hidden spot, the widower kills him with a single blow and is placed on trial. Although acquitted, Mat's brother Maurice "Morry" Brady, who is in love with Ally and who has always looked upon Hurrish as a father figure, feels himself obliged to avenge his evil brother's death because of an unwritten code which demanded that crime against one's own blood must not go unpunished. Morry fatally wounds Hurrish, but is forgiven in the dying man's last wishes. Ally becomes a nun and Morry moves to the USA where he is shunned as an informer and where he "led a rather uncomfortable life amongst his compatriots, who persisted, rightly or wrongly, in looking askance at him, and regarding him as a traitor to the national cause, and the assassin of his own best friend".¹⁰ As Murphy states, the "informal law of rural resistance is brutal, castigating the in-former more than the crime".¹¹

    Although *Luke Talbot; or, the Cliffs of the Mullawn-Mor* by County Carlow native *James Murphy* (1839–1921) is set some eighty years before its publication, the subject of land conflict is still at its core. Luke Talbot, the proud owner of a small plot of land is in conflict with the local land-owner Sir Robert Graham and his agent, the evil M'Nab. Both Luke and M'Nab are in love with the same girl, Kate Redmond, and when Graham berates his agent for his treatment of Luke, M'Nab kills his master using Luke's gun. Luke is blamed for the crime but, unaware of the murder, he sets off for Dublin only to be press-ganged on the way. After surviving a shipwreck, he arrives in Spain, fighting the French in the Peninsular War. Meanwhile in Ireland M'Nab is prospering, managing the late Sir Robert's estate for an absentee landlord. Joe Foley, a local peasant who witnessed the crime but suffered from amnesia, later recovers his memory, but M'Nab conspires to have him imprisoned as insane in order to protect his secret. When Luke eventually returns to Ireland he is arrested and sentenced to

9    James H. Murphy, *The Oxford History of the Irish Book. Volume IV. The Irish Book in English 1800–1891* (Oxford: Oxford University Press, 2011), 419.
10   Emily Lawless, *Hurrish: A Study* (Edinburgh: Blackwood, 1886), 338.
11   Murphy, *Irish Novelists*, 179.

death while M'Nab attempts to marry Kate. The final resolution owes more
to coincidence than to investigation, with M'Nab's ignominious death in a
bog and Luke's marriage to Kate owing more to the romance than to crime
fiction, but, as in *Hurrish* and so many other Irish novels of the period,
the law is represented as being something which only serves to uphold the
domination of a privileged few and, in a society "without a centre of legit-
imation" the legal apparatus is recognisably alien.[12]

The Dubliner *Kathleen O'Meara* (1839–88) is perhaps best known
for *The Bells of the Sanctuary* (1879), but the writer, who spent most of
her life in Paris, also produced *Narka: A Novel* (1888), which deals with
anarchist and socialist plots in Czarist Russia and which, with its down-
trodden peasants, secret societies and evil landlords, can easily be read as a
convincing allegory for the contemporary situation in Ireland, with both
countries blighted by "the law of might and cunning".[13] The two volumes
of *Narka* also reveal a disturbing anti-Semitism. The murder victim, Count
Larchoff, is "a liar and a hypocrite; as cruel as a tiger, and as greedy as a
wolf; cowardly as a rat, and dishonest as a Jew".[14] In a similar vein, Sybil,
sister of Basil, the novel's hero, is appalled when she hears that her brother
is to marry Narka because she does not want "that abomination of abom-
inations, Jewish blood" in her family.[15]

Elizabeth Thomasina Meade (1854–1914), known professionally as
*L. T. Meade*, suffers from a critical neglect which contrasts with the enormous popularity she enjoyed in her lifetime. The author of over 300 novels
and collections of short stories, Meade is nowadays mostly remembered as
"probably inventing the girl's boarding school novel",[16] but can also claim
to be the writer who published "the first series of mysteries featuring a
physician as a protagonist, the first book of impossible crime stories, the

---

12   Ibid., 179.
13   Kathleen O'Meara, *Narka: A Novel* (London: Richard Bentley & Sons, 1888), 18.
14   Ibid., 14.
15   Ibid., 200.
16   Winnie Chan, "The Linked Excitements of L. T. Meade and ... in the *Strand
     Magazine*" in *Scribbling Women and the Short Story Form: Approaches by American
     and British Women Writers*, ed. Ellen Burton Harrington (New York: Peter Lang,
     2008), 60.

first series of short stories about a female murderer" as well as "an early
group of stories about a female sleuth".[17] Born in the Ascendancy enclave
of Bandon, West Cork, to an Anglican clergyman father, Meade relocated
to London after her father's remarriage. In the English capital, she fre-
quented the British Museum Reading Room where she finished her first
novel, *Ashton Morton*, published anonymously in 1866.[18] Meade became
"the archetypal New Woman figure",[19] acting as a committee member for
the Pioneer Club, a member of the Men and Women's Club founded by
the eugenicist Karl Pearson, as well as writing articles in defence of women's
colleges.[20] Her girls' school novels create the figure of the "New Girl",[21]
her slum novels raise awareness of social conditions in London, while an
early medical novel, *The Medicine Lady*, contains, according to James H.
Murphy, the subtext of the need for women to be able to procure proper
medical training.[22]

Her mystery fiction is notable for its sheer quantity and originality,
and while she replicates many of the tropes of the crime narrative of the
period, her innovation and experimentation with the limits of the genre is
of enormous interest. Although she wrote several works in collaboration
with three male co-writers, Clifford Halifax, Robert Eustace and Robert
K. Douglas, the authoritative voice in the fiction is that of Meade, while
the three male authors are basically responsible for the addition of scientific
and medical information unavailable to her. Craig and Cadogan's claim
that Eustace's collaboration possibly "helped to inject vigour into Meade's
narrative style" is patently unsustainable, as the narrative strength of much
of Meade's solo work, such as *An Adventuress* (1899), *The Blue Diamond*

17    Introduction to L. T. Meade and Robert Eustace, *The Detections of Miss Cusack*,
      ed. Douglas C. Greene and Jack Adrian (1892, Shelbourne, Ontario: The Battered
      Silicon Dispatch Box, 1998), vii.
18    Tina O'Toole, *The Irish New Woman* (London: Palgrave Macmillan, 2013) 45–63.
19    Ibid., 12.
20    Sally Mitchell, "Children's Reading and the Culture of Girlhood: The Case of L. T.
      Meade", *Browning Institute Studies* 17 (1989), 54.
21    Sandra McAvoy, "The 'Wild Irish Girl' in Selected Novels of L. T. Meade" in
      *Adolescence in Modern Irish History*, ed. Catherine Cox and Susannah Riordan
      (London: Palgrave Macmillan, 2015), 64.
22    Murphy, *Irish Novelists*, 207.

(1901) or *The Necklace of Parmona* (1909) can never be called into doubt. As in Richard Dowling's later fiction, Meade confronts the contradictions and concerns of the late nineteenth century and foregrounds modern inventions and ideas, while juggling with the apparent contradictions to be found in the fashionable science and pseudo-science of mesmerism, phrenology and physiognomy, which, together with evolutionary biological theories, were beginning to present an alternative to traditional religious beliefs and practices, and which created "fertile ground for the development and popularity of religion".[23]

In Meade's first mystery novel, *A Ring of Rubies* (1892), Rosamund is a modern female protagonist who, living in gentile poverty with her parents and two brothers in London, is determined to study art at the Slade School. When her father declines to help her fulfil her wish, she visits Geoffrey, a rich miser and her mother's cousin, to request financial assistance to help her in her quest for an educational opportunity. Telling her that he will consider her request, Geoffrey dies before he can answer, but leaves her a beautiful ruby ring under the condition that she must not sell it. The novel introduces a number of the concepts and themes which would become familiar in Meade's fiction, with elements such as the modest but ambitious young woman, the dissolute brother and the importance of inheritance. It also contains a mysterious room, the "Chamber of Myths", a staple of much late nineteenth-century fiction, which reflects the influence of the gothic, and the physical embodiment of the mystery, in this case, the ring itself which is identified as a product of colonial heritage and which possesses a secret compartment.

In 1876 Meade had published her first economically successful novel, *Great St. Benedict's: A Tale*, which was set in a London teaching hospital. She would return to the world of medicine with *The Medicine Lady* (1893), which features Cecilia Harvey, a middle-class orphan who becomes a nurse and marries the taciturn and formal Dr Digby, who is working on "the new doctrine of heredity" and for whose experiments Cecilia offers herself as

---

23    Tatiana Kontou, "Sensation Fiction, Spiritualism and the Supernatural" in *The Cambridge Companion to Sensation Fiction*, ed. Andrew Mangham (Cambridge: Cambridge University Press, 2013), 142.

a guinea pig.[24] The plot centres on the attempts of the "evil genius" – and tremendously rich and ruthless – Dr Phillips, to obtain Cecilia's husband's papers, following rumours that Digby had discovered a cure for consumption.[25] After her husband's death, Cecilia thwarts Phillips' attempts to secure Digby's notes and herself pursues his research with, eventually, disastrous consequences. A woman, Meade would seem to suggest, can play an important role in helping her husband, but once she attempts to assume sole prominence her limits are revealed.

The same year as the publication of *The Medicine Lady*, Meade produced her first collaborative novel, *This Troublesome World* (1894), co-authored with Clifford Halifax, the pseudonym of Huddersfield-born physician Edgar Beaumont (1860–1921). Meade and Halifax started working together in 1893 with a series of short stories published in *The Strand* magazine. *The Strand* was at the height of its popularity in the 1890s as, what had started as a risky attempt to challenge the dominance in the market place of serial-based magazines by producing a journal that featured quality short fiction in which scientific method and accuracy were prominent.[26] The first series of what was to become *Stories from the Diary of a Doctor* were issued in *The Strand* between 1893 and 1894 and collected in book form in 1894. This first series ran at the same time as Conan Doyle's Sherlock Holmes stories in the magazine, which reached formidable sales figures and prompted the creation of a second series, published in book format in 1896.

*Stories from the Diary of a Doctor* purports to be the journal of a practising medical doctor, Clifford Halifax, who is faced with many situations that require the use of his medical, scientific and detection skills to solve the mysteries. In the first story, readers encounter a newly qualified Halifax who is called to the house of Ogilvie, a friend, to treat his sick wife. His visit is interrupted by the appearance of an old woman who is the mother of the friend's late first wife and who, according to the woman, is still alive. Ashamed of the situation, Ogilvie attempts to poison both his wife and

24    L. T. Meade, *The Medicine Lady*, 3 vols. (London: Cassell and Company, 1893), vol. 1, 228.
25    Ibid., vol. 2, 141.
26    LeRoy Lad Panek, *After Sherlock Holmes: The Evolution of British and American Detective Stories 1891–1914* (Jefferson, NC: McFarland & Company, 2014), 58.

himself, only to be detained by Halifax who uncovers the truth – the first wife is, in fact, dead – and manages to save both Ogilvie and his wife. This story, "My First Patient", although not particularly typical of the stories in the two series, does reveal how the doctor's detection of criminal activity is not necessarily related to his scientific skills but rather to his assessment of human intentions. Medical knowledge is called on to save the two poison victims, not to resolve the problem. Similarly, in "The Heir of Chartepool", "The Horror of Studley Grange" and "An Oak Coffin" from the first series, or "A Doctor's Dilemma", "On a Charge of Forgery" and "The Small House on Steven's Heath" in the second series, Halifax solves the cases with little or no medical or scientific input. The most satisfying stories from the *Diaries* are, however, arguably those in which the combination of medical and detection skills are jointly employed to resolve an apparently contradictory mystery. In "The Ponsonby Diamonds", for example, from the first series, Halifax helps Beryl Temple to find employment as a nurse for Lady Violet, engaged to the wealthy Lord Ponsonby. When the aristocrat gives lady Violet a diamond necklace, Beryl is allowed to try on the necklace which subsequently disappears. The nurse is accused of the theft and, when detectives are called in they believe that she is responsible. Halifax, however, is convinced that Beryl is not responsible for the crime and sets out to prove her innocence. He determines that Lady Violet is not in love with Lord Ponsonby, and that her aversion to marrying him has resulted in her developing a medical condition of acute and momentary kleptomania, determining that she herself has taken the necklace but has since forgotten her actions.

In *Stories from the Diary of a Doctor*, and most especially in the second series, a number of the stories are of a topical nature. In "The Seventh Step" Halifax, by discovering the false paralysis of a character, is able to determine that the woman is, in fact, Olga Krestofski, a nihilist leader, reflecting the fears generated by anarchist and nihilist groups in the 1890s.[27] Likewise, a number of the stories, such as "The Hooded Death" and "With the Eternal Fires", translate colonial concerns to the centre of the Empire.

27    Maurizio Ascari, *A Counter-History of Crime Fiction: Supernatural, Gothic, Sensational* (London: Palgrave Macmillan, 2007), 162.

Halifax describes himself as being "only so far a detective that I have made human nature the one study of my life".[28] His medical knowledge is an important, if not essential part of his detective skills. In "To Every One His Own Fear" from the second series, for example, he discerns that the supposed drowning of a young man is not a result of his verified catalepsy but rather of a hole which has been drilled in the boat in which he suffered the accident. The great English Golden Age writer Dorothy L. Sayers credits Meade with "paving the way for great developments in a scientific age – the medical mystery story",[29] and more recently Christopher Pittard believes that "there is a strong case for crediting Meade with the invention of the subgenre of the medical mystery".[30] Heather Worthington agrees with this viewpoint, seeing Meade's Dr Halifax as matching "the scientific and the rational against the irrational and supernatural, with science triumphing every time",[31] while Sally Mitchell adds that the "twist" used by Meade and Halifax is to "base plot on new scientific discoveries or bizarre medical information".[32] LeRoy Lad Panek, however, notes that while the stories in the *Diaries of a Doctor* "superficially follow the pattern of notebook literature" by "providing the allure of a behind-the-scenes look at the way members of a profession perform said profession", in fact only a small number of the short stories in the two collections actually follow up their initial promise of basing their denouement on the use of scientific or technical knowledge.[33]

It is difficult to determine the extent to which Halifax collaborated with Meade, but if we are to study the Irish writer's individually written

28    L. T. Meade and Clifford Halifax, *Stories from the Diary of a Doctor (Second Series)* (London: Bliss, Sands and Foster, 1896), 277.

29    Dorothy L. Sayers, "The Omnibus of Crime" in *Detective Fiction: A Collection of Critical Essays. Twentieth Century Views*, ed. Robin W. Winks (Englewood Cliffs, NJ: Prentice-Hall, 1980), 72.

30    Christopher Pittard, "From Sensation to the *Strand*" in *A Companion to Crime Fiction*, ed. Charles J. Rzepka and Lee Horsley (Chichester: Wiley-Blackwell, 2019), 114.

31    Heather Worthington, *Key Concepts in Crime Fiction* (London: Palgrave Macmillan, 2011), 22.

32    Mitchell, "Children's Reading", 54–55.

33    Panek, *After Sherlock*, 59.

novels and stories it is difficult to discern any stylist or thematic difference. It is tempting to see Halifax and her two later collaborators as acting merely as providers of technical, scientific and medical background, and Winnie Chan would seem to corroborate this belief when she observes that, because the target readership of *The Strand* was made up largely of "socially aspirant middle-class professionals" Meade was "compelled to link her name to pseudonyms of scientifically credentialed male collaborators".[34] She would continue to collaborate with Halifax throughout the decade and into the new century. In *Dr. Rumsey's Patient* (1896) they revive the formula of the diary, this time using the format of the novel, in which the eponymous doctor solves a case of homicide involving a family whose male line has suffered a hereditary curse after an ancestor had made an "inconvenient marriage" to a West Indian creole heiress who "had coloured blood in her veins" and who possessed a "deformed figure".[35] Although the family had believed that the curse had been removed thanks to the sanitising marriage of his grandfather to a Scottish wife, a "healthy-minded daughter of the North", the current heir, guilty of accidental homicide, suffers from amnesia and has no memory of the incident for which another man is convicted.[36] Dr Rumsey successfully demolishes the myth of the family curse by blaming the young heir's amnesia on nervous problems brought about by his constant dwelling on the supposed curse of his house and lineage. The novel is interesting in that Rumsey uses medical knowledge – in this case of a psychological nature – not only to unveil the mystery, but also to dismantle the racist assumptions displayed at the beginning of the story and which, it must be supposed, were shared by many of the readers of the work.

The collaboration continued with *When the Shoe Pinches* (1900) and *A Race with the Sun* (1901), both collections of short stories featuring, respectively, Dr Wallace and Paul Gilchrist as the amateur detectives involved in solving the cases. These cases are in many ways similar to those of the earlier *Diary*, and Wallace, a doctor who through his profession comes

34  Chan, "Linked Excitements", 61.
35  L. T. Meade and Clifford Halifax, *Dr. Rumsey's Patient: A Very Strange Story* (New York: Hurst & Company, 1896), 17.
36  Ibid., 19.

across "all sorts and conditions of men"[37] is essentially a slightly altered version of the fictional Halifax from the earlier stories. Paul Gilchrist is "a man whose life study has been science in its most interesting forms"[38] and who would appear to be an experimental scientist rather than a physician. The stories in *A Race with the Sun* make use of numerous scientific and pseudo-scientific devices and procedures. X-rays are used to determine that a missing diamond has been swallowed by an Indian servant ("The Snake's Eye"), Gilchrist goes to India with a "spectroscopist" and uses cyphers for communication ("Lady Tragenna"), and there are Hindu palm-reading chiromancers ("The Sleeping Sickness") and hypnotists ("The Panelled Bedroom"). These later collaborations are in general more sophisticated than the earlier narratives and Chan suggests that the heroes of these stories are more similar to the detectives who appear in conventional crime fiction of the period rather than being mere observers.[39] Meade's final collaboration with Halifax would be a single story in *Silenced* (1904), which also contained two individual contributions and three tales jointly written with Robert Eustace, by this time a habitual collaborator.

Apart from her collaborative writing, Meade wrote prolifically in the 1890s, and among her published works are several mystery novels that were highly successful in both Britain and the USA. *In an Iron Grip* (1894) sees a young actress, Esther, sentenced to five years' imprisonment for forging a cheque in the name of her stepfather in order to help Frank Forbes, the leading actor in her company, a self-indulgent wastrel who has persuaded the young woman to lend him her support. Discovering she is pregnant, Esther is forced to give up the baby while she serves her sentence. The descriptions of prison life are noteworthy, and the author's sympathy for the plight of the young mother lends pathos to a tale which comes close to tragedy but ends in a slightly unconvincing manner with Esther, her debauched and unfaithful beau and their son, now a young boy, making a new life for themselves in Australia. Along with her girls' school stories,

37   L. T. Meade and Clifford Halifax, *Where the Shoe Pinches* (London: W. R. Chambers, 1900), 1.
38   L. T. Meade and Clifford Halifax, *A Race with the Sun* (London: Ward, Lock & Co., 1901), 5.
39   Chan, "Linked Excitements", 64.

Meade also wrote an abundant number of "slum novels", a subgenre popular at the end of the nineteenth century, which was concerned with life in the most economically deprived areas of a city, usually London, and with the attempts of good-hearted middle-class philanthropists to mediate in situations of gross social inequality. One of these, *A Princess of the Gutter* (1895), is particularly interesting in that it contains a murder plot within a love triangle, which leads to a false confession, a death sentence and a deathbed revelation, and follows a number of the conventions of the murder mystery. *The Voice of the Charmer* (1895) also contains as much romance as it does mystery, but is mostly of interest for its extended dramatic use of the fashionable concept of mesmerism.

*A Son of Ishmael* (1896) is a fully fledged detective mystery novel with a long, intricate plot and a cleverly paced use of suspense, with gradual revelation leading to a series of carefully construed surprises. Dr Follet and his daughter Nancy live in the gothic darkness of an English mansion house, where the doctor laments the unsolved Paris murder of his son and heir. Nancy, meanwhile, is courted by the handsome Adrian Rowton who, despite his good looks is, we are told, "too dark for the conventional Englishman".[40] Wary of this foreign-looking suitor, Follet seeks out the London detective Crossley to find the truth behind his son's murder and, simultaneously, to find out what he can about the background of Rowton. When the old doctor dies, Adrian and Nancy marry, but she becomes gradually more suspicious of her husband and his activities which, despite his status as a wealthy landowner, include unexplained trips to Madrid and his apparent involvement with "The Silver School", a gang in the London slums. The evidence presented to the reader seems to point towards the implication of Adrian in the death of his wife's brother, and his obdurate behaviour leads Crossley, the detective, to believe in his guilt. The final surprise, which undermines the detective's theory, provides a satisfying ending to a novel which, despite the large number of narrative strands, is a fine example of late nineteenth-century crime fiction. Crossley is a fascinating figure as the professional and slightly self-important detective, "a man of middle height, dressed in the correct garb of an ordinary gentleman" and

40   L. T. Meade, *A Son of Ishmael* (London: F. V. White and Company, 1896), 3.

who "had a pleasant face and looked eminently respectable"[41] who builds up the suspense by telling Nancy that he has information regarding the death of her brother but asking her to have patience as she would "know all in a few minutes".[42] The ironic revelation that the information he imparts is, in fact, false, adds a certain sardonic pathos to the detective's behaviour.

Although in Meade's school stories there often appears the figure of the Irish girl, generally unconventional and socially progressive, Irish characters and settings are relatively infrequent in the author's work. *The Siren* (1898) is one of the few works in which Irish characters are prominent and, although set largely in England and Russia, the plot, which is centred around the relationship between the Irish Nugent family and Russian nihilists, leads Janis Dawson to comment on the extent to which this reflects contemporary "anxieties about terrorist tactics of continental arsonists and Fenians".[43] *On the Brink of a Chasm: A Record of Plot and Passion* (1898) introduces, once again, the then topical subject of mesmerism, and *An Adventuress* (1899) uses the narrative device of two identical girls, one rich and one poor, each called Kate. *The Blue Diamond* (1901) features both mesmerism and continental nihilists, again reflecting dominant concerns of the contemporary middle class.

During the 1890s Meade also collaborated with Sir Robert Kennaway Douglas (1838–1913), an oriental scholar who, after a period of diplomatic service in China, became Professor of Chinese at King's College, London. The short stories they co-wrote were collected in *Under the Dragon Throne* and present a view of Anglo-Chinese relationships tarnished with the brush of xenophobia, despite Douglas's presumed sympathy towards the subject. In the first of the five stories in the collection, "Richard Maitland, Consul", an Englishman marries a Chinese woman. Despite this apparently liberal step, the story is festooned with racial stereotypes such as "a Chinaman will do anything for spoil"[44] or "the Chinese are remarkable for their cunning

41   Ibid., 266–267.
42   Ibid., 271.
43   Janis Dawson, "'Write a Little Bit Every Day': L. T. Meade, Self-Representation, and the Professional Woman Writer." *Victorian Review* 35, no. 1 (Fall 2009), 144.
44   L. T. Meade and Robert K. Douglas, *Under the Dragon Throne* (London: Gardner, Darton & Co. 1897), 23.

and duplicity".[45] A more lasting, and more profitable collaboration was that which Meade was to initiate with Robert Eustace and which would result in what by many are considered her finest achievements. Eustace was the pen name for Eustace Robert Barton, a divisional surgeon for the Metropolitan Police who would later collaborate with Gertrude Warden, Edgar Jepson and Dorothy L. Sayers. His birthdate is variously given as 1854, 1868 and 1871, although there is consensus to the fact that he died in 1943. It can be assumed that Eustace's role was similar to that of Douglas or Halifax, basically advisory, and that the literary aspects of the works they jointly produced was left largely to Meade. In her introduction to *The Oracle of Maddox Street* (1904), Meade states that several of the stories in that collection were written with the collaboration of Eustace "to whose genius I owe the extraordinary and original ideas contained therein",[46] and Greene and Adrian say that it "is generally conceded that Meade did the actual writing while Eustace supplied the scientific gimmicks and gadgets".[47] Although their first collaboration dated back to a short story in 1894, their first book-length publication was *A Master of Mysteries* (1898). The six stories of which the volume comprises are classic mystery narratives based on seemingly impossible situations. The narrator, John Bell, insists that the stories he relates at first appear to possess supernatural origins but, after his scientific detection, are all explainable in rational terms. In the first story, "How Siva Spoke", for example, Bell is called upon to look into the case of Edward Thesiger, an Englishman who has lived in India and who has stolen an idol from the house of a Brahmin. Thesiger, it appears, is going mad, believing that the idol is speaking to him in Hindu. Bell discovers that the voice of the idol in fact belongs to the fiancé of Thesiger's niece, Jasper Bagwell, who had been speaking through the water pipes to try to drive his uncle mad and thus inherit his property. This formula, of supposedly occult problems having practical solutions which only needed the intellect of the rational scientific detective to solve them, proved highly popular with Meade's readers, and *A Master of Mysteries* was a commercial success.

45   Ibid., 45.
46   L. T. Meade and Robert Eustace, *The Oracle of Maddox Street* (London: Ward, Lock & Co., 1904), 6.
47   Greene and Adrian, Introduction to *Detections*, ix.

*The Gold Star Line* (1899) repeats the formula to a certain extent, but in this case, the rational detective is the purser of an ocean-going luxury liner for the shipping line of the title who narrates a number of the cases which he has solved on his voyages. The voyages take the ship to Singapore, Ceylon, Sydney and Melbourne, New Guinea and Mandalay, and the mysteries presented reflect the relationship between the metropolitan British and the colonial subject. An English soldier is returning from India with the jewels of a maharajah concealed in his belt, one of the passengers amongst the squatters and bushmen sailing to Sydney is a human cypher needed to reveal the secrets of a gang of anarchists, and an expert conchologist's granddaughter is tricked into believing that a talking parrot can reveal the whereabouts of a rare shell in Colombo. Meade's pro-Empire stance is apparent, and the rights of the colonists to take their pickings from their colonies are never called into question; one character proclaims that "even a black fellow is a human being".[48] *The Brotherhood of the Seven Kings* (1899) is related by another scientific narrator. Norman Head has studied physiology at Cambridge when a young man but had never qualified, and now having independent means worked at biology and physiology for the pure love of the subjects. In *The Brotherhood of the Seven Kings*, Head's scientific genius is pitted against Madame Koluchy, an evil master criminal and leader of The Brotherhood, who is rumoured to be able to restore youth and beauty through her almost magical powers. The Brotherhood is a secret society founded in Italy, which is now causing terror in London and which Scotland Yard is unable to contain. Madame Koluchy is probably the first female gang leader and certainly the first female serial killer in crime fiction, and her skills as a beautician would later be used by Meade and Eustace for their characterisation of Madame Sara in *The Sorceress of the Strand*, which would be published four years later.

As well as producing the first female gang leader, Meade and her collaborator also published a series of stories featuring Florence Cusack, "one of the most significant of early professional female detectives", which appeared in the *Hamsworth Magazine*, later retitled *The London Magazine*, between April 1899 and March 1901, but were not collected in book form

48    Meade and Eustace, *The Detections of Miss Cusack*, 213.

until a Canadian publisher issued an edited collection in 1998,[49] the editors of which, Douglas C. Greene and Jack Adrian, claim that the collection forms "one of the most important series of Victorian detective stories never previously collected in book form".[50] Florence is presented in "Mrs Bovey's" as "a young and handsome woman" who possesses "to all appearances abundant health", and whose "energies were extraordinary, and her life completely out of the common".[51] She lives alone in Kensington and keeps "a good staff of servants", is beautiful with a "slender figure", "eyes of the darkest blue" and has "raven black hair and clear complexion".[52] The narrator is a Dr Lonsdale who bears a similar relationship to the detective as that of Watson to Holmes, although Craig and Cadogan stress that "his admiration for Florence seems avuncular and a little less awe-ridden than Watson's for Holmes".[53] Florence, we hear, "was a power in the police courts"[54] and "highly respected by every detective in Scotland Yard".[55] In the cases presented she variously disguises herself as a servant in order to discover a trap and shows the police how gold coins have been melted down and hidden, discovers the complex use of scents used to communicate the names of horses in a racing swindle, and by sensing the use of Valerian discovers how a cat has been used to take cablegrams from one place to another. Cusack's detective skills are often of a sensory nature, and the crimes she investigates are usually those of theft, fraud or connected with the world of gambling. She always insists that she lives on private means and undertakes detective work out of personal interest rather than for financial reasons, and often hints at a secret reason why she takes on these tasks. The reason, however, is never revealed, and the character of Florence Cusack, unfortunately, is never fully developed. Her position is important however as,

---

49   Greene and Adrian, Introduction to *Detections*, xi.
50   Ibid., xi.
51   Ibid., 3.
52   Ibid., 3.
53   Patricia Craig and Mary Cadogan, *The Lady Investigates: Women Detectives and Spies in Fiction* (London: Victor Gollancz, 1981), 30.
54   Greene and Adrian, Introduction to *Detections*, 4.
55   Ibid., 5.

with McDonnell Bodkin's Dora Myrl, she provides a fascinating example of a New Woman detective created by an Irish author.

*The Sanctuary Club* (1900) marks another effort of collaboration between Meade and Eustace. The narrator, Dr Cato is "a man of day-dreams and a doctor by profession" who uses his inheritance to go into partnership with his rich friend Henry Chetwynd, founding the Sanctuary Club.[56] The primary objective of the club is to "cure maladies that were in any way curable without sending the patients away from England".[57] Members paid fifty pounds as an entrance fee and a further ten pounds annually to receive treatment in conditions aimed at replicating those of foreign countries to which patients were often sent. Somewhere between a collection of inter-related stories and a novel, *The Sanctuary Club* sees Cato solve a number of mysteries involving his patients and eventually coming into conflict with a new partner, the evil Dr Horace Kort who, although coming from a "good half-English, half-German family" and having "considerable outward charm" was a keen vivisector, as well as being a mesmerist and, as Cato belatedly discovers, a mass murderer.[58] The two novels published in 1902, *The Lost Square* (with Eustace) and *A Double Revenge* (written alone) are notable for the way in which they reflect contemporary misgivings towards foreigners. In the former, a dying British secret service agent in Paris puts the life of his dissolute young friend Rupert Phenays in danger when he confides a secret which leads to contact with the dangerous Francesca Delacourt who, after being seen disguised as a Portuguese noblewoman, is later revealed to be a spy from the Transvaal. In *A Double Revenge*, the melodramatic tale of Sicilian vendetta in the unlikely setting of a Cornish farm eventually leads to the execution of the female murderer.

*The Sorceress of the Strand*, again written by Meade with input from Eustace, is generally considered to be the author's finest work. Originally published in volumes XXIV and XXV of *The Strand* magazine between July 1902 and June 1903, the six stories introduce Meade and Eustace's most memorable character, Madame Sara who, like Madame Koluchy in *The*

---

56    L. T. Meade and Robert Eustace, *The Sanctuary Club* (London: Ward, Lock & Co., 1900), 7.
57    Ibid., 8.
58    Ibid., 115.

*Brotherhood of the Seven Kings*, "aspires to no higher purpose than artifice" and threatens the social order through a mixture of her gender, foreignness, and scientific knowledge.[59] Madame Sara is a "professional beautifier" who "claims the privilege of restoring youth to those who consult her" and has "the ability to make quite ugly people handsome".[60] Herself of great beauty, "very fair, with blue eyes, an innocent, childlike manner, and quantities of rippling gold hair", her age is indeterminate. Although she looks to be about twenty-five, one character confides that Sara was bridesmaid at her mother's wedding some twenty years previously. Madame Sara uses her powers to win the confidence of gullible young women, usually married to members of the establishment, who she later uses to obtain financial benefits from their husbands or male members of their families. Elizabeth Carolyn Miller notes how the character is based on that of the real-life Madame Rachel, a notorious female criminal of the 1860s, whose exploits in the field of fraud were earlier novelised by Wilkie Collins in *Armadale* (1864–66).[61] Madame Rachel's full name was Sarah Rachel Leverson so, Miller argues, the connection would be obvious to the contemporary readership.[62] Leverson, like Madame Sara, purportedly helped women to look younger with her beauty secrets, and was given the inordinately long sentence of five years imprisonment, being judged, according to Miller, as much for fraud as for her condition as being "illiterate, thrice-married, separated from her husband, and Jewish".[63] Madame Sara is of foreign parentage, her mother was Indian and her father Italian, and the women she exploits are

59   Chan, "Linked Excitements", 70.
60   L. T. Meade and Robert Eustace, *The Sorceress of the Strand* (London: Ward, Lock & Co., 1903), story 1 "Madame Sara", <http://digital.library.upenn.edu/women/meade/sorceress/sorceress.html#I>, accessed 4 October 2019.
61   Elizabeth Caroline Miller, "'Shrewd Women of Business': Madame Rachel, Victorian Consumerism, and L. T. Meade's *The Sorceress of the Strand*", *Victorian Literature and Culture* 34 (2006), 34, 311.
62   Ibid., 311.
63   Ibid., 314.

often of foreign blood who are either married or are soon to be married to respectable upper-class English gentlemen.[64]

Madame Sara as a woman, alien and scientific genius poses a threat to English masculinity and the patriarchy which constitutes the establishment. According to Miller, the problem created both by the real Madame Rachel and the fictional Madame Sara is based upon "a vexed entanglement of gender, ethnic, and economic anxieties" which "symbolize threats to English national identity posed by feminism, immigration and cosmopolitanism, and consumerism".[65] She is opposed by two male figures, neither of whom is able to trap or curtail her activities. Dixon Druce, the proud possessor of what is believed to be the most sophisticated private science laboratory in London, is the manager of Werner's Agency, "the Solvency Inquiry Agency for all British Trade", a defender, therefore, of state-supported capitalism.[66] He is aided by his friend Dr Eric Vandeleur, a police surgeon and confirmed rationalist. The problem for Druce and Vanleur, however, is that the rationalism and scientific ability of Madame Sara is greater than theirs, and she is constantly capable of outwitting them. Her tricks are varied and horrific. She tattoos incriminating information disguised in the form of a cross on a girl's neck using silver nitrate so that any exposure to light would kill the victim. Using her skills in dentistry she inserts a poisoned capsule into a victim's tooth. She rigs up an explosive device in a palm tree that disperses poisonous gas. Although a beautician, her laboratory and its surgical equipment suggest more sinister purposes:

> There stood a polished oak square table, on which lay an array of extraordinary-looking articles and implements – stoppered bottles full of strange medicaments, mirrors, plane and concave, brushes, sprays, sponges, delicate needle-pointed instruments of bright steel, tiny lancets, and forceps. Facing this table was a chair, like those used by dentists. Above the chair hung electric lights in powerful reflectors, and lenses like bull's-eye lanterns. Another chair, supported on a glass pedestal, was kept there,

---

64   Jennifer A. Halloran, "The Ideology behind *The Sorceress of the Strand*: Gender, Race, and Criminal Witchcraft", *English Literature in Transition (1880–1920)* 2 (2002), 175.

65   Miller, "Shrewd Women", 313.

66   Meade and Eustace, *Sorceress*, story 3, "The Face of the Abbot".

Madame Sara informed me, for administering static electricity. There were dry-cell batteries for the continuous currents and induction coils for Faradic currents.

Madame took me from this room into another, where a still more formidable array of instruments was to be found. Here were a wooden operating table and chloroform and ether apparatus.[67]

The suggestion, of course, is that Madame Sara, like Madame Rachel, was also suspected of performing putative abortions.[68] Her superiority over her male adversities has underlined the fact that she gets the better of them in five of the six stories and, in the final tale only her death prevents a final victory. Druce and Vandeleur, as representatives of the establishment, are forced to follow the letter of the law and play, as it were, by the rules, while Madame Sara, as a foreigner and, we are led to understand, as a female, is not susceptible to the norms of male fair play. As Halloran says, her "feminine, foreign nature allows her not only to imagine what for other criminals seems unimaginable but to act on impulses in a way that is completely unexpected by her pursuers".[69]

   *The Oracle of Maddox Street* (1904), although containing some satisfying stories, is, in most respects, much less accomplished than *The Sorceress of the Strand*, lacking the internal unity of its predecessor and giving the impression of being more a collection of unconnected fragments rather than a unified collection. The framing premise relies on one Edward Dering, the narrator, a man of over sixty who, after travelling widely, is now back in England where he has apparently been urged by friends to "annotate and publish" his stories.[70] Again international settings abound, from Brazil to South Africa, and the stories contain modern scientific discoveries such as radium, a spectroscope and ether waves applied to wireless technology and, in "The Love Adventures of Primrose Ward", an interesting independent New Woman. *Micah Faraday, Adventurer*, is another linked collection situated somewhere between a collection of short stories and a novel narrated in short, curt sentences by Micah, a graduate in medicine who, unwilling

---

67    Meade and Eustace, *Sorceress*, story 2 "The Blood-Red Cross".
68    Miller, "Shrewd Women", 327.
69    Halloran, "Ideology *Sorceress*", 187.
70    Meade and Eustace, *Oracle*, 7.

to tie himself down to "the homely work of the ordinary medical practitioner"[71] partakes in a number of adventures where his combined skills of scientist and detective overcome all apparent odds. As in *The Sanctuary Club*, there is a recurring villain throughout the stories, in this case, Harold Fisher, an eerie combination of scientist and stock dealer who, in the final stages of the work and on his deathbed, lures Micah into the death chamber which he has made airtight, setting off a poison intended to kill both the dying villain and young Faraday.

Meade's later mystery fiction is of a mixed quality, with weak romantic novels involving blackmail, hereditary curses and Italian aristocrats as seen in *The Necklace of Parmona* (1909). Such works sit uneasily alongside more substantial narratives such as *The House of Black Magic* (1912), which introduces John Fuller, a professional detective, and the presence of competent police officers. In 1911 the author published *Ruffles*, a work which merged her girls' fiction with her mystery narratives. This book involves a fifteen-year-old girl who solves mysteries and, according to Sally Mitchell, its "tone leads one to suspect there might have been sequels had Meade not died shortly afterwards".[72] The sheer volume of Meade's immense output, however, should not conceal the importance of her contribution to crime fiction in the English language and the original and varied formats, ruses and solutions she proposes in her work.

71   L. T. Meade, *Micah Faraday: Adventurer* (London: Ward, Lock & Co., 1910), 8.
72   Mitchell, "Children's Reading", 56.

# CHAPTER 6

# "I just go by the rule of thumb, and muddle and puzzle out my cases as best I can." Detection and Mystery at the Turn of the Century

The two cousins Edith Anna Oenone Somerville (1858–1949) and Violet Florence Martin (1862–1915) published their first novel *An Irish Cousin* (1889) under the pseudonyms "Geilles Herring" and "Martin Ross", although subsequent works would be published using the names *Somerville and Ross*. *An Irish Cousin*, initially given the pre-publication title *The Shocker*, is, "despite being generally dismissed as an awkward piece of Gothic apprentice work",[1] an interesting debut with "elements of sensation and mystery about it".[2] The narrator, Theodora Sarsfield is a young Irishwoman who, after spending her childhood between Germany and Switzerland has returned from Canada, where she has been staying since the death of her parents, to visit her father's cousin, her Uncle Dominick, and his son Willy at Durrus, the gothic family mansion. Theo soon discovers that the mansion holds a secret; the visitation of the mad former housekeeper Moll Bryan and her strange daughter, Dominick's alcoholic hallucinations and the discovery of a secret paper lead her to the realisation that her father's death was neither of natural causes nor on the date that her uncle had previously claimed, and that she is the true heiress to Durrus. Theo is courted in the novel by both her cousin and a neighbour, the initially irascible Nugent O'Neill, whose family have historically been in dispute with the Sarsfields. Theo's growing love for "The O'Neill", whose name betrays his native Irish roots, would appear to imply that the

---

1   Vera Kreilkamp, *The Anglo-Irish Novel and the Big House* (Syracuse, NY: Syracuse University Press, 1998), 115.

2   James H. Murphy, *Irish Novelists and the Victorian Age* (Oxford: Oxford University Press, 2011), 186.

O'Neills, who had first been seen as the Other are not, in fact, the enemy, and that the real Other inhabits the family Big House. The marriage between Theo and Nugent can be seen, therefore, as an attempt at national reconciliation.

*Naboth's Vineyard* (1891) is set in the context of the Land War and takes the action away from the Big House and into the native Irish community of Rossbrin, an imaginary fishing village. John Donovan, hotel owner and leader of the local branch of the Land League, uses his position of power to carry out a private vendetta and encourages a boycott of the land farmed by the widow Mrs. Leonard and her daughter Ellen. Richard "Rick" O'Grady, who has returned to Rossbrin from the USA, realises that Donovan's intentions against the Leonards are more personal than political and foils an attempt by the publican to use its previous owner, Malony, to burn down the farm. The plot is complicated by the jealousy of Donovan's wife, Harriet, a former lover of Rick's, and the rivalry between him and Dan Hurley, the Leonards' farm-hand, for the love of Ellen. Harriet's refusal to warn her husband about the existence of a trap which Dan has set to kill Rick leads to the death of both Donovan and Dan, and the trial of Mahony reveals Donovan's duplicity. The novel does not attack the Land League as such, but criticises the way in which a political conflict can be used to satisfy personal grudges by unscrupulous leaders. Somerville and Ross are best known, of course, for their three volumes of tales: *Some Experiences of an Irish RM* (1899), *Further Experiences of an Irish RM* (1908) and *In Mr. Knox's Country* (1915). These tales ostensibly show Major Yeates, an ex-army Resident Magistrate, administering justice in rural south-west Ireland, but are mostly remarkable for their humorous portrayal of the various representatives of the different strata of Irish society and their relationship with authority.

*J. Fitzgerald Molloy* (1858–1908) was born in New Ross, County Wexford and produced a number of novels and non-fiction works, including a biography of Lady Blessington. His fictional output was initially published in magazines such as *Temple Bar*, *English Illustrated Magazine*, *Graphic* and *Illustrated London News*, and includes a number of melodramatic works featuring crime and its detection, such as *A Modern Magician* (1887), *His Wife's Soul* (1893) and *A Justified Sinner* (1897). Arguably his most accomplished work is *An Excellent Knave* (1893), in which Hugh Moreland, a painter and the "younger son of an Irish squire, impoverished by reckless ancestors and made bankrupt by wanton extravagance"[3] is the main suspect in the murder of Charles Forrester on the London to Paris train. The case is investigated by Inspector Jacob Inquies of Scotland Yard and, in his defence, Hugh seeks out the private detective Geoffrey Gillesby. Unlike many crime writers of the period, Molloy portrays both Inquies and Gillseby in a positive light, emphasising their professionalism and alacrity. While Inquies is a "man of education" who "spoke the language of every nation in Europe with fluency",[4] Gillesby is a master of disguise and possesses a fine analytical brain. The conclusion, involving a cross-dressing "New Woman", is enhanced by an excellently written court scene in which the reader sees how Gillesby gradually develops his hypothesis.

Dublin-born *Abraham "Bram" Stoker* (1847–1912) is, of course, best known for his *Dracula* (1897), a work which brilliantly fused the gothic with the detective mystery and the invasion narrative, and which touched on such varied concepts as colonialism, the treatment of the "Other", the role of women, sexuality and immigration. Apart from *Dracula*, however, crime is always present in Stoker's fictional output, and many of his works contain echoes of the crime and mystery fiction of the era. Interestingly, he contributed, along with Arthur Conan Doyle and others, in *The Fate of Fenella* (1892), a round-robin mystery, and his first published narrative, *The Primrose Path*, which featured in *The Shamrock* magazine in 1875, is a topical temperance novel with the drunken murder of a wife by her husband at its core. Both *The Snake's Pass* (1890), set in Ireland, and *The Watter's Mou* (1895), set in Scotland, feature evil, criminal money-lenders and plots which include hidden treasure and smugglers.

*Miss Betty* (1898), like *The Shoulder of Shasta* (1895), is a somewhat insubstantial romance whose main interest lies in a repentant highwayman who returns the money he has stolen and serves a year as a slave on a Turkish galley. *The Mystery of the Sea* (1902), again set in Scotland, connects the

---

3   J. Fitzgerald Molloy, *An Excellent Knave*, 3 vols. (London: Hutchinson, 1893), vol. 1, 34.
4   Ibid., 57.

then-contemporary Spanish-American War with tales of missing bullion and gold from the Spanish Armada, and combines gothic features of a ghostly procession and an old castle riddled with secret tunnels with a New Woman, coded clues and the use of a "Kodak" camera to take photographs of the evidence. *The Jewel of the Seven Stars* (1903) and *The Lair of the White Worm* (1911) also link a gothic past with incipient modernity. The former is particularly noteworthy in a study of crime fiction for its portrayal of the competent, professional police officers, Sergeant Daw and Superintendent Dolan, whose sophisticated techniques include the mastery of the locksmith's art and the use of a magnifying glass to examine the evidence.

Of *Dracula* (1897), of course, much has been written, and the figure of the main character, who also appears in the posthumous short story collection *Dracula's Guest and Other Weird Stories* (1914), is now a well-recognised cultural icon. It can be stressed, however, that *Dracula* contains numerous features of the detective novel, and many of its concerns are those of the contemporary crime narrative being produced at the same time by writers such as L. T. Meade and Richard Dowling. The influence of Sheridan Le Fanu, although most obvious in the debt Stoker owes to his fellow Dubliner's "Carmilla", is also apparent in the figure of Professor Abraham Van Helsing. This distinguished supernatural detective owes much to Le Fanu's Hesselius, and W. J. McCormack even reminds us that this debt is also reflected in the name of Stoker's character.[5]

*The Picture of Dorian Gray* (1891), by Stoker's fellow Dubliner *Oscar Wilde*, contains a murder and blackmail, and Wilde parodied the contemporary fashion for crime writing in "Lord Arthur Saville's Crime", published in *The Court and Society Review* in 1887 and reprinted in *Lord Arthur Saville's Crime and Other Stories* (1891). Saville, who has "the doom of murder hanging over his head", is told by a chiromantist that his future path, as seen in his palm, is that of a murderer.[6] Believing himself to be unable to marry until he has fulfilled his destiny, Arthur tries to carry out

5   W. J. McCormack, "Irish Gothic and After (1820–1945)" in *The Field Day Anthology of Irish Writing: Volume* II (Derry: Field Day Publications, 1991), 842.
6   Oscar Wilde, *Lord Arthur Saville's Crime and Other Stories* (London: James R. Osgood, McIlvaine & Co., 1891), 39.

a murder with hilarious results. The story subverts the conventions of the developing genre, and even permits the mockery of the contemporary forces of law and order. The German anarchist who provides Saville with a bomb disguised as a carriage clock, which Arthur wants to send to the Dean of Chichester, comments on the English police:

> If it is for the police or any one connected with Scotland Yard, I am afraid I cannot do anything for you. The English detectives are really our best friends, and I have always found that by relying on their stupidity, we can do exactly what we like. I could not spare one of them.[7]

Wilde's family had been depicted by Wexford-born caricaturist *Harry Furniss* (1854–1925) who, in 1905, published a curious comic crime novel entitled *Poverty Bay: A Nondescript Novel*, which featured an endearingly unreliable narrator, the unwitting heir to a smuggler's fortune, and an apparently supernatural crime featuring a cross-dressing hero/heroine, a superstitious lawyer who doubles as an aristocratic postman, and a female painter who is also a barber, palm-reader and phrenologist. The resolution at one point seems so difficult that it is described as "a task fitted for one who should be a cross between Sherlock Holmes and the president of the Psychic Society".[8]

*Robert Cromie* (1856–1907), a resident of Belfast, was best known for his early science fiction works, including *A Plunge into Space* (1890), which included an introduction by Jules Verne. He merged crime and science fiction in *The Crack of Doom* (1895), where the misanthropic Brande uses atoms to create a bomb which he intends to use to destroy the world, and in *The Lost Liner* (1898), where the wreck of a seemingly unsinkable liner brings two passengers of different social classes together on an uncharted island with the remains of the ship and a fortune in gold. Cromie will be remembered as a writer of crime fiction, however, for his *The Romance of Poisons: Being Weird Episodes from Life* (1903), written in collaboration with T. S. Wilson. A series of stories which originally appeared in *Black and*

7    Ibid., 55.
8    Harry Furniss, *Poverty Bay: A Nondescript Novel* (London: Chapman & Hall, 1905), 187.

*White, The Romance of Poisons* features the detective pairing of Surgeon-Colonel Hedford, an ex-army doctor and specialist in venomous substances and Inspector Trowbrigg, a former Scotland Yard officer who now works as a "Private Enquiry Agent".[9] Together Hedford and Trowbrigg investigate several cases of poisoning or suspected poisoning, using their respective medical knowledge and investigative brilliance to entrap a corrupt MP and his accomplice, a nurse, an aristocratic Russian nihilist and an Indian man-servant. In keeping with the jingoism apparent in much turn-of-the-century fiction, the foreign or colonial origin of much of the poison and many of the poisoners is stressed, and although Trowbrigg is portrayed as a professional detective, Hendon follows the norms of the gifted amateur whose investigation is carried out for purely altruistic motives.

*Matthew Phipps Shiel* (1865–1947) was born in the West Indian island of Montserrat to parents of Irish descent, and although, in the words of John Wilson Foster, "the claim for his Shiel's Irishness is tenuous", his visionary writing was influential for future generations of writers. Credited with producing "the first future-history series in science fiction", Shiel also produced some noteworthy short crime fiction, including "The Pale Ape", "Huguenin's Wife" and "The Case of Euphemia Raphash".[10] "Euphemia Raphash" was first published in *Chapman's Magazine of Fiction* in 1895 and later reprinted in the collection *The Pale Ape and Other Pulses*. Reviewing the Tartarus Press re-edition of *The Pale Ape*, William P. Simmons stresses Shiel's "ethereal wedding of cosmic awe and emotional unease beyond the grasp of his peers"[11] and notes the influence of both Poe and Le Fanu while pointing out the influence of Shiel on writers such as Lovecraft and Arthur Machen. Narrated by Parker, the secretary of Dr Arnot Raphash, the story details the investigation carried out by the doctor and his secretary to unveil

9   Robert Cromie and T. S. Wilson, *The Romance of Poisons: Being Weird Episodes from Life* (London: Jarrold and Sons, 1903), 15.
10  Christopher Fowler, "Forgotten Authors No. 28: Matthew Phipps Shiel", *Independent*, 22 March 2009. <http://www.independent.co.uk/arts-entertainm ent/books/features/forgotten-authors-no28-matthew-phipps-shiel-1648079. html>, accessed 6 March 2013.
11  William P. Simmons, "The Pale Ape and Other Pulses by MP Shiel", *Infinity Plus*, <http://www.infinityplus.co.uk/nonfiction/paleape.htm>, accessed 6 March 2013.

the murderer who has killed Euphemia, the doctor's sister. Acting as detectives, the two seek to explore avenues untouched by the official forces of detection because, as Dr Raphash says, "deeps, black to the eye of a policeman, may lighten to the eye of a thinker".[12] The investigation moves, however, to Parker's eventual doubting of his mentor. The behaviour of the doctor, who believes the search for his sister's killer "is a task we must not leave to the crude intellects of the recognised authorities",[13] starts to raise questions in his hitherto faithful assistant, who soon comes to understand that he is Watson to a highly unreliable Holmes.

*Matthias McDonnell Bodkin* (1850–1933) is, perhaps, one of the most overlooked crime writers from the period between the end of the nineteenth and beginning of the twentieth century. Julian Symons believes that Bodkin does not deserve such neglect, and that the members of the author's Beck family are the "best Plain Man detectives of their era".[14] Bodkin was a barrister who later became a judge, and who served briefly at Westminster as the nationalist MP for North Roscommon. His early writing consists of a number of quirky tales, such as those collected in *Pat O'Nine Tales and One More* (1894), and in 1897 he published his first mystery novel *White Magic*. This contains many of the features that would characterise his later detective fiction, such as the incursion of modernity through technological advances, the presence of the New Woman, the dissolute male heir and the perceived deficiencies of the official services of law and order. One of the characters, Jenny, who wants to become a "lady journalist" is seen trying on her new bicycle costume "with the door locked and the blind down" so that her aspiring New Woman status is not ridiculed.[15] Mr Jacob Merlyn, the stereotypical Jewish banker (and miser) is obsessed with his tape telegraph and his telephone, which "were the familiars of this nineteenth-century magician, whispering mysteriously of money to be made in every

12    M. P. Shiel, *The Pale Ape and Other Pulses* (1911, Carlton, North Yorkshire: Tartarus Press, 2006), 28.

13    Ibid., 30.

14    Julian Symons, *Bloody Murder. From the Detective Story to the Crime Novel* (1972, Harmondsworth: Penguin, 1985), 83.

15    M. McDonnell Bodkin, *White Magic* (London: Chapman & Hall, 1897), 50–52.

corner of the globe".[16] The detectives called in to investigate the murder of Merlyn are "vastly mysterious and self-important"[17] and are never close to solving the case or recovering the money and gold taken from the dead financier. Although primarily set in London, a substantial sub-plot takes place in Ireland where Gerald Daly and his mute sister Grace are left penniless after the death of their father and are forced to sell their land and move to Dublin. Gerald, in many respects an autobiographical version of Bodkin himself, contests a parliamentary election as a nationalist candidate which, again like Bodkin, he wins with a narrow majority and moves to London to take his seat in the House of Commons. Gerald falls in love with Dorothy, Merlyn's beautiful daughter and, aided by the lip-reading powers of Grace, the banker's killer is revealed and his riches recuperated. The ending is conventionally happy, with a honeymoon in Ireland included, but *White Magic* is an interesting first novel within the limited scope of late-nineteenth-century mystery fiction.

*A Stolen Life* (1898) also features a semi-autobiographical character in John Trevor, a lawyer who becomes a judge and whose behaviour is influenced by his opposition to the death penalty. The novel is notable mainly for its ingenious use of mesmerism as a narrative tool, going beyond the conventional use of the hypnotist's art in fin-de-siècle mysteries with a memorable battle of wills between two mesmerists who attempt to mesmerise each other. The year 1898 would also see the publication of the first in Bodkin's Paul Beck series. *Paul Beck, the Rule of Thumb Detective* is a collection of interlinked short stories featuring the eponymous protagonist, an unassuming, self-effacing private detective who is, however, reputed to be "one of the cleverest detectives in London" and who "had puzzled out mysteries where even the famous Mr Murdock Rose had failed".[18] The reader, especially in the 1890s, will immediately recognise in this famous detective the resonance of Sherlock Holmes, to whom Beck would appear to be the diametrical opposite. LeRoy Lad Panek praises the figure of Beck who he calls "a master of minutiae possessed of encyclopaedic knowledge

16    Ibid., 29.
17    Ibid., 62.
18    M. McDonnell Bodkin, *Paul Beck, The Rule of Thumb Detective* (London: C. Arthur Pearson, 1898), 8.

and exhaustive scientific background".[19] The detective is introduced in "The Vanishing Diamonds" in the following terms:

> He was a strong, stoutly built man in dark grey tweed, suggesting rather the notion of a respectable retired milkman than a detective. His face was ruddy and fringed with reddish brown whiskers, and his light brown hair curled like a water dog's. There was a chronic look of mild surprise in his wide-open blue eyes, and his smile was as innocent as a child's.[20]

The cases Beck solves are generally concerned with theft, forgery and blackmail, although the perpetrators, often of foreign extraction like M. Grabeau, Signor Montifero or Signor Madaveski, also commit murder. They use hypnotism and diverse creative methods in their criminal activities: the sun reflecting on a piece of glass is employed in one murder, and vanishing ink is used for fraudulent purposes. The "ordinariness" of Beck is constantly stressed by Bodkin, who mentions the detective's stolidity as representing his most salient characteristic, stating that he "had nerve to any amount, but no nerves".[21] Beck himself describes his method:

> A little common sense, Miss, that's all. I have no more system than the hound that gets on the fox's scent and keeps on it. I just go by the rule of thumb, and muddle and puzzle out my cases as best I can.[22]

For Panek, Beck's "rule of thumb" emphasises his "common sense and routine versus genius", and he considers the Beck stories to parody the Sherlock Holmes stories, claiming that the hero's "proletarian lack of method" reveals his true detective genius.[23]

Another collection of short stories, *Dora Myrl, The Lady Detective* (1900), introduces Dora, a "dainty little lady" with the "face of a bright

19   LeRoy Lad Panek, *After Sherlock Holmes: The Evolution of British and American Crime Fiction* (Jefferson, NC: McFarland & Company, 2014), 74.
20   Bodkin, *Rule of Thumb*, 8.
21   Ibid., 37.
22   Ibid., 30.
23   Panek, *After Sherlock*, 74.

schoolgirl" and a "keen bird-like look".[24] While Bodkin is at pains to stress that there "was certainly nothing of the New Woman" about this character, readers, like Kathleen Gregory Klein, would have no difficulty in identifying Dora as "the archetypal New Woman of fiction" who in terms of "appearance, education, occupation and recreation" are those of "the Girton girl whose independence so challenged her countrymen".[25] Dora, we learn, is a Cambridge Wrangler and a Doctor of Medicine, who, although yet to find a vocation, has worked as a telegraph girl, a telephone girl and a lady journalist.[26] She rides a bicycle, and for Craig and Cadogan shows "an exuberant type of independence that suggests a leap into the modern crime story genre".[27] By the end of the first story in the collection, "The False Heir and the True", Dora has solved her first case and found her true vocation, that of Lady Detective. Despite her evident skill and dexterity, Dora is constantly under-rated and disparaged by male characters. In "The Palmist" Dr Phillimore sees her profession as being "somewhat incongruous for a charming young lady";[28] in "The Last Shall Be First" Sir Warner considers her to be a "bright, piquant little woman whose pretensions as a detective he regarded with good-humoured amusement"; while in "The Clue" Sir Charles finds "a world of humour in the notion of unsophisticated Dora as a lady detective".[29] Ironically, of course, these same male characters are generally highly flawed and their gullibility, stupidity, vanity and unjustified self-righteousness only help to cast the astute, subtle and unassuming Dora in a better light. While Dr Phillimore is obsessed with theosophy, astrology, phrenology and palmistry, Dora is cracking cyphers, tracking down murderers using cunning disguises and exposing fraudulent practices of all types.

24  M. McDonnell Bodkin, *Dora Myrl, The Lady Detective* (London: Chatto & Windus, 1900), 2.

25  Kathleen Gregory Klein, *The Woman Detective: Gender and Genre*, 2nd edn (Urbana: University of Illinois, 1995), 58.

26  Bodkin, *Dora Myrl*, 6.

27  Patricia Craig and Mary Cadogan, *The Lady Investigates: Women Detectives and Spies in Fiction* (London. Victor Gollancz, 1981), 33.

28  Bodkin, *Dora Myrl*, 72.

29  Ibid., 114.

Dora, along with L. T. Meade's Florence Cusack, is considered to be one of the first female detectives not only in Irish crime fiction but in the universal history of the genre. James H. Murphy remarks that Bodkin's Dora "most helped to champion the woman detective",[30] although Craig and Cadogan criticise Bodkin's inability to sustain the initial impulse of the stories throughout the volume.[31] There is no doubt, however, that Dora Myrl is an important addition to the roster of detectives created by Irish writers and a notable precursor to later female detective figures. LeRoy Lad Panek remarks that, while most early women detectives were "dipped rather deeply in sentiment", Dora Myrl proves an exception to this rule.[32] Somewhat less successful, perhaps, is Bodkin's next detective character. In *A Modern Robyn Hood* (1903), Robyn, the upper-class detective, observed by his friend and Watson-like narrator Jack Tresham, solves several minor crimes in a world of cycle races, duels with insulting Frenchmen and cheating at cards games. Typical of early twentieth-century crime writing, Bodkin makes use of numerous modern technical devices in order to trap the miscreants. The most notable of these in this particular volume is an animatograph camera with a slow-motion reel, which is used to catch a card thief in "A Living Picture".

Paul Beck returns in *The Quests of Paul Beck* (1908), another collection of short stories in which the "rule of thumb detective" once again excels against a variety of evil thieves, fraudsters and killers. In "Trifles Light as Air" Bodkin displays one of the rare instances in crime fiction in which a member of the official forces of the law shows unabated respect for the private detective, as a member of the local police "regarded the detective with the profound veneration of the small boy for the head of school".[33] In this volume Beck states that he has his own personal wealth owing to both his work and his gains on the stock market, leaving him in the liminal status between professional private detective and gifted amateur. In "The Ship's

---

30  Murphy, *Irish Novelists*, 208.
31  Craig and Cadogan, *Lady Investigates*, 33.
32  LeRoy Lad Panek, *An Introduction to the Detective Story* (Bowling Green: Bowling Green State University Popular Press, 1987), 108.
33  M. McDonnell Bodkin, *The Quests of Paul Beck* (London: T. Fisher Unwin, 1908), 42.

Run" Beck, posing as a South African millionaire, uncovers an on-board lottery swindle on an ocean liner called the Gigantic, an early name for the Titanic, while in "Twixt the Devil and the Deep Blue Sea" Beck, employed by Lloyds, captures a dynamiter planning to blow up a ship on a sea voyage to Hong Kong. *The Capture of Paul Beck* (1909) takes the character out of the context of the short story and into the novel format. It is possible that a character such as Beck who, despite his skill and modesty is somewhat one dimensional, is more suited to the shorter format, and *The Capture of Paul Beck* is more noteworthy for its bringing together, romantically and professionally, of Beck and Dora Myrl, than for its convoluted plot which initially pits the two detectives against each other but finally brings them together in marriage.

*Young Beck* (1911) is similar in many respects to *A Modern Robyn Hood* and, unfortunately, equally forgettable. The hero is, with a total lack of verisimilitude, the son of Dora and Paul who, like his parents, is pitted against a series of mesmerists, anarchists and evil actors. The most interesting feature of the book, a series of interconnected tales, is the self-referential attitude it reveals with references to other Beck and Myrtle fiction – Young Beck is "a mother's pet" who is "more like a girl than a boy"[34] and who has "read all the old Beck stories and Dora Myrl stories", preferring the latter as he found his father "too meek and modest".[35] The book is topical, with references to the Irish Question and the "German scare"[36] but lacks the originality of works like *Paul Beck, the Rule of Thumb Detective* or *Dora Myrl, The Lady Detective*. In *Pigeon Blood Rubies* (1915), Bodkin returns with another Paul Beck novel in a "frankly sensational"[37] story which sees the detective and his club friends confront the killers of the male members of the Tresham family who, it would appear, are heirs to the secret of how to make rubies using a secret formula. The novel sees Beck bonding with his male friends but leaves Dora at home, her domestic role replacing her earlier verve and active intelligence in what can only be seen as a lamentable turn of events. Similarly, the frame text of *Paul Beck, Detective* (1919), finds

34   M. McDonnell Bodkin, *Young Beck* (London: T. Fisher Unwin, 1911), 14.
35   Ibid., 24.
36   Ibid., 106.
37   M. McDonnell Bodkin, *Pigeon Blood Rubies* (London: Eveleigh Nash, 1915), 11.

Dora rummaging in the lumber-room of their home when she discovers several earlier cases solved by her husband, at times with her involvement. The cases are presented as short stories and, while retaining certain of the salient features of the earlier short stories, are disappointing in the subservient role in which Dora is presented. Craig and Cadogan lament that Dora was "doomed as a detective when marriage and motherhood caught up with her" and how she is "not allowed to carry on the role of partner or even assistant to her husband".[38] Some of the better stories in the collection such as "The Phoenix" and "A Bird of Prey" are set in Ireland, and Bodkin's playful self-referencing is once again apparent in "The Dream and the Waking" where Paul finds a copy of *The Quests of Paul Beck* in the murderer's bedroom.

Bodkin's final mystery novel, published four years before his death, was *Guilty or Not Guilty* (1929). A stand-alone work which does not feature the Becks, this novel, set entirely in Ireland, is a satisfying hybrid which draws features from the mystery fiction of the 1890s with which Bodkin's career had commenced and the conventions of the new Golden Age fiction, predominant in the 1920s and 1930s. In Golden Age fashion, the amateur investigator is assisted by a friend who is a writer of crime fiction and who, through the analysis in clues in footprints and types of shoes is able to solve the murder despite the technological advantages possessed by the official police investigators.

Belfast-born *Samuel Robert Keightley* (1859–1940) is best known for his poetry and for several historical novels such as *The Crimson Sign* (1894) and *The Pikeman* (1904). In his only crime novel, *A Man of Millions* (1901), the titular hero is Percival, who had been forced to abandon his native Ireland after falsifying his father's signature on a cheque on the instigation of his cousin, Christopher. Taking advantage of Percival's absence, Christopher marries Marion, his cousin's fiancée. Percival arrives in Wickham, England, a rich man, having made his fortune after discovering diamonds in South Africa. He is accompanied by a Chinese servant, Ah Sin who, somewhat predictably, is said to possess a "yellow unreadable countenance".[39] When

---

38   Craig and Cadogan, *Lady Investigates*, 33.
39   Samuel Robert Keightley, *A Man of Millions* (London: Cassell, 1901), 161.

Christopher and an accomplice attempt to trick Percival with the offer of a Paraguayan concession, Christopher is murdered and the initial blame is placed on his cousin. The son of the local cleric, Dicky Wells, believes Percival to be innocent and, with the aid of his gang the League of Blood he discovers the real murderer, whose identity, most probably, will surprise nobody accustomed to the endemic racism of the period.

*Erskine Childers' The Riddle of the Sands* (1903) is widely regarded to be one of the earliest modern espionage novels and the author has been seen as "the first writer to successfully shape the war prophecy story into a spy novel" and the first "who joins the schoolboy story to the elements of espionage to unify his fiction and make it mean something beyond the transitory warning that the Germans are coming".[40] Childers (1870–1922) was born in London to an Anglo-Irish mother and a diplomat father and served in the British armed forces in both the Anglo-Boer campaign and the First World War. He later converted to Irish nationalism, becoming "the unlikeliest of all revolutionaries".[41] He formed part of the Irish delegation for the negotiation for the Anglo-Irish Treaty in late 1921, but his opposition to the terms of the Treaty led him to support the anti-Free State side in the Civil War. He was arrested by Free State forces and tried for the possession of a small calibre pistol and hurriedly executed in November 1922. Childers' son, also named Erskine, would become the fourth President of Ireland in 1973. *The Riddle of the Sands* begins when Carruthers, a civil servant in the Foreign Office joins a friend, Davies, for a sailing holiday in the Baltic Sea. They discover a plan to invade England by the German navy with the aid of Dollmann, an Englishman who is committing treason out of an alleged respect for the Kaiser and contempt for his fellow countrymen. Although complicated by a romantic twist – Davies is in love with Dollmann's daughter – the two English navigators reach England with information of the proposed invasion and the threat is averted. Although David Seed sees the work as belonging to the sub-genre of invasion fantasies

---

40    LeRoy Lad Panek, *The Special Branch: The British Spy Novel, 1890–1980* (Bowling Green: Bowling Green State University Popular Press, 1981), 32.
41    Andrew Boyle, *The Riddle of Erskine Childers* (London: Hutchinson, 1977), 25.

which started with *The Battle of Dorking*, a pamphlet published in 1871,[42] and for LeRoy Lad Panek, the insistence on the use of excessive technical information "ruins the book as a novel",[43] critics are agreed on the importance and influence of the work on future writers of espionage mysteries. Dennis Butts states that by "beginning slowly and lingering over so much apparently unnecessary detail, the story achieves a hard-won authenticity", and the use of an "amateur agent, the accidental discovery of mystery, the gradual discovery of the mystery's serious implications, and the hero's ultimate defeat of the conspiracy" were to become recurring features in the genre.[44] Childers' novel is seen as "straddling two genres" in one of the earliest examples of a work which fuses a tale of adventure with one of detection,[45] and for Panek, Childers, like twentieth-century detective writers, "conceives the plot as a riddle to which Davies and Carruthers (not the readers) seek an answer".[46] Indeed the novel pioneers this fusion of adventure and detection in a format that would become increasingly popular as the twentieth century progressed, and would condition the plot of much international spy fiction, revealing a "sphere of action which seems to be beyond the law, its characters use aliases and inverted identities, typically it progresses from apparently disparate fragments of information towards a more complete account of action".[47]

James Owen Hanny (1865–1950), writing under the pseudonym of *George A. Birmingham*, published over sixty novels and volumes of short stories, and in 1912 he was named by *Newsbasket*, the house magazine of newsagent chain W. H. Smith, as the biggest selling author of the year.[48]

---

42   David Seed, "The Adventure of Spying: Erskine Childers's *The Riddle of the Sands*" in *Spy Thrillers: From Buchan to Carré*, ed. Clive Bloom (London: Macmillan, 1990), 40.

43   Panek, *Special Branch*, 35.

44   Dennis Butts, "The Hunter and the Hunted: The Suspense Novels of John Buchan" in Bloom (ed.), *Spy Thrillers*, 46.

45   Seed, "Adventure of Spying", 37.

46   Panek, *Special Branch*, 37.

47   David Seed, "Crime and the Spy Genre" in Rzepka and Horsley (eds), *Crime Fiction*, 233.

48   John Wilson Foster, *Irish Novels 1890–1940: New Bearings in Culture and Fiction* (Oxford: Oxford University Press, 2008), 28.

Born in Belfast Hanny, a Protestant minister, after schooling in London, Methodist College in Belfast and undergraduate studies at Dublin's Trinity College, spent most of his life in Westport, Co. Mayo. His first novel, *The Seething Pot* (1905) was followed by *Hyacinth* (1906), which sees the hero attempting to apply nationalist principles to his father's clothing business, only to reject the cause after disillusionment both with the beautiful militant Finola and with what he sees as the hypocrisy of those supposedly committed to the cause. After three political novels, Birmingham produced the first of his humorous mystery novels which would characterise his future output.

In *Spanish Gold* (1908), the author introduces the Reverend J. J. Meldon and Major Kent, both or either of whom would reappear in a total of twelve subsequent novels, although not always bearing the same names. Meldon, "a deflator of pomposity and undeserved reputation",[49] is "a superbly comic character, possessed of an amiable and endearing realism".[50] Meldon, a Church of Ireland curate, and Kent, a third-generation Anglo-Irish landowner, go in search of some hidden gold, reputedly coming from the Spanish Armada and believed to be concealed on an island off Ireland's west coast. Finding the treasure in the home of intrepid islander Thomas O'Flaherty Pat, both Meldon and O'Flaherty are captured by rival gold hunters and held captive. The curate manages to trick his captors into spilling the gold and, with the help of the local Catholic priest and a group of islanders, led by O'Flaherty's granddaughter Kate, manages to seize the thieves and recover the gold. The gold is distributed among the islanders and Kate and Meldon marry, to go and live in an industrial town in Lancashire. *Spanish Gold* is interesting for a number of reasons other than its providing the first version of a formula for which the author would become famous. The collaboration between Meldon and Father Mulcrone, the Church of Ireland curate and the Catholic priest, and that of the Catholic islanders and the Protestant landowner reveals the ecumenical inclusiveness which Birmingham supports, while the difference in the way the various characters

---

49  Brian Taylor, *The Life and Writings of James Owen Hanny (George A. Birmingham) 1865–1950* (Lewiston: The Edwin Mellen Press, 1995), 90.

50  A. Norman Jeffares, *Macmillan History of Literature: Anglo-Irish Literature* (London: Gill & Macmillan, 1982), 215.

interpret the law hints at the depth of divisions still underlying Irish society. Meldon returns in *The Search Party* (1909) and, with Kent, in *The
Simpkins Plot* (1911). In this latter novel the curate attempts to rid the
town of an English writer who he believes to be a murderer by having her
marry, and the woman, innocent of the crime, ends up marrying the staid
and formal Major Kent.

    *The Red Hand of Ulster* (1912) is another political novel which foresees
the introduction of partition in Northern Ireland, while *The Adventures of
Dr Whitty* is a series of short stories featuring a thinly disguised Meldon
as the doctor of the title. A satirical political work, *General John Regan*
(1913) created a scandal when adapted for the theatre and angry crowds in
Westport rioted and burned an effigy of the author. Dr Whitty again appears in *Gossamer*, another linked short story collection relating conflicts
between the nationalist population, the police and Castle bureaucracy. The
First World War provided the background for *The Island Mystery* (1918),
a novel in which an American millionaire buys the crown to the sparsely
inhabited island in the Balkans for his daughter, and Birmingham's fiction
of the 1920s largely followed the patterns of his earlier work. In 1930 the
publication of *The Hymn Tune Mystery* saw a change in style for the author,
and the work owes much more to the contemporary Golden Age novel
than the beginning-of-the-century mystery fiction of his earlier works. The
Reverend John Dennis, an Irish Anglican canon at the fictional English
cathedral of Carminster, joins Inspector Smallways and retired Scotland
Yard detective Sergeant Hodson in the search for Lady Carminster's stolen
emeralds and the person responsible for the related murder of the cathedral
organist. *Two Fools* (1934), despite a convoluted plot involving the murder,
in Ireland, of an Albanian dictator, is of interest primarily for its self-reflexive
comments on crime fiction. The two fools of the title are renamed versions
of Meldon and Kent, and both are in love with Mary Maintree. When
the Albanian attacks Mary, her maid defends her by hitting the "fiddling
gipsy" over the head with a poker.[51] Reverend Augustine Grantwood, the
Meldon figure, is a keen reader of detective novels and when he and his

51    George A. Birmingham, *Two Fools* (London: Methuen, 1934), 175.

romantic rival Henry McNeice (Kent) try to bury the Albanian they discuss the differences between such an action in crime fiction and real life.

    *Dorothea Conyers* (1869–1949) was born Minnie Dorothea Spaight
to a landowning Ascendancy family in County Limerick. She produced
one novel per year between the publication of *The Thorn Bit* (1900) and
*The Witch's Samples* (1950), and although most of her work centres on
romance within the Ascendancy hunting set, some of her works contain
considerable elements of crime narrative. *Lady Elverton's Emeralds* (1909)
provides an interesting example of early twentieth-century Anglo-Irish detective fiction. Set largely in a country house which, although nominally in
England contains all the features of the Irish Big House, with a background
of horse racing and parties, the theft of Lady Elverton's famous jewels is
initially blamed on Reeves, a disgraced former rider and trainer, who has
spent time in prison, wrongly accused of theft. The case is investigated by
Inspector Jones of Scotland Yard, "a hard-bitten, dark little man",[52] aided
by a local officer, Inspector Jones, who is incompetent and rude. It is decided, however, to call in a private detective, as the aristocratic victims of
the crime want an investigator like Sherlock Holmes, one who could "see
you'd been to bed day before yesterday, and what soap you'd used in your
tub".[53] Despite the efforts of both official police detectives and an unofficial private investigator, this latter disguised as a new valet, it is Reeves, the
morally inscrutable, ill-treated amateur who eventually solves the case, winning his innocence, the love of his former sweetheart and the management
of an estate with horses in Worcestershire. *The Experiments of Ganymede
Brown* (1917) also mixes horse breeding, inheritance and crime, this time
with an explicit Irish setting.

    Detective features also appear in some of Conyers' numerous short
stories. In "Escape" from the collection *A Mixed Pack* (1915), for example, a
clerk who kills his employer after being dismissed for losing company money
through gambling is discovered through his own guilt and through the skill
of a commercial traveller who is interested in detective stories. Both *Grey
Brother* (1927) and *Hunting and Hunted* (1930) are collections of short

---

52    Dorothea Conyers, *Lady Elverton's Emeralds* (London: Hutchinson, 1909), 88.
53    Ibid., 172.

stories, most of which feature "the great detective" Mervyn Henderson who is in the habit of recounting his cases to groups of assembled listeners in comfortable surroundings and in true Golden Age fashion. In *Grey Brother* Henderson explains that he had initially trained to be a doctor but that he "dreamt on, attended criminal trials, studied the methods of thieves and murderers, deduced and surmised" until, eventually, he took up his "sleuth-hound's work".[54] Many of the stories are incredibly intricate, and Henderson works on a moral compass which is refreshingly pragmatic. In "Justice Evaded" from *Grey Brother*, the detective's friend Fred is in love with Denys, who is married to Dennison, who is in love with another woman. Dennison attempts to trick Fred into his wife's bedroom, claiming that she is dying. Dennison is subsequently found to have been killed and, although Fred is the initial suspect, a hand-written note points to suicide. Telling the tale to his guests, Mervyn Henderson claims that he, the detective, has in fact killed Dennison, justifying the murder by saying that "vermin are best out of the way".[55] The context of the frame text, however, allows for doubt, and Mervyn's listeners, like Conyers' readers, are left questioning the reliability of the narrator. Stories like "The Poisoning of Hector Althuser" and "An Alibi" from *Hunting and Hunted* are competently written detective stories which help to show the importance of Dorothea Conyers as a link between the turn-of-the-century fiction by writers such as Meade and Bodkin, and the new Golden Age fiction of the interwar years.

54    Dorothea Conyers, *Grey Brother* (London: Hutchinson, 1927), 98.
55    Ibid., 113.

# CHAPTER 7

# "Too sharp to be absolutely wholesome." The Golden Age I: Freeman Wills Crofts

The years between the end of the First World War in 1918 and the beginning of the Second World War in 1939 have been characterised as what has been called the Golden Age of crime fiction, a period of incredible popularity for the genre, in which certain writers such as Agatha Christie, Dorothy L. Sayers, Ronald Knox, G. D. H. Cole, and E. C. Bentley dominated the literary market place. Although essentially an English phenomenon, three Irish writers were among the pioneers of Golden Age fiction and two of these, Freeman Wills Crofts and Nicholas Blake, are considered to be amongst its most accomplished practitioners. Golden Age, or Classic Detective Fiction uses a self-referential and "highly contrived"[1] formula in which "the plot is elevated above all considerations".[2] It is characterised by wide use of the "clue puzzle", closed settings (such as a country house), easily identifiable suspects and a rational detective who is able to uncover the truth using largely circumstantial evidence. The murderer in Golden Age fiction is "rarely a conventional criminal" and "invariably of the same social group as the other suspects".[3] The detective, on the other hand, is "closely identified" with the ruling class, and the crimes solved "are no more than ripples on the surface of an otherwise comprehensible, largely benevolent universe".[4] The narratives are highly formalised, often listing and displaying a number of rules and involving the reader actively in the process of detection. Such formality

---

1   Lee Horsley, *Twentieth-Century Crime Fiction* (Oxford: Oxford University Press, 2005), 12.
2   John Scaggs, *Crime Fiction* (London: Routledge, 2005), 35.
3   Ibid., 46.
4   Horsley, *Twentieth-Century*, 39.

was exemplified by the existence of the Detection Club, a group of writers founded in 1930 and which, among other activities, drew up a prescribed set of rules for authors of detective fiction. It also encouraged the publication of collaborative works by its members, the most successful of which was the "round-robin" novel *The Floating Admiral* (1931–32) which, edited by Dorothy L. Sayers, counted the participation of Freeman Wills Crofts, G. K. Chesterton and Agatha Christie, among others.

*Freeman Wills Crofts* (1879–1957) was born in Dublin, the son of an army surgeon who died before the child's birth. When his widowed mother remarried, the family moved to Belfast where, at the age of seventeen Crofts became an engineer in the Belfast and Northern Counties Railway. His first novel was published in 1920, and nine years later he gave up his engineering post to become a full-time writer. Martin Edwards describes Crofts as "a thoroughly decent man with strong spiritual values",[5] and Curtis Evans notes that the writer's two great influences were railways and religion.[6] Julian Symons famously referred to Crofts as "the best representative of the Humdrum school of detective novelists whose work poured from the presses during the decade, and indeed for long afterwards".[7] For Symons, the "humdrum" writers were those who made an excessive use of puzzles and placed less apparent emphasis on the literary aspects of their writing.[8] Symon's poisoned compliment is perhaps unfair, and although Crofts at his worst can seem over-methodical, his focus on the everyday practicalities of police detection has led to his being seen by no less a figure than W. H. Auden as a precursor to writers of the police procedural novel.[9] Crofts published a total of thirty-eight books, including his collections of short

5   Martin Edwards, *The Golden Age of Murder: The Mystery of the Writers Who Invented the Modern Detective Story* (London: HarperCollins, 2015), 169.
6   Curtis Evans, *Masters of the "Humdrum" Mystery: Cecil John Charles Street, Freeman Wills Crofts, Alfred Walter Stewart and the British Detective Novel, 1920–1961* (Jefferson, NC and London, McFarland & Company, 2012), 147.
7   Julian Symons, *Bloody Murder: From the Detective Story to the Crime Novel*, 2nd edn (Harmondsworth: Penguin, 1985), 104.
8   Ibid.
9   W. H. Auden, "The Guilty Vicarage" in *Detective Fiction: A Collection of Critical Essays. Twentieth Century Views*, ed. Robin W. Winks (Englewood Cliffs, NJ: Prentice-Hall, 1980), 24.

stories between the publication of *The Cask* (1920) and *Anything to Declare?* (1957), and between the 1920s and 1940s achieved enormous popularity.

*The Cask* contains many of the features which would be of lasting importance in Crofts' fiction. It is built around an "alibi plot", a device which the author was to use regularly throughout his career. The "alibi plot" became Crofts' "trademark", and in *The Cask*, as in later novels, "the one character in a Crofts story who could not possibly have committed the crime will in the end be shown to have done just that".[10] Using such a device, Crofts attempts to make the reader believe that it is impossible that the suspect could have committed the crime, and the attempts to uncover the alibi only lead, at first, to making this alibi appear even more solid and unbreakable. The investigating officers, painstakingly thorough professionals in Crofts' works, eventually discover the flaws in the alibi, leading to the arrest and conviction of the culprit. In *The Cask*, the murderer, who hides his victim's remains in a cask which is shipped between France and England, has a supposedly watertight alibi.

*The Cask* is notable for its meticulous attention to detail, in the setting and mechanics of the commercial shipping industry, in the inquiries carried out by the investigators, and, importantly, in the background, motivation and commitment of the detectives themselves. Even the humblest of police officers presented in the novel, Constable John Walker, reads the works of Conan Doyle and Austin Freeman, practises in his free time "observation and deduction", and has ambitions, "the chief of which was to become a detective officer".[11] Inspector Burnley, a forerunner to Crofts' later Inspector French, is pensive, intuitive and cosmopolitan, feeling equally at home in Paris as in London. Scotland Yard is aided by the efficient machinery of the French police, which uses three female detectives to obtain information about the victim's clothes from Parisian clothing shops, and by the efficient private detective Georges La Touche, half-English and half-French.

*The Ponson Case* (1921) is also centred on a seemingly credible alibi, and when the coroner suspects an apparent suicide to be murder, Inspector

---

10   Howard Haycraft, *Murder for Pleasure: The Life and Times of the Detective Story* (1941, New York: Carroll and Graf, 1984), 123.

11   Freeman Wills Crofts, *The Cask* (London: Collins, 1920), 39.

Tanner of Scotland Yard is called in. While not as overtly brilliant as
Inspector Burnley, he is "a painstaking and conscientious man" who "never
took probabilities for granted".[12] In *The Pit-Prop Syndicate* (1922), Crofts
compares the effectiveness of amateur and professional detection. In the
first part of the novel, a smuggling conspiracy is investigated by two young
friends, Merriman, a junior partner in a wine merchants and Hilliard, a low-
ranking customs officer before, in the second part of the book, Inspector
George Willis of the Criminal Investigation Department at Scotland Yard
takes over. After the boyish enthusiasm of Merriman and Hilliard, Willis
brings a reassuring stability to the case:

> George Willis was a tall, somewhat burly man of five-and-forty, with heavy, clean-
> shaven, expressionless features which would have made his face almost stupid, had it
> not been redeemed by a pair of the keenest of blue eyes. He was what is commonly
> known as a safe man, not exactly brilliant, but plodding and tenacious to an extra-
> ordinary degree. His forte was slight clues, and he possessed that infinite capacity
> for taking pains which made his following up of them approximate to genius. In
> short, though a trifle slow, he was already looked on as one of the most efficient and
> reliable inspectors of the Yard.[13]

*The Pit-Prop Syndicate* is particularly notable for the detailed descriptions of police activity, and the techniques used, the methodical investigation and the easy camaraderie between officers all look forward to later
police procedural patterns. Simplicity and rigorous preparation are the
key to his success:

> His preparations were simple. He had only to arrange for a couple of plainclothes
> men and a photographer with a flashlight apparatus to accompany him, and to bring
> from his room a handbag containing his notebook and a few other necessary articles.
> He met the police doctor in the corridor and, the others being already in waiting, the
> five men immediately left the great building and took a car to the station.[14]

---

12    Freeman Wills Crofts, *The Ponson Case* (London: Collins, 1921), 45.
13    Freeman Wills Crofts, *The Pit-Prop Syndicate* (London: Collins, 1922), 145.
14    Ibid., 146.

Crime, it is suggested, can only be solved by scrupulous attention to detail: typewriter keys, the makers' labels on items of clothing, fingerprints and duplicated purchases all present inestimable clues.

*The Groote Park Murder* (1923) featured a South African police officer, Inspector Vandam, and the Scottish Detective Inspector Ross in a murder mystery in which the role of victim and killer is skilfully reversed. In 1925 Crofts published *Inspector French's Greatest Case*, the first of many works which would feature this officer. French is an amalgam in many ways of the author's previous detective figures, although, unlike these, he is given a home life and a wife, Emily, who at times helps with her husband's armchair detection. French has a "natural kindness of heart" and "the gift of the imagination",[15] and he was "destined by his superiors for even greater and more remunerative responsibilities in the early future".[16] The case in this first novel takes the "comparative stay at home"[17] Inspector to the Netherlands, France, Spain and Portugal, using ships and trains with a keen eye always on the timetables, which control the progress of the investigation but also help to make and break the alibis which are so important in Crofts' fiction.

*Inspector French's Greatest Case* is a fascinating work and, despite the success of Crofts' earlier novels, and despite superficial similarities, it is arguably the high point of his early fiction. Unlike his previous works, it also contains a certain amount of socio-political commentary not generally associated with Crofts' narratives. In Barcelona, for example, the Inspector is told that "both the race and language is different from the rest of Spain" and that the Catalan people are "more go-ahead and enterprising than the people further south".[18] French, an Englishman, answers that "that sounds a bit like Ireland", mentioning that he has "been both in Belfast and in the south, and the same thing seems to hold good".[19] French returns in *Inspector French and the Cheyne Mystery* (also known as *The Cheyne Mystery*, 1926), which repeats to some extent the structure of *The Pit-Prop Syndicate*, with the case being investigated by an enthusiastic

15  Freeman Wills Crofts, *Inspector French's Greatest Case* (London: Collins, 1925), 170.
16  Ibid., 177.
17  Ibid., 70.
18  Ibid., 72.
19  Ibid., 72–73.

if shady private detective before "the machinery of the law" is brought in and the Inspector appears to resolve.[20] *Inspector French and the Starvel Tragedy* (also known as *The Starvel Hollow Tragedy*, 1927) uses the triple murder of a miser and his servants, which has been made to look like an accident, to take French to Yorkshire, France and Scotland, even though the detective "loathed working away from his headquarters, bereaved of his trained staff and of the immediate backing of the huge machine of which he was a cog".[21] This emphasis on the importance of teamwork and the negation of individuality is again something which would be typical of late twentieth- and early twenty-first-century crime fiction but which, until Crofts, had been unheard of. As in all of his works, the author shows his tendency "to divide people into good and evil",[22] and his belief in moral absolutes tends to disorientate the modern reader. For this reason Curtis Evans insists that French should be regarded as "an archetypal Everyman figure" who is responsible for "bringing good out of dauntless industry" and not as a realistic character as such.[23]

In *The Sea Mystery* (1929) French and Dr Crowth discuss a case which the reader identifies as that presented in Crofts' own *The Cask*. When the doctor comments that the case seems more like a novel, French attempts to clarify the distinction between real and fictional criminal investigation. There is, he says a difference between a novel and real life, in that in the former "the episodes are selected and the reader is told those which are interesting and which get results", whereas in real life "we try perhaps ten or twenty lines which lead nowhere before we strike the lucky one. In each line we make perhaps hundreds of inquiries, whereas the novel describes one. It's like any other job, you get results by pegging away. But it is interesting on the whole, and it has its compensations".[24] *The Sea Mystery*, in which French uses a "Molesworth" – *Molesworth's Pocket Book of Engineering*

20   Freeman Wills Crofts, *Inspector French and the Cheyne Mystery* (London: Collins, 1926), 61.

21   Freeman Wills Crofts, *Inspector French and the Starvel Mystery* (London: Collins, 1927), 50.

22   Evans, *Masters of Humdrum*, 152.

23   Ibid., 158.

24   Freeman Wills Crofts, *The Sea Mystery* (London: Collins, 1928), 24.

*Formulae* – and *The Box Office Murders* (1929), in which he manages tide and train timetables, both present apparently unsolvable cases which the detective resolves using his own intelligence and these textual resources.

*Sir John Magill's Last Journey* (1930) is the first of Crofts' novels in which the action takes place to a great extent in an Irish setting. French is requested to participate in the investigation of the murder of a leading member of the Orange Order in "one of the most important cases that had taken place in Northern Ireland for many a long day".[25] The detective agrees to go to Belfast although "as a rule he disliked working with a strange police force", as he is fully aware that "with the best will in the world strangers could not give him the help he was accustomed to by his own trained staff".[26] Despite his reluctance, however, the Inspector's views on the Royal Ulster Constabulary (RUC) are highly positive. He expresses the opinion that "Northern Ireland men had nothing to learn from London",[27] and affirms that the "detective force of Northern Ireland had abundantly vindicated itself, in fact it had shown the way to this experienced officer of the C.I.D.".[28] James Murphy complains that "Crofts is too engrossed in the extraordinary intricacies of evidence, red herrings, testimonies, hypotheses, and dead ends to register the tense politics of a fledgling statelet feeling itself under siege from the Irish Free State".[29] The point is a good one, but it could also be argued that Crofts in his novel is giving visibility to the existence of that "statelet" and the revelation of the cause for the downfall of Sir John Magill, his gambling debts, prefigures much subsequent Northern Irish crime fiction, which would emphasise the ethical problems of a hypocritical unionist ruling caste that preaches austere Christian values but is simultaneously involved in morally impeachable and criminal activities.

*Sir John Magill's Last Journey* is also of interest for the visit French makes to Dublin and his opinions on the new Free State. The policeman had been to the Irish capital before, but that was during the "troubles" of

25   Freeman Wills Crofts, *Sir John Magill's Last Journey* (London: Collins, 1930), 101.
26   Ibid., 23.
27   Ibid., 49.
28   Ibid., 192.
29   James H. Murphy, *Irish Novels and the Victorian Age* (Oxford: Oxford University Press, 2011), 379.

the early 1920s (which prompts the reader to ask in what capacity), but is now "impressed by the air of smartness which the city wore".[30] Now, he notes, the city "seemed cleaner than before and the new buildings made O'Connell Street a really imposing thoroughfare".[31] The novel must have generated some interest in Ireland as, along with *The Pit-Prop Syndicate* (in 1933), it is one of the two of Crofts' novels to be translated into the Irish language (in 1935).[32] *Mystery in the Channel* (also known as *Mystery in the English Channel*, 1931) and *Death on the Way* (also known as *Double Death*, 1932) are of particular interest in that they, perhaps coincidentally, both feature Irish culprits. In the former, the unscrupulous Nolan (who peppers his speech with "faith" and "sure") is guilty of the murder of two company directors, while in the latter Carey, a "thorough paced scoundrel",[33] manipulates his friend, a railway engineer, in the murder of a colleague. *Sudden Death* (1932) uses an experimental narrative pattern, in which the murder of a woman with mobility problems is analysed by her housekeeper and by Inspector French.

In 1933 Crofts changed his London publisher, moving from William Collins to Hodder & Stoughton. The change only lasted for three books, *The Hog's Back Mystery* (also known as *The Strange Case of Dr Earle*, 1933), *The 12.30 from Croydon* (also known as *Wilful and Premeditated*, 1934) and *Mystery on Southampton Water* (also known as *Crime on the Solent*, 1934). The first of these is remarkably domestic for an Inspector French novel, taking place entirely in the county of Surrey, also the county of Crofts' residence at that time. Interestingly, although little of French's background is ever hinted at in the novels, we learn in *The Hog's Back Mystery* that French, while watching labourers in the earthworks where the missing person is thought to be buried, "had an Irishman's love of doing other people's jobs".[34]

In *Mystery on Southampton Water* French, newly promoted to Chief Inspector, investigates a murder committed in the context of the rivalry

---

30   Crofts, *Sir John Magill*, 252.
31   Ibid.
32   Murphy, *Irish Novels*, 379.
33   Freeman Wills Crofts, *Death on the Way* (London: Collins, 1932), 275.
34   Freeman Wills Crofts, *The Hog's Back Mystery* (London: Hodder & Stoughton, 1933), 134.

between two cement companies, each of which is trying to develop a low-cost, fast-drying cement. As well as providing a fascinating glimpse into an early example of industrial espionage, the novel also raises pertinent questions regarding the amoral, profit-based nature of business. As Martin Edwards notes, the "conservatively inclined Freeman Wills Crofts became a persistent critic of business mores"; he "understood industry better than most detective novelists, and his descriptions of how businessmen (they almost always were men) operate are as convincing as any of the period".[35] This is further seen in *The 12.30 from Croydon* in which a factory owner facing ruin because of the economic crisis is compelled to contemplate the murder of his wealthy uncle. *The 12.30 from Croydon* also provides the first clear example of the "inverted mystery", a format which Crofts would use with regularity and a certain mastery throughout the rest of his career. In the "inverted mystery" the culprit is revealed in the early stages of the work, with the mystery being transferred to other factors such as motivation or the methods employed. In *The 12.30 from Croydon* Crofts also uses the classic form of the denouement of Golden Age fiction by gathering a group together, in this case including a writer on criminology, and explaining to them the intricacies of the case.

*Crime at Guildford* (also known as *The Crime at Nornes*, 1935) marked Crofts' return to William Collins, which in the mid-1930s was a publisher almost synonymous with detective fiction. Again using a murder committed in an industrial milieu, the novel highlights the cooperation between the British, French and Dutch police forces and the efficiency of the police machinery. Crofts' importance in the development of the police procedural formula is nowhere more apparent than in this novel:

> Norne rang off and French quickly made several other calls. Firstly he repeated the story in an even more condensed form to Sir Mortimer Ellison, the Assistant Commissioner under whose supervision he worked, and obtained his approval for his giving the case his personal attention. Next, he instructed his assistant, Sergeant Carter, to be ready to accompany him. Two more calls secured the services of a finger-print expert and a photographer, while a fifth requisitioned a fast car. Then picking up his emergency case, which always stood packed with apparatus likely to

---

35  Edwards, *Golden Age*, 262.

be used in preliminary investigations, French hurried from his room. Within six minutes of the receipt of Norne's call, the little party turned out of the Yard gates on to the Embankment.[36]

Crofts' two novels published in 1936, *The Loss of the Jane Vosper* and *Man Overboard* (also known as *Cold Blooded Murder*) combine, like much of his fiction, the author's interest in the worlds of industry and transport. Both are concerned with shipping companies and both involve murder and the theft of industrial secrets. Curtis Evans believes that the former is the work in which the author came closest to the format of what would later become the police procedural sub-genre.[37] In *Man Overboard* French returns to Northern Ireland where he reencounters some of the characters from *Sir John Magill's Last Journey*. The narrative variations Crofts experimented with in *Sudden Death* are continued here, with three narrators expressing their points of view, highlighting the perspective of the fiancée of the innocent man accused of murder ("As Pamela Grey Saw It"), that of an RUC officer ("As Detective Sergeant M'Cling Saw It"), and that of French ("As Chief Inspector French Saw It"). Comments on Northern Ireland are few, but the author makes an interesting reference to the "unhappy division of the country".[38]

One of the techniques most commonly employed by Crofts is that of the belated appearance of his detective figure. French does not usually appear until late in the novel, often in the second half. Such a technique allows readers to consider the circumstance by themselves, weigh up the different possibilities and, if possible, create a hypothesis as to the identity of the culprit, their motivation or methods, depending on the mystery involved. This, of course, was very much in keeping with the ludic tendencies of much Golden Age crime fiction, and proved extremely popular with readers. This is evident in *Found Floating* (1937), the novel which marked Crofts' second and definitive move to Hodder & Stoughton, and in *The End of Andrew Harrison* (1938), where the first part uses one of the characters, Markham Crewe, who has been left almost penniless after speculation on

36   Freeman Wills Crofts, *Crime at Guildford* (London: Collins, 1935), 39.
37   Evans, *Masters of Humdrum*, 160.
38   Freeman Wills Crofts, *Man Overboard* (London: Collins, 1936), 4.

the stock exchange, as the single focaliser, before moving on to the view-point of French in the second part of the novel.

*Antidote to Venom* (1938) is criticised by Martin Edwards for the author's "limited skills of characterization", although the same critic praises the experimental nature of the work, which combines "an inverted crime story with a straight account of police detection" and which makes an ori-ginal "effort to tell a story of crime positively".[39] The novel also reveals the extent to which Crofts' religious principles influence his writing. As a reli-gious "puritan", he supported the Oxford Group founded by the American Frank Buchman and also backed, in the late 1930s, the associated campaign of "Moral Re-Armament". As a result, his books often came to resemble "moral parables".[40] In *Antidote to Venom*, for example, the culprit is "faced with a choice between right and wrong" and not, as he initially believes, "between two evils" and, in the end, finds redemption through God.[41]

*Fatal Venture* (1939) takes French, who only appears in the second half of the work, on a trip around Ireland with his wife, who also appears in *Golden Ashes* (1940). Emily, who he calls "Em", is supportive of her hus-band, but is never fully developed as a character. Her role is basically that of a sounding board for her husband's theories and hypotheses, and *Fatal Venture* provides one of her few appearances outside a domestic setting. *Golden Ashes* again divides the story between two narrative perspectives, "As Betty Stanton Saw It" and "As Chief Inspector French Saw It", and features Crofts' usual paraphernalia of ingenious mechanical devices, train timetables and French's ubiquitous copy of *Molesworth*. Rail, air and taxi times are all used to assert possibility and the reading of the mileage on a hired car is used to determine where the suspect might have driven to.

*The Losing Game* (1941), *James Tarrant, Adventurer* (1941) and *Fear Comes to Chalfont* (1942) are competent murder mysteries. The first of these sees Chief Inspector French help a struggling crime writer develop credible plots. *The Affair at Little Wokeham* (1943) contains an interesting frame device in which the Chief Inspector is hospitalised and is visited by Freeman

39  Edwards, *Golden Age*, 386.
40  Evans, *Masters of Humdrum*, 147.
41  Edwards, *Golden Age*, 386.

Wills Crofts. The author asks his character which of his cases should be used for the next novel, and French suggests that of Little Wokeham, even though the events had taken place before the war. Such a framing device obviously exonerates the author from producing a topical, wartime mystery, but also reveals yet again the playful, self-referential details which Crofts often brings to his works and which do not, it could be argued, seem like the ideas of a humdrum writer. *Fear Comes to Chalfont* is a fine Golden Age mystery, but one which, like much of his later long fiction, tends toward excessive sentimentality.

The war is introduced in *Enemy Unseen* (1945) and *Death of a Train* (1946). The former starts with the theft of a quantity of grenades from a Home Guard depot in Cornwall, and when a grenade is used to commit murder, Scotland Yard, in the figure of French, is called in. French holds an interesting discussion with Wickham Crane, a writer of thrillers living in the Cornish village where the crime takes place. Crane tells French his idea of the distinction between thrillers and detective fiction. Detective stories, he suggests, are "the story of the elucidation of a problem" whose solution "is reached by inference and deduction from the given facts" and, in which "all the facts are given to enable the reader to find out the truth for himself".[42] In a thriller, however, "Premise and deduction take a second place and conflict is in the forefront: the struggle of the criminal and the police, or of the evil gang and their righteous pursuers".[43] *Death of a Train*, again set in England during the Second World War, takes Crofts' obsession with railways to a new level detailing, as it does, in anthropomorphic terms, the biography of a train which takes up the first half of the novel. Although French appears in the second half of the work, and a German spy ring is exposed, the narrative audacity of the opening chapters reveals the kind of playful experimentation which remains one of the chief, if unrecognised, achievements of Crofts and other Golden Age authors.

Howard Haycraft suggests that there is a "hoodoo that has always hovered over boy detectives".[44] This was true for McDonnell Bodkin's *Young*

---

42    Freeman Wills Crofts, *Enemy Unseen* (London: Hodder & Stoughton, 1945), 125.
43    Ibid., 124.
44    Haycraft, *Murder for Pleasure*, 173.

*Beck*, and it is true for Crofts who, in *Young Robin Brand Detective* (1947), created what is arguably his least successful character. The young detective is staying with a school friend, Jack, whose father is a railway engineer. Together they investigate the kidnapping of Jack's three-year-old stepsister, taking plaster casts of footprints and drawing up a list of suspects. One of Jack's father's colleagues is a young engineer, Cyril French, nephew of the great detective, and through him, they contact the Chief Inspector who gives them advice. The most memorable feature of the novel is peripheral to the plot but provides a fine explanation of the writer's craft as envisaged by Crofts. Speaking in the voice of a young engineer with ambitions to becoming a writer of detective fiction, Crofts asserts:

> "If I want to plan the layout of a station yard," he said, "I begin by working out what movements are required: trains in and out, empties to carriage sidings, engines to and from the Loco yard, and so on. Then I plan a layout that will enable these things to be done. Similarly", he went on, "in starting a book I begin with the important adventures or happenings, and then I plan the necessary characters and situations and locations to enable these adventures to take place.[45]

The year 1947 also saw the publication of the first collection of short stories, *Murderers Make Mistakes*. The volume is divided into two parts, the first of which consists of a series of "double stories" which contain the information about the crime, followed by French's solution, while the second part contains "single stories" outlined by French. The characters in the stories are similar to those in all of Crofts' fiction, including a signalman who is killed by a colleague, a junior assistant engineer who is also a murderer, a research chemist who kills to stop being blackmailed, and a novelist who plans to murder an invalid colonel to win the colonel's wife. The culprits use several original techniques; a time fuse is used by a solicitor who kills his neighbour; a clock is deliberately short-circuited to stop at a determined hour; a hand grenade aimed at killing a victim fails because the killer has not allowed the time between the removal of the pin and the explosion in his calculations. French, of course, has the ability to solve all

---

45  Freeman Wills Crofts, *Young Robin Brand, Detective* (London: Hodder & Stoughton, 1947), 68.

of these crimes and it could be said that the short story format brings a new freshness to the works. By the late 1940s Crofts' novels had started to lose some of their earlier lustre, but the translation into the shorter mode adds a new breath of life to them. Crofts' problems with characterisation are of less importance in the short story, and the emphasis on plot and inventive solution are helped by the brevity required. This is evident when the stories are compared with the writer's next two novels, *Silence for the Murderer* (1949) and *French Strikes Oil* (also known as *Dark Journey*, 1952). The meta-textual elements in Crofts' works are generally to be welcomed by the reader, but the clumsy authorial intrusion in *Silence for the Murderer* is little short of annoying. Halfway through the book, the reader is told that she or he "has now been given all the information which enabled Inspector French to prove what really occurred" and is challenged to provide the solution.[46] *French Strikes Oil* finds the detective, and most probably the author, highly critical of post-war England. He is "sick to death of these hooligan youngsters with their guns and their coshes and their attacks on defenceless old women".[47] It is almost possible to envisage the author sitting in the garden of his Guildford home reading *The Daily Telegraph* as he blames "the war, housing, careless parents" and "the general lowering of moral standards" for the state of 1950s' England.[48]

   *French Strikes Oil* was followed by two volumes of short stories. *Many a Slip* (1955) contains some stories which had been previously published in *The Evening Standard* and, once again, Crofts alludes to the ludic nature of his work. "They are murder tales," he states, "and in all of them the criminal makes a mistake which gives him away".[49] The author proposes a game with the reader, in which "he wins if he spots these before they are revealed, and (so to speak) I do if he doesn't".[50] The crimes are committed by the usual middle-class criminals, a solicitor with financial problems, a junior architect in debt and a schoolteacher who kills his rival for the headmaster's

46   Freeman Wills Crofts, *Silence for the Murderer* (London: Hodder & Stoughton, 1949), 139.
47   Freeman Wills Crofts, *French Strikes Oil* (London: Hodder & Stoughton, 1952), 54.
48   Ibid., 54.
49   Freeman Wills Crofts, *Many a Slip* (London: Hodder & Stoughton, 1955), 5.
50   Ibid., 5.

post at their school. *The Mystery of the Sleeping Car Express and Other Stories* (1956) shows less internal cohesion than the other two volumes of stories, largely because these appear to be taken from different periods in the writer's career. French is present, but not in all of the tales. "The Motive Shows the Man", for example, is ostensibly written by a serving CID detective, and "The Raincoat" features a new detective, Inspector Hubbard, who relates his case to his former head, Inspector French.

In Crofts' last novel, *Anything to Declare?* (1957) a plan to smuggle watches from Switzerland is foiled by an attempt at blackmail, and when the blackmailer is murdered French is called in. This is not the pro-active detective of the earlier works, however, and as "it was no longer French's habit to undertake outside inquiries like this one"[51] he ostensibly delegated the case to his subordinate, Inspector Rollo. French, however, is still French, and it is his reasoning and tenacity which eventually solve the case. Although the gang are arrested and set to be convicted, the lack of a body means that they will only be charged with smuggling and not with murder – the ageing detective persists and succeeds in discovering the body.

For Jeffrey Symons, Crofts was typical of the Golden Age writers, most of whom "came late to writing fiction", and few of whom "had much talent for it".[52] The critic also insisted that Crofts "knew nothing about Scotland Yard and did not feel it important that he should learn details of police procedure, perhaps thinking that a detailed knowledge of railway timetables was enough".[53] Howard Haycraft notes, in the later works, "evidence of weariness in the methodical Inspector's adventurings" and, he believes, the author "becomes too greatly preoccupied with time-tables and menus to serve the best interests of fiction" although, he admits, this may be "justified and inherent in the factual method when it gets out of hand".[54] Norman A. Jeffares, however, praises Crofts' precision, noting how his "realistic crime novels depend upon careful attention to detail, an insistence on

---

51  Freeman Wills Crofts, *Anything to Declare?* (London: Hodder & Stoughton, 1957), 129.
52  Symons, *Bloody Murder*, 104.
53  Ibid., 104.
54  Haycraft, *Murder for Pleasure*, 124.

the slow logical gathering of information".[55] For Stephen Knight, Crofts "gave special qualities of patience and insight to individualistic heroes",[56] and for Heather Worthington, in Inspector French, he had created an "ordinary police detective" as a protagonist, and French's focus on the practical aspects of police detection can be seen as a precursor to the modern police procedural.[57] Although the "novelty" of Crofts' police detective was later copied in the 1930s by writers such as the New Zealander Ngaio Marsh, the Scot Michael Innes or, notably, the Belgian Georges Simenon,[58] the Dublin-born writer's reputation has suffered over recent years. Although the current fashion is for the police procedural as the dominant format in detective-centred crime fiction, the standing of the more individualistic amateur detectives of writers such as Agatha Christie has continued to grow. It is possible that the contemporary police procedural contains popular elements which were missing in Crofts' work, most notably, perhaps, the personal aspect. Present-day writers of the police procedural examine every part of their detectives' home and family lives: their marital problems and their extra-marital affairs, their children or lack thereof, their problems with alcohol or their inability to pay their mortgage. Little of Inspector French's private life was revealed. His wife Emily, "Em", "sits placidly at home and acts as nothing more distinctive than a sounding board for her husband's ruminations".[59] Despite Em's apparent passivity, however, as Susan Rowland notes, in *Inspector French's Greatest Case*, although her husband travels around Europe in a fruitless attempt to catch the suspect, he is only able to solve the case with the help of his wife, who never leaves

55    Norman A. Jeffares, *Macmillan History of Literature: Anglo-Irish Literature* (London: Gill & Macmillan, 1982), 225.
56    Stephen Knight, *Form and Ideology in Crime Fiction* (London: Macmillan, 1980), 168.
57    Heather Worthington, *Key Concepts in Crime Fiction* (London: Palgrave Macmillan, 2011), 68.
58    Leroy Lad Panek, *An Introduction to the Detective Story* (Bowling Green, OH: Bowling Green State University Popular Press, 1987.
59    Patricia Craig and Mary Cadogan, *The Lady Investigates: Women Detectives and Spies in Fiction* (London: Victor Gollancz, 1981).

her home.[60] This lack of a private life is also true of other Golden Age detectives who are still held in esteem, two obvious examples being Christie's Hercule Poirot and Miss Marple. The Golden Age novel was "notoriously impersonal", and the intrusion of the personal into detective mysteries has been "one of the major developments in recent crime fiction".[61] Although Crofts may have been "the first of modern writers to find fictional possibilities in the step-by-step methods of actual police routine",[62] his legacy has been largely ignored, but his works stand as one of the most outstanding contributions of an Irish writer to the history of crime fiction.

60  Susan Rowland, "The Classical Model of the Golden Age" in *A Companion to Crime Fiction*, ed. Charles J. Rzepka and Lee Horsley (Oxford: Wiley-Blackwell, 2010), 121.

61  Hans Bertens and Theo D'haen, *Contemporary American Crime Fiction* (New York: Palgrave, 2001), 58–59.

62  Haycraft, *Murder for Pleasure*, 122.

# CHAPTER 8

# "A deceptive air of docility." The Golden Age II: Nicholas Blake and Mrs Victor Rickard

The term "Golden Age" was supposedly first employed by John Strachet in his article "The Golden Age of English Detection" which appeared in the *Saturday Review* in January 1939.[1] Works which belong to this period are generally considered to be those written and published between the two World Wars, although stylistic Golden Age features can be found in much post-1945 fiction. Critics usually regard Agatha Christie's first novel, *The Mysterious Affair at Styles* as the first Golden Age novel, although it is significant that Freeman Wills Crofts' first novel, *The Cask*, was published in the same year. Christie and Crofts would represent two different strands within the mode but, despite the obvious differences, both used a style of detection which "is rational rather than active or intuitional, a method which fits with the unemotional presentation of the crime".[2] Unlike Freeman Wills Crofts' police detectives, most Golden Age sleuths were amateurs, usually pertaining to the same social group as the victim and suspects. Most Golden Age fiction is set in the English heartland, and "few Golden Age mysteries seem to bother with what is felt or thought beyond the Home Counties".[3] Initially, Golden Age fiction followed the pattern set by Conan Doyle's Holmes: the detective had an assistant who was often used as a substitute for the reader, the focus was

---

1    Victoria Stewart, *Crime Writing in Interwar Britain* (Cambridge: Cambridge University Press, 2017), 6.

2    Stephen Knight, "The Golden Age" in *The Cambridge Companion to Crime Fiction*, ed. Martin Priestman (Cambridge: Cambridge University Press, 2003), 78.

3    Hans Bertens and Theo D'haen, *Contemporary American Crime Fiction* (New York: Palgrave, 2001), 2.

on the process of detection, the crime occurred early on in the narrative, and the reconstruction of the events was told in a retrospective fashion.[4]

Whereas late nineteenth-century crime fiction had dealt mainly with economic offences, the central criminal activity in Golden Age narratives is murder.[5] While Holmes and his like operated largely within an urban context, Golden Age mysteries are usually set in a rural atmosphere.[6] Golden Age fiction is "cosy", as it reflects "the preference for plots in which a comfortable recognizable pattern [...] is acted out in a familiar domestic setting, with the restoration of reassuring orderliness guaranteed".[7] Many of the mysteries from the period are set within a closed community in which the victim, detective and several suspects are congregated. While this space can be a school, a hospital, a prison or a cruise ship – to give just a few examples used – Golden Age mysteries are most often set in a country house. Such a setting provides a marker for the social class of the protagonists who, except for the servants (and police officers, often given the status of servants in these works) are usually upper-middle- or upper-class. The country house is also conveniently isolated from the wider community, creating, as it were, a sort of vacuum in which the events take place. It stands, according to Susan Rowland, for "a structure that can be opposed to all the social instabilities created by modern capitalism".[8] It is tempting, perhaps, to see these country house mysteries as close cousins to the Irish Big House novels, works in which the residents, members of the Ascendancy community, lived in "splendid isolation", cut off from their hostile neighbours and enclosed within the claustrophobic atmosphere of Big House and demesne. Golden Age fiction is notably formulaic, and followed "clue puzzle" techniques which, in other circumstances, may have seemed excessively restrictive. Although the Decalogue of "Ten Rules for Detective

---

4   Heather Worthington, *Key Concepts in Crime Fiction* (London: Palgrave Macmillan, 114.
5   Bertens and D'Haen, *Contemporary American*, 81.
6   Worthington, *Key Concepts*, 117.
7   Lee Horsley, *Twentieth-Century Crime Fiction* (Oxford: Oxford University Press, 2005), 38.
8   Susan Rowland, *From Agatha Christie to Ruth Rendell: British Women Writers in Detective and Crime Fiction* (New York: Palgrave Macmillan, 2004), 44.

Fiction" presented by the author and priest Ronald Knox in 1929 is often tongue-in-cheek (the rule prohibiting the appearance of "Chinamen", for example), most of his rules were, unwittingly or not, followed by writers.

The clue-puzzle mystery, which was distinguished by its use of "multiple suspects and the rational analysis of determinedly circumstantial evidence",[9] was more suited to the length and diversity of the novel than to the brevity of the short story which had earlier been the prominent format within the genre.[10] Although short stories in the crime genre were still popular during the 1920s and 1930s, these were mostly consumed by male readers, while the gender shift that had occurred in readership following the First World War meant that 75 per cent of the novels which were being borrowed from lending libraries were read by women, and a large number of these were mystery novels.[11] The popularity of the Golden Age novel can be explained by a number of factors, often related to the socio-political climate of the interwar years, including the growing influence of women and the generalised middle-class fears of working-class attempts to copy the Bolshevism of their Soviet counterparts. The "central fear", however, voiced or unvoiced in Golden Age crime fiction, is that "the threat of social disruption comes from within".[12] These novels tend to present a world, again like that of the Anglo-Irish, in which the outside world is hermetically excluded until, as the result of a disruption, such as a murder, the peace is broken. While the "domestic scale of the action" in Golden Age fiction "shuts out much that is disquieting in early twentieth-century politics and society",[13] it is unable to free itself from the deviant element which now resides, not outside, but within the hermetic social milieu. LeRoy Lad Panek points out that the years of Golden Age crime fiction were also "the golden ages of publishing and advertising".[14] The market conditions were right for the

9　Knight, "Golden Age", 79.
10　Ibid., 81.
11　Ibid.
12　John Scaggs, *Crime Fiction* (London: Routledge, 2005), 46.
13　Lee Horsley, "From Sherlock Holmes to the Present" in *A Companion to Crime Fiction*, ed. Charles J. Rzepka and Lee Horsley (Oxford: Wiley-Blackwell, 2010), 32.
14　Leroy Lad Panek, *An Introduction to the Detective Story* (Bowling Green, OH: Bowling Green State University Popular Press), 120.

launching and promotion of a product which was to gain enormous popularity and whose influence – and the reactions against it – were to critically
affect the world of crime fiction over the following decades.

*Nicholas Blake* was the pseudonym used by the poet Cecil Day-Lewis
for the twenty crime novels he would write between 1935 and 1968. This
name would also be used for the radio play *Calling James Braithwaite*
(1940), based on a script he had written for the film *The Colliers*. Day-Lewis
was born in Balintubbert, Queen's County (now County Laois) in April
1904. His father was a Church of Ireland curate, and both parents were
descendants of English families who had settled in Ireland in the nineteenth
century. When Cecil was around eighteen months old the family moved
to England, where his mother died in 1908. Day-Lewis was raised by his
father and his aunt, his mother's sister, who would take the boy on holiday
to Ireland every summer until 1914. Reared within the English public
school system, he became a schoolmaster after leaving Oxford, publishing
his poetry initially in small private editions. He started writing mystery
novels while teaching in Cheltenham, primarily as a source of much-needed
income to pay for repairs to the roof in the house the schoolteacher shared
with his first wife Mary. According to his son Sean, Day-Lewis started
writing detective fiction for three main reasons. Firstly, of course, there
were the imperative financial reasons. The wages of a junior master at a
public school were small, and his poetry did not as yet bring in any income.
Secondly, the poet was an avid reader of crime fiction; in his son's words he
was "an addict who wanted to introduce others to the habit".[15] The third
reason was what Day-Lewis referred to as the "guilt motive".[16] This he connected with the erosion of religious belief in contemporary society and the
difficulty faced by the modern subject, unable to find solace in the belief in
a God capable of relieving the individual from the burden of guilt. As such
the author saw the detective novel as "a kind of substitute religious ritual
with the detective and the murderer representing the light and dark side
of man's nature; two sides which could be identified with by the reader".[17]

---

15    Sean Day-Lewis, *C. Day-Lewis: An English Literary Life* (London: Weidenfeld &
      Nicolson, 1980) 86.
16    Ibid.
17    Ibid.

The Detective triumphs in the end because "he has more or less supernatural powers; if he is not a god he is at least a fairy godmother".[18]

The decision to take a pseudonym formed part of a strategy designed to keep the two facets of his career apart. According to biographer Peter Stanford, Cecil Day-Lewis was worried that writing crime novels might harm his reputation as a poet, quoting him as saying that he believed that "people who read detective novels don't like the detective novelist to be anything like a serious poet".[19] Although many people knew that Day-Lewis was Blake, this was not officially revealed until 1959 when, called as an expert witness at the Penguin obscenity trial, the writer publicly admitted that he was in fact "Nicholas Blake". The first novel written under the "Nicholas Blake" alias, *A Question of Proof* (1935), introduces Nigel Strangeways, Blake's fictional sleuth who was, initially at least, modelled on Day-Lewis's friend and fellow poet W. H. Auden, towards whom Day-Lewis felt "real competitiveness".[20] Strangeways is, in this first novel, an extravagant character whose credentials as a "private enquiry agent" are aided by the fact that his uncle is Assistant Commissioner at Scotland Yard. A struggling poet, Nigel had left Oxford after failing his examinations which he had answered in limericks before deciding on a career in the investigation of crime which, he believed, "was the only career left which offered scope to good manners and scientific curiosity".[21] Strangeways is, for George Grella, an example of the "witty connoisseur" figure who, he believed, had replaced the "sardonic savant" as represented by Sherlock Holmes.[22] Set in the closed atmosphere of an English public school, the novel is in many ways typical of much of the "Golden Age" fiction of the interwar years. Nigel is approached by the school to investigate the murder of unpopular and unlikeable schoolboy Algernon Wyvern-Wemyss who has been discovered strangled in a haystack, reminiscent of the Hay Feast which

---

18  Ibid.
19  Peter Stanford, *C. Day-Lewis: A Life* (London: Continuum, 2007), 129.
20  Ibid.
21  Nicholas Blake, *A Question of Proof* (London: Collins, 1935), 64.
22  George Grella, "The Hard-Boiled Detective Novel" in *Detective Fiction: A Collection of Critical Essays. Twentieth Century Views*, ed. Robin W. Winks (Englewood Cliffs, NJ: Prentice-Hall, 1980), 92.

Day-Lewis had participated in as a youth at Sherborne School. The main suspect is Michael Evans, a teacher who had been a friend of Strangeways at Oxford. Nigel is "a kind of human microscope" who uses "psychological induction" to find the real killer.[23] For this detective, the physical evidence is of less importance than the psychological observations and deductions he makes from his study of the characters involved. His treatment of the killer, once he is discovered, is also unconventional. The murderer, a religious fanatic, is encouraged to commit suicide by the detective who knew that if the killer were sent to trial he would be committed to an asylum and would not be hanged. Strangeways has, he says, "no use for keeping lunatics alive, criminal or otherwise".[24]

The novel, which "boasted the added ingredients of gleeful adultery and sexual repression as a motive for murder" was successful and proved popular with readers.[25] It paid for the repairs to the leaking roof of its author's house, but also caused some unexpected problems for Day-Lewis. Although the general reading public was not aware of the poet's authorship of this mystery thriller, this anonymity did not protect him in his immediate environment. In the novel, a young teacher is having an affair with the wife of the headmaster. In *The Buried Day* (1960), Day-Lewis relates how the authorities of the school in which he was teaching at the time strongly disapproved of the suggestion of inter-marital infidelity in an educational institution which they feared might be identified as their own.[26] The author was reprimanded by the school governors and this incident was to prove crucial in leading him to the decision to leave teaching and concentrate on writing in a full-time capacity. While he considered his poetry to be of greater importance, he realised that his crime fiction provided a profitable – and enjoyable – side-line.

The second Nicholas Blake novel, *Thou Shell of Death* (1936) is a Golden Age classic, with many of the characteristics of the sub-genre, including a party at a large country house, anonymous threatening notes and

23    Ibid., 69.
24    Ibid., 158.
25    Martin Edwards, *The Golden Age of Murder: The Mystery Writers Who Invented the Modern Detective Story* (London: HarperCollins, 2015), 273.
26    Cecil Day-Lewis, *The Buried Day* (London: Chatto & Windus, 1960), 201.

a restricted cast of suspects. Strangeway's uncle gives his nephew the task of investigating several threats made against the flamboyant Irish airman and adventurer Fergus O'Brien. The poet-detective is invited to a Christmas house party at the Irishman's mansion Dower House in Somerset where, it is supposed, the issuer of the threats is to be found among the guests. On Boxing Day, however, O'Brien is found dead, and Strangeways is obliged to investigate more than just the threats. He realises that the secret behind this death lies in O'Brien's past, and he goes to Ireland to probe into the Irishman's early life. In Ireland, Nigel is surprised to feel so much like a foreigner, and he constantly reflects on the differences between the habits of the Irish and those of the Home Counties English. His investigations lead to the story of O'Brien's youth as under-gardener in a Big House where he had fallen in love with the daughter of the house, providing vital clues for the unravelling of the mystery. The novel is tight, well-paced and reveals a more skilful approach both to plotting and characterisation than its predecessor. The language is powerful and convincing and the literary allusions abound.

If *A Question of Proof* introduced a promising newcomer to the world of classic detective fiction, *Thou Shell of Death* presents the reader with a master who already dominates his craft. The novel also introduces two characters who will become important in future novels – the beautiful and adventurous Georgia Cavendish and Detective Inspector Blount, the plodding police detective, "a man of middle height, with a bland, youngish face, but almost entirely bald" who "would have been mistaken anywhere for a bank manager".[27] Georgia would later become Strangeways' wife, while Blount would be his foil, the inefficient voice of officialdom constantly out-thwarted by the superior intuition and intelligence of the gentleman sleuth. A new Nicholas Blake novel would appear uninterruptedly each year from 1935 until 1941, when the war brought a hiatus in the production of these mysteries. In *There's Trouble Brewing* (1937), Nigel is invited to give a literary lecture at a Dorset village, where he is asked by the owner of a local brewer to look into the violent death of his dog in a pressure cooker. On investigating, Strangeways discovers that a man, who he initially believes

27    Nicholas Blake, *Thou Shell of Death* (London: Collins, 1936), 105.

to be the owner of the brewery, has also been killed in the large cooker. This and two succeeding murders are successfully resolved by the private investigator, despite the blundering presence of the local police.

The Beast Must Die (1938), "one of the few Golden Age novels where a child is a key figure",[28] is based on an incident in which Day-Lewis's eldest son Sean was nearly run over by a car.[29] Mystery writer Frank Cairnes seeks out the hit-and-run driver who has killed his son. This tale of revenge starts with extracts from Cairnes' diary revealing the conflicting feelings of anger and guilt he feels as a bereaved father. Nigel Strangeways is called in to look into the death of the driver, George Rattery, and is aided by the adventuress, Georgia Cavendish, now his wife. Detective Inspector Blount also appears, and his character is further evolved as he is revealed to be a dour Lowland Scot. The Beast Must Die was filmed by French director Claude Chabrol in 1969 as Que la bête meure and has been widely praised by critics. H. R. F. Keating believes that The Beast Must Die is "a good deal more" than a straightforward detective story, and that with its publication "seriousness was shouldering its way into the plaything genre".[30]

In The Smiler with the Knife (1939), Georgia is given a leading role, with Strangeways being relegated to the part of a supporting player. In this top-ical thriller, Nigel's uncle, Sir Strangeways, asks Georgia to infiltrate English Banner, a secret ultra-right-wing group. The climate of economic and social unease of the immediate pre-war period is evoked in a narrative in which the fascist menace is given a particularly English face. Malice in Wonderland (1940) returns Nigel to prominence in a murder mystery set in an English holiday camp. The murders, apparently committed by a practical joker called the Mad Hatter, are confused with the story of a German spy who is allegedly seeking out military secrets on the coast of England, and once again Nigel Strangeways is called in to resolve the situation. Strangeways insists in this novel that he is not an amateur sleuth, but rather that he is paid for his detecting skills. In The Corpse in the Snowman (1941), Nigel and Georgia are invited to a large country house, ostensibly to investigate

28   Edwards, Golden Age, 275.
29   Sean Day-Lewis, C. Day-Lewis, 109.
30   H. R. F. Keating, Crime & Mystery: The 100 Best Books (New York: Carroll & Graff, 1987), 61.

mysterious psychic incidents, although they are given a murder to solve. The novel, written at the beginning of the Second World War, as well as echoing the tensions of the "phoney war", explores the nature of evil and the "dreadful relish for power" in a world at war with fascism.

Day-Lewis spent the war years working for the Ministry of Information, and this experience would be reflected in the first post-war Nicholas Blake novel, *Minute for Murder* (1947), with the author's place of work transformed into the "Ministry of Morale". Strangeways is now a widower, Georgia having been killed during the Blitz – Sean Day-Lewis recalls his father saying he had "got bored" with her[31] – and is engaged in war service in the Visual Propaganda Division of the Ministry. A poison capsule brought back from Germany triggers off a "closed room" mystery which Nigel resolves with his usual psychological insight. The novel is noteworthy, perhaps, for the portrayal of another complex Irish character, Merrion Squires. This work was followed two years later by *Head of a Traveller* (1949), arguably one of the most satisfying of the Blake novels. Nigel Strangeways is called in to investigate a murder in a large country house in rural England. Although the English setting is emphasised, the allusions to Ireland (Peadar Mayo, the Irish poet, Finny Black, the dwarf) and the importance attributed to the possession of land give the novel a distinctively Anglo-Irish feel.

By the 1950s Blake's detective had lost most of the traits which linked him to the figure of Auden. Nigel Strangeways is now more perceptibly Cecil Day-Lewis himself, reflecting, as Sean Day-Lewis suggests, the decreasing influence of the American-born poet on his father.[32] *The Dreadful Hollow* (1953) sees Strangeways hired to look into a number of poison-pen letters circulating in an otherwise apparently idyllic English village. Nigel's patron, the rich entrepreneur, is subsequently murdered and the detective sets out to uncover the killer. As is usual in the Blake novels, the local police are inefficient and unintelligent – Sergeant Clotworthy is "slow of speech and slower of thought",[33] while Inspector Randall "stands like a farmer appraising

---

31　Sean Day-Lewis, *C. Day-Lewis*, 169.
32　Ibid., 86.
33　Nicholas Blake, *The Dreadful Hollow* (London: Collins, 1953), 33.

stock".[34] The subsequent resolution by Nigel, aided by Inspector Blount –
a character who becomes more sympathetic as the series progresses – is
intricate and shows just how well Day-Lewis could successfully negotiate
the intricacies of tight plotting in these mature mystery novels.

*The Whisper in the Gloom* (1954) is a Cold War thriller, notable for
the first appearance of Nigel's new "love interest", Clare Massinger, and a
rather unlikely gang of boys from mixed social backgrounds. The next year's
*A Tangled Web* (1956) is the first of the Blake novels in which Strangeways
does not appear. It tells the story of Hugo, an ex-public school cat burglar
who is accused of murdering a police officer. One of the strong points of
the novel is the skilful characterisation apparent in the evil abortionist Dr
John "Jacko" Jaques and Hugo's innocent lover, Daisy. Towards the end of
the novel there is a marvellous identity parade scene "like some macabre
version of a children's party".[35] Strangeways returns in the next Nicholas
Blake novel, *End of a Chapter* (1957), now living with Clare in a new sexually liberated atmosphere. The novel makes use of Day-Lewis's experiences
of working in the world of publishing as director and senior editor at
Chatto & Windus. A case of libel is followed by the murder of romantic
novelist Millicent Miles and the subsequent investigation by Nigel, who
has to discover the culprit from among a flamboyant cast of suspects. One
of these suspects is the Irishman Arthur Geraldine, who leads Strangeways
to reflect on "the paradoxical Anglo-Irish alternations of boisterousness
and ceremoniousness, hauteur and horse-play, glibness and reticence".[36]

*A Penknife in My Heart* (1958) is another psychological thriller, the
second of the Blake books not to feature Nigel Strangeways. In the novel
two men each agree to murder someone for the other, thus providing
both with convincing alibis. The coincidence of this plot with Patricia
Highsmith's *Strangers on a Train* (1950) led to the author being criticised
and accused of plagiary. In a postscript, he states that he had "discovered
that the basis of its plot is similar" to that of *Strangers on a Train* but he
had neither read the novel nor seen the film and that his own treatment

34   Ibid., 85.
35   Nicholas Blake, *A Tangled Web* (London: Collins, 1956), 200.
36   Nicholas Blake, *End of a Chapter* (London: Collins, 1957), 149.

"is very different from Miss Highsmith's", while thanking her "for being so charmingly sympathetic over the predicament in which the long arm of coincidence put me".[37] Strangeways and Clare return in *The Widow's Cruise* (1959). The holiday cruise that the investigator and his lover are enjoying is disturbed by a disappearance and a murder. The closed setting of the ship at sea and the limited number of suspects recall earlier Golden Age mysteries, providing the novel with a pleasantly nostalgic air that would all but disappear from the five final Blake novels, which were to appear in the next decade

*The Worm of Death* (1961) is not one of Blake's strongest novels, but it is notable for the prominence given to Nigel's sculptor girlfriend, Clare Massinger, and for the excellent descriptions of Greenwich, where Day-Lewis was living at the time. Strangeways describes himself as a viper who "insinuates himself into the confidence of the suspects" and "worms his way along, deeper and deeper through the secret passages of people's lives".[38] In *The Deadly Joker* (1963), Blake once again dispenses with the figure of Strangeways. Set in a Big House in the Dorset countryside, the novel is narrated by a retired Inspector of Schools and features the exotic Vera Paston, the Indian wife of a rich local businessman, modelled on an Indian novelist with whom Day-Lewis was involved romantically at the time.[39] More rewarding, perhaps, are the next two novels, *The Sad Variety* (1964) and *The Morning after Death* (1966). Both works feature Strangeways and Clare, and while the former takes the characters to a typical English country house, the latter sees Nigel visiting the USA where he is a guest researcher at an Ivy League university. In *The Sad Variety*, Nigel is hired by a British government security department to look after the scientist Professor Wagley, his Hungarian wife Elena and their daughter Lucy. The professor has a secret, which a Russian agent, Petrov, and English fellow-traveller, Paul Cunningham, are determined to discover. Lucy is kidnapped, and the situation is complicated by the fact that the Russians are holding Elena's son Ivan, who has been trying to escape from Hungary. The plot is

37   Nicholas Blake, *A Penknife in My Heart* (London: Collins, 1958), 85.
38   Nicholas Blake, *The Worm of Death* (London: Collins, 1961), 85.
39   Sean Day-Lewis, *C. Day-Lewis*, 232.

tight and lucid in this undemanding but enjoyable Cold War thriller which contains a significant amount of early 1960s' colour, with a jazz singer, a drug dealer and a depraved rich girl who is a member of the Campaign for Nuclear Disarmament (CND).

*The Morning after Death* is the last Nigel Strangeways novel, set in Hawthorne House at the fictional Cabot University, near Boston. Despite seeking rest and intellectual nourishment, Strangeways is once again forced to uncover the murderer of a professor, one of three brothers. Blake's usual literary allusions are multiplied in a work which, unsurprisingly, has something of a valedictory tone. Nigel reflects on the nature of crime fiction which, he claims, is not an art form "but an entertainment".[40] He also acknowledges that the role of the individual private investigator is no longer valid in the complexity of the modern world, as "crimes of violence can only be dealt with now by teams of professionals".[41] With these words, Strangeways seems to herald the belated death of the Golden Age and foresee the advent of the police procedural which would dominate crime fiction from the next decade onward.

The final Nicholas Blake novel, *The Private Wound* (1968), is the fourth of his works not to feature Nigel Strangeways, and is in all probability the most autobiographical of the Blake novels. Set in Ireland in 1939, the novelist Dominic Eyre takes up residence in an isolated cottage to write. His friendship with the local squire leads to an affair with this man's younger wife, Harriet "Harry" Leeson, who is later murdered. Dominic, an Irishman long resident in England, is the initial suspect, and subject to the anti-English sentiments of the local inhabitants, themselves victims of the tensions of the pre-Emergency times, with talk of Blueshirts, fascism and the perceived threat of a Nazi-supported Irish attack on the six counties of Northern Ireland. Eyre is treated as a British spy and ruefully declares that never before had he felt "so complete a stranger in the land of my birth".[42] Eyre is Anglo-Irish – "West British" he calls himself – and constantly compares the work of the Irish Guards unfavourably with that

---

40   Nicholas Blake, *The Morning After Death* (London: Collins, 1966), 17.
41   Ibid., 18.
42   Nicholas Blake, *The Private Wound* (London: Collins, 1968), 93.

of their British counterparts. The discovery of the actual killer is cleverly delayed by the author, and the closing chapter, apparently written in 1967 by Eyre's literary executor casts fresh doubt on the events and their consequences. Apart from the Anglo-Irish background of Dominic, there are other autobiographical features in the novel. The affair between Dominic and Eyre is seen as being a thinly disguised recreation of the love affair Day-Lewis had with a neighbour's wife, Billie Currall between 1939 and 1940.[43] Although Day-Lewis considered writing a final Nicholas Blake mystery, with the participation of Nigel and Clare and tentatively entitled *Bang Bang, You're Dead*, the writer gave up the project on page seventy-seven "after apparently running out of impetus".[44]

Jessie Louise Moore (1876–1963), writing under the name of *Mrs Victor Rickard*, in memory of her late husband, is the third and least well known of the three Irish members of the Detection Club, the academy of Golden Age detective fiction. Born in Dublin, the daughter of a Protestant canon, Rickard is also remembered for her patriotic works set in the First World War. Her mystery fiction is unfortunately largely forgotten, and while the works of Wills Crofts and Blake have been reprinted since their deaths, those of Rickard are mainly confined to the elusive first editions only to be found in the larger libraries. These mystery novels are generally competent, however, and the best of them can be favourably compared to more famous and successful Golden Age mysteries. Her first crime novel *A Fool's Errand* (1921) is a light tale in which Quentin Dillon, recently returned from action in the First World War, falls in love with a beautiful girl he sees in a London art gallery. He then meets a man who, coincidentally, shares his surname. William Dillon tells his namesake that he is obliged, against his wishes, to sail out to Rangoon to take up employment in the Burmese capital. Quentin agrees to go instead of William, and, again coincidentally, finds that the girl from the gallery, Marion Keith, is also a passenger onboard the ship to Rangoon. On arrival, he takes up his employment to discover that he is mistaken for his namesake who has been keeping several illegal and immoral actions secret, and the burgeoning love affair with

43  Sean Day-Lewis, *C. Day-Lewis*, 282.
44  Ibid.

Marion is temporarily frustrated. Naturally, all turns out well in the end, but the mystery in this novel – who is William and what exactly has he done and why? – is secondary to the romantic tale. It does, however, offer various interesting features, especially in the figure of the returned middle-class soldier, forced to seek employment but alienated from his peers, the rootlessness of the British colonists in Rangoon, and the effects of bigamy.

In *Upstairs* (1925) Rickard produces an excellent murder mystery set in a claustrophobic London of lodging houses and inquisitive neighbours, of fortune-tellers and aristocrats and the alienation produced by life in the metropolis. Daniel Harrington who is "temperamentally inquisitive"[45] returns to London from a spell working in the Gold Coast, physically and psychologically crippled. Obsessively observant, he spies on his neighbours, detecting the disappearance of the evasive Sir Hector Montagu, a director of the Cassiopean Mining Company and seemingly romantically linked to both Lady Vanessa, his widowed sister-in-law, and the mysterious Mrs Rupert Chance, whose bigamous second husband has been imprisoned in France. Harrington's amateur sleuthing is reinforced by the enigmatic "private inquiring man",[46] Cosmo Rouselle and the unremarkable Inspector Frazier of the Criminal Investigation Department (CID). *Upstairs* is a fascinating work which merges topics of sensation fiction – divorce, bigamy, fortune-telling, returned colonial subjects – with elements of interwar mystery writing and traces of the urban angst of modernism.

*Not Sufficient Evidence* (1926) is another fine mystery, drawing this time from the real-life Charles Bravo "murder at the priory" poisoning case, an unsolved crime from 1876. This case had previously been treated in Sir John Hall's non-fiction work *The Bravo Mystery and Other Cases* (1923), and would also inspire a later novel, Marie Belloc Lownde's *Letty Lynton* (1931), corroborating, as Victoria Stewart notes, the popularity of Victorian criminal cases in interwar crime fiction,[47] and showing just how many Golden Age writers were "influenced by their Victorian predecessors not just in their subject matter but in their form and style".[48] Set in

45   Mrs Victor Rickard, *Upstairs* (London: Constable, 1925), 169.
46   Ibid., 98.
47   Stewart, *Interwar Britain*, 28.
48   Ibid., 54.

London, *Not Sufficient Evidence* tells the story of Nydia Brenner, daughter
of the Anglo-Irish aristocrat Lord Clantalbot. Nydia is obsessed with the
sinister, red-bearded Clive Stretton, psychologist and "mental healer".[49] In
a chemist's shop, which will play an important part in the novel's development, she meets the handsome young solicitor Robert Esmond, who
immediately falls in love with the rich young heiress. He faces opposition
from two sides, however: from his mother who, before her marriage had
been one of the Pallisters, another Anglo-Irish family which hated the
Clantalbots, and from Florrie, Nydia's paid lady companion who favours
her mistress's relationship with Clive. Against his mother's wishes, Robert
marries Nydia, but to sow discord between them Florrie tells him of his
new wife's previous relationship with the psychologist. Robert is later poisoned, and although it is first believed to have been suicide, Nydia and her
companion are soon suspected. London society, encouraged by a vociferous
press, initially blames Robert's death on the victim's "Irish blood", but later
rectifies this and places the blame on Nydia and Florrie.[50] The court case
with which the novel concludes is as good a piece of crime writing as any
that came out of the Golden Age period, and the open-ended conclusion
is highly satisfying. *Not Sufficient Evidence* contains several salient features,
including an Anglo-Irish rivalry which has crossed over from Ireland to
London, an early appearance of a sinister psychiatrist, the hiring of a private detective (by Robert, to follow Nydia). The use of the poison and
the probable means of its administration are also highly original, while
Rickard's portrayal of the relationship between Florrie and Nydia hints
with no great subtlety at the former's lesbian attraction to the latter, stating
that she, Florrie, had never cared for any man as much as she did for Nydia.

In *The Empty Villa* (1929) Rickard introduces the criminal Baccarat
Club led by the evil Sir Ulick who uses his tricks and an unwitting
charwoman's daughter to steal valuable emeralds. The Baccarat Club returns in *The Mystery of Vincent Dane* (1930), titled *The Baccarat Club* in
the USA, and both this novel and *The Dark Stranger* (1930) were originally serialised in the *Dundee Evening Telegraph* and *Post* before their

---

49    Mrs Victor Rickard, *Not Sufficient Evidence* (London: Constable, 1926), 27.
50    Ibid., 179.

publication in book format. The latter novel features an interesting femme fatale, Dolores Castell, the "dark angel" of the title, a drug addict and poisoner.[51] *Murder by Night* (1936) is a well-constructed if somewhat old-fashioned murder mystery which, like most of Rickard's fictions, owes much to the sensation fiction of the previous century. The sudden death of Lady Skelton, although initially believed to be a heart attack, is suspicious, and the blame moves from one to another of the young members of the rich old lady's family. Although, as is typical in Rickard's novels, the police (and private detectives) do become involved, it is once again the amateur work carried out by friends or acquaintances of the suspects which eventually uncovers the truth.

Golden Age crime fiction was, as we have seen, a peculiarly English mode, rooted in the English middle and upper classes and generally set in the English Home Counties. Ireland, it could be argued, had different problems with which to involve itself in the 1920s, and the decade in which the clue puzzle novel was at the peak of popularity saw the country first fighting for its independence (or that of twenty-six of its counties), then being involved in a Civil War, and finally trying to consolidate its newly won status. Writers like Liam O'Flaherty had other concerns than whether the killer was the vicar, the housemaid or the retired general. As Brian Cliff notes, there is, and has been, a tendency in Irish writers to avoid the Golden Age style, and "the brilliant amateur, the locked room, the cosy village mystery" are generally uncommon in Irish crime fiction.[52] Notwithstanding, three of the great writers of the Golden Age were Irish, and their influence and importance should not be undervalued.

---

51   Mrs Victor Rickard, *The Mystery of Vincent Dane* (London: Hodder & Stoughton, 1930), 14.
52   Brian Cliff, *Irish Crime Fiction* (London: Palgrave Macmillan, 2018), 12.

# CHAPTER 9

# "Among the poor the police are never regarded as the upholders of the common law, but as agents of the rich to oppress those without property." Post-Revolutionary Ireland

The events of the Easter Rising of 1916 and subsequent reaction contributed towards the Sinn Féin landslide victory in the elections of December 1918. The declaration of independence in January of the following year led to the Irish War of Independence or Anglo-Irish War, which lasted from January 1919 until July 1921. The signing of the Anglo-Irish Treaty ended this conflict, with ensuing partition of the island and the creation of the Irish Free State in the South and Northern Ireland in the six counties of the north-east. The conflict between those in favour of and those opposed to the Treaty resulted in the outbreak of Civil War, which lasted from June 1922 to May 1923. Partition brought about changes in the policing in both the Free State and in Northern Ireland. In the twenty-six counties which constituted the former, the RIC was replaced with the Civic Guard, the Garda Síochána, the Guardians of the Peace, while in Northern Ireland the RUC took on the command structure, territorial distribution and duties of its island-wide predecessor. While the newly created province in the north largely endorsed the sectarian principles behind its foundation, the Free State was immersed in over a decade of conflict and political turmoil. Such an atmosphere would mark the literary production of the period, and this would be reflected in the crime writing from the revolutionary and post-revolutionary periods. In England, the interwar years would be dominated by the Golden Age murder mysteries, the "cosy" fiction where the "clue puzzle" mystery predominated in works which took pains never to "mention the tensions and dangers that threatened the precarious stability of the Twenties and Thirties".[1] Crime, however, in the Free State, existed but, as William Meier and Ian Campbell Ross point out, this has been largely ignored by historians, and "rarely receives a mention as a feature of the social, economic, or cultural landscape in narrative texts of Irish history".[2] Similarly, we see no crime fiction from the early years of the Free State that deals with sexual abuse committed by representatives of the Catholic Church, nor adventure stories centred on the intensive smuggling activity that was taking place on both sides of the newly drawn-up border.

While the Anglo-Irish writers Freeman Wills Crofts, C. Day-Lewis (Nicholas Blake) and Jessica Louise Rickard (Mrs Victor Rickard) would specialise in Golden Age mysteries – generally with an English setting – crime writing or writing centred on criminal activity taking place in Ireland was, significantly, scarce. In 1918 *John Weldon* (1890–1963), writing under the pen name of *Brinsley MacNamara*, had published the hugely con-troversial *The Valley of the Squinting Windows*, which involves a case of murder in the closed, judgemental and hypocritical world of small-town rural Ireland. As a young woman, Nan Brennan, fell in love with Henry Shannon, a well-to-do local farmer. When it is revealed that she is preg-nant with his child, he rejects her and she leaves Garradrimna in disgrace after giving birth, believing the new-born child to have been murdered. She moves to England where she marries and has a child, John, who she dearly hopes will become a priest. She and her husband Ned return to Ireland, but after hearing gossip about his wife's past, Ned begins to beat his wife. John, now a seminarian, is attracted to Rebecca Kerr, a young schoolteacher who has started to work in Garradrimna, but her attentions are also sought by Ulick, a local youth and erstwhile friend of John. When John hears that Rebecca is pregnant by Ulick he kills him in a fit of fury, hiding his weighed-down body in a nearby lake. He is then ridden with

1    George Grella, "The Formal Detective Novel" in *Detective Fiction: A Collection of Critical Essays*, ed. Robin W. Winks (Englewood Cliffs, NJ: Prentice-Hall, 1980), 101.
2    William Meier and Ian Campbell Ross, "Editors' Introduction: Irish Crime since 1921", *Éire-Ireland*, 49, nos. 1 & 2 (Spring/Summer 2014), 9.

grief when he discovers that Ulick was really his half-brother, the son his mother thought had been killed and buried in her garden.

The *Valley of the Squinting Windows* provides a wonderful portrayal of crime, guilt and remorse in rural Ireland, revealing the damaging power of gossip and the claustrophobia of rural communities, and creating a pastoral tragedy which is both poignant and credible. Written during the Easter Rising of 1916, MacNamara's novel provoked riots in his home town of Delvin, Co. Westmeath, whose inhabitants saw themselves and their forefathers depicted unfavourably in the work by their compatriot who, O'Farrell claims, was "the first to write a novel of rural Irish life from his own experience".[3]

Three of the writers who would produce crime fiction in the Ireland of the post-Civil War period, Robert Brennan, Eimar O'Duffy and Liam O'Flaherty, had actively taken part in the revolutionary activities. *Robert Brennan* (1881–1964) was a member of the Irish Volunteers before 1916 and had participated in the events of the Easter Rising, being sentenced to death for leading the insurgent forces in Wexford. This sentence was commuted to imprisonment, and Brennan's political activities continued throughout the pre-independence period, and during the Civil War he was head of publicity in the anti-Treaty Irish Republican Army. Brennan, who was to become Ireland's first Minister Plenipotentiary to the USA, and was the founding editor of *The Irish Press*, wrote three mystery novels and several short stories that were published in *Flynn's Mystery Magazine* between July 1926 and January 1927, and which feature the two detectives who would later appear in *The Toledo Dagger* (1927).

*The False Finger Tip* (1921), published under the pseudonym *Selskar Kearney*, is an important work within the history of Irish crime fiction, as it is one of the first detective novels by an Irish writer to be set in contemporary Ireland. It is the story of the Dublin medical student, Christy Kirwan, who tells his friend Sam Lanagan that he believes he has killed someone and, although there is no news of it in the press, he believes it to be Jemmy Delaney, a youth who has been reported missing. Kirwan's

---

3    Padraic O'Farrell, *The Burning of Brinsley MacNamara* (Dublin: The Lilliput Press, 2013).

amnesia about the events is complicated by the discovery of the fingertip of the title inside a glove with a diagram, and the revelation that Delaney is now living under the name of Edward Collins (Nemo), and that, obviously, he has not been killed by Kirwan. Jemmy Delaney (Collins) recalls having been present at a fire in a house of O'Connell Street where his miser friend Fintan McCabe was found dead and from which Delaney had saved the safe containing a large sum of money and valuables. This somewhat convoluted plot contains some wonderful Dublin dialogue and captures the spirit of the Dublin of the second decade of the twentieth century. A Dublin Metropolitan Police officer is ironically referred to as "Vidoq" in a work which examines humorously the talent of the Irish towards the art of detection:

> Our Irish annals present us with a specimen of detective art where Fionn McCumhaill displayed his genius in tracing Diarmuid and Grainne utilizing the unbroken bread they left behind. Indeed, the Celtic race has a particular aptitude for the detective work. It is one of the greatest pities in the world that our people are against the government. Were it otherwise we could rival creation in producing successful detectives; and as it is, look at the New York police![4]

*The Toledo Dagger* followed a series of ten short stories published, as we have noted, in *Flynn's Mystery Magazine*, set mainly in France and featuring Oscar Van Duyven, an American millionaire, and Pierre Lemasse, his young prodigy, from Paris but of Breton origin. While in the short stories the two investigators travel around France seeking mysteries, in *The Toledo Dagger* they are staying at the French Riviera home of M. Rodin and his daughter Jacqueline plus a selection of house guests which apparently included the ghost of old Queen Jeanne the Unquiet of Naples. Oscar and Pierre are forced to investigate the murder of Darracq, one of the guests, of which M. Rodin – found guiltily replacing the titular dagger – is accused. The locked-room mystery is solved largely by Pierre's cunning – the Duyven and Lemasse stories are almost unique in that the young sidekick is more skilled in detective practices than his apparent superior – and the novel ends with the revelation of usurped identity, blackmail and with one

---

4    Selskar Kearney, *The False Finger Tip* (Dublin: Maunsel and Roberts, 1921), 10.

of the few cases in detective fiction where it can honestly be said that the butler committed the murder, albeit to save his master and mistress from the blackmailer.

Brennan's final crime novel *The Man Who Walked Like a Dancer* (1951), which, like *The Toledo Dagger* was published under his own name, is set in contemporary Ireland. The unlikely hero is Peter Rosegarden, the owner of an insurance company and a hotel, who, after stumbling upon what he believes to be the murder of a woman by a man who "walks like a dancer", reports his experience to the Guards. The supposed murderer is one Rupert Delaclaire who, despite the name "is as Irish as you or me" and who, it appears, is both a blackmailer and a murderer.[5] This slight, romantic mystery has as its climax a swordfight between Peter and Delaclaire and the former's engagement to the sister of the Guard to whom he had reported the murder.

*Eimar O'Duffy* (1893–1935) wrote three crime novels between 1932 and the year of his early death in 1935. The son of an Anglo-Irish dentist, O'Duffy was estranged from his family after refusing to follow his father's wishes of entering the British army and instead joined the Irish Volunteers, reaching the rank of captain. A supporter of Eoin MacNeill, O'Duffy opposed the 1916 Easter Rising for tactical reasons and disassociated himself from the nationalist movement after the events at the General Post Office (GPO). The author of numerous plays and poems, he is best remembered for his novel set in the period of the Rising, *The Wasted Island* (1919), and his satirical trilogy of *King Goshawk and the Birds* (1926), *The Spacious Adventures of the Man in the Street* (1928) and *Asses in Clover* (1933).

He apparently wrote his "pot-boilers" out of pure economic necessity, taking about three months to write each one and, despite what Robert Hogan calls their "uneven merit", they hold intrinsic value within the history of Irish crime fiction.[6] Indeed, *The Bird Cage* (1932) is a fine, if flawed, piece of crime writing which incorporates the author's satirical mode and economic radicalism into a highly readable mystery novel that has been unjustly forgotten. Set in an English coastal town which "has been sadly

5    Robert Brennan, *The Man Who Walked Like a Dancer* (London: Rich and Cowan, 1951), 109.
6    Robert Hogan, *Eimar O'Duffy* (Cranbury, NJ: Associated Universities Press, 1972), 14.

neglected by the speculative builder and the entertainment contractor",
the novel is a murder mystery which also includes blackmail and fraud.[7]
The body of a man is discovered in a hotel room, but the head has been so
mutilated by the hammer blow which caused his death that correct identification is not possible. The initial investigation carried out by ambitious
police officer Inspector Cranley, "an alert young man in a grey flannel suit",
follows the apparent clues leading to the perpetrators of an important international forging syndicate which has recently carried out a huge operation
in the Central American republic of San Felipe.[8] The forgery thread, which
turns out to be a red herring, is nevertheless used by the author to provide
a radical discourse of the nature of forgery under capitalism:

> To talk of ruin, of course, is only to adopt once again the artificial language of the
> sham science which rules this unreal civilization of ours. In no real sense was there
> danger of ruin to anybody. The crops still ripened in the sun; the earth still yielded
> its minerals to the seeker; human hands and brains had not lost their strength or
> cunning. San Felipe had not lost a pennyworth of wealth because somebody had been
> monkeying with the tokens of exchange. In a civilization dominated by money, an
> altogether disproportionate degree of heinousness has been attached to the crime of
> counterfeiting. Though his motives are not altruistic, the counterfeiter is in actual
> fact a public benefactor in a small way. That is to say, he increases the amount of
> money in circulation: and since, owing to a flaw in our economic system, there is
> never enough money in the people's pockets to buy more than a part of the generous
> output of goods produced by modern industry, this is all to the good. When the
> same thing is done by a government in financial difficulties, it is called "inflation".
> When it is done (as it is habitually done) by the bankers, it is called "expansion of
> credit". But the principle is the same.[9]

The same tone of satirical critique is apparent throughout the novel,
which pits the official police investigation led by Cranley with the unofficial
investigation run by Robert Cardwell's Investigations, Ltd., who had set
up the agency after the war instead of resuming his law studies. Cardwell
is, however, a flawed detective, who "took a keen intellectual pleasure in

---

7    Eimar O'Duffy, *The Bird Cage: A Mystery Novel* (1932, New York: H. C. Kinsey &
     Company, 1933), 1.
8    Ibid., 3.
9    Ibid., 10.

piecing fragments of evidence together and deducing events from them, but the business of arduously hunting for clues and practically tracing the criminal himself was not much to his mind".[10] He employs two young men, Allingham, a failed novelist, and Agnew to help with the case, and after Cranley is murdered they take over the investigation. Their relationship with the police is strained, the latter regarding the former as "amateur interlopers", although Inspector Cranley becomes totally subservient to his private rival as the case develops. The novel contains a number of the self-referential features so beloved by Golden Age writers, but O'Duffy's stance is entirely ironic, and his satire is directed towards the world of finance, the psychological and social conditions which lead the criminal to crime, the genre itself and the role of women in modern society. Inspector Cranley's girlfriend, Miss Philpot, helps him in his investigations because her ambition is to "buy a dream house in the country, not too far from London, where Cranley would set up as a private detective and become as famous as Sherlock Holmes",[11] but she feels belittled because she is female, arguing that if a man had made her suggestions he would have taken them seriously and thought them over, but "because I'm a girl you just waved them aside".[12]

O'Duffy comments ironically on the crime novelist's responsibility towards the reader:

> The detection of crime is but the preliminary to its punishment, and we, therefore, take it to be the duty of the mystery-monger to follow his tale to the bitter end. Let it be recorded then, for the moral gratification of all concerned, that the law duly took its course with the criminals.[13]

The cynical narrator sees the eventual hanging of the killer "as a punishment for his sins, and as a deterrent against murder, – or at any rate against getting found out".[14] This flippancy is also seen in the next mystery novel O'Duffy wrote, *The Secret Enemy* (1932). Harry Quinlan, an

---

10    Ibid., 98.
11    Ibid., 32.
12    Ibid., 37.
13    Ibid., 177.
14    Ibid., 178.

artist living in Montparnasse, is invited by his rich aunt to spend some time with her in her Surrey residence where, it would appear, a "phantom burglar" has been in operation. Spiritualists are consulted, but when the eccentric vegetarian, naturalist, stamp-collecting neighbour Fotheringay is poisoned, Harry is immediately suspected. Roy Thacker, a modernist poet and amateur detective, reputed to be "like Edgar Allan Poe" is called in to investigate what is essentially a locked-room mystery.[15] O'Duffy playfully uses the conventions of Golden Age detective fiction with the country house setting, the unconventional detective, the hero wrongly accused, the romantic sub-plot and quasi-gothic devices such as the poltergeist, burglar and sleepwalking, in a novel which retains the parodic and satirical strengths of *The Bird Cage*.

In *Head of a Girl* (1935) three upper-class friends, Stella, Dicky and Ethel, decide to investigate a series of murders that have occurred in London. Stella has been putting off marrying Dicky until he can prove himself by doing something worthwhile with his life. She was rich but hard-working and "believed that women ought to work to show their independence of men, and that people with private incomes had no right to consume without producing".[16] She agrees to marry Dicky if he is able to solve the three murders brilliantly, so he sets up as a private detective with the aid of his Irish valet, Coffey and his friend Ethel. After a fourth murder and the kidnapping of the Home Secretary, Inspector Cude of Scotland Yard consults Dicky and Ethel, showing suitable respect to their aristocratic position. Dicky, who starts to realise that he is more in love with Ethel than with Stella, is kidnapped, and during his absence chapters are narrated by Coffey and Ethel. By the end of the novel it is obvious to the reader that Ethel, a modern, smoking girl detective, is far more efficient in the role than Dicky, and after an attempt to kill her with gas fails, the evil genius behind the murders, who has been experimenting with atomic energy, is killed before he can be brought to justice. In true Golden Age fashion, Dicky and Ethel are together at the end of the novel, enacting the social restitution brought about by the removal of the threat to society.

---

15    Eimar O'Duffy, *The Secret Enemy* (London: Geoffrey Bles, 1932), 51.
16    Eimar O'Duffy, *Head of a Girl* (London: Geoffrey Bles, 1935), 38.

Like the two earlier novels, *Head of a Girl* abounds with ironic commentary on several issues, and also, like the earlier novels, is full of whimsical references to the genre itself. Dicky thinks "it would be rather fun to play the private sleuth"[17] but is worried that his social position might prove a hindrance as "detectives didn't take valets around with them".[18] There are references to Holmes, Poe and others throughout the novel, which also discusses American detective magazines, which Dicky dislikes because of the "machine-made villainy, the complete absence of character in the people, the laboriously manufactured 'thrills', the cheap smartness of the writing, the dreary clichés when the supply of this ran short".[19] It is tempting to see in such criticism O'Duffy's own views on certain aspects of crime writing. It is also tempting to wonder whether, if the author had lived beyond 1935 he would have continued to write crime fiction. His skill, sense of humour and highly developed sense of satire and irony have, in these three hastily written novels, given Irish crime fiction a notable figure in the genre in this crucial interwar period.

*Liam O'Flaherty* (1896–1984) was born on Inishmore, the largest of the Aran Islands. After being severely injured and suffering shell shock while serving in the British army during the later stages of the First World War, he became involved in revolutionary politics, participating in the anti-Treaty side in the Civil War and in the proclamation of the Irish Soviet Republic at the Rotunda hospital in central Dublin in January 1922. James Howard O'Brien divides his fourteen novels into three groups, namely those that deal with the Irish Revolution of 1916–23, those that centre on the historical roots of the Irish psyche, and those that deal with the psychic condition of the New Ireland.[20] The first novel he wrote, *The Black Soul* (1924), is largely autobiographical, based on the return to Ireland of a damaged, shell-shocked demobbed soldier who settles in an inhospitable community on the author's native Aran Islands. The Stranger, later identified as Fergus O'Connor, takes lodgings with a couple of islanders,

---

17    Ibid.
18    Ibid., 41.
19    Ibid., 267.
20    James Howard O'Brien, *Liam O'Flaherty* (Cranbury, NJ: Associated Universities Press, 1973), 37.

the tall, beautiful Little Mary, and her husband, the physically deformed, red-haired dwarf, Red John. Mary and John have never consummated their marriage, and she is immediately attracted to the handsome former soldier who, initially, takes great pains to reject her advances. When they do commence to have sexual relations, Red John seeks out his rival and, in an impressive cliff-top scene, they fight and the dwarf is killed. Although it is not a murder mystery in the true sense, tension is created in this myth-like tale through the uncertainty over Red John's death, and whether this was premeditated murder, manslaughter or, as it transpires, death due to natural causes in the exertion of the fray.

Despite its terse, brittle style, little in *The Black Soul* could anticipate the brilliance of O'Flaherty's next work, *The Informer* (1925). Set in the labyrinthine backstreets of Dublin in the aftermath of the Civil War, *The Informer* follows the fortunes of "Gypo" Nolan, a former policeman and current member of an unnamed revolutionary group. Fellow revolutionary Frankie McPhillip has murdered the secretary of a local branch of the Farmers' Union, and Nolan reports this to the police. With this action, Gypo has become that most abysmal of outcasts, the informer, a word which "was whispered with fear and hatred",[21] and whose horror can "be understood fully only by an Irish mind".[22] The novel contains powerful descriptions of the "criminal and pauperized circles"[23] of Dublin's underclass:

> Casual workers, casual criminals and broken old men, their connection with the ordered scheme of civilized life, with its moral laws and its horror of crime, was so thin and weak that they were unable to feel the interest that murder arouses in the tender breasts of our wives and sisters.[24]

Through this world Nolan wanders "like some primaeval monster just risen from the slime in which all things have their origin",[25] hunted down by his former comrades for whom he has become a pariah. For Derek

---

21    Liam O'Flaherty, *The Informer* (1925, San Diego: Harcourt, Brace & Company, 1980), 34.
22    Ibid., 46.
23    Ibid., 5.
24    Ibid., 10.
25    Ibid., 80.

Hand, *The Informer* is "a remarkably dense piece of writing that at once consciously harks back to nineteenth-century detective novels with its incessant reference to precise time and place over the period of eight hours of the story".[26] Indeed, O'Flaherty stated that *The Informer* was created with the idea of its being "a sort of highbrow detective story" with "its style based on the technique of the cinema".[27] The novel was itself given two cinematic adaptations, with a silent English version in 1928 and John Ford's acclaimed Hollywood version in 1935. The language of religion, sin and redemption which pervades the closing pages of the novel look forward to many of the late twentieth-century "Troubles" novels, like Bernard McLaverty's *Cal* (1983),[28] and for *Jennifer Malia The Informer* reveals O'Flaherty's "disillusionment with political violence as a means to further a revolutionary cause".[29]

*Mr Gilhooley* (1926) is a tale of love, betrayal and jealousy set in lower-working-class Dublin in the 1920s, which culminates in a sordid murder. It has been described as "a wasteland of the heart"[30] which shows "modern man's sense of the void".[31] *The Assassin* (1928) returns to the activities of revolutionary politics explored so successfully in *The Informer*, with a story based on the topical assassination of Kevin O'Higgins, Minister for Justice, the year before the publication of the novel. Dublin is seen as a hive of detectives and spies, and the central theme of a lack of trust is highlighted in the varying and doubtful loyalties of the characters. The spiritual burdens of modern life are carefully explored, and the three conspirators are skilfully portrayed compendiums of a number of psychological states, ranging from

---

26  Derek Hand, *A History of the Irish Novel* (Cambridge: Cambridge University Press, 2011), 173.

27  Liam O'Flaherty, *Shame the Devil* (1934, Dublin: Wolfhound Press, 1981), 189.

28  Elmer Kennedy-Andrews, "The Novel and the Northern Troubles" in Foster (ed.), *Irish Novel*, 246.

29  Jennifer Malia, "Liam O'Flaherty's Disillusionment with Irish Revolutionary Martyrdom in *The Informer* and *The Assassin*", *Pacific Coast Philology* 44, no. 2 (2009), 193.

30  O'Brien, *Liam O'Flaherty*, 79.

31  Ibid., 79.

McDara's obsession with his mother, to Kitty's almost religious fanaticism, to Fetch's dull thuggery.

*The House of Gold* (1929) is set in Barra, a town in the west of Ireland closely based on Galway, and this work holds the unfortunate record for being the first novel to be banned in the Irish Free State. In the figure of Nora, *The House of Gold* also presents, perhaps, the Free State's first femme fatale. *The Puritan* (1932) is a work which, despite being, for Derek Hand "perhaps his greatest work", has been unjustly ignored.[32] While examining the character of its protagonist, Francis Ferriter, the puritanical representative of the new Catholic middle-class, it also examines the morality of the new Free State, a morality which had led to the censorship of *The House of Gold*. Ferriter, sick in mind and body, becomes a vigilante, fighting against the vices of drink and prostitution taking place around the north Dublin boarding houses in which the novel is set. His need for a blood sacrifice echoes the foundational myths of the Free State, and the police investigation into the murder provides one of the first fictional representations of the Garda Síochána, the Civic Guards. Chief Superintendent John Lavan "had risen almost to the top of his profession, principally by virtue of that energy and ambition which is typical of public officials in this generation since the establishment of the Free State".[33] Lavan was "a man of considerable information and culture, entirely devoid of that heavy and brutal manner which has come to be regarded as the classical attribute of the police officer" but, unfortunately, he "looked like a smart French army officer, more interested in glory and love affairs than in the detection and prevention of crime".[34] *The Puritan* relentlessly scrutinises all strata of Free State society, from publicans and prostitutes to judges and lawyers, journalist and editors, to professors and priests, and analyses the state control of the press, the police and the courts, and its use of vigilantes who burn books that are "immoral or a danger to the community".[35] Like "Gypo" Nolan, Francis Ferriter attempts to find God, but while the informer encounters a form of redemption before Frankie McPhillip's mother in a church, all Francis

32    Hand, *History of the Irish Novel*, 174.
33    Liam O'Flaherty, *The Puritan* (1932, Dublin: Wolfhound Press, 2001), 34.
34    Ibid.
35    Ibid., 36.

discovers is the probable non-existence of God in a randomly constructed but state-regulated world.

While considering the work of Liam O'Flaherty, it is also worth mentioning the 1930s' writings of *Seán O'Faoláin (John Whelan, 1900–91)* and Frank O'Connor. Both also participated in the events leading up to the creation of the Free State, and among their short stories are some of the finest narratives to take as their starting point the revolutionary period. O'Faoláin's first collection of short stories, *Midsummer Night Madness and Other Stories* (1932), contains notable narratives set in the Anglo-Irish War, including "The Bombshop", "Fugue" and "The Patriot", all of which "present the gruesome attrition of the freedom fighters: their initial steadfast and elated faith in the Rebellion succumbing to solitude, hunger and the terror foisted on them by the Black and Tans".[36] John Grant notes how, although ostensibly set during the War of Independence, stories like "The Bombshop" and "Fugue" in fact reflect the author's experiences in the Civil War and this ambivalence necessarily "enhances the suspicion that the writer is finding it difficult to absolve the harrowing experiences inflicted by Civil War".[37] In 1935, two years after publishing his first novel, *A Nest of Simple Folk* (1933), O'Faoláin wrote an article for *The Spectator* which gave his views on crime fiction in the 1930s. "Give Us Back Bill Sikes" is critical of detective fiction, although the models he uses are restricted to those of Holmes and the clue puzzle narratives of the Golden Age. He attacks the genre against what he styles the "novel proper", but makes some interesting suggestions regarding the relative importance of detective and criminal:

> The detective-story [...] deflects of necessity from the main road of literature. It picks up where the novel proper arrives at a climax, and dives inside the periphery of the brain to a side-track. The detective is an ancillary to the criminal, who, by rights, should be the main character, and it runs to a new climax – the discovery and capture of the damned soul.[38]

36 Christelle Chaussinand, "Love and Love of One's Fatherland: Aspects of Patriotic 'Ex-Istences' in Sean O'Faolain's Short Story "The Patriot", *Journal of the Short Story in English*, 34 (Spring 2000), 139.

37 John Grant, "'I Was Too Chickenhearted to Publish It': Seán O'Faoláin, Displacement and History Re-Written", *Estudios Irlandeses* 12 (2017), 50.

38 Seán O'Faoláin, "Give Us Back Bill Sikes", *The Spectator*, 15 February 1935, 242.

The perfect detective novel should, he argues, be turned upside down; we should "hunt not Bill Sikes but Superintendent Blank", in order to have, at least, "a fair view both of the hare and hounds".[39] The ideal crime narrative, for O'Faoláin, "instead of beginning with a murder and ending with a revelation, begins with a live thug and ends with a dead detective".[40] It is tempting to wonder what might have occurred had the author dedicated at least part of his formidable talents to writing crime stories. They may have been capable of changing the face of Irish crime fiction in the 1930s.

*Frank O'Connor* (*Michael O'Donovan*, 1903–66), like O'Faoláin, used his experiences in the struggle for independence as an important part of his first volume, *Guests of the Nation* (1931). The story which gives its name to the collection is the harrowing tale of republican volunteers interacting with two British soldiers they are holding prisoner. They play card games together and pass the time talking, but neither captives nor captors are initially aware that the soldiers are hostages who will be killed if the British do not release their Irish prisoners. The ending is, of course, tragic and leaves a feeling of profound emptiness. Other stories in the collection such as "Attack" and "Machine Gun Corps in Action" deal with the conflict, while special attention should be paid to "Jumbo's Wife" in which an abused wife unintentionally causes her husband to be sentenced to death by the republicans as an informer. The concept of the informer also comes up in "In the Train" from O'Connor's second collection, *Bones of Contention and Other Stories* (1936) where a woman is returning to her home village after a court case. Accompanied by police officers and witnesses, she has been acquitted after having poisoned her husband. Facing being hanged for the offence, charges had had to be withdrawn after neighbours refused to give evidence against her for fear of being branded informers.

Although not known specifically for her crime writing, there are, as Sandra Kemp indicates, "plenty of murders in *Elizabeth Bowen's* fiction".[41] Bowen (1899–1973) is one of the greatest English-language writers of the

---

39    Ibid., 243.
40    Ibid.
41    Sandra Kemp, "But One Isn't Murdered: Elizabeth Bowen's *The Little Girls*" in *Twentieth-Century Suspense*, ed. Clive Bloom (London: Palgrave Macmillan, 1990), 130.

interwar years, and her second novel, *Last September* (1929) is justly considered to be a masterpiece. Set in rural Cork in 1920, the novel looks at the War of Independence but, unlike O'Faoláin and O'Connor, she does so from the perspective of the Ascendancy class to which she belonged. *Last September* takes place in Danielstown, a sprawling estate in whose Big House a group of Anglo-Irish residents and visitors gradually awaken to the new reality facing the country. As in much of Bowen's fiction, the novel is seen through the viewpoint of "an imaginative, delicately responsive, quite young woman", Lois Farquar.[42] Lois, again like many of Bowen's central characters, lives with proxy parents, in this case, her uncle, Sir Richard Naylor, and his wife Myra, Lady Naylor. She is uncertain about her future and the nature of her relationship with Gerald Lesworth, an English officer in the British army. While the action in *Last September*, again like that in most of Bowen's work, takes place within the minds of her protagonists, there are moments within the novel which link it to the thriller. Gerard's murder, although attributed to the insurgent friend of Peter Connor, the Catholic neighbour who Gerald had made prisoner (and who never "appears" in person in the novel), remains unsolved. The frightening encounter that Lois and her cousin Marda have with a group of insurgents in the woods, the murder of Gerald and the final act of arson all contribute to the underlying tension present in the novel.

Bowen's *To the North* (1932) ends with a dual murder and suicide, while many of her short stories contain substantial features of the crime mystery. J. A. Morris states that Bowen is "par excellence a short story writer of suspense".[43] This suspense, which Morris describes as "the building up of a particular type of nervous tension", is achieved by the means Bowen uses to prevent the reader from "seeing or telling with any precision what is really going on beneath surface events while, at the same time, experiencing powerfully the sense of what might be described as 'a hidden agenda' of threat or horror".[44] The title story from *The Cat Jumps and Other Stories*

---

42  Bruce Harkness, "The Fiction of Elizabeth Bowen", *The English Journal* 44, no. 9 (December 1955), 499.

43  J. A. Morris, "Elizabeth Bowen's Short Stories of Suspense" in Bloom (ed.), *Twentieth-Century Suspense*, 114.

44  Ibid., 114.

(1934) sees how a family changes after purchasing a house in which a murder has been committed, while "Brigands" (1932), published in a collection of children's stories edited by Celia Asquith, featured two child detectives.[45] Of special interest, however, is a story which was serialised over three issues of *Home and Country*, the official journal of the National Federation of Women's Institutes in the summer of 1938. This serial, recently uncovered by Clara Jones, was specially commissioned for the magazine and is a light detective mystery which, nevertheless "overlaps thematically with Bowen's other interwar short stories" and is "[s]elf-reflexively concerned with the status of the writer in the community".[46] Veronica Philbeam, living with her aunt and her uncle, the local doctor, in the sleepy English village of Sutton Plover, is one of Bowen's "imaginative" and "delicately responsive" young heroines, who lived with surrogate parents, and who "would bicycle round the country, simply looking for trouble".[47] She is a member of the local archaeological society, although "not really interested in archaeology; it was mystery that she chiefly liked".[48] When The Lilacs, an empty house in the village, receives new tenants, Virginia is interested, especially when she sees the young man, Denis, who is accompanying his aunt, Mrs Clarke-Moberly. The new tenants arouse her curiosity, but she is alarmed to see that Denis has a pistol, which falls from his pocket while she is visiting him. In the second instalment of the serial, Sutton Plover is in uproar about a novel which is circulating and which would appear to reveal, using disguised names, secrets of many of the villagers, who wonder who the writer, acting under the pseudonym of Antrobus Grey, might be. Virginia sees local landowner Sir Horace Hammer behaving suspiciously, and when Denis tells her that his aunt has disappeared she starts to search for suspects, centring her attention on Sir Horace and Denis himself.

The next day Denis tells Virginia that his aunt really has disappeared. He reveals that the staged disappearance of the day before was a ruse, and

---

45    Clara Jones, "'Mystery at the Lilacs' (1938): Elizabeth Bowen's Serial for *Home and Country*", *Literature and History* 27, no. 1 (2018), 8.

46    Ibid., 3.

47    Elizabeth Bowen, "Mystery at the Lilacs: Part One", *Home and Country*, June, 1938, 233.

48    Ibid., 233.

that Mrs Clarke-Moberly was really Lucinda Bradnitt, the famous author. She had been commissioned to write a detective novel but had "always rather despised detective stories believing their psychology is unsound" and that "all the people in them behave, re-act, so unnaturally".[49] To help her compose her story, she was to stage "a disappearance, an apparent murder".[50] Denis was to report back on the reactions of the villagers, and she would use this information in her novel. The next morning, however, Lucinda had actually disappeared, and Virginia helps Denis to search for her. Suspecting Sir Horace, they hide out in his garden and at night discover the two in a semi-abandoned belvedere. Lucinda admits that she had seen Sir Horace and recognised him as fellow-author Antrobus Grey with who she shared a publisher. She threatened to reveal that "the scandalous novelist and the highly respected squire were the same man" if he did not help to conceal her in his grounds.[51] Swearing to keep their secret, Denis and Virginia announce their betrothal, gaining the blessing of Lucinda who tells them that she "meant her detective story to end with a romance".[52]

Although apparently so slight, "Mystery at the Lilacs" is a fascinating text in that, like Seán O'Faoláin's "Give Us Back Bill Sikes", it provides a rare view of an Irish writer of the interwar period giving her opinions on the contemporary trend of the detective story. Bowen, Clara Jones notes, was an "avid reader of detective fiction and a habitual viewer of 'cinematic thrillers' throughout this period".[53] Indeed, at the time of writing the serial, she and her husband were lodging as a house guest with Billy, son of the Scottish novelist John Buchan who, at the time, was completing an apprenticeship under suspense master Alfred Hitchcock at Lime Grove Studios in Shepherd's Bush, West London.[54] Lucinda's comments on the detective story are of great interest, and her views would seem to coincide with those of Bowen's friend, Virginia Woolf, and "a certain version of highbrow elitism

49    Elizabeth Bowen, "Mystery at the Lilacs: Part Three", *Home and Country*, August 1938, 325.
50    Ibid., 326.
51    Ibid.
52    Ibid.
53    Jones, "Mystery", 9.
54    Ibid.

in currency during the interwar period with which Virginia Woolf was identified".[55] Jones also believes, however, that Lucinda contained elements of Bowen herself, as well as of the author of *To the Lighthouse*, noting that the character is "not just self-reflexive but self-satirical".[56]

Towards the end of her life, Bowen would return to the crime genre, and once more would give her own particular twist to the form. In *The Little Girls* (1963) she introduces "all the paraphernalia of murder – a buried box, a knife, a gun, a suicide" and "the prototypical eccentric and bohemian detective" with "her admiring but slightly stupid foil".[57] The problem is, of course, that despite all the paraphernalia, despite the atmosphere, and despite the apparent adherence to the clichés of the genre, *The Little Girls* is a murder mystery without a murder. Bowen "sets up the structures of the detective story, only to subvert them",[58] and successfully "parodies the object-as-clue convention".[59]

*Maurice Walsh* (1879–1964) was born near Listowel in County Kerry and is best known for his short story "The Quiet Man" from *Green Rushes* (1935), made into a famous Hollywood film by John Ford and starring John Wayne and Maureen O'Sullivan. Before the creation of the Free State in 1921, Walsh had worked as an excise officer for the British customs authority, mostly in northern Scotland. There he met and befriended fellow excise man Neil M. Gunn, later to become a key figure in the Scottish Literary Renaissance of the late 1920s and early 1930s and one of the founding voices in the restructuring of Scottish nationalism.[60] Although Walsh returned to Ireland after the creation of the Free State, his Scottish experience and friendship with Gunn, who allegedly helped him develop his early plots,[61] led to the publication of light, Highland-set works involving whisky, poaching and fishing, such as *The Key Above the Door* (1926) and

55   Ibid., 10.
56   Ibid., 11.
57   Kemp, "But One", 130.
58   Ibid., 140.
59   Ibid., 135.
60   Richard Price, *Neil M. Gunn: The Fabulous Matter of Fact* (Edinburgh: Edinburgh University Press, 1991), 47.
61   J. B. Pick, *Neil M. Gunn* (Tavistock: Northcote House, 2004), 8.

*The Small Dark Man* (1929). *The Road to Nowhere* (1934), although primarily a romantic adventure story in which a former rugby international travels around south-west Ireland with a group of tinkers, contains a murder mystery which is investigated by the Civic Guard, "an intelligent police force".[62] The book, according to Steve Matheson, "caused a considerable outcry amongst the establishment in Ireland which thought that the 'itinerant' problem should be recognised as a serious matter of social concern and not idealised in that way".[63]

*The Hill is Mine* (1940), set once again in the Scottish Highlands, is an insubstantial mystery novel with clichés about the nobility of the Scottish clan system and stereotyped characters, many of whom, like the Scottish woman Kirsty "who had lost her young Irishman tragically in an Irish rising, and [whose] daughter had been born three months later" reinforce Walsh's vision of Scottish-Irish unity.[64] *The Spanish Lady* (1943) is another murder mystery set in Scotland, involving the murder of local landowner Major-General Harper, which is at first blamed on his Basque wife Ann Mendoza and his Paraguayan nephew, Don Diego Usted, who has been fighting in a British commando unit and is recovering from wounds sustained at Dunkirk. Diego and Mendoza originally suspect each other, but gradually develop feelings for each other, which seek them to look together for the true culprit as mystery takes second place to romance. Matheson refers to it as a crime story, but stresses that "it is not a thriller in the usual sense and has no detective".[65]

Walsh's first *bona fide* detective novel is *The Man in Brown* (1945). When rich farmer Marcus Aitken is murdered, his Canadian nephew, Peter Falkner, with whom he had quarrelled, is immediately suspected. A number of the facts surrounding the case seem to point, however, to Peter's innocence, and the existence of a mysterious "man in brown" seen on the date of the murder leads Con Madden, a private investigator, to investigate the case. Madden had been a police detective, but had been dismissed for assaulting a senior officer, and now worked for a small detective agency

---

62    Maurice Walsh, *The Road to Nowhere* (Edinburgh: Chambers, 1934), 78.
63    Steve Matheson, *Maurice Walsh, Storyteller* (Dingle: Brandon, 1985), 80.
64    Maurice Walsh, *The Hill is Mine* (Edinburgh: Chambers, 1940), 67.
65    Ibid., 120.

which is a "sort of free-lance organisation" that chooses its own cases. The novel, full of clues, counter-clues, red herrings and broken alibis functions as a piece of detective fiction at its most whimsical, with a final twist and happy ending included. Somewhat more substantial is *Danger under the Moon* (1956), which sees Dave Daunt, a convicted killer, return home to Ireland after serving time for the murder he did not commit. Daunt seeks to clear his name, but is afraid that by so doing he might implicate the woman he loves, Jean, the widow of the victim, Daunt's cousin. The investigation is interesting, as is the positive representation of the local guards, initially suspicious but later supportive of Daunt, but once again the work finally degenerates into pure romance.

One of the stated aims of the Free State government in the early years of independence was the need to support and encourage the use of the Irish language, which, especially in urban areas, had been in decline for many years. Before the creation of the Free State there existed no central agency "with the power and resources to investigate and ultimately impose any significant reform".[66] Now, however, after independence, "the new state had that kind of clout"[67] – clout to debate the norms of orthography and grammar, clout to find against the intrusion of Anglicisation, but also clout to produce Irish-language texts aimed mainly at strictly didactic targets; at young readers, at learners of the language or at native speakers who were illiterate in Irish. It is normal, therefore, that such texts should be aimed to please the tastes of their target readerships and, as such, many of these books were genre-based works, a significant number of which used the crime mode. More popular, however, were the detective serials which, as in the English-language *Ireland's Own*, began to appear in a variety of Irish-language or bilingual magazines. Philip O'Leary has detailed a large number of popular series from such diverse sources as the *Cork Weekly Examiner*, *An Gaedheal*, *The Rock* and the bilingual *Our Boys* which appeared during the 1920s and 1930s, while Ian Campbell Ross stresses the relevance of the Holmes and Watson-like detectives created by An t'Athair Seoirse Mac

---

66    Philip O'Leary, *Gaelic Prose in the Irish Free State: 1922–1939* (University Park, PA: Penn State University Press, 1994), 25.
67    Ibid., 25.

Clúin whose tales appeared in *An Sguab* as early as 1922.[68] The creation of the state-sponsored agency, An Gúm, a subsidiary of the Free State's new Department of Education in 1926 saw the arrival of "the single most important and controversial force in Gaelic literature".[69] An Gúm provided a massive boost for Irish-language publishing, but its success was qualified by accusations of cronyism and complaints that most of the work commissioned by the agency consisted of translation from English into Irish. Ian Campbell Ross hails *Oidhche I nGleann na nGealt* (1939) by Ciarán Ó Nualláin, brother of Flann O'Brien, as the first crime novel in the Irish language, followed closely by *An Doras do Plabafdh* by Seoirse Mac Liam (1940). Despite the efforts of An Gúm, however, and despite occasional successes, such as the works of Cathal Ó Sandar in the third quarter of the century or Ruaidhirí Ó Baílle in the 1980s, Irish-language crime writing would never find a large mainstream market until the twenty-first century when writers such as Anna Hessauf, Éilis Ní Dhuibhne or Mícheál Ó Ruairc would produce commercially successful high quality crime novels in Irish.

---

68    Ross, Ian Campbell, "Irish Crime Fiction" in *The Oxford Handbook of Modern Irish Fiction*, ed. Liam Harte (Oxford: Oxford University Press, 2020), 357.

69    O'Leary, *Gaelic Prose*, 505.

# CHAPTER 10

# "A kind of private eye and general trouble-shooter." Irish Hard-Boiled and Pulp

Hard-boiled and noir as modes of crime fiction first appeared in the USA in the 1920s, at the same time that British – and some Irish – writers were embracing the clue-puzzle mysteries of the Golden Age. For Lee Horsley, a noir narrative is one which takes a subjective viewpoint, includes protagonists who frequently interchange roles, which reveals the difficult relationship between the protagonist and society, and which includes elements of socio-political critique.[1] Hard-boiled crime fiction usually contains an "alienating urban setting, frequent violence and fast-paced dialogue", with, unlike its Golden Age equivalent, little or no analysis of clues.[2] The detective is usually an amateur, and in most cases self-employed, and "it is this independence and self-sufficiency, inherited from the frontier hero, that contributes to the hostility that the private eye typically displays for the forces of law and order".[3] The character – exclusively male in the early hard-boiled narratives – is tough, but often reveals a startling degree of sensitivity, is intelligent, but not usually intellectual, is not averse to the use of physical violence if he considers it to be necessary, and generally enjoys a relationship of mutual hostility with the law enforcement agencies, and "nominally, at any rate, shares their aim to restore and maintain the social order".[4] While Horsley believes that the hard-boiled style is "only one of the means of expressing the noir vision,[5] she is also of the view that much of the best noir fiction that has been

1   Lee Horsley, *The Noir Thriller* (London: Palgrave Macmillan, 2001), 8.
2   John Scaggs, *Crime Fiction* (London: Routledge, 2005), 56.
3   Ibid., 60.
4   Ibid., 61.
5   Horsley, *Noir Thriller*, 7.

written is hard-boiled.[6] The style has also retained an enormous popularity, and the "iconographic elements of the hardboiled world (private eyes with a whisky bottle in the filing cabinet, femme fatale, rich – and usually corrupt – clients) remain as sure-fire a combination today as when they were freshly minted, despite a million parodies".[7]

The hard-boiled style was initiated in the "pulp" magazines of the USA, and it was in *Black Mask*, a popular monthly founded by the controversial journalist and critic H. L. Mencken in 1920, that the hard-boiled crime story is believed to have begun. By 1922 *Black Mask's* popularity was such that it took to a twice-monthly format and, in December of that year, Carroll John Daly published "The False Barton Combs", believed to be the first story in the new style. In June of the next year, in the same magazine, Daly published "Knights of the Open Plan", his first story to feature private detective Race Williams, for many the model on which future hard-boiled private detectives would be based. The hard-boiled detective narrative reached maturity in the 1930s and 1940s, with writers such as Dashiell Hammett and Raymond Chandler (whose mother was from County Waterford). Unlike the Golden Age mystery, hard-boiled stories "have never included an emphasis on closure".[8] There are no "tidy victories" for the hard-boiled private eye, the results of his investigations yield only "small, local and temporary" rewards.[9] In hard-boiled fiction the police can no longer be assumed to have the general goodwill as their main objective; they are often corrupt or are helping to conceal the corruption of others. The hard-boiled private detective "does not compete against the moronic Prefect of past detective stories, he struggles with police who can solve crimes, but who will not because of their complicity in them".[10]

6　Ibid., 23.
7　Barry Forshaw, *Crime Fiction: A Reader's Guide* (Harpenden: Oldcastle Books, 2019), 43.
8　Karin Molander Danielsson, *The Dynamic Detective: Special Interest and Seriality in Contemporary Detective Series* (Uppsala: Diss Acta Universitatis Upsaliensis, 2002), 52.
9　Scaggs, *Crime Fiction*, 63.
10　LeRoy Lad Panek, *An Introduction to the Detective Story* (Bowling Green, OH: Bowling Green State University Popular Press, 1987), 157.

The detective is often linked to the knight of old, and his personal quest is usually given at least as much importance as the case he is investigating.[11] This quest, like the case itself, often contains veiled or overt ideological implications, and is usually "inflected with political assumptions", even where these assumptions are unclear or complex".[12]

Although the hard-boiled detective novel was largely an American mode, its popularity soon spread to other countries, including the UK and Ireland. In both these countries publications were generally poor imitations of the American originals, with a marked tendency "not to confront specific socio-political concerns" while still creating "lively variations" on the themes used by American writers.[13] In the UK, the hard-boiled detective story "became tough-guy fiction".[14] Unlike in America, there was no sympathy shown towards the armed villain,[15] and even the toughest novels still managed to display an at-times disconcerting sense of civic loyalty to the police and institutions such as the monarchy.[16] Britain, like France, had a large market which eagerly purchased novels featuring private detectives in cheap, paperback editions, but the market in both countries was "primarily dominated by novelists who pastiche American hard-boiled crime fiction".[17] Early British novelists who used the format were James Hadley-Chase (René Lodge Brabazon Raymond) and Peter Cheyney. This latter was included by Peter Haining in his anthology *Great Irish Detective Stories* (1994), under the mistaken belief that he "was born in County Clare, where his forebears had lived for at least two centuries" when, in fact, the author was born in Whitechapel, East London, and had no known Irish ancestors.[18]

---

11   Heather Worthington, *Key Concepts in Crime Fiction* (London. Palgrave Macmillan, 2011), 123.
12   Andrew Pepper, "The Hard-Boiled Genre" in *A Companion to Crime Fiction*, ed. Charles J. Rzepka and Lee Horsley (Oxford: Wiley-Blackwell, 2010), 141.
13   Horsley, *Noir Thriller*, 100.
14   Panek, *Detective Story*, 144.
15   Horsley, *Noir Thriller*, 61.
16   Ibid., 100.
17   Ibid.
18   Peter Haining, *Great Irish Detective Stories* (1993, London: Pan Books, 1994), 197.

The most notable – and prolific – Irish writer of early hard-boiled fiction was the Dubliner *James Brendan (J. B.) O'Sullivan*. His early novels, set largely in the imaginary American metropolis, Tower City, were published by small popular Dublin publishers before the author moved to the London publishing houses of Werner Laurie and, as of 1956, Ward, Lock. O'Sullivan's first novel, *The Case of the Three Black Crows*, perhaps somewhat fortuitously published by the Dublin Catholic Truth Society in 1945, introduced several characters, including Lieutenant Peter Tracey of the Tower City Police Department, Edgar Davis, an alcoholic crime reporter, and the private detectives Ben Bishop and Mike Abbott. Bishop and Abbott would seem to enjoy a surprisingly modern partnership: they live together in their office, and Bishop's tiny figure is contrasted with that of his huge partner who, however, "looks incongruous in a flowered apron".[19] Their first case involves Henry Vanston who, after the murder of his brother, fears that he will be the next victim, as he, like his late brother, had a dead crow delivered to his home. Bishop and Abbott discover the truth behind the murders, when Ben, through details discovered on a set of false teeth, realises that the man who has hired his services has, in fact, tricked him. On discovering the truth, Ben reveals his integrity by returning the fee to his client, not wishing to be a party to what he considers to be immoral gain. This example of the morally honourable private detective would obviously have done much to win the good grace of the Dublin Catholic Truth Society, but was also indicative of how O'Sullivan had grasped the American model of the lone investigator, showing himself to be morally superior to his counterparts in the police, and endorsing, perhaps, George Grella's claim that hard-boiled writers "ultimately wrote more romantic rather than realistic fiction".[20]

The same characters reappear in J. B. O'Sullivan's second novel *Cherry in the Wineglass* (1945), published in the same year as his debut, but this time by another small Dublin publisher, Grafton. In this novel, Ben Bishop

19    J. B. O'Sullivan, *The Case of the Three Black Crows* (Dublin: Dublin Catholic Truth Society, 1945), 3.
20    George Grella, "The Hard-Boiled Detective Novel" in *Detective Fiction: A Collection of Critical Essays. Twentieth-Century Views*, ed. Robin W. Winks (Englewood Cliffs, NJ: Prentice-Hall, 1980), 118.

is convinced that the death of police officer "Tex" Riley is no accident, and, at no charge, sets out to investigate what he believes to be a murder. His search leads him to "The Cherry", a Washington DC nightclub where Riley's girlfriend Jean Verne works as a cabaret singer, and his discovery of a forgery ring operating from the club leads him to suspect the gangster owner of "The Cherry" as being responsible for Riley's death. Jean Verne, who presumably would have been unacceptable to the author's previous publisher, is the first of a long line of femmes fatales in O'Sullivan's fiction. The figure of the sexually attractive but potentially dangerous woman was, of course, a staple in the male-dominated world of hard-boiled fiction, and represented an "antithesis to the hard-boiled private eye, in that she reverses the normal dialectic of tough surface and sensitive depth that characterises the private eye hero".[21]

*The Castle of Death* (1945), also published by Grafton, introduces a new detective, Steve Silk, who would go on to feature in seventeen novels over the next twenty years. The novel opens with Silk playing poker with Lieutenant Tracey and crime reporter Edgar Davis, taking over, as it were, the central role of Bishop and Abbott, who are excluded from the rest of the author's canon. In this novel Silk is hired by an insurance company to investigate the suspected murder of Warren Spencer. Believing the death to be related to a false insurance claim, the detective solves the case after finding the bodies of two children who had also been killed by the suspect. *The Death Card* (1945) was published by Pillar, a Dublin publisher which released numerous popular novels in the mid-1940s, including five works by O'Sullivan. This novel, involving a carnival, a lost child, a palmist (who is also a nightclub singer), and Italian gangsters, maintains the typical features of the writer's fiction, when the Mayor is murdered by his wife's lover after being blackmailed by gangsters who wanted him to lose the election. In *Casket of Death* (1946), Silk is present when a stage magician is killed in what would appear to be an onstage accident. The detective is recruited to find out the truth when it is revealed that the magician was really an undercover FBI agent looking into organised crime in Tower City, and after several suspects are cleared, including an infamous gangster and Silk

---

21  Scaggs, *Crime Fiction*, 77.

himself, the real killer is discovered to be someone who was close to the murdered magician.

In *Death Stalks the Stadium* and *Death on Ice* (both 1946), O'Sullivan has Silk investigate, respectively, the murder of a boxer in the ring and that of a skater at an ice rink. In both cases Silk collaborates with Lieutenant Tracey, providing the insight necessary to solve the case. In the same year, the author published two other works which did not feature the character of Steve Silk, who would not reappear until O'Sullivan's first publication with Werner Laurie some seven years later. *It Could Happen to You* (1946) is a collection of short stories, all of which have in common the central presence of a confidence trickster. Of special interest are the stories with an Irish setting – notably "Light Fingers", "Christmas Charity" and "Monkey Business" – which represent the first fiction with a non-American setting and, as such, anticipate the author's later "Irish" crime novels. The other work was a pulp western, *The Third Horseman* (1946), published in Dublin by the Mellifont Press. All of these early Dublin-published works are interesting, in addition to their texts, for their presentation. While cheap paperback "pulp" hard-boiled novels from both the USA and from other European countries usually featured lurid coloured covers containing scantily dressed women, O'Sullivan's novels were comparatively staid and restrained, a result, it must be supposed, of the censorship in Ireland in the 1940s and 1950s. With the publication of his novels in London from 1953, the covers are more typical of those common in the genre, where the figure of the partially dressed femme fatale in a sexually suggestive pose was typical of the 1950s, "a period during which sex became one of the major ingredients in the paperback boom".[22]

Steve Silk returned in *Nerve-Beat* and *I Die Possessed*, both published in London in 1953 by Werner Laurie. In *Nerve-Beat* Silk celebrates his thirtieth birthday – in the last novel of the series published in 1968 he would be thirty-five – and once again investigates a case related to The Cherry nightclub, although no reference to the previous case involving the same club is made. Longer, and somewhat more sophisticated than his Dublin-published pulp thrillers, *Nerve-Beat* contains all the blackmail

22    Horsley, *Noir Thriller*, 125.

and murder, insurance frauds and political corruption usually found in the Steve Slick novels. Working on a broader canvas, O'Sullivan introduces a young inventor, an Irish maid and a sharp-eyed lawyer in a work in which his erstwhile foil in the Tower City police, Lieutenant Peter Tracey, has been replaced by Lieutenant Paul Talbot, who shares the same initials and most of the characteristic attributes of his predecessor. Talbot also appears in the next Steve Slick novel *I Die Possessed*, narrated posthumously by the murder victim and in which the lieutenant's ex-girlfriend Marion is the main suspect. In *Don't Hang Me Too High* (1954), published in New York, the father of a beautiful femme fatale is murdered at a poolside party. The private detective and the police officer combine their talents to discover the identity of the mysterious blonde killer after, as is almost par for the course in the Slick novels, the private eye is originally considered to be the prime suspect. While the characters in the short, earlier books of the serious were only slightly sketched with basic character traits, the Werner Laurie novels attempt a more consistent and credible characterisation of the main protagonists. Thus in *Don't Hang Me Too High*, Silk and Talbot are seen to share objectives but to differ in methods, and while they "did not like each other, [...] each knew the other's capability and shared a grudging respect".[23]

*Someone Walked Over My Grave* (1954) represents, perhaps, a turning point in the Steve Slick thrillers, in that it takes the private detective to Ireland, revealed to be his ancestral home. This would, with the exception of some of the short stories contained in *It Could Happen to You*, be O'Sullivan's first fictional use of his own country. The novel is narrated in first person by Jimmy, an Irish journalist who had met Steve in the USA, and who now welcomed the private eye, accompanied by his friend Edgar Davis, revealed for the first time to be of Irish birth, to his home in the small town of Drumgoole. Silk is soon drawn into the investigation surrounding the murder of the English owner of the local Big House, Beresford Hall, who had opposed the marriage of his son, Gerald Humbert, to a local girl because of her brother's involvement in the IRA. Although Gerald is the initial suspect, he is not the only one, as his father had many enemies,

23    J. B. O'Sullivan, *Don't Hang Me Too High* (New York: Pocket Books, 1954), 39.

having been a member of the dreaded Black and Tans in the revolutionary period in Ireland. *Someone Walked Over My Grave*, despite its pulp status, contains numerous informed references to Irish history and the changes which had taken place in Irish society in the first half of the twentieth century. Beresford Hall, for example, is the typical Big House which had changed dramatically over the years, having "passed down the scale from one family of the British ascendancy class to another, until now all that remained of it was in the hands of Jonathan Humbert, scrap-metal dealer".[24]

*Someone Walked Over My Grave* is also notable for its portrayal of the Irish police, with a treatment of the Gardaí which is largely sympathetic. The local sergeant, O'Hara, with "a good-humoured ruddy face and a luxurious moustache"[25] who "believed in avoiding trouble and waiting patiently for a pension", may appear to conform to the common stereotype of the rural Guard, but his superior, Superintendent George Tubridy, is shown as a competent, intelligent officer with whom Steve Silk shares a mutual respect.[26] Tubridy would later appear in further novels written by O'Sullivan, and in this, his debut, the quiet but assertive, youthful-looking, pipe-smoking Irish detective presents an interesting figure in the world of Irish crime fiction. Silk, who in the novel defines himself as "just a hard-boiled private eye, who locates missing husbands, protects innocent suspects, breaks up blackmail plots – all strictly for cash",[27] is forced to give credit to the efforts of the Irish police who, he admits, are "a pretty smart lot".[28] In *The Stuffed Man* (1955), Silk is still in Ireland, having, he claims, left the USA and the "gumshoe business" a year before.[29] He receives a request from a female acquaintance to help her husband, who has been dismissed from his job after being robbed in a raid on the GPO for which he was considered to be a suspect. Using his new friendship with George Tubridy, known by the nickname of "Bruno the boy detective" because of

24    J. B. O'Sullivan, *Someone Walked Over My Grave* (London: Werner Laurie, 1954), 24.
25    Ibid., 36.
26    Ibid., 39.
27    Ibid., 17.
28    Ibid., 88.
29    J. B. O'Sullivan, *The Stuffed Man* (London: Werner Laurie, 1955), 22.

his youth and boyish looks, Steve investigates the case, uncovering a fraud scheme which organised payroll robberies like the one in which the innocent husband had been involved.

*The Long Spoon* (1956), *The Death Seat* (1957), *Raid* (1958) and *Choke Chain* (1958) find Steve Slick back in his home town of Tower City. The first of these is a topical Cold War thriller involving the FBI, Italian mobsters and a "red ring" of communist supporters, in which Silk, who describes himself as "a trouble-shooter, a man with a conscience" is asked to help save the world from the apparent menace of communism.[30] In *The Death Seat*, Silk helps solve a case of gambling debts, blackmail and attempted murder, where he discovers a world of police corruption and protection schemes. *Raid* and *Choke Chain* both feature cases of kidnapping, blackmail and murder, and in the latter, Steve finds himself in love with the guilty party. Between these Steve Silk novels, O'Sullivan also published a stand-alone thriller, *Disordered Death* (1957), featuring American police officer Sergeant Glen Moore, who becomes accidentally involved with the daughter of Nicky Valencia, the most powerful racketeer in the city. Moore is obliged by the gangster to shoot his chief rival, Macardi, but when the police officer shoots the wrong man, he incurs the wrath not only of Valencia but of the whole underworld, including that of police colleagues discovered to be in the pay of the criminals. *Guilt Edged* (1959) is another non-series thriller in which the hapless protagonist is accidentally responsible for the death of the man who has tried to rescue him from drowning in a failed suicide attempt, provoking attempts at extortion by feared gangster Eddie Mocamba.

In *Gate Fever* (1959), Slick is undergoing financial difficulties because of the lack of work received from his habitual source of income, the insurance companies of Tower City, and is forced to leave his usual place of residence, a suite in the luxurious Brenner Hotel. In these circumstances, he agrees to help Danny, a childhood friend who has been wrongfully imprisoned and who wants him to help locate the mysterious Kerry Swanton, aka Kay Wyngard. When Danny is killed after escaping from prison, Steve is suspected of being an accomplice by Lieutenant Vitelli, the police officer in charge of the case and who Silk compares to a Keystone Cop.[31] *Backlash*

---

30   J. B. O'Sullivan, *The Long Spoon* (London: Ward, Lock, 1956), 189.
31   J. B. O'Sullivan, *Gate Fever* (London: Ward, Lock, 1959), 178.

(1960) sees Silk return to Ireland, where once again he is accompanied by his writer friend Jimmy, engaged in the writing of a biography of Roger Casement. The events take place in Lake Lacken, a resort in the Wicklow Mountains owned by Texan oil millionaire Paul Tyrell, where Silk is recuperating from the loss of a lung. Fellow resident Rose Brentwood disappears from the resort, but Steve's erstwhile accomplice Superintendent Tubridy rejects the private detectives offer to help, telling him that they "manage quite nicely without private investigators in this country".[32] When Rose is later discovered to have been murdered, however, it is Silk who gets to the bottom of the complex plot involving local gangster, bootleg poteen and stolen emeralds.

Cold Chisel (1960) is another stand-alone mystery, but its entertaining plot and credible description of criminal and police activity in the Ireland of the late 1950s make it an important contribution to the field of Irish crime fiction. The novel shows a group of professional criminals led by Squad Hogan, a local Dublin gangster, with his two English associates Winthrop and Duke, who plan and execute a payroll heist resulting in the death of O'Halloran, a special branch officer in charge of the safekeeping of the money. The Irish police force is well represented by Detective Garda Sean Brannagan, Inspector O'Rourke and Detective Sergeant Bob Rafferty, all depicted as competent modern guards with access to the efficient resources of the Garda Technical Squad. Cold Chisel is one of the first novels to treat the Irish guards as human beings with a life outside their official function, who worry about promotion and the possibility of depositing a down payment on a "new house in Dundrum".[33] The success of the police investigation into the case is clearly attributed to the cooperation between the various departments of the force and between individual officers, with crucial information being obtained from a junior Tallaght Guard who "would show the smart sergeant from Dublin that the local police had a special function, getting to know the natives and keeping in touch with them".[34]

---

32    J. B. O'Sullivan, *Backlash* (London: Ward, Lock, 1960), 64.
33    J. B. O'Sullivan, *Cold Chisel* (London: Ward, Lock, 1959), 30.
34    Ibid., 166.

*There is One S.O.S.* (1961) is again set in Ireland, and is the third novel to feature Superintendent Tubridy, this time without Steve Slick. Liam Holland, a nine-year-old Dublin boy, is missing from his home and, as Tubridy suspects, the child has been kidnapped as a means of getting hold of the money which the boy's father, Frank Holland, had recently won on the Irish Sweep lottery. Frank is contacted by a man calling himself Vulcan who tells him that he has kidnapped Frank's son and demands money for his safe release. Frank, estranged from Liam's mother, confides in his lover, Jane, who suggests he contact a private investigator. The private detective chosen is one Nick Carroll, an ex-police officer and proprietor of the Carroll Private Enquiry Agency situated just off Dublin's St Stephen's Green. Carroll's agency is manned by the owner himself, assisted by his nephew and a cat, but despite his modest resources, he is able to track down Liam's three captors, an ex-convict, a white-collar thief and the former's girlfriend and, with the help of Tubridy and his officers manage to free the boy.

Nick Carroll, one of Ireland's first fictional private detectives, is also featured in O'Sullivan's next novel *Hue and Cry* (1961). Like O'Sullivan's Irish stand-alone fictions and the previous Tubridy and Carroll novel, this is a better-written work than those of the Steve Silk series, and the author lingers on characterisation, descriptions of atmosphere and subtleties of plot much more than in the earlier novels. *Hue and Cry* follows the life of Dave Nolan, a former IRA volunteer who has just been released from Portlaoise prison after serving a three-year sentence for bank robbery. Disenchanted with his former comrades and feeling remorse for his part in the death of an RUC officer in a cross-border mission, Nolan laments the factors that had led him first to an armed uprising, and later to crime, in words that seem far from the staccato prose of the Silk novels:

> And as the night wore on and he considered Jimmy's plight his anger grew, inflaming his mind with many hatreds. Against so-called friends; against the poverty of his father who had fought to free his country from the British tyrant yoke in the 1916–21 period; against the smug, self-seeking politicians and their "jobs for the boys" policy; against the corruption of public life and the mismanagement of the country's finances – the foreign investment of its capital that should be used at home to reduce unemployment

and emigration, the "peaceful" plantation of Ireland by British capitalists who could buy up the land when it was no longer feasible to conquer it by force.[35]

On his release, Nolan is hunted by his partners-in-crime who believe he has hidden the money taken from the bank, and also by the dangerous gangster Red Crawford whom Nolan had crossed in prison and who now seeks revenge and a share of the missing loot. Nick Carroll participates in the search for this money, and is on hand to save Nolan's life in a confrontation which sees Crawford shot dead – a death which Carroll hides from Nolan in order to spare the ex-convict's conscience. The scarce details of Nick and his assistant Bennie which were afforded in *There is One S.O.S.* are expanded slightly in this, the second novel in which the characters appear. We learn that Carroll had been expelled from the Gardaí for having allegedly extracted confessions by force and that Bennie, his twenty-year-old nephew, had been taken on only after his sister, the boy's mother, had implored to do so, as young Benny Cooke "had failed the Clerical and Executive Officers' examinations for the Civil Service; he had not qualified for a cadetship in the army; and he had not impressed the Dublin Corporation, the E.S.B., the Sugar Company, *Bórd na Móna* or C.I.E. with his talents" and so, "naturally, [...] the only place for him was a private detective agency".[36] Benny, who "looked like one of those unwholesome 'beatniks' that you saw too many of these days in cafés and dance halls" provides intertextual references as he compares his and his uncle's situation to that of American writer Rex Stout's characters Archie Goodwin and Nero Wolfe.[37]

*Double Negative* (1962) is again set in Ireland, and features Superintendent Tubridge, a pipe-smoking Guard detective who, despite the slightly changed name, shares all the main characteristics (and also the assistant, Sergeant Wallace) of George Tubridy. It is an intelligent noir thriller which begins when Harry Meredith, an ambitious and unscrupulous Dublin advertising agent awakes to find a dead woman in his house. Set on marrying Helga, a rich lager heiress, Harry cannot explain how the woman came to be in his house and is unsure whether he is responsible

35   J. B. O'Sullivan, *Hue and Cry* (London: Ward, Lock, 1961), 49–50.
36   Ibid., 92.
37   Ibid., 94.

for her death. When, furthermore, he is blackmailed by a photograph showing himself and the dead woman together, on the night before her death, Harry is considered to be the main suspect. Tubridge, who believes the case to be more complex than first impressions would suggest, investigates and is able to piece together the events which prove Harry's innocence. In *Pick-Up* (1964), Tubridy reverts to his original surname and, with his faithful sidekick, the intuitive Sergeant Wallace, is called in to investigate the murder of a missing woman. The initial suspect, the woman's husband, is having an affair with a young teacher, and, when the murder weapon, a poker, is found in his car, the proof against him seems to be overwhelming. Although the man is found guilty, Tubridy is not happy with the verdict, and his tenacity is revealed to be justified when the real guilty party – the victim's friend's husband with whom she was having an affair – commits suicide, leaving a note confessing to the crime.

*Make My Coffin Big* (1964) heralds the return of Steve Silk in a minor thriller which sees him once again working with – and against – his two police foils, the sympathetic Lieutenant Paul Talbot and the openly hostile Lieutenant Vitelli. Silk falls in love with a girl whose brother is sought by gangsters to whom he owes gambling money. When he is present at the shooting of a man named Winslow in a trailer park, Silk once again becomes the suspect on whom Vitelli tries to pin the murder. *Lunge Wire* (1965) marks O'Sullivan's return to an Irish setting, with Tubridy as the main investigator again, but sharing prominence with Detective-Sergeant Patrick Reilly, whose love of the circus leads to him being present at the death of a trapeze artist, which Tubridy investigates as murder and which brings to light the suspicions, jealousies and secret relationships present in the closed circus community. Although less satisfying than the earlier Tubridy mysteries, *Lunge Wire* again pays significant attention to the role of the An Garda Síochána as a modern, functioning police force, which is shown to combine the individual brilliance of detectives like George Tubridy with technological innovation and "sheer, dogged, foot-slogging, hard work".[38]

O'Sullivan's final novel would be, quite fittingly, perhaps, a Steve Silk novel set in Ireland, and with the collaboration of Superintendent

---

38    J. B. O'Sullivan, *Lunge Wire* (London: Ward, Lock, 1965), 53.

Tubridy and his faithful assistant, Sergeant Wallace. *Murder Proof* (1968) sees Silk, once again in financial difficulties, accepting the job of bodyguard to Richmond, an American millionaire visiting Ireland with his daughter. The plot, with counterfeit money being circulated and the false identity of Richmond – in fact, a convicted bank robber – and his daughter, is typical of O'Sullivan, although the Ireland depicted in the novel has lost much of the innocence it had when the fictional private investigator first visited the country in 1954. Tubridy laments that there is an "alarming increase of narcotics in Dublin"[39] and the superintendent – who "Richmond" believes to be "a kind of police janitor"[40] – has difficulty in sharing his modern views of policing with some of his more recalcitrant colleagues who defend the use of "a few good old-fashioned hidings"[41] against Tubridy's belief that "a police force that is feared, but not respected is a fragile instrument of justice".[42]

The Dublin Catholic Truth Society, which had been responsible for the publication of J. B. O'Sullivan's first novel in 1945, also published *Frances McBride's Death in the Cathedral* (1946). The copy held in the National Library in Kildare Street contains no biographical information, and only the name and place of publication suggest the writer is Irish. Set in the fictional factory town of Greenvale in what may be Ireland or the UK, a body is discovered in the boys' vestry of the Catholic cathedral of Saint Margaret's and the crime is investigated by Detective Inspector Jim Fleming. The last words of the victim claiming that no one but he, the victim, was to blame for his death, complicates the case for Fleming, who eventually respects the secret of confession and destroys his report, effectively privileging the religious concepts of remorse, guilt and divine justice over the terrestrial system of law. McBride's work is interesting in that it brings to crime fiction the moral and theological arguments of the staunch and often fundamentalist Catholicism which characterised the De Valera years and which is of such prominence in other aspects of life in Ireland during the middle decades of the twentieth century.

39    J. B. O'Sullivan, *Murder Proof* (London: Ward, Lock, 1968), 46.
40    Ibid., 61.
41    Ibid., 79.
42    Ibid., 80.

*Brian Moore* (1921–99), the talented Belfast novelist, published several crime novels under his own name and the pseudonyms Bernard Mara and Michael Bryan before producing the novels which would make him famous. Taking advantage of the post-war paperback original boom, Moore published two hard-boiled novels for Harlequin in 1951. Moore called his pulp works "poor clones of Chandler and Dashiel Hammett" and admitted to personally hating detective stories,[43] although his biographer Patricia Craig is of the opinion that the seven potboilers he wrote "were all perfectly efficient and enjoyable exercises in production-line intrigue".[44] Written for purely financial reasons, these early works led to Moore being offered membership of the association of Mystery Writers of America, an invitation he declined.[45]

Both *Wreath for a Redhead* (also issued as *Sailor's Leave*) and *The Executioners* (1957) are set in Canada and bear little of the stamp which Moore's later novels would show. *Wreath for a Redhead* is standard post-war pulp, with John Riordan, a "prairie sailor" from Saskatchewan, who meets Joan Mansfield, "a redhead, tall and with a beautiful build" on a train travelling to Montreal.[46] After they sleep together at her suggestion, she disappears from a French restaurant leaving behind her address book. She returns for the book, but, shortly after, he reads in the newspaper that she has died and that he, Riordan, is being sought by the police as the main suspect. Posing as a private detective he investigates, uncovering a gang running illegal ventures and blackmail operations across Canada. One of the victims of blackmail is Simone Portier, a "mongrel" who is half-Irish and half-French, and with whom Riordan falls in love.[47] In *The Executioners*, Mike Farrell sees a confidence artist tricking a man and stops them before they can rob their victim. Their victim is Tomas Wasky, an important European political figure who offers Mike the job as his bodyguard. Wasky's daughter Janina is kidnapped by Suvarov, an agent of the NKVD, the Soviet law-enforcement agency, who tortures her to obtain information

43 Patricia Craig, *Brian Moore: A Biography* (London: Bloomsbury, 2002), 114–115.
44 Ibid., 116.
45 Ibid., 139.
46 Brian Moore, *Wreath for a Redhead* (Toronto: Harlequin, 1951), 7.
47 Ibid., 80.

about her father's involvement in the Polish resistance. Naturally, Mike saves her, and Suvarov is killed, and the two marry after the safe escape of the surviving members of the resistance.

*French for Murder* (1954), was published under the Bernard Mara pseudonym, a name he had chosen "because it could be easily pronounced in any language", and is set in Paris.[48] The story is narrated by Noah Cain, an American ex-serviceman who accidentally discovers the body of a murder victim in a hotel. The woman who is beside the corpse claims that the man is her husband and that his death has been suicide. When Cain sees that she is concealing a large amount of money, the woman knocks him out and escapes. Immediately being cast in the role of a suspect by the Paris police, Cain sets out to find the woman, who he discovers to be Stella Webster, the wayward daughter of wealthy Americans, in a pursuit that takes him through the districts of the French capital and down south as far as Marseilles. In Provence, he finds not only Stella, but also a conspiracy involving Polish and Hungarian intelligence working in conjunction with the French underworld to smuggle nuclear components out of the country. *A Bullet for My Lady* (1955), again written under the name of Bernard Mara, is set largely in Spain. Joshua Camp arrives in Barcelona to meet his friend, like him, a former pilot, only to be told by Nina Fontana that he has died after falling from a hotel balcony. Unconvinced by this account of his friend's death, Cain decides to investigate and becomes involved in a fantastic plan to find the coffin of a cardinal who had been buried centuries before wearing vestments inlaid with jewels. The novel, much of which Moore wrote while living in Spain, contains numerous clichés about the country, including the "shabbily-dressed, heavily-armed civil guards" with a *frontón*, bull-fighters and their *peones*.[49] *This Gun for Gloria* (1956) is the final work published under the Mara name. Mitchell Cannon, a failed freelance reporter living on the Left Bank in Paris after an acrimonious divorce, is contacted by an American woman seeking her missing daughter. After initially refusing, Cannon accepts the task and searches Paris for the girl while he himself is tailed by North Africans and the corrupt police officer Inspector Git. Cannon eventually finds Gloria in Versailles, about to get married and victim

---

48  Craig, *Brian Moore*, 116.
49  Bernard Mara, *A Bullet for My Lady* (New York: Fawcett Gold Medal, 1955), 6.

of a drug trafficking ring in which she has been involved. The main strengths of the work, however, lie in the portrayal of cosmopolitan Paris with its Arab, Senegalese, German and rich American ex-patriots mixing with the locals in a world of drugs, prostitution and hedonism.

The publication of *Judith Hearne* in 1955 (re-published as *The Lonely Passion of Judith Hearne* the following year) saw the start of Moore's career as a successful "mainstream" novelist, but continuing financial problems led him to continue publishing pulp thrillers over the next two years. *Intent to Kill* (1956) is the first of two novels published under the name of Michael Bryan. Set once again in Montreal, the novel focusses on an attempt by subversives to kill South African President Menda who is undergoing an operation in the Canadian city. When they kill the wrong man, Dr McLaurin investigates the case and, despite the initial protests of his superior, MacNeill, he realises that this has been an attempt to murder the foreign politician, and the police are called in. One of the plotters, Flores, the South African ambassador, is having an affair with Menda's wife, but he kills her when she learns of her lover's involvement in the attempted coup. Another of the gang captures McLaurin and his lover, Nancy, a hospital resident, but the doctor, wounded by a bullet from Milo, the hitman, manages to escape and go after the conspirators. At the novel's end, both McLaurin and Sergeant O'Brien of the Mounted Police are invited by Menda to live in South Africa. The second Bryan novel is *Murder in Majorca* (1958), set on the Balearic island, scarcely recognisable and shown in less than flattering terms. The taxi that takes the hero, American magazine photographer Greg Fall is a "motor museum piece",[50] the hotel "looked like a flea trap"[51] and the island itself is "filthy with colourful characters"[52] and included the homosexuals who "had their own uniform: sandals, tight jeans and silk blouse" and "moved in chattering groups from café to café, stopping to gossip and giggle with others of their number".[53] The storyline is, despite there being no murder, of sufficient interest to keep the reader entertained. The novel shows an early use of the concept of the mule – in this case, students or tourists who wanted a free flight home – smuggling jewels, and the characters,

---

50   Michael Bryan, *Murder in Majorca* (London: Eyre & Spottiswoode, 1958), 8.
51   Ibid., 9.
52   Ibid., 42.
53   Ibid., 37.

especially Freitag, the sinister former Waffen SS officer, are in general more rounded than in the earlier thrillers.

After *Murder in Majorca* Moore's career as a writer of pulp thrillers came to an end as he concentrated on the fiction he really wanted to write. Despite this, however, he showed a continuing respect for good genre writing, lamenting the fact that traditional forms of narrative and genre-based writing had been left in the hands of inferior authors and expressing his desire to reclaim these forms for mainstream literature.[54] In the author's later career, the thriller format is still recognisable in some of his most acclaimed works.

Irish hard-boiled fiction of the 1940s and 1950s made no significant contribution to the genre as a whole, and will generally go uncelebrated in histories of the noir narrative. In an Irish context, however, the works of J. B. O'Sullivan (and to a lesser extent the pulp of Brian Moore in his various guises) are of some importance. They showed a willingness on the part of Irish writers to enter into a transnational dialogue with other writers working within the genre, and gave the Irish reading public a small but nevertheless significant taste of modern crime narratives written by home-grown authors. O'Sullivan's growing use of an Irish setting gave a prominence to the country in crime narratives it had never before enjoyed, and his portrayal of the Irish police as an efficient and competent body helped to shed some of the earlier prejudice which had hampered the genre and its development in Ireland in previous years. That a famed American detective, Steve Slick, could come to Ireland and be able, there, to enlist capable and expert help from the local forces of law and order contributed to giving Irish crime fiction some of the self-confidence it had lacked. Writers like Nigel Fitzgerald, therefore, owe a great debt to J. B. O'Sullivan, and although his works can never be regarded as classics, they did introduce the hard-boiled style to Ireland, and the interest in the hard-boiled would persist, eventually resulting in the re-writing of the hard-boiled by many of the major figures of the wave of Irish crime writers who would emerge in the first two decades of the twenty-first century.

54    Craig, *Brian Moore*, 242.

# CHAPTER 11

# "Not too quiet for crime." Irish Crime Fiction in the Mid-Twentieth Century I

The years of the Second World War were known in Ireland, somewhat enigmatically, as the "Emergency". The Free State's professed – and often questioned – neutrality did little to avoid the economic harshness and a sense of uncertainty which seemed to permeate political life over the period. In the early twenty-first century several writers would use this era as the background for crime and espionage novels, but during the 1940s, references to international affairs were few and far between in works by Irish crime writers. Both Nicholas Blake and Freeman Wills Crofts used the wartime period for some of their works, most particularly the former's *Minute for Murder* (1947), in which detective Nigel Strangeways' wife, Georgia, is killed in the London Blitz, or Crofts' *Enemy Unseen* (1945), where grenades which had been stolen from a Home Guard depot are used to commit murder.

The "Emergency" does appear, however, as a background to the first two of the four crime novels published by *Sheila Pim* (1909–90) between 1945 and 1952. These are of enormous interest to the student of Irish crime fiction, as they present the first example of, although belated, Golden Age crime within an Irish location. While Freeman Wills Crofts and Nicholas Blake both, with the exceptions mentioned, used mainly English settings, Pim locates her narratives within the context of post-independence Ireland. Pim's novels represent, perhaps surprisingly, an important milestone in the history of the genre in Ireland. These unashamedly "cosy" mysteries make use of an Irish setting which, although privileging a somewhat arcane Ascendancy milieu, are among the first Irish crime novels to treat the Garda Síochána as a modern, coordinated and generally competent and efficient police force. Indeed, her final publication in 1952, *Hive of Suspects*, high-lights a thoroughly competent piece of detection in which the city police officers and their country counterparts pool resources to resolve the crime in question.

In *Common or Garden Crime* (1945), Lucy Bex is living with her brother Linnaeus, a crime writer, in the small village of Clonmeen in the early years of the "Emergency". The domestic arrangements have adapted to the abnormal conditions created by the war, where flour is being "illegally sifted to a pre-war whiteness",[1] and the brown "emergency bread was generally unpopular".[2] Lucy and her brother come from an Anglo-Irish family; his son is fighting in the British army and their lives revolve around the small village events such as the annual Flower Show. Lucy seems unaffected by the political and social change which the events of the twenty previous years had brought about in Ireland. Although the Flower Show had previously been little more than "a sideshow at the annual garden fête of the Protestant church",[3] with the new state of affairs people like the Naylors, "well-to-do sociable Roman Catholics",[4] had been asked to join the committee. The friction between the two communities at times comes to the fore. A member of the Protestant community objects to the local TD opening the show, because this would mean that the national anthem, the *Soldiers Song* would be sung. The theft of fruit and vegetables had increased since the outbreak of war, and after the theft of some green figs from one of the gardens, the Gardaí – here the Civic Guards – are called and instructed to "look out for traces of tar on the clothes of the Houlihans or the Slatterys, two neighbouring families who were automatically suspected in any case of this kind".[5] When a newly arrived resident is killed using deadly monkshood root poison, Lucy, as an amateur detective, and the guards, suspect it to be murder.

This is one of the first crime novels in which the Gardaí are involved, and the description of the working of this police force and the reactions to

---

1    Sheila Pim, *Common or Garden Crime* (1945, Boulder, CO: Rue Morgue Press, 2001), 21.
2    Ibid., 26.
3    Ibid., 69.
4    Ibid., 106.
5    Ibid., 29.

their work by the Protestant community are most interesting. One Anglo-Irish resident comments on the supposed inefficiency of the Guards:

> "Needn't expect those fellows to find out anything. All they're fit for is interfering with the likes of you and me. Can't cut a branch without having one of them on the doorstep. Spend their lives getting out forms for this and that. Waste of the taxpayer's money. But as for catching a murderer – why, they can't even catch a little boy stealing fruit. Has your father ever heard who took his fig crop, Wendy? No, nor he won't. Call themselves a police force! Ah, they're not the old R.I.C."[6]

Lucy herself notices that the Guard barracks seems unhomely, with a high turnover of officers, none of whom "had made much of a success of the garden", and she also doubts their efficiency.[7] On visiting the Garda headquarters at Dublin Castle, however, she is more impressed, seeing that they are awaiting a report from the technical bureau and appear to exude efficiency. The main Guard character, Inspector Lancey, is described as being like the "machinery of the law", methodical if impersonal, but he is never given much prominence in the search for the killer.[8] The ending, with the killer sentenced to hang, sees Lucy respectfully singing the *Soldier's Song* at the end of the Flower Show, having listened to the TD's speech in Irish.

In *Creeping Venom* (1946), the "scion of an old Ascendancy dynasty"[9] who had enlisted in the Irish army and taken to calling himself Liam, despite being named after William of Orange, falls in love with and plans to marry a Catholic girl. In the sleepy village of Brainborough, his rich cousin, the 80-year-old Miss Hampton, threatens to cut him out of her will if he goes ahead with his plans. The subsequent death of the old lady places suspicion on Liam, but the case is investigated by Trinity College student Tim Linacre, a distant cousin of Miss Hampton and second in line for the inheritance. Tim is an amateur detective in the mode of Lucy in *Common or Garden Crime*, and like Lucy, his methods of investigation run parallel to those of the Guards. Brainborough is described, "in police jargon, only a one and three village; that is, one sergeant and three guards were the barracks

6    Ibid., 116–117.
7    Ibid., 131.
8    Ibid., 147.
9    Sheila Pim, *Creeping Venom* (1946, Boulder, CO: Rue Morgue Press, 2001), 14.

staff".[10] The local Guard sergeant is "laborious", and he "asked questions twice over and slowly".[11] The village police are aided, however, by an arrival from the Dublin detective branch, Inspector Devlin, who "looked a harmless little man" but was soon believed to be thoroughly professional.[12] Such is his admiration for the Dublin-based detective that Tim decides that he would like to become a Guard, although his mother believes the idea to be "rather morbid".[13] *Creeping Venom* is a well-constructed "cosy" fiction, which employs several Golden Age tropes within a modern Irish context. The declaration that "Once you start suspecting people, there's no end to it. It's like some dreadful creeping venom" gives rise to a number of suspects being placed in the spotlight before being discarded.[14] The author herself communicates with the reader using a footnote in which she states that, as the investigator knew all the relevant facts, the reader should likewise be privy to such information. The ending, in which it is discovered that the death was due to the causes of a natural venom and not murder, also echoes a typical Golden Age trope of surprise.

*A Brush with Death* (1950) is concerned with the histrionic painter Fergus Gandon, who, believing he is being poisoned, goes to stay with his sister in Dublin to recover. The Garda Sochaána again play an interesting role and, although Fergus calls them "great gobdaws" who are always tramp, tramp, tramping off along false trails", they are seen in general terms as a relatively efficient modern police force.[15] The description of criminal life in Dublin is worth citing:

> Dublin cannot be called a very wicked city, as cities go. There is a dearth of ex-public school jewel thieves, beautiful foreign spies, international crooks, sinister Chinamen of the old school, mad inventors of death rays, and much that makes life interesting for the police of other countries. The human side of the work, apart from the perpetual filling up of forms, is mostly concerned with habitual criminals born and bred in the slums who go drifting in and out of jail all their lives without very much

10    Ibid., 51.
11    Ibid., 56.
12    Ibid., 96.
13    Ibid., 58.
14    Ibid., 102.
15    Sheila Pim, *A Brush with Death* (1950, Boulder, CO: Rue Morgue Press, 2001), 26.

option, unemployables to whom no more respectable form of existence is open. Improvements in housing, education, the penal system and the probation system may reduce their numbers, but can hardly completely rid society of its inevitable substratum. Experience, for a detective, largely consists in getting to know the criminal classes and all their relations. Between the Civic Guards and the habitual criminal it is all very much in the family. Mere ordinary householders who get robbed are only of minor, incidental importance.[16]

*A Brush with Death*, unlike the two preceding novels, contains several tongue-in-cheek comments on the new Ireland of the late 1940s. The novel is set in one of the "old big houses, in which, as may be gathered from many novels and plays about Ireland, everybody except the peasantry at one time used to live".[17] This is in contrast to the new "modern labour-saving villas in garden suburbs in which the whole population will be housed in a few years' time".[18] The guards stationed in the village "made an odd pair".[19] One of these, Nolan, was "the big St. Bernard dog type of Guard, all patience and caution", while the other, Devlin, had "the strong point for detective work of being one of those people whose appearance it was impossible to remember", and takes out his false teeth when he needs a disguise.[20] As in *Creeping Venom*, no murder is actually committed, although in *A Brush with Death* homicide is at least attempted, and here also Pim encourages the reader to guess the outcome of the investigations.

In Pim's next and final novel, *A Hive of Suspects* (1952), a local entrepreneur, whose hobby is beekeeping, dies after eating honey from his own hives. Although other local beekeepers believe that bees have been feeding on poisonous plants, the Guards are suspicious and uncover various motives for murder. In this final novel, the Gardaí assume the full weight of the investigations, with important differences being stressed between the rural and urban arms of the force. Dublin-based Inspector Grace is smart and

16    Ibid., 45.
17    Ibid., 7.
18    Ibid.
19    Ibid., 71.
20    Ibid.

effective, "in contrast to the thin, grey, shabby country Superintendent"[21] and the overall view is of quiet efficiency:

> All major crime in Ireland is transferred to the Detective Branch in Dublin. There are detectives attached to county districts who investigate the ordinary run of petty offences, but important investigations require trained men, searchers, photographers, fingerprint experts, with the backing of laboratories and records. Colonel Tunney said he would try to get a good man sent down in time for the inquest and would also ask the Branch to produce an expert on honey toxins.[22]

*A Hive of Suspects* is, in many respects, a more modern work than the other three of Pim's novels, in that it introduces the studied use of forensics and scientific analysis of evidence, "a pet subject of Grace's".[23] For the detective:

> "Even negative evidence is something. To my mind, it's detail that counts. If you don't find what you're looking for you may stumble on something else. Time and time again I've known that to happen. A chemical stain on a piece of cloth, or a piece of dust from a trouser turn-up – things like that can hang a man."[24]

The four Sheila Pim novels mark a significant development within the field of Irish crime fiction. Although rooted in the somewhat unreal world of an anachronistic Protestant Anglo-Irish community, they show crimes being committed (or not, as is the case of one of the four novels) in Ireland and being resolved, by Irish detectives.

*Eilis Dillon* (1920–94) wrote three crime novels between 1953 and 1956. These deal, like the work of Sheila Pim, with crime in an Irish setting. They are notable for, among other virtues, their portrayal of the Gardaí, and especially the contrast between modern officers such as Mike Kenny in *Death at Crane's Court* (1953) and *Death in the Quadrangle* (1956) and Inspector Pat Henley in *Sent to His Account* (1954) and the more traditional "culchie" Guards such as Sergeants MacDonagh, Lawler and McCarthy in *Death at Crane's Court*, *Sent to His Account* and *Death in the Quadrangle*

---

21    Sheila Pim, *A Hive of Suspects* (1952, Boulder, CO: Rue Morgue Press, 2001), 58.
22    Ibid., 42.
23    Ibid., 59.
24    Ibid.

respectively. *Death at Crane's Court* is set in the eponymous hotel near Galway, where the new owner, John Burden, has made enemies of many of the guests and staff. When Burden is murdered, the Gardaí are called in to investigate. The detectives are the urbane Mike Kenny, "a Galwayman, born and bred" who "had a deep understanding of his people, which up to now, he believed, was the reason for his success as a detective",[25] and Sergeant McDonagh, who is from the Aran Islands and "has led a very sheltered life".[26] The guests at the hotel are among the suspects, and seem like stock characters from a typical Golden Age novel. They include George Arrow, a wealthy bachelor who has retired to the hotel on medical advice, Major Dunlea, Colonel Waters and Professor Daly, while other suspects are Barbara Henry, the niece of Crane Court's previous owner who stands to inherit the property, and Eleanor Keane, the manageress. The denouement, however, shifts culpability away from the hotel's residents and staff, and onto the more convenient relationship of the victim with criminal activity in Dublin.

*Death in Crane's Court* is interesting for its portrayal of the two police officers, its perceptive analysis of social class and its defence of the Irish language. The plot is adroitly managed by the author, herself an Irish speaker and author of numerous non-genre works in both Irish and English. *Sent to His Account* (1954) introduces a different pair of police officers, while maintaining a similar contrast between them: Inspector Pat Henley, Dublin-born, efficient and diligent, and Sergeant Lawlor who was noted for his impartial attitude. For this latter "a farm labourer with an unlit bicycle and a drunken gentleman driving home from a hunt ball were simply two bipeds breaking the law".[27] Miles de Cogan is a Dublin bookkeeper who inherits a lavish estate in County Wicklow on the death of his cousin, a baronet. Miles has several radical ideas which he wants to put into effect on the estate, including the conversion of the flour mill into a cooperative. His ideas are welcomed by the local populace, one neighbour, Tom Reid, is planning to build on the estate, which infuriates the other villagers. When

---

25   Eilis Dillon, *Death at Crane's Court* (1953, Boulder, CO: Rue Morgue Press, 2009), 69.
26   Ibid., 63.
27   Eilis Dillon, *Sent to His Account* (1954, Boulder, CO: Rue Morgue Press, 2009), 95.

Reid is murdered, the investigation unveils the hidden secrets which lie beneath the surface of the apparently idyllic rural community.

In *Death in the Quadrangle* (1956), Mike Kenny is reintroduced in a case which takes him to the fictional King's University in Dublin to investigate the murder of the college president. Professor Daly, one of the residents at Crane's Court in the previous novel, is asked to deliver a series of lectures at his old university where the atmosphere is tense, a result mainly of the unpopular regime installed by the new college president, Professor Bradley, who, he is told, has been receiving threatening mail. When Bradley is murdered, Daly asks for help from his old friend Kenny to investigate the killing and to decide which, of all the many suspects on the campus, is responsible for the president's death. The university atmosphere is skilfully created and Dillon, whose father was a professor of chemistry at University College Galway and whose husband at the time of writing *Death in the Quadrangle* was professor of Irish at University College Cork, uses her inside knowledge well. These three crime novels form only a small part of Dillon's output, and she was known as a respected writer of non-fiction works, historical novels and stories for young readers in both English and Irish. Her maternal grandfather was Joseph Mary Plunkett, one of the seven signatories of the Proclamation of the Irish Republic who was executed at Kilmainham Gaol after the Easter Rising of 1916, and her daughter is the famed Irish poet Eiléan Ní Chuilleanáin. Her son Cormac Ó Cuilleanáin is a professor at Trinity College, Dublin, and as Cormac Millar has written two crime novels, including *The Grounds* (2006), set like *Death in the Quadrangle* in King's College, Dublin, and which enters into a fascinating extemporal dialogue with his late mother's work

*L. A. G. Strong* (1896–1958), born in Plymouth, England, of Irish parents, was a highly prolific writer who produced a series of detective novels in the 1940s and 1950s. Strong, who had taught at Summer Fields Preparatory School along with C. Day-Lewis (Nicholas Blake) and was a friend of W. B. Yeats, published the collection of linked short stories *Odd Man In* in 1938. These stories featured Peter Black, a graduate who has had numerous jobs after leaving Cambridge. Given work in a strange City office, Peter realises he is actually being used as a "fence" and helps the police to end the scheme, after which a police officer recommends he enrol in Police

College. The subsequent stories have Peter as a police detective who uses his university education to help resolve several cases, helped by his friend, the reporter Jimmy Garstin.

*Slocombe Dies* (1942), Strong's first crime novel, looks at a murder from an unusual point of view. Two friends, Everard Wilson, a crime writer, and John Matthews, a police officer, discover a possible murder scene. With no obvious reasons, Matthews challenges Wilson to come up with a feasible explanation, not as to who committed the murder, but to why the murder was committed in the first place. The rest of the novel is dedicated to the narrative the crime writer concocts and reads to his friend. Wilson's story involves a complex love story in which the two rivals, the shell-shocked Captain Slocombe, now teaching at the village school and considering himself to be "a safeguard against Bolshevism" and Charlie Bird, who has returned to the village after studying at the College of Modern Studies in Plymouth, are in love with the same girl.[28] The attempts by Slocombe to discredit Charlie, and the former's death, according to Wilson's narrative, produce the corpse discovered by the two friends at the beginning of the novel. The main strength of this light novel lies in the contrast between Captain Sam Slocombe, a representative of the traditional values held in the village, and Charlie, the returned exile, schooled in modernity. The village canon comments on this, believing that young men like Charlie Bird "get enough town to unsettle them, and make them discontented with home, but not enough to make them leave home".[29]

After this second attempt at crime writing, Strong created, in *All Fall Down* (1944), the detective who would feature in all his subsequent crime novels. Ellis McKay, a cultured Scotland Yard officer, is also a musician who frequently berates his "horrid trade".[30] In his first outing, Ellis investigates the murder of an elderly bibliophile who is found dead under a pile of books.[31] The most interesting feature in this novel is how the detective finally realises that he has been right about the identity of the murderer, but has been completely wrong concerning the motives, thus reversing the

28    L. A. G. Strong, *Slocombe Dies* (London: Collins, 1942), 24.
29    Ibid., 152–153.
30    L. A. G. Strong, *All Fall Down* (New York: Doubleday, Doran & Co., 1944), 97.
31    Ibid., 97.

standard clue-puzzle conventions in which the detective's logical reasoning and subsequent deduction construct the narrative of the crime. *Othello's Occupation* (1945), published in the USA under the title *Murder Plays an Ugly Scene*, has Ellis McKay investigating a murder in the closed atmosphere of a stage school, where the principal has been killed. McKay is described as having "thin reddish hair" and "rubicund face", looking like a "dissatisfied cockatoo",[32] although one of the characters further describes him as a "little fat man".[33] Inspector "Bradders" Bradstreet, McKay's uncouth colleague, who has a thick Devon accent, acts throughout the series as Ellis's foil.

In *Which I Never: A Police Diversion* (1950), Ellis and "Bradders" investigate the disappearance of some missing girls in a novel which features an ex-commando, a wartime Irish spy and an investigation which McKay describes as:

> A muddle from start to finish. I do nothing right. Finally, with no alternative, I blunder on the truth, and have to be hoiked out by an overgrown hobbledehoy who's disobeying his orders. Look at the case! All loose ends. An exhibition of our inefficiency and incompetence.[34]

The self-effacing – and self-critical – Detective Inspector makes his last outing in *Treason in the Egg* (1958), a Cold War thriller in which the Scotland Yard detective is drawn into an elaborate intelligence plot to find secrets from a nearby nuclear plant while lecturing, in a private capacity, on music at a modern art seminary at Armada House in the English countryside. The cast consists of refugee psychologist, secret service operatives, poet, painter, nuclear scientist and rich spinsters, and McKay discovers that the cocaine discovered at the beginning of the novel was simply a ruse to cover the more serious dealing in nuclear secrets. Again the detective's diffidence and apparent blundering is made clear, as Strong has Ellis comment that "I wander along in my own way, step by silly step".[35] *Treason in the Egg*, with its background in the Cold War, saw McKay become involved in the

---

32    L. A. G. Strong, *Othello's Occupation* (London: Collins, 1945), 17.
33    Ibid., 135.
34    L. A. G. Strong, *Which I Never: A Police Diversion* (London: Collins, 1950), 249.
35    L. A. G. Strong, *Treason in the Egg* (London: Collins, 1958), 172.

murky world of espionage, a theme which was becoming increasingly well-liked in popular literature throughout the 1950s, and which would reach a peak in the 1960s when Ian Fleming's James Bond novels were filmed, inspiring numerous imitators.

The fashion for spy fiction would, perhaps surprisingly, be embraced fairly quickly by Irish writers, with Manning O'Brine and John Welcome writing thrillers featuring cases of international espionage. *Manning O'Brine* (1913–74), born in Connemara to Irish and Italian parents, introduced his hero, at times journalist, broadcaster, writer, secret service agent, and private investigator, the flamboyant Michael "The" O'Kelly in *Killers Must Eat* (1951), the first of seven titles published in the 1950s with the same protagonist. All these have The O'Kelly travelling between Italy, Egypt, Syria and other hotspots, with the criminal foil usually being provided by remnants of Nazi organisations now re-finding their feet within the context of the Cold War. True to the spirit of the 1950s' thriller, the novels contain a copious use of beautiful women, drugs and fast cars. In *Killers Must Eat* O'Kelly is in Rome when a group of terrorists attempt to blow up the British Embassy building. With the help of colleague Mario Cercarelli, an American of Italian descent, and Luigi, a friendly taxi driver, Michael, who considers himself to be "a pratie-eating, pig-in-the-parlour, bred-in-the-bog shamus, equally at home in Ireland, England and the USA", sets out to unmask the terrorists.[36] The book, as well as being anti-Nazi, is also virulently anti-German, a trait that would be repeated throughout the writer's career. *Corpse to Cairo* (1952) finds O'Kelly suspected of the murder of two drug dealers on a voyage to Egypt. The men, the Dutchman Leytmans and the Egyptian Basil have been trailed by Hamish Fergusson, an undercover special branch agent who reveals to Michael that the Dutchman had been a Nazi informer in the Second World War and was wanted for jewellery theft, blackmail, drugs and treason. The novel, told by its protagonist in hard-boiled fashion, also presents four *femmes fatales*, two of whom are killed, and a treacherous Englishman, Gerald Wainwright, who awaits the Nazi jewels which Leytman and Basil had been carrying in Cairo.

---

36 Manning O'Brine, *Killers Must Eat* (London: Hammond, Hammond & Co., 1951), 218.

In *Dodos Don't Duck* (1953), also published as *Dead as a Dodo*, O'Kelly is in Mauritius where he comes across a series of unexplained death and is himself left for dead after finding the body of a young woman. After the death of Kilo, a private investigator, O'Kelly takes on the task, discovering a plot which began in Vichy France in 1945 and which was being played out amid drug smuggling and the machinations of former Yugoslavian Nazis and French collaborationists on the island. *Deadly Interlude* (1954) is set in Tangier where O'Kelly is beaten up and robbed and loses his memory. Helped by Heloise, wife of a Portuguese fascist living in the North African city, he is given an Egyptian passport and starts to regain his memory but is then accused of the murder of Reagan Collins, an Irishman who worked for British intelligence. Trying to clear his name, O'Kelly uncovers a web of corrupt police, former Nazis and blackmail. In *Passport to Treason* (1955), Michael is given a job as a private detective in London. Initially commissioned to find a missing Maltese man, his investigations lead to him to Spain as he tries to uncover a spy ring with connections to fascist pretenders from England, Germany, Poland and Spain.

*The Hungry Killer* (1956) finds O'Kelly showing a rich American woman, Helen, and her stepdaughter, Mairhi, around Europe at the behest of their husband and father, Senator Allardyce, a noted American anti-vice campaigner. In Naples, where the girl has persuaded Michael to take her despite being expressly forbidden, they visit a casino where they meet Fortunati, a gangster who has been deported from the USA and who bears a grudge against the senator. After disappearing with Dallapiccola, a cohort of Fortunati's and "a greasy wop with a smooth manner",[37] Mairhi accidentally kills him. She and her mother are kidnapped by Fortunati, but O'Kelly frees them, chasing the Italian to Sicily and then on to Marseilles. At the end of the novel Michael leaves Marseilles for Egypt, and in *Dagger Before Me* (1957), the final O'Kelly thriller, he has become a full-time writer; after the discovery of the body of an American diplomat in an ancient tomb he joins forces with Pia, a beautiful British agent, in the fight against the notorious Lodestone gang, led by the former Nazi officer Krapps.

37   Manning O'Brine, *The Hungry Killer* (London: Hammond, Hammond & Co., 1956), 48.

The later novels *Mills* (1969), *Crambo* (1970) and *No Earth for Foxes* (1974) are all more fitted to the type of thriller being written in the 1950s than the late 1960s and early 1970s. All feature Mills, a British agent who is trying, unsuccessfully, to leave the secret service. We first see him as he travels to San Martino in Italy, a place where, during the war, he had led a partisan raid which had brought about harsh German reprisals. Again, Nazis are central to the plot, and again the underlying chauvinism is most apparent – the works are unfortunately as anti-German as they are anti-fascist. O'Brine's final novel, *Pale Moon Rising* (1978), is a stand-alone thriller featuring Patrice, an Italian war refugee who has been living in Ireland with his Irish grandmother. He is recruited by the SAS, who fly him into France to work with the local resistance groups and train them in sabotage against the occupying forces. He falls in love with Solange, a French woman, but both are betrayed to the Nazis and forced to use their wits and skill to escape in what has become for the Italian "a private vengeance".[38] The narrator claims that the "anti-Nazi German is a myth that will not become a reality until defeat",[39] while the language of the occupying forces is described as the "Neandethral noises that pass for the German language".[40]

John Needham Huggard Brennan (1914–2010) wrote several novels under the pseudonym of *John Welcome*. As longstanding chairman of Wexford Racecourse and a senior National Hunt Steeplechase Steward, Welcome's novels are primarily concerned with the world of horse racing. After a non-crime debut, *Red Coats Galloping* (1949), Welcome produced a series of thrillers featuring Simon Herald, an amateur racing driver, and Richard Graham, who, in *Run for Cover* (1958), is introduced as an amateur steeple-chaser who had been "a moderately successful gentleman rider".[41] In this initial thriller, Graham searches for Rupert Rawle, his wartime comrade and erstwhile rival, who some years after his apparent death, publishes his memoirs. The search takes the amateur jockey to the south of France where he uncovers Soviet involvement in the mystery. *Stop at*

38    Manning O'Brine, *Pale Moon Rising* (London: Futura, 1978), 190.
39    Ibid., 139.
40    Ibid., 191.
41    John Welcome, *Run for Cover* (New York: Harper and Row, 1958), 70.

*Nothing* (1959) introduces Herald who, at the age of forty, is residing in Ireland to avoid taxes and is living a degenerate lifestyle which includes "Benzedrine for breakfast".[42] Like *Run for Cover*, much of the action takes place in Provence where Herald, helping the young jockey Roddy Marston, is a guest of the millionaire Mantovelli who, it transpires, is involved in the production and use of a formula for hormone treatment in racehorses, which he intends to use to help him win the derby.

   *Wanted for Killing* (1965) sees the pairing of two of Welcome's heroes, Richard Graham and Simon Herald. Graham is in Corsica visiting Herald and his wife, Roddy's sister, Sue, when he becomes involved in stopping a coup against French President De Gaul, which is being planned by a group of false Legionnaires and angry veterans of the Algerian war. Both Herald and Graham are accused by Manahan, a shady lawyer, of being anachronistic amateurs and, at the end of the novel Graham, influenced by the British secret service chief Sir William Bellamy, decides to become a professional agent. *On the Stretch* (1969), is narrated in the first person by Graham, now a member of the "doubtful and discredited trade" of the secret service. He has been trailing Sam Hanaker, a Yorkshire millionaire and arms manufacturer who British intelligence are maintaining under vigilance and, having won his way into the Yorkshireman's confidence, Graham has been entrusted to look after his racing interests in Ireland, paying attention to the machinations of Arthur Ravidge who, Hanaker believes, wants to disable his prize racehorse, Rollo. In Ireland, at Tigerstown racecourse and in Dublin, amid the remnants of the Ascendancy and the mysterious German neighbours, Herr Meller and his nephew Herr Manfred Kruntze, Graham discovers a conspiracy to steal the plans for a secret missile which would potentially jeopardise world peace.

   In *Hell Is Where You Find It* (1970), Richard is almost bankrupt after losing heavily on the stock market. He decides to return to racing, although he still works secretly for Sir William Bellamy's Brigade, described as a secret, almost private army within the British secret service. When Bellamy's friend and colleague Giles Bryson is killed, Bellamy asks Graham to investigate the death and the victim's circle of acquaintance. Richard

---

42   John Welcome, *Stop at Nothing* (New York: Harper and Row, 1959), 104.

follows one of Bryson's colleagues, Derek Marley, to Paris where he sees him make contact with Manahan, the deceitful lawyer from *Wanted for Killing* shortly before being killed under the Paris metro. With Marley's daughter Virginia, who Graham eventually discovers is also working for Bellamy, and his jockey friend Roddy Marston, the secret agent follows the leads to the south of France where the full story of treachery, double agents and murder is unveiled. In *Go for Broke* (1972) Graham, who is working as a freelance racing journalist as well as continuing to be in the pay of the British secret service, finds himself hounded by Eric Vaughn, a millionaire who seems determined to destroy him at any cost without any apparent reason. In this, the last of the Richard Graham novels, the secret agent is once again in Ireland where he is framed by Vaughn, who accuses him of cheating at cards, of using marijuana and of being involved in rape, and who, it appears, will not stop until he has finished with the former jockey and spy.

Bellary Bay (1979) and *A Call to Arms* (1985) are historical novels which trace the life of an Anglo-Irish family involved in the world of horses through the twentieth century from the time of the First World War and the Black and Tan War in Ireland to life in colonial Africa. With *A Painted Devil* (1988) Welcome returns to the thriller, with a horse racing setting that finds Mike Ashley, a young solicitor and amateur rider who is sent by his law firm to evaluate the claims made by two cousins – Sonia, a trained horse instructor, and Piers – over a series of sporting paintings valued in millions of pounds. When Sonia disappears, Ashley, whose only experience has been in "several leg-work, semi-investigative jobs",[43] sets out to find her, and, drugged by a suspicious foreigner and confused by the appearance of a dwarf who apparently bears proof to a family curse, he is finally capable of seeing the way he has been manipulated by his own company and why this has been done.

In *Reasons of Hate* (1990) Charles Hampton, who has been rearing horses in the area of the Persian Gulf, returns to Ireland when his cousin Jo tells him of the murder of her father, his guardian. Although the death is originally believed to have been part of an aborted IRA arms raid led by

43    John Welcome, *A Painted Devil* (London: Collins, 1988), 10.

Francis O'Shaughnessy, a bloodstock agent and republican volunteer with a historical grudge against Manners, Charles discovers that the murder has its roots in events which had happened in France during the Second World War when the murdered man had worked for special operations and where Amory Brayne, a millionaire chemist and horse breeder, had betrayed friends from the French resistance. *Royal Stakes* (1993) is a historical mystery featuring Danny de Lacey, a gentleman horse racer in the 1920s, whose father, a trainer, suffers a stroke after being investigated for the alleged doping of a horse. In his attempt to clear the old man's name, de Lacey stumbles upon a plot to assassinate the then Prince of Wales before going on to win the Grand National.

Interestingly, perhaps, Welcome incorporates in his fiction two of the main tendencies that would predominate in Irish crime fiction during the 1960s and early 1970s; that is, on the one hand, the introduction of international glamour against a background of espionage, and, on the other, a renewed interest in Irish settings.

# CHAPTER 12

# "The law after all is just a machine that suspects everyone on general principles." Irish Crime Fiction in the Mid-Twentieth Century II

Edward Plunkett, 18th Baron of Dunsany (1878–1957), who published under the name of *Lord Dunsany*, is best known as an author of fantasy tales, club tales and as a playwright. Dunsany, who had started writing under the influence of the Irish Revival, was born in England, but lived most of his life in his ancestral residence in Castle Dunsany, County Meath. His contribution to crime fiction is mainly apparent in his volume of short stories *The Little Tales of Smethers and Other Stories* (1952), which is a fascinating collection of old-school detective fiction influenced as much by the late nineteenth-century short crime story as by the Golden Age. The first part of the volume is dedicated to a series of tales narrated by Smethers, a travelling salesman for a brand of relish, and unlikely amateur detective. Smethers shares an apartment with Linley, an "Oxford man" whose favourite occupation is the solving of puzzles and who claims that "There's not the mystery in ten murders that there is in one game of chess".[1]

In the first story in the collection, "The Two Bottles of Relish", the amateur sleuth concludes that the evil Steeger, Linley's nemesis in several of the stories, has murdered his wife because he has bought two bottles of relish, making it obvious that he wanted to eat her. Dunsany's crime stories are generally "thinly-disguised parodies of the genre", and these parodies are given particular strength by the impassive and prosaic voice of Smethers, the narrator.[2] Linley and Smethers, an improbable Holmes

---

1   Lord Dunsany, *The Little Tales of Smethers and Other Stories* (London: Jarrolds, 1952), 10.

2   S. T. Joshi, *Lord Dunsany: Master of the Anglo-Irish Imagination* (Westport, CT: Greenwood Press, 1995), 159.

and Watson, face their own Moriarty, Steeger, in all of the tales, and the evil antagonist manages to outwit them until he is captured and hanged in "Once Too Often", the last of the four stories narrated by Smethers. These stories also see the participation – and death – of an inept police officer, the aptly named Constable Slugger. The means of solving the mysteries is similar in all four stories, and Linley's investigation is purely intellectual. An apparently insolvable crime is resolved when a murder is discovered to have been committed using a bullet made of ice, and in "Kriegblut's Disease" an apparently invisible spy is discovered when the amateur sleuths uncover the enemy agent, Steeger, who has disguised himself as a "stage spy", a stereotypical German so obvious to come initially under no suspicion.

The non-Smethers stories are also of considerable interest. In "An Alleged Murder", the narrator relates the entries from a diary written by a girl who is in love with a murderer; in "The Waiter's Story" we hear how a man is murdered by being bought too much alcohol; and in "The Speech" a group, believing that an impending speech by an MP may provoke a future war, successfully prevents him from delivering the speech by killing the politician's father, a peer, thus giving the MP automatic promotion to the House of Lords and, therefore, becoming ineligible to speak in the House of Commons. Despite these somewhat outmoded plot devices, there are also hints at modernity. In "A Victim of Bad Luck" the robbers are caught thanks to electric signals emitted by the radio, and in "The New Master" a robotic chess machine becomes jealous of its owner's growing relationship with his radio, and kills him. In "The Pirate of the Round Pond" there is a hint at paedophilia, when as the young schoolboy narrator playing with model boats on a park pond notices "one or two men mopping their faces with white handkerchiefs and making funny little signs".[3]

The final stories in the volume are narrated by Ripley, a retired detective who reminisces on old cases in which he has been involved. In "Among the Bean Rows" he infiltrates a Russian revolutionary gang operating from the British Museum, while in "Murder by Lightning" he explains how a sabotaged lightning conductor had been used as a murder weapon in a case he had solved as a young detective.

---

3    Dunsany, *Little Tales*, 118.

Writing under his *Flann O'Brien* pseudonym, Brian O'Nolan (1911–66) wrote *The Third Policeman* between 1939 and 1940, although the work would not see publication until 1967, a year after the writer's death. In what might arguably be the world's first "metaphysical" crime novel, O'Brien introduces a nameless, one-legged narrator, who is obsessed with the works of scientist and philosopher De Selby, to which he has dedicated his life. When he wants to publish his findings, he is encouraged by his friend, Divney, to murder Mathers, a rich farmer in the rural Irish townland in which the action is set. After Divney hits Mathers with a bicycle pump, the narrator kills him with a spade, allowing his friend to escape with the victim's cash box. Divney, however, refuses to either give the narrator the money or to reveal the whereabouts of the box, and the narrator sets out on a quest to find this. During his search he finds himself conversing with the murder victim, with his own soul – who he calls Joe – and visiting a strange police barracks manned by Sergeant Pluck and Policeman McCruikseen, apparently suffering from a bicycle obsession, and the mysterious Fox, the nocturnal third policeman of the title. The surprising ending, significantly, owes much to the mystery genre which the whole nature of the narrative simultaneously rejects and embraces. For John Connolly, *The Third Policeman* is one of the few works of genre fiction which draws on the Irish fantasy tradition, in what he describes as "essentially an anti-rationalist crime novel" that manipulates genre conventions.[4] Terence Browne sees the work as a "grim tale of crime and punishment in a hell that is indistinguishable from the Irish Midlands at their most stultifying",[5] where the narrative shifts from "curiously deadpan prose" of hard-boiled crime fiction to the gloom of the gothic.[6]

*Nigel Fitzgerald* (1906–81), whose first novel, *Midsummer Malice*, was published in 1953, is a highly original author who adopts with swaggering

4    John Connolly, "No Blacks, No Dogs, No Crime Writers: Ireland and the Mystery" in *Down These Green Streets: Irish Crime Writing in the 21st Century*, ed. Declan Burke (Dublin: Liberties, 2011), 54.

5    Terence Brown, "Two Post-Modern Novelists: Samuel Beckett and Flann O'Brien" in *The Cambridge Companion to the Irish Novel*, ed. John Wilson Foster (Cambridge: Cambridge University Press, 2006), 216.

6    Ibid., 218.

disdain a variety of the possibilities open to the genre in the period. He makes use of an Irish setting in which crimes are committed and solved, but at the same time embraces the contradictions which lie between the cosy post-Golden Age and the sexually frank and geographically unlimited cosmopolitanism of the new thriller. Hence Fitzgerald's novels work within the same neo-Big House framework used by Sheila Pim, and to some extent Eilis Dillon, while introducing the fast cars, promiscuous *femmes fatales* and Martini cocktails of Manning O'Brine, John Welcome and the various incarnations of the pulp version of Brian Moore.

Fitzgerald's main protagonist, Superintendent Duffy, continues in the new tradition of enlightened, efficient guards, although he is aided in at times by the effusive and cosmopolitan actor/director Alan Russell. Indeed, the world of the stage and film features regularly in Fitzgerald's works, reflecting the author's own involvement as a professional actor in several films and television series. The novels, apart from *This Won't Hurt You* (1959), which is set in London, are largely located in Ireland, mostly in the remote West. The conflict in Fitgerald's fiction is one between the self-aware artificiality of the "natives" – generally an odd mixture of Anglo-Irish aristocrats, middle-class professional Catholics and unremorseful, if at times irascible, peasants – and the perceived threat of outsiders. Thus, in *Midsummer Malice* (1953), the tranquillity of Cahirmore and the Ascendancy gothic of Castle Talbot are destroyed by the murders of two young women. One is the daughter of an English baronet, and the other a seemingly promiscuous member of a troupe of touring actors. *The Rosy Pastor* (1954) again highlights the effects on a local community of the arrival of an outsider, in this case, the "Yank", Denis O'Rourke. Alan Russell, in *Midsummer Madness*, one of the suspect thespians, here provides an unlikely but surprisingly efficient foil to Superintendent Duffy, being at once of "the gentry" but also providing a refreshingly logical mind.[7]

*The House is Falling* (1955) represents, perhaps, the essence of his fiction in this period, containing as it does his favoured themes of degenerate Big House, returned outsider/insider, the intrusion of modernity on the perceived antiquity of the West of Ireland and, of course, murder. Hugh

7    Nigel Fitzgerald, *The Rosy Pastor* (London: Collins, 1954), 67.

Barry returns from his self-imposed exile in England to the home of his childhood many years after being wrongfully disinherited in favour of the crippled "Argentinian-Irish" Oliver Cliffe-Barry and his beautiful wife, Carol. The house of the title is a gothic monstrosity which, at the time of Hugh's return is also inhabited by his strange aunt, Veronica, the stunningly sexual Consuelo, the degenerate Vaughn and the unlikely Brigadier Poodle, while nearby lives the eccentric Professor Lake and his beautiful niece Hilary. The Professor writes detective fiction under the pseudonym of Simon Strang, featuring the nymphomaniac investigator Dahlia Delancey.

*The House Is Falling* is set during a race-week, so the suspicious death of Carol Cliffe-Barry who falls down the elaborate staircase of the house her husband has, according to some of the residents, unlawfully inherited, is seen as a crime which brings to light the secrets of a past which some had hoped to bury. The novel is particularly interesting, however, in that it provides a fascinating view of Irish crime fiction in the mid-1950s. The Irish setting, the fascination with the past, the international ramifications and the position and actions of the investigating officers, together with the attempted representation of a cross-section of contemporary Irish society lend to the novel the sensation that it has been lost in time, at a period when the Irish crime novel struggled to search for its own identity.

Hugh Barry, for example, as the returned exile, is representative of a concurrent figure in many types of Irish fiction, not just, of course, the crime novel. More specifically, in Fitzgerald's work, he is the continuation of characters like Denis O'Rourke and the foregoer of the likes of Benedict Carey, Standish Wyse and Hector O'Brien Moore. It is not, perhaps, surprising to note that the novel contains many of the clichés of Ascendancy fiction. The retired army man, Brigadier Poodle is a jingoist defendant of the values of Empire, who still talks of the "wogs" in Africa.[8] The tinkers who appear in their habitual role of initial suspects and are quickly ruled out are treated with forceful eviction by the rank and file Civic Guard who "shepherded" them off the Barrys' land.[9] Aunt Veronica, the eccentric remnant of the pre-Free State aristocracy, laments her lack of formal education,

8    Nigel Fitzgerald, *The House Is Falling* (London: Fontana, 1955), 27.
9    Ibid., 8.

which she blames on her parents' reluctance to let her go off to school because of the "troubles" of the 1920s when "like so many of her age and class" her normal development was stunted.[10] The land, and inheritance, is at the centre of the plot, and Hilary's statement that "whether he knows it or not, an Irishman always hates anyone who comes between him and the land" gives the novel its keynote.[11] Likewise, the figure of the eccentric crime writer, Professor Lake, is another crime fiction staple which harks back to an earlier age, and the conversion from crime writer to amateur detective as seen in Lake's declaration "I am Simon Strang, and I propose to solve this crime" echoes that of numerous Golden Age fictions.[12]

As ever, though, in Fitzgerald's work modernity is, as it were, at the door and peeping through. There are, for example, foreign workers who speak the Irish language, a phenomenon which would surprise many in the Ireland of the Celtic Tiger. In this novel, these foreign workers are not Polish meatpackers but German servants working in the Big House; their use of the language provokes mirth and the comment by one of the characters that the "funny thing is that Wolfgang hasn't realized yet that Irish isn't the language of the country".[13] This jocular comment leads the returned exile, Hugh, to contemplate the nature of the language and his own fractured relationship with it. Hugh is "surprised both at the idea that his countrymen should speak their own language, and at the fact that it should seem strange to him".[14] The subsequent discussion on the use of Irish in "modern times" leads to the somewhat surreal and "healthily Rabelaisian" search for "the Irish for hot pants".[15] "Hot pants", because Fitzgerald encompasses the sexuality of transatlantic pulp, in which the young female characters wear bikinis which are "so exiguous to be practically non-existent".[16]

10    Ibid., 130.
11    Ibid., 42.
12    Ibid., 76.
13    Ibid., 21.
14    Ibid.
15    Ibid.
16    Ibid., 46.

The detection in itself is, however, modern and efficient. Superintendent Duffy is revealed as one of the new enlightened guards, whose efficacious investigations are easily on a par with those of his British or American counterparts, before the works of Sheila Pim, Ellis Dillon and Fitzgerald himself, the main role models for functioning law enforcement agency in Irish detective fiction. Like Pim and Dillon, Fitgerald contrasts his rational, educated guards with the more stereotypical "culchies" – "let ye be moving on now, and find some other amusement"[17] – but this, if anything only serves to further emphasise the cultured efficiency of the physically unimpressive Duffy.

The theatrical background present in so much of Fitzgerald's fiction is also highlighted in *Imagine a Man* (1956), but the localised theatricals of the earlier novels is substituted for a more internationally oriented threat in the world of film. The drama is even displaced towards Italy and the then topical *Dolce Vita* of *Cinecittà*, and the denouement, in which amateur sleuth Guy Murrough marries the Italian starlet Toni and settles down to breed Jersey cattle on a Kerry farm, resolves an intricately internationalised elaboration on the plots of the earlier novels. *The Student Body* (1958) takes the action out of the West of Ireland into late 1950s' Dublin, although the stage theme remains central, and the murder of a Hungarian duchess and the involvement of an Irish woman who is resident in Brazil add an international touch to the novel. *Suffer a Witch* (1958) returns the narrative to the Irish west, again with touring actors amongst the protagonists. In what is one of the author's most sophisticated and complex narratives, Superintendent Duffy investigates a murder in the village of Dun Moher which, the locals believe, is connected with witchcraft. Even though "[b]oth the practice and the persecution [of witchcraft] were practically unknown in Ireland", the tales of the fourteenth-century Witch of Castlebawn resonate in the area and Vanessa, who believes herself to be a witch, is murdered under strange circumstances.[18] Duffy, joined by O'Riordan, another actor-manager and friend of Alan Russell, sorts through the eclectic selection of neighbours before discovering the cause behind the girl's death.

17    Ibid., 40.
18    Nigel Fitzgerald, *Suffer a Witch* (London: Fontana, 1958), 49.

*This Won't Hurt You* (1959) transfers the action to London, where the Cold War theme of *The Student Body* is replayed amongst a cast of disconcerting Irish expatriates. It also introduces an interesting detective, Detective-Superintendent Charles Laude, the son of an Anglican bishop, and a series of memorable characters, including the Irish dentist Brian Carty who "looked like a half-witted leprechaun" or Schweitzer, an Armenian impresario and former actor, who used his dramatic skills to successfully disguise himself and impersonate an Irishman.[19] *The Candles are All Out* and *Ghost in the Making* (both 1960) make use of highly charged gothic settings. In the first of these Alan Russell, unable to stay at the local hotel because of overbooking, is invited to lodge at Inislahan House on the island of Invermore in Connemara, during the fiercest of storms in living memory. When the bridge to the mainland collapses due to flooding, the murdered body of one of the guests is found, and the suspects are limited to the Standish family and their guests who have been stranded on the island. This classic Golden Age mystery, with a limited cast of suspects in a closed location, is solved by Alan after the murderer tries to kill him. *Ghost in the Making* finds Alan – who now has "the reputation of being something of a detective, of being almost an honorary member of the CID"[20] – at a party in Hunter's Hall, a large house which is reputedly haunted. Again the house is cut off from the rest of the world, this time by a crashed truck which blocks the access road so, when a young woman is killed, the owner of the house, Lord Lisduff, asks Alan to investigate, given that he has already been "mixed up in this detection lark".[21]

*Black Welcome* (1961) and *The Day of the Adder* (1963) combine the degenerate Big House theme with that of the returned outsider who once was part of the family, a subject that would characterise the later Fitzgerald novels. In the first of these, when Hector O'Brien Moore, an American, returns to his ancestral home of Newton Moore, he is faced with the murder of Joan Alison, a student who had been carrying out research into the family history. Superintendent Duffy again investigates, believing the girl's

---

19    Nigel Fitzgerald, *This Won't Hurt You* (London: Fontana, 1959), 159.
20    Nigel Fitzgerald, *Ghost in the Making* (London: Fontana, 1960), 14.
21    Ibid., 233.

death to be related to some family secret she has unwittingly uncovered. Another returned outsider, John Cane O'Corram, features in *The Day of the Adder*, published in the USA as *Echo Answers Murder*. O'Corram, living in London with his English wife, Dora, returns to Ireland alone for his mother's funeral. The ancestral castle no longer belongs to the family, but the O'Corrams are still highly respected by the people in the area. John is collected at the station by Cornie Smith, a newly rich local entrepreneur, and they, in turn, pick up Nellie Davoran, a former lover of John's. After a night drinking with Americans, the sound of what the villagers believe to be a Banshee is heard, presaging in local tradition a sudden death. Ness's body is discovered and Duffy is once more called in to investigate the murder. Again, the homecoming of someone who has left the community is the event which triggers off the homicide, but as is usually the case in Fitzgerald's works, the killing has its roots in the community and the outsider is not the guilty party. *Affairs of Death* (1967) was Fitzgerald's last novel. Standish Wyse, an actor, attends a party in which the guests perform a black magic ritual involving the burning of effigies. Shortly after, two girls are killed and, although Duffy appears to investigate, it is Standish, the talented amateur, who discovers the murderer amid a host of suspects.

Both Desmond O'Neill and Liam Redmond published notable novels in the latter part of the 1950s which, unfortunately, and despite their quality and interest, were not followed up by further works of crime fiction. *Desmond O'Neill* was, in fact, the pseudonym of Eoin Neeson (1927–2011), editor of *The Kerryman*, a weekly newspaper published in Tralee, who went on to become government press secretary and to publish a non-fiction work, *The Irish Civil War* (1966). His only crime novel, *Life Has No Price* (1959), is set in 1950s' Dublin and follows the attempts by Donal Roe O'Connell to investigate the causes of an intentional killing he has witnessed off Stephen's Green. Formal police presence is limited to that of Donal's friend Brian, a Guard in the Dublin Castle CID, who advises his friend not to become involved in the investigation. Suspicion of the police is deep-rooted and visible throughout the novel. One old man in a pub, on seeing Donal and Brian, "winked at the barman behind their backs and tossed his head in the manner of one Irishman to another when he spots a policeman".[22] The Dublin underworld, with the gangsters Simpson and Coughlan, and the smugglers from the North, Wee Willie and Long John, suggests a society still smarting from the divisions of the Civil War and the austerity of the "Emergency".

*Death is So Kind* (1959) by actor and writer *Liam Redmond* (1913–89) is set in the early years of the Irish independence and evokes an atmosphere similar in some respects to that of Liam O'Flaherty's *The Informer* and *The Assassin*. After the erstwhile leader is killed by the police, Joe Corcoran, "as slick as an eel in a bucket of snot", is elected leader of an IRA group operational in Dublin and fighting against the forces of the Free State.[23] His one-time friend, Charlie Horgan, is now working for the new administration and manages to convince Joe's comrades that he is an informer. Corcoran is hounded by both his own side and that of the government, which aims to use the figure of Joe to push through the Coercion Act repealing Habeas Corpus and effectively allowing republican volunteers to be arrested on suspicion. Despite being allowed to execute Horgan for the murder of student activist Sonny Coughlan, Joe is tried by his own side for collaborating with the Free State and sentenced to death. He escapes, but his eventual killing at the hands of a police detective brings a strange kind of peace to the revolutionary, tired of the double-dealing and treachery on an internecine conflict which shows no signs of abating.

*Leonard Wibberley* (1915–83) is probably best known for his comic novel *The Mouse that Roared* (1955), famously converted into a film starring Peter Sellers. Born in Dublin, Wibberley spent most of his life living in the USA, publishing under a series of pseudonyms, which included Patrick O'Brien, Christopher Webb and Leonard Holton. *The Mouse that Roared* tells of an imaginary English-speaking Duchy in the Alps which, in the height of the Cold War declares war on and then invades the USA. This highly successful work was followed by a prequel *Beware of the Mouse* (1958) which chronicles the founding of the Duchy by an Irish knight in the fourteenth century and two sequels, *The Mouse on the Moon* (1962) and *The Mouse on Wall Street* (1969), which dealt respectively with the Duchy

22    Desmond O'Neill, *Life Has No Price* (London: Victor Gollancz, 1959), 13.
23    Liam Redmond, *Death is So Kind* (New York: Devlin-Adair, 1959), 12.

of Grand Fenwick's entry into the space race using local wine as fuel and the tiny state's cataclysmic influence on world markets after the Duchy's shares in American bubble gum manufacturers soar when anti-smoking campaigns cause a slump in the market for tobacco.

Besides these comedy thrillers, Wibberley also wrote a series of eleven crime novels under the pseudonym *Leonard Holton,* featuring the clerical private detective Father Bredder and his friend, the Los Angeles police detective Lieutenant Minardi, and this latter's daughter, Barbara, a founding member of her school's detective agency and an aspiring sleuth. Father Bredder, a Franciscan priest who works at the convent where Barbara Minardi is a pupil, has a colourful history as an ex-professional boxer and marine, and is quickly establishing a reputation as an excellent private investigator. These light, often wistful novels do, perhaps surprisingly, contain a certain amount of physical violence, despite the priest's own personal aversion, and the murders he is called in to investigate – a task which he undertakes as a spiritual exercise and for which he makes no charge – are often of a brutal nature. Bredder's contacts among the underworld of inner-city Los Angeles, contacts which generally date back to the priest's boxing days, help him to mingle with life in the underbelly of the city.

Bredder and Minardi are introduced in *The Saint Maker* (1959), where a human head appears in a bag in Bredder's chapel in place of the melon that had been expected by the convent's Reverend Mother. The police are initially suspicious of the priest, and more so when his underworld contacts offer to help him escape from the country. The head is discovered to belong to a young woman who had been involved in the movement of illicit heroin hidden in match heads, and while trying to solve the mystery Father Brennan is also able to save the life of Barbara Minardi from the killer, a demented parishioner who had killed her sea-captain husband. The novel details Bredder's motivation, the priest seeing himself as a "policeman of God",[24] whose investigative methods took on a spiritual sense, differentiating him from a secular detective like Minardi who used "the approach of someone who searched for a person and not a soul".[25]

24    Leonard Holton, *The Saint Maker* (New York: Dodd, Mead, 1959), 145.
25    Ibid., 128.

In *A Pact with Satan* (1960) Bredder helps Minardi solve a case involving the apparent death of a dentist, which reveals that the victim is, in fact, the murderer of his wife and their chauffeur. Here once again the priest's spiritual approach proves more helpful than that of the police officer, prompting Bredder to muse that faith, intuition and instinct are stronger than mere reason, for the Franciscan "the weakest of human faculties".[26] *Secret of the Doubting Saint* (1961) sees Bredder investigating the murder of a television producer and the connection between this death and the disappearance of a priceless Indian diamond, while in *Deliver Us from Wolves* (1963) he travels to Fátima in Portugal where he uncovers a drug-smuggling racket which uses the insides of cheap religious souvenirs and which has at its centre an evil Portuguese countess and a gothic castle, reputedly haunted by a werewolf. Narcotics are also featured in *Flowers by Request* (1964), in which Father Bredder is forced back into the ring as he discovers a Sicilian Mafia operation which supplies Californian flower shops with drugs imported from Mexico.

Both *Out of the Depths* (1966) and *A Touch of Jonah* (1968) reflect the author's love of the sea and sailing. The former has a Cold War theme involving a murdered diver and missing atomic formula, and once again the priest, impersonated by a criminal, is briefly regarded as a suspect. In *A Touch of Jonah*, Bredder joins the crew of a luxury yacht on an ocean race and investigates the disappearance and suspected murder on board of the yacht's skipper, Sir Harry Stockton. In *A Problem in Angels* (1970) the clerical private eye is faced with killings which have their roots in the betrayal of Jewish prisoners during the Second World War, while *The Mirror of Hell* (1972) finds Barbara – now a rapidly maturing sixteen-year-old – at the centre of a series of murders committed at and around the university where she is taking a summer cheer-leading course. Drugs are again of crucial importance, although the 1970s are charmingly portrayed in the persons of a radical poet and young hippies. In *The Devil to Play* (1974), Bredder is required to infiltrate the structure of a professional baseball team after a star player is shot during a game, and in the final novel of the series, *A Corner of Paradise* (1977), Bredder helps Minardi with the problems

26    Leonard Holton, *A Pact with Satan* (New York: Doss, Mead, 1960), 143.

faced by Barbara, now recently married to a black activist who is wrongly accused of murder.

The Father Bredder mysteries are light, clerical detective tales which, nevertheless, are skilfully written and which, at their best, present the disturbing but still somehow familiar Southern California of the late 1950s, 1960s and early 1970s through the eyes of the ethical, apparently spiritual but deceptively worldly priest. While the influence of Chesterton's Father Brown is present, Holton's Bredder – who frequently denies having any Irish ancestry – is a refreshingly altruistic private eye in a world in which many would regard him to be an anachronism.

*Patricia Moyes* (1923–2000) published nineteen novels featuring the police detective Henry Tibbett between 1959 and 1993. These light, clue-puzzle novels take Tibbett and his wife Emmy on several adventures in different parts of the world, with significant works being set in the West Indies where the Dublin-born Moyes had her residence for the last years of her life. Chief Inspector Henry Tibbett is the typical self-effacing, unassuming police detective so beloved by many writers of "cosy" mysteries. In the first novel in which he makes an appearance, *Dead Men Don't Ski* (1959), the reader is told that Tibbett is "not a man who looked like a great detective" but is "a conscientious and observant policeman, with an occasional flair for intuitive detection which he called 'my nose'".[27] Although possessing a "card-index memory",[28] he is "the kind of bird you'd pass in the street without a second glance".[29] Tibbett is an "unremarkable, sandy-haired man in his forties, with gentle blue eyes, a diffident manner and a quiet voice", but, nevertheless, "his air of mild vagueness was as deceptively simple as any of Monnier's little black dresses".[30] Tibbett's cases are often solved through the combined intuition of Tibbett and his omnipresent wife. *In Dead Men Don't Ski*, the detective uses a timetable to discover the murderer among the hotel guests involved in a drug-smuggling ring in the Italian Alps.

While *The Sunken Sailor*, also published as *Down Among the Dead Men* (1961) involved a case of inheritance and the conflict over land leading

27    Patricia Moyes, *Dead Men Don't Ski* (1959, New York: Henry Holt, 1989), 8.
28    Ibid., 159.
29    Patricia Moyes, *Falling Star* (1964, New York: Henry Holt, 1982), 8.
30    Patricia Moyes, *Murder à la Mode* (1963, New York: Henry Holt, 1989), 29.

to two murders in rural Norfolk, *Death on the Agenda* takes the detective and his wife once again to continental Europe, to Geneva, where an interpreter at the conference Tibbett is attending is murdered. The involvement of international drug syndicates complicates the investigation in which Henry himself is the initial suspect. In *Murder à la Mode* (1963) and *Falling Star* (1964), Tibbett investigates murders in the world of fashion and that of film respectively. *Johnny Under Ground* (1965) sees Tibbett looking into the disappearance of an RAF fighter pilot, with whom Emmy had been in love, some twenty years before, while Murder Fantastical has the detective and his wife investigating a murder in the company of the eccentric Mancible family. The Mancibles, of Irish origins, reveal Moyes' skill as a comic writer, and reappear in the last Tibbett novel, *Once in a Blue Moon* (1993). *Murder Fantastical* also introduced a colonial theme that would become apparent in many of the author's later works. *Death and the Dutch Uncle* (1968) takes Tebbit and Emmy to the Netherlands, where Patricia Moyes was living at the time, to examine a case in which the murders are connected with a border dispute between two African states and the peacekeeping international unit, the fictional PIFL.

In *Who Saw Her Die* (1970), published in the USA as *Many Deadly Returns*, Tibbett is back in England investigating the strange death of Lady Balaclava, a follower of the occult, at her country estate, and *Season of Snows and Sins* (1971) is set once again at a ski resort in the Alps. The action in *The Curious Affair of the Third Dog* (1973), in which Henry laments the difference between real and fictional murder, takes place in the world of legal and illegal dog-racing tracks where the main suspect is reported to have "tendencies to compulsive gambling, transvestism, homosexuality, violence, and – above all – slumming".[31] *Black Widower* (1975), *To Kill a Coconut* (1977), published in the USA as *The Coconut Killings*, *Angel Death* (1980) and *Black Girl, White Girl* (1989) are all set in Tampica in the Seaward Islands, a fictional ex-British colony in the West Indies. The novels touch on aspects of racism and the effects of colonialism, while retaining the whimsical tone of the series. In *Black Widow* Henry – accompanied as

---

31    Patricia Moyes, *The Curious Affair of the Third Dog* (New York: Holt, Rinehart & Winston, 1973), 208.

usual by Emmie – investigates the murder of the Tampican ambassador's wife at their embassy in Washington, which may have been related to the islanders' disagreement with the ambassador's inter-racial marriage. In *To Kill a Coconut*, it soon becomes apparent that the initial suspect and his motive are the result of a complex plot in which American geopolitical interests are of fundamental importance. Tibbit's normally uncommitted stance wavers slightly as he describes the Tampicans as "volatile and emotional".[32] In both *Angel Death* and *White Girl, Black Girl* drug smuggling is at the centre of the narrative, the "white girl" of the latter apparently referring to cocaine. Both novels echo concerns which were common among many writers of the 1980s, with the drug cartels being depicted as all-powerful and posing a real threat to the extent that they are in a position to take over the running of an entire state, in this case, the newly independent country of Tampica. Interestingly, Henry Tibbett argues that the islanders are more independent than most peoples, as they possess "complete internal autonomy" along with "the power of Great Britain behind them on matters of defence".[33] With this in mind, it is not, perhaps, surprising that the newly jingoistic detective should compare the islanders with the Irish, as they "tend to say what they think one wants them to hear – very much like the Irish".[34]

Other novels published in the later years of Moyes' career, such as *Who is Simon Warwick?* (1978), *A Six-Letter Word for Death* (1983), *Night Ferry to Death* (1985) and *Twice in a Blue Moon* (1993) reveal the mature author as a skilful craftswoman in the construction of tightly plotted clue-puzzle mysteries. In the first of these, Moyes reworks the age-old mystery story theme of the two claimants for a single inheritance. In *A Six-Letter Word for Death*, the self-referential nature of classic crime fiction is once again shown when Chief Inspector Tibbett receives a number of crossword puzzle clues which turn out to have been sent by members of a group of mystery writers calling themselves the "Guess Who Club". The weekend house party, to which Tibbett is invited as guest expert and lecturer, results in a

32   Patricia Moyes, *The Coconut Killings* (New York: Holt, Rinehart & Winston, 1977), 20.
33   Patricia Moyes, *Black Girl, White Girl* (London: Diamond Books, 1989), 339.
34   Moyes, *Coconut Killings*, 197.

death with each of the club members being in some way under suspicion. *Night Ferry to Death* is another locked-room mystery, the room in question being the passenger lounge of a ferry on the route from the Netherlands to England. The final Tibbett mystery, *Twice in a Blue Moon*, published seven years before the author's death in the British Virgin Islands, has Henry investigating a death of over twenty years ago and a more recent poisoning in the world of high-class cuisine.

Patricia Moyes wrote novels which fit clearly, if belatedly, into the British Golden Age model. Despite being a Dubliner, Moyes' references to Ireland are few and rarely complimentary. Her detective, Henry Tibbett is, as mentioned, a typical product of the British modestly diffident school of detectives, although at times, and especially in the later novels, there is a sense of awareness that he is not only a maverick individual but a cog in the larger machine of justice. He frequently involves himself – and his wife – in his cases on a personal level while trying to remain "the outsider, the impersonal representative of the law".[35] He refers to the "maw of the police machine"[36] and states that he belongs to "a big and reasonably efficient organization",[37] which has "all the facilities of a superbly organized police force at his fingertips".[38] Despite such protestations, however, Moyes' mysteries are far from the police procedural to which they are linked in only a temporal sense. The position of Henry's wife, Emmy, is as a helpful accomplice who, as in Bartholomew Gill's McGarr series, challenges the reader's credibility somewhat. Moyes also wrote an interesting young adult novel, *Helter-Skelter* (1968), an adventure story set on the English coast with the murder of a "tinker" and the presence of an Irish spy which, perhaps paradoxically, is far less "cosy" than her adult thrillers.

35    Patricia Moyes, *Death on the Agenda* (1962, New York: Henry Holt, 1992), 44.
36    Moyes, *Murder à la Mode*, 182.
37    Patricia Moyes, *Johnny Under Ground* (London: Chivers Press, 1965), 31.
38    Patricia Moyes, *Season of Snows and Sins* (New York: Holt, Rinehart & Winston, 1971), 167.

# CHAPTER 13

# "His father had been on the wrong side in the Civil War." Irish Spy Fiction in the 1960s and 1970s

The international spy thriller reached enormous heights of popularity in the 1960s and 1970s. LeRoy Lad Panek regards the novel of international intrigue to be of a mixed form, which embraces "the territory of detective story, romance, gangster book or treasure hunt tale".[1] Martin Kayman notes how espionage had been part of the crime narrative since early times, with nineteenth-century detectives making regular use of "quasi-criminal and spy-like activities" such as disguise, infiltration, entrapment, the intimidation of witnesses, the use of false information, and illegal vigilance and search.[2] The figure of the fictional spy, even in his parodic version such as Fleming's James Bond, owes much to the character of the hard-boiled detective, and when "everyone around him is a potential (or real) enemy, the secret agent must be detached, unemotional, dispassionately observant – in a word, cool".[3] This, for Cawelti and Rosenberg, is "his legacy from the Raymond Chandler hard-boiled detective".[4] The spy in Irish fiction had had a notable beginning, with Erskine Childers' *The Riddle of the Sands* being widely considered as almost a foundational text for the genre. Since then, Irish fictional spies had been whimsical amateurs such as Manning O'Brine's Michael O'Kelly or John Welcome's Richard Graham and Simon Herald. By the early 1960s, however, writers like Brian Cleeve and Jack Higgins were beginning to follow the global

---

1   LeRoy Lad Panek, *The Special Branch: The British Spy Novel, 1890–1980* (Bowling Green, OH: Bowling Green State University Popular Press, 1981), 2.

2   Martin A. Kayman, *From Baker Street to Bow Street: Mystery, Detection and Narrative* (London: Macmillan, 1992), 119.

3   John Cawelti and Bruce A. Rosenberg, *The Spy Story* (Chicago: Chicago University Press, 1987), 75.

4   Ibid.

fashion for contemporary spy thrillers which highlighted the "ethical opposition between the national and the international".[5] These new spy narratives shared many of the characteristics of the detective novel, in that their "sphere of action seems to be beyond the law", their "characters used aliases and inverted identities" and their action tends to progress "from apparently disparate fragments of information towards a complete account of action".[6] Cleve, Higgins and the later O'Brine moved the Irish spy novel out of the 1950s, but they still combined the production of spy fiction with that of more mainstream crime novels. Although in their espionage narratives the Cold War is at times present, these early Irish writers would often prefer to centre their narratives in the past, and many novels deal with the Second World War, either directly, or in narratives where its effects are of significant importance. By the beginning of the 1970s, Higgins would start to write spy thrillers which used the contemporary Northern Irish Troubles as background, but his most successful works would still be those which, like *The Eagle Has Landed* (1975), dwelt on fictional events from the Second World War.

*Brian Cleeve* (1921–2003), born in England to an Irish father and English mother, was a prolific author who started to write mystery novels at around the same time as he started to work for Ireland's newly founded television station, RTE, in 1961. In *Assignment to Vengeance* (1961) a retired British intelligence agent, John Trent, is called back into service after fifteen years of inactivity following a failed final mission during the Second World War. Branded as unreliable, he is tasked with finding the whereabouts of Hans Stelling, a Nazi officer who had escaped from Berlin and was now living somewhere in Switzerland. Tracking him down to a Swiss monastery, Trent discovers that Stelling is being sought after not only by British intelligence but also by a devious fascist group called the Sons of Charlemagne who want to use the old German as the standard-bearer for a new Nazi organisation. Forced to reconsider the situation when confronted

5    Michael Woolf, "Ian Fleming's Enigmas and Variations" in *Spy Thrillers: From Buchan to Le Carré*, ed. Clive Bloom (London: Macmillan, 1990), 93.
6    David Seed, "Crime and the Spy Genre" in *A Companion to Crime Fiction*, ed. Charles J. Rzepka and Lee Horsley (Oxford: Wiley-Blackwell, 2010), 233.

by Stelling's daughter Helga, Trent falls in love and completes the path towards redemption that he took when accepting the mission.

*Death of a Painted Lady* (1962) is a murder mystery set in Ireland. The rape and murder of Elaine, a woman who has a local reputation of being of easy virtue, initially throws up three suspects, all connected with the Dublin art world. Tadg O'Connor, an alcoholic painter, is initially charged, and the alibi of gallery owner Geraghty is found to be false, but the discovery of a blood-stained shirt switches the blame towards Paul Traynor who had been in love with Elaine. When O'Connor admits to the rape but denies murder the guards are forced to widen the scope of their investigation. Although containing the stereotype of a red-faced Kerry Guard, the leading officer in the case, Inspector Quinn, is given a highly positive portrayal as a good professional who is objective, patient and methodical.

*Vote X for Treason* (1964) is Cleeve's second spy novel and the first to feature Sean Ryan, a character who would also appear in three further works. According to Bruce, Cleeve saw the need to replace Trent, as the earlier protagonist "would be a little too old now to compete with a generation of fictional secret agents, and probably not as ruthless either".[7] Although John Trent does, in fact, make an appearance at the end of the novel, married now to the daughter of the former Nazi, Stelling, the protagonist here is Ryan, who, it is hinted but never explicitly stated, is a former IRA volunteer, anticipating, perhaps, the later heroes of Jack Higgins' thrillers, Liam Devlin and Sean Dillon. At the beginning of the novel, Ryan is in prison serving a sentence for unspecified terrorist offences. He is offered parole if he agrees to infiltrate the New Party, a neo-fascist political party which appears to be growing in influence and membership. During a trip to Ireland with New Party members, a shoot-out in the Wicklow Mountains results in Sean being sought for murder. He escapes to Wales and is able to inform the British government about New Party plans to create a crisis in the Middle East which will lead to war. At the end of the novel, Ryan's usefulness is acknowledged and he accepts a permanent post in the British Intelligence service. In *Dark Blood Dark Terror* Ryan is again involved in

---

7    Jim Bruce, *Faithful Servant: A Memoir of Brian Cleeve* (Raleigh, NC: Lulu, 2007), 109.

trying to halt a right-wing plot involving international fascist organisations from Portugal, Spain, Rhodesia and Germany and the impenetrable Guardians of the Fortress from South Africa. His mission involves him working closely with the South African special branch, and Sean ponders on his own situation, working for the British when "he can never really be one of them".[8] In *The Judas Goat* (1966), published in the USA as *Vice Isn't Private*, Ryan must neutralise the threats to blackmail a senior British cabinet minister, while in the last Ryan novel, *Violent Death of a Bitter Englishman* (1967) he once again fights against another right-wing group, Shadow Force, while again having to destroy photographs of a top-ranking British politician shown beside a German woman dressed in a Nazi uniform.

In *You Must Never Go Back* (1968) Wolf, an engineer living in Peru, returns to Italy where fifteen years previously he had escaped from an attack which had killed his parents at a campsite in the mountains. Determined to discover the truth behind the attack, Wolf discovers that his father had been a British agent involved with Italian partisans at the end of the Second World War and that surviving members of the force had suspected him of taking for his own use the legendary quantities of Mussolini's gold lost in the area. In *Exit from Prague* (1970), Tony Brett is a television reporter working in Prague who finds himself caught up in a spy ring involving the South African communist Julius Goldman and an old Jewish woman and her niece who use Brett to send photos out to the west. *Cry of the Morning* (1971) is effectively Cleeve's last thriller, as his future fictional output would mainly consist of historical novels with female protagonists. *Cry of the Morning* in many ways anticipates later novels of political corruption, in this case during the period of economic and cultural transformation in Ireland in the late 1960s. Francis O'Rourke is a property developer who wants to build a huge office complex in Dublin city centre, and he has the support of the suspiciously secretive Catholic interest group the Guardians of the Flame. As the area set aside for development houses slum dwellers who stand to be evicted, O'Rourke's plans are opposed by liberal sectors of society, including playwright Felicity O'Connor, TV presenter John Lennox, Lady Honoria Gandon, an Anglo-Irish aristocrat who leads the

8    Brian Cleeve, *Dark Blood Dark Terror* (London: Hammond, 1965), 75.

campaign against the destruction of Georgian Dublin, and Father Herbert Tracey, a priest who is a committed social campaigner. Similar in many respects to novels that would appear during the Celtic Tiger period some three decades after its publication, *Cry of Morning* gives a fascinating view of Dublin society of the period.

Also active in the 1960s was Harry Patterson (b. 1929), who, using the pseudonym *Jack Higgins*, would gain worldwide fame in later decades for his formulaic international thrillers. Patterson was born in Newcastle-Upon-Tyne, but spent a large part of his childhood in Northern Ireland with his Irish mother, who had separated from his Scottish father. The influence of the years living in Belfast can be perceived in much of Patterson's highly popular thriller output, where Irish characters such as Liam Devlin and Sean Dillon are prominent. His first novel, *Sad Wind from the Sea* (1959), published under his own name, is an interesting debut in which Rose Graham, the exotic offspring of an Indo-Chinese mother and a Scottish father, seeks out the American adventurer Mark Hagen in Macao to help her rescue, alleging humanitarian reasons, a quantity of sunken gold from the River Kwai. The influence of Hemingway is apparent throughout, and Hagen is himself told that he "looks like something out of a Hemingway novel",[9] and that he "is like a man out of Hemingway", in case any readers are unaware of the supposed similarities.[10] *Sad Wind from the Sea* commits many of the sins of the Cold War thriller, with the treatment of Hagen's adversaries, the communist Chinese, in clichéd racist terms. Hagen believes he is "familiar with the oriental mind and its refinements in cruelty and contempt for human life",[11] and speaks of a "pockmarked, evil face",[12] and of a "little yellow bastard",[13] warning his crew members about the duplicity of "wog traders" and reflecting on the sanitary conditions of the Chinese

---

9   Harry Patterson [Jack Higgins], *Sad Wind from the Sea* (London: Harper, 1959), 132.
10  Ibid., 194.
11  Ibid., 41.
12  Ibid., 227.
13  Ibid., 75.

army, which were "indications not only of the standards of Chinese sol-
diery, but also of their stupidity".[14]

Hagen's plans for the future include his retirement to Ireland, but the
Ireland to which he aspires is that of the Ascendancy: "A country house
with plenty of liquor and good horses".[15] His crewmate, O'Hara, reminisces about boyhood fishing and hunting in Ireland, prompting Hagen to
fabricate his own "memories" about "fairy pools" constructing his vision
of a country "outside" the world as such, a retreat to which he could go
to escape and where, he believed, the world could continue without him.
Ireland is central to Patterson's second novel, *Cry of the Hunter* (1960), set
in Northern Ireland and featuring Martin Fallon, a former hero of the IRA,
here referred to simply as The Organisation, who, after serving nine years
in prison has converted to pacifism but who, after his release, is forced to
participate in one final mission, the liberation of the head of the IRA from
police custody. *Cry of the Hunter* introduces many of the themes which
Patterson would later incorporate into his Jack Higgins novels, with the
tortured idealist, the essential goodness of certain members of both sides
of the political divide, the essential evil of others from both sides, and the
angelic female love interest who both respects and shares the hero's idealism
and sense of sacrifice. Fallon reappears in *A Prayer for the Dying* (1973), in
which the "strange, small man" is forced to flee from both an IRA execution squad and the police.[16] Although the novel ends with Fallon's death,
many of his characteristics (including the annoying habit of overusing the
expression "girl dear") would be passed on to Higgins' later Irish heroes
Liam Devlin and Sean Dillon.

*The Thousand Faces of the Night* (1961), *Comes the Dark Stranger* and
*Hell is Too Crowded* (both 1962) are all set in England, and explore different
avenues in crime and thriller writing. In the first, Hugh Marlowe, released
after five years in prison, seeks to recover the money he has hidden, and
is pursued throughout the novel by a series of adversaries. In *Comes the
Dark Stranger*, Martin Shane, a former prisoner-of-war in Korea, returns to

14    Ibid., 221.
15    Ibid., 59.
16    Jack Higgins, *A Prayer for the Dying* (London: Harper, 1973), 184.

discover the whereabouts of the friend who has betrayed him, only to fall in love with that same friend's sister. *Hell is Too Crowded* finds its American hero, Matt Brady, wrongfully imprisoned after being improperly charged with murder, escaping from jail to track down those who have framed him.

*The Testament of Caspar Schultz* (1962), later retitled as *The Bormann Testament*, was the first novel to be published under the pseudonym of Martin Fallon, and to feature Paul Chavasse, his troubled secret agent who is sent to post-war Germany to recover a manuscript written by Schultz – the real-life Martin Bormann – and to bring the former Nazi leader to trial, if he is still alive. Chavasse, a blueprint for later Higgins heroes, worries about his role in the world of international espionage, wondering whether he is "a sort of twentieth-century mercenary who enjoyed the game for its own sake",[17] and realises he has much more in common with his opposite number in the KGB than "with any normal citizen" of his own country.[18] Chavasse also features in *Year of the Tiger* (1963), *The Keys of Hell* (1965), *Midnight Never Comes* (1966) and *A Fine Night for Dying* (1969), set in Tibet, Albania, the UK and the English Channel Islands respectively.

*The Dark Side of the Island* (1963) a stand-alone thriller set in the Greek islands, was followed by one of Patterson's rare departures from stock situations and characters. In *Pay the Devil* (1962), set in the aftermath of the American Civil War, a Confederate officer relocates to Ireland where, as a secret outlaw, he wages war on the landlords in favour of the Irish tenant farmers during the Land Wars. *Seven Pillars to Hell* (1963), later republished as *Sheba* (1994), was the first Patterson novel to bear the pseudonym "Hugh Marlowe" and features Gavin Kane who, in 1939, is sent to try to find Cunningham, a fellow archaeologist who has disappeared while searching for the Temple of Sheba, accidentally stumbling on a Nazi base which is preparing for a sabotage attack on the Suez Canal. The Marlowe pseudonym was also used for *Passage by Night* (1964), a routine Cold War espionage narrative set in Cuba, but *A Phoenix in the Blood* (1964), *Thunder at Noon* (1964), *Wrath of the Lion* (1964) and *The*

---

17    Martin Fallon (Jack Higgins), *The Bormann Testament [The Testament of Casper Schultz]* (1962, New York: Berkley, 2006), 223.
18    Ibid., 58.

*Graveyard Shift* (1965) were all published under Patterson's own name. *The Graveyard Shift* introduced a new series hero, Nick Miller, who would also feature in *Brought in Dead* (1967) and *Hell is Always Today* (1968). Miller is unique amongst Patterson's heroes, in that he is a serving British police officer who possesses a law degree and lives with his millionaire brother. These police novels provide an interesting hiatus in the Higgins/Patterson trajectory and beg the interesting question as to what success Higgins might have had as a writer of conventional detective fiction instead of the international thrillers which brought him fame.

*The Violent Enemy*, also known as *A Candle for the Dead* (1966) is attributed to Hugh Marlowe, and introduces another Irish anti-hero, Sean Rogan, again a former member of the IRA who, after serving a long sentence, has difficulty in coming to terms with the changed circumstances after breaking out of prison. The organisation he had formed part of has changed since he was imprisoned, and Rogan can no longer identify with the ideals that have come into play after the end of the Border Campaign. *The Violent Enemy* is interesting in its implicit support of political status for paramilitary prisoners, criticising the system in the UK which is "the only country in the civilised world that doesn't make special provision for political offenders",[19] leading one of the characters, a police officer, to comment that Rogan, as a political detainee, should not be treated as a felon: "Rogan's no criminal. He's a political offender. That doesn't mean I think he's right, but it doesn't mean I have to agree with a system that condemns him to the same treatment as a criminal".[20]

*The Savage Day* (1972) is the first Higgins thriller to be set with a background in the Northern Irish Troubles of the 1970s. Simon Vaughn, a former major in the British army whose mother was Irish and whose grandfather had been an IRA hero in the 1920s, is sentenced to a term of imprisonment after an incident involving officers from the Greek army. Vaughn is given the chance of receiving a pardon in exchange for undergoing a dangerous mission in Ireland, disguised as an arms dealer, to recover a shipment of

---

19  Hugh Marlowe (Jack Higgins), *The Violent Enemy (A Candle for the Dead)* (1966, London: HarperCollins, 2008), 13.
20  Ibid., 69.

stolen gold in the hands of the IRA. Vaughn discovers that the IRA is divided into two different factions, and is used by both, and also by the British government. *The Savage Day* sees Higgins taking an initial stance on the events in Northern Ireland, believing that the army had been sent in in 1969 to "protect the Catholic minority", and that this had been "working until the IRA got up to their old tricks again".[21] The split the author describes in the IRA allows him to differentiate what he regards to be its moderate and its fanatic elements, while his depiction of the British intelligence service is critical, anticipating to some extent the position the writer adopts in later novels, especially those in the Sean Dillon series. The plot, however, makes unnecessary demands on the reader's credibility, and this early Troubles thriller is little more than "a ludicrously improbable adventure story set in a never-never land called 'Northern Ireland'".[22] Simon Vaughn would reappear in *Day of Judgement* (1978), set some years before the action in *The Savage Day*, at the time of President Kennedy's famous visit to Berlin.

*The Eagle Has Landed* (1975) was the first novel to feature Liam Devlin. Made into a film in 1976, it follows a faux-documentary style with a frame story that starts with the discovery of thirteen German graves in an English country churchyard and goes on to unearth the attempt by a group of elite German forces to kidnap British Prime Minister Winston Churchill and to take him back to Germany with them. The novel is notable for its surprisingly sympathetic treatment of the German paratroopers and the character of Liam Devlin, an anti-Treaty IRA veteran who is co-opted by the Germans to help in their endeavour. Devlin, who reads poetry in Irish, insists that, although he is helping the Germans, he does not hate the English, despite being highly critical of their politics. Devlin defends his Irishness before Germans and English alike, telling the local Norfolk girl, Molly Prior, who helps him to escape: "Molly, I'm Irish, that means I'm as different from you as a German is from a Frenchman. I'm a foreigner. We're not the same just because we speak the same language with different accents. When will you learn, you people?"[23]

---

21    Jack Higgins, *The Savage Day* (1972, New York: Open Road, 2010), 60.

22    James MacKillop, "Ulster Violence in Fiction" in *Conflict in Ireland*, ed. E. Sullivan et al. (Gainesville, FL: Florida University Press, 1976), 149

23    Jack Higgins, *The Eagle Has Landed* (1975, London: Penguin, 1998), 319.

The popularity of *The Eagle Has Landed* led to a less successful sequel, *The Eagle Has Flown* (1990), while the character of Liam Devlin would re-appear in *Touch the Devil* (1982) and *Confessional* (1985), as well as having a minor role in four of the later Sean Dillon novels. In *Touch the Devil* the former IRA man is kidnapped by British intelligence and forced to capture a KGB assassin, while in *Confessional* Devlin is again sent to discover a Soviet agent, son of an IRA activist and Russian mother, who has been given the task of assassinating the Pope on a visit to Canterbury Cathedral in England in 1959. *Confessional* also re-introduces the ageing British spymaster Charles Ferguson who had previously appeared in *The Iron Tiger* (1966) and *Touch the Devil*, and who would feature in the Crete-based *Solo* (1980), the Falkland War thriller *Exocet* (1983) and *A Season in Hell* (1989), which would also introduce the characters of Sean Egan, a Sean Dillon prototype, and Tony Villiers. Ferguson would also appear in many of the Sean Dillon novels, while the character of Brigadier Munro is Ferguson in all but name and historical period in *Cold Harbour* (1990) which, along with *The Eagle Has Flown*, published in the same year, signalled a temporary end for the series of successful Second World War novels which had started with *The Eagle Has Landed* and continued with *Storm Warning* (1976), *The Valhalla Exchange* (1976), *A Game for Heroes* (1979), *To Catch a King* (1980), *Luciano's Luck* (1981) and *Night of the Fox* (1986).

Sean Dillon first appeared in *Eye of the Storm* (1992), and was to dominate Higgins' literary production for the next twenty-five years. Although Dillon's biography is revealed gradually in the more than twenty novels in which he features, the basic details are as follows. Born in 1952, Dillon started to work as an assassin for the IRA when, at the age of nineteen and about to embark on a career as an actor, his father was killed by the British army. Disillusioned with the IRA, Dillon started to hire out his services as a trained assassin when, after an unsuccessful attempt to kill British Prime Minister John Major, he is forced to work for Brigadier Charles Ferguson, commander of British elite anti-terrorist unit Group Four, answerable only to the Prime Minister. Apart from Dillon and Ferguson, the novel also features Martin Brosnan, from *Touch the Devil* and Liam Devlin, now over eighty years of age but, for Brosnan, better than "the kind of rubbish the IRA employs these days".[24] In *Thunder Point* (1994) Ferguson ensures Dillon's continued loyalty by freeing him from a Croatian firing squad before entrusting him with the mission to rescuing the Windsor Protocol, a document implicating members of the British royalty in Nazi interests, which had been lost in a briefcase belonging to Martin Bormann in a German U-boat which had sunk off the Virgin Islands at the end of the Second World War.

*Angel of Death* (1995) is set in Ireland against the backdrop of the Troubles of the 1990s, when Dillon is sent to his native land to try to stop a new terrorist organisation, "January 30". This had been named after the date of Derry's Bloody Sunday, and its members target not only British but also American and Soviet, Arab and Israeli intelligence agents, as well as members of both Protestant and Catholic paramilitary forces in Northern Ireland, and as a result are seen to be damaging the prospects of the ongoing peace process.

With the Sean Dillon series, Higgins seemed to have found a successful formula, which would see him well into the twenty-first century. The Dillon novels continued to appear, at the rate of virtually one a year and to use as their background many of the topical historical conflicts of their age, but these later works suffered from their over-reliance on increasingly formulaic features.

*John Kelly* (1931–91), a noted Irish jurist and politician, wrote two novels in the 1960s. The first of these, *Matters of Honour* (1964) was published under the pseudonym of John Boyne, and its protagonist, the young Irish student Raphael Houlihan, is, like the author had been, studying at the University of Heidelberg. With a background in spying and the Cold War, Houlihan becomes suspicious of his German girlfriend when he discovers lists of American army officers in her room and overhears her talking to an old man who "earns his living by doing some kind of intelligence work for the East German government".[25] *The Polling of the Dead* (1993) was also written in the 1960s but was not published until after the author's death, this time using his real name. Redmond Byrne, a politician party hack, is

24    Jack Higgins, *Eye of the Storm* (London: Signet, 1992), 173.
25    John Boyne (John Kelly), *Matter of Honour* (London: New Authors, 1964), 86.

shocked when the body of his friend and Opposition candidate Daithi Flood is discovered at the bottom of a refuse chute just before polling day. Redmond investigates his friend's death, discovering clues which cast suspicion on an expelled alien, who turns out to be a German businessman who is now a supporter of the party. His inquiries are thwarted by the political interests which, given the proximity of the elections, are determined to suppress any potentially damaging information. The political world that Kelly describes is one of corruption and nepotism in which the guards, heavily stereotyped figures who are all from "the country"[26] are treated as little more than personal aids to the politicians.

A native of Carrickfergus, *Shaun Herron* (1912–89) spent most of his life in Canada, and in *Miro* (1969) he introduced the secret service agent of the same name. Professional and distinctly unromantic, Miro is pitted against a far-right conspiracy aimed at showing the world "how easy it is to make us hysterical".[27] Working for the unspecified "Firm", he is sent to Canada, a country which seems to echo many of the quirks and problems of Northern Ireland. Miro's charming cynicism is shown in his answer to a colleague who asks him if he hadn't been told that they, the secret service agents, were outlaws in the service of law and order, to which he responds: "They didn't and we're not".[28] Miro returns in *The Hound and the Fox and the Harper* (1970) in which, after fleeing from the Firm, he and his pregnant wife Eva move to the fictional Irish village of Killyroe where he intends to write a book revealing his career as a spy and the Firm's "sanctioned criminality".[29] Miro is captured twice, and Eva is abducted by the East Germans, but the combined strength of the villages, including the fire brigade, the undertaker and a group of tinkers with a harper, trap the East German agent and allow Eva and her new-born baby to escape. In *Through the Dark and Hairy Wood* (1972) Miro, who has published his revealing memoir, goes to Northern Ireland at the behest of Captain Strong, a populist Unionist politician. When a bomb narrowly avoids killing the

---

26    John Boyne (John Kelly), *The Polling of the Dead* (Dublin: Moytura Press, 1993), 73.
27    Shaun Herron, *Miro* (London: Coronet, 1969), 193.
28    Ibid., 20.
29    Shaun Herron, *The Hound and the Fox and the Harper* (London: Coronet, 1970), 155.

captain and injures his wife, Miro starts to suspect that the bomb was aimed at him. When, however, he is kidnapped, he realises that Strong himself was behind the attack and is more dangerous than he first appeared to be.

*The Whore-Mother* (1973) moves away from the world of Miro, but remains within the Northern Irish situation of the early 1970s. John McManus, a middle-class Catholic, has joined the Provisional IRA but feels uncomfortable among the working-class Belfast men who make up his unit and the violence they represent. His decision to leave the organisation leads to him being followed when he tries to escape across the whole of Ireland, as his former colleagues, led by the brutal Powers who rapes and murders John's sister. The Whore-Mother of the title is Ireland herself, and the novel stresses the importance of the figure of the informer in the Irish collective consciousness: "Your father could rape half the women on the street and you could live it down, but if your great-grandfather informed, your great-grandchildren would pass the mark of it to theirs".[30] Herron as a young man had participated in the Spanish Civil War, and *The Bird in Last Year's Nest* (1974) makes use of his experiences there. Although set in the Basque country at the beginning of the 1970s, the events of the conflict which had brought the Franco regime to power resonate throughout the novel. Mauro Ugalde, the headstrong student son of Dion, a village doctor in Navarre, has become involved in ETA, the Basque separatist movement. Captain Basa, head of the Civil Guard and builder of a new prison for political prisoners, is Dion Ugalde's friend and, torn between duty and loyalty to his friend, attempts to warn the doctor of his son's implication in the separatist group. When, however, Mauro is captured and imprisoned for terrorist attacks and attempted kidnap, Dion joins with his son's comrades, men who he neither trusts nor agrees with, to help liberate the boy. Herron's detailed depiction of the doctor, who reveals to his son his own involvement with the republican resistance during the Civil War, draws interesting parallels between the situation in the Basque Country and that in contemporary Ireland, and the problems of conscience shown by Dion reflect those of McManus in *The Whore-Mother*.

---

30   Shaun Herron, *The Whore-Mother* (New York: M. Evans, 1973), 28.

*The Private Sector* (1971) by *Joseph Hone* (1937–2016) introduces Peter Marlow, an Irish secret agent, who is sent to Cairo in the weeks leading up to the Arab-Israeli War of 1967 to find fellow spy Henry Edwards who has disappeared. To complicate matters, Marlow's ex-wife Bridget has become romantically involved with Edwards and all three become involved in a plot to overthrow Egyptian President Nasser. Marlow, closer to Le Carré's Smiley than to Fleming's James Bond, is wrongfully imprisoned, and in *The Sixth Directorate*, he is released, taking the identity of George Graham, a British secret service and Soviet KGB double agent. *The Paris Trap* (1977) is another spy novel, but instead of Marlow, it features Harry Tyson, who is a writer of spy fiction and a film director, as well as being a spy himself. While filming a project in Paris concerning Palestinian terrorists, his girlfriend and his daughter from his estranged wife are kidnapped by Palestinians who want to use the kidnapping as pressure on Tyson to make the film more sympathetic to the Palestinian cause. Peter Marlow reappears in both *The Flowers of the Forest* (1980) and *The Valley of the Fox* (1982). Having retired to the Cotswolds, the spy is recalled to track down Lindsay Phillips, a missing high-ranking secret service officer. The search takes him to Yugoslavia where the personal enigmas which Phillips had harboured are found to be as important as the professional enigmas involved and, as often occurs in Hone's work, lies about parenthood take on substantial significance. *The Valley of the Fox*, the final Marlow novel, finds the spy facing the murder of his new wife and the kidnapping of his step-daughter and once again must leave his rural retreat to combat international forces of terror, this time in the deceptively tranquil English countryside.

Hone's last novel, *Goodbye Again* (2011), is the only one of his works to be set almost entirely in the writer's native Ireland. Ben Contini, half-Italian, half-Irish, is a painter who, after his mother's death, discovers a valuable painting by Modigliani in the family home in Kilkenny. Attempting to find where the painting has come from, Ben is obliged to change his opinion about his father who, he had believed, had been a Jewish Italian refugee, and is forced to face up to the fact that his progenitor had been involved in Nazi art thefts and the trafficking of art treasures. He also meets his grandmother in Italy, who sheds light on the name of his grandfather, a famous Italian painter.

*Michael Kenyon* (1931–2005), an Englishman from Huddersfield, wrote several crime thrillers set in Ireland during the 1960s and 1970s. In *May You Die in Ireland*, Dr William Folley, an obese American professor of mathematics inherits an Irish castle and travels to Ireland to take possession. He becomes inadvertently involved in a scheme to smuggle secret microfilm into the country and is pursued by spies, gangsters and members of the Irish guards. *The 10,000 Welcomes* introduces Detective Superintendent O'Malley who is specially endowed with what at times seems like a supernatural gift. He "never forgot a face" and dreamt of events before they happened.[31] This apparent clairvoyance helps him to outwit the criminal Finn McQuaid who, with the aid of his gangster brother recently arrived from the USA, steals St Patrick's Cross from the Rock of Cashel as part of a plan to hold the Irish government to ransom. O'Malley returns in *The Shooting of Dan McGrew* (1972), where he investigates the disappearance of two Canadian prospectors working for Invernia Exploration in Kilkelly, Ireland on a new site. O'Malley, again relying on his premonition and photographic memory, is helped – or hindered – by Henry Butt, a geologist from Invernia sent from Canada to find his compatriots. In the final O'Malley novel, *A Sorry State*, the detective is sent to the Philippines to bring back an Irish prisoner, a paramilitary gunrunner Paddy Byrne. *The Rapist* (1977), published under the name of Daniel Forbes, returns to Kenyon's common theme of the outsider recently arrived in Ireland and, in this case, alarmingly, manages to concoct another of his light farcical crime novels with the subject of sexual violation.

31   Michael Kenyon, *The 10,000 Welcomes* (London: William Collins, 1970), 23.

# CHAPTER 14

# "Being Irish, you had a certain innate guile that allowed you to think like a criminal and keep one step ahead of them." Irish Crime Writing in the 1970s and 1980s

The 1970s was not a particularly fruitful decade for Irish crime fiction. The popularity of international thrillers, which had begun in the 1950s and continued during the following decades, was still on the rise, and Jack Higgins and others produced a steady stream of works which sold large quantities. Towards the end of the decade Patrick McGinley published his highly inventive works, most of which used some of the strategies of crime fiction, while Bartholomew Gill would inaugurate his ground-breaking McGarr series, the first series in a roughly procedural model to feature Irish police officers. In the early part of the decade, however, Irish lovers of crime fiction had to seek out foreign imports or follow the weekly adventures of Miss Flanagan in *Ireland's Own* magazine. *Ireland's Own*, is a "weekly magazine devoted to all that is best about Ireland and being Irish, published in Wexford town, in the Sunny South East of Ireland without interruption since 1902".[1] The weekly prides itself on "the diversity of interesting material that can be packed into one magazine every week; and all this without indulging in sexual titilation [*sic*] or offensive language".[2] With its avowed aim of setting out "to entertain, educate and inform", from its inception *Ireland's Own* had devoted space to accounts both of true crime and crime fiction narratives.[3] The introductory issue contained the first part of a serial, "Tracked by His Crime" by C. J.

---

1   <https://www.irelandsown.ie/about/>, accessed 18 September 2016.
2   Ibid.
3   Ibid.

Hamilton, set in England and Sligo, which lasted for nine issues over the
months of November and December of 1902, and January 1903.[4] This was
followed by "The Room of the Murder" by Victor Power, and a succes-
sion of stories and serials which contributed to the magazine's popularity
over the years.[5] In 1971 *Ireland's Own* introduced the first story to feature
Inspector McCarthy in "The Casebook of Inspector McCarthy". Written
by John J. Dunne, the series featured Guard detective Michael McCarthy
in several stories until, in March 1972, the series shared the limelight with
a new detective figure, Miss Flanagan. Miss Flanagan was, in many respects, a light, Irish version of Agatha Christie's Miss Marple, but she
achieved enormous popularity in Ireland, and her name became almost
synonymous with that of the magazine. Introduced in the St Patrick's
Day Special edition of *Ireland's Own* on 11 March 1973, Miss Flanagan
is the sister of Monsignor Flanagan. A schoolteacher and a spinster, she
announces her retirement from teaching in the first story, "The Case of
the Broken Ring", along with her intention to become a private investigator. Although apparently staid and gentile, Miss Flanagan admits to
having been "quite a flighty bit" when younger.[6] In her first case she is approached by Mr Verdon, a man who suspects his wife of being unfaithful
and seeks evidence against her. Miss Flanagan, however, on becoming a
private investigator "was determined to be different", and this difference
included putting the ideas of her Catholic faith and concurrent family
values before the supposed wishes of her clients. In keeping with this doctrine Miss Flanagan solves the case by procuring tickets for a school play
in which the Vernons' children were to appear, and engineering the presence of the parents at the show. As a result, both realised the importance
of their family ties. Miss Flanagan's cases are often couched in Catholic
ideas, echoing the dominant ideology of *Ireland's Own* and its readership, but these anonymous tales (presumably written by a number of
commissioned authors) have remained popular well into the twenty-first
century, and continue to appear today. Although other detectives have

---

4    C. J. Hamilton, "Tracked by His Crime", *Ireland's Own* 1, nos. 1–9 (1902–3).
5    Victor Power, "The Room of the Murder", *Ireland's Own* 1, no. 10 (1902), 6–7.
6    John J. Dunne, "The Case of the Broken Ring", *Ireland's Own* 11 March 1973, 11.

been introduced – Tara Bell and Oscar Rafferty were both well received – none has achieved the general admiration of Miss Flanagan.

Mark C. McGarrity (1943–2002), an American who lived for a long period in Dublin, wrote his crime mysteries, all set in Ireland, under the penname of *Bartholomew Gill*. His sixteen novels feature Peter McGarr, a police detective working for the Dublin police. McGarr was first introduced in *McGarr and the Politician's Wife* (1977), later republished as *The Death of an Irish Politician*, where he is 44 years old and "looked like a minor civil servant or a successful racetrack tout".[7] He had worked some twenty years in Europe for Interpol, and his acquired cosmopolitanism is used throughout the series to offset his acclaimed upbringing in the inner city slums of Ireland's capital. McGarr is often accompanied by his wife Noreen, whose involvement in many of the cases circumvents the limits of strict realism. His colleagues include Hughie Ward, Liam O'Shaughnessy, Bernie McKeon, and Ruth Bresnahan, who appear continually throughout the series, contributing not only to the professional but also to the social ambience and helping to create what is arguably the first police procedural series set in Ireland. In *McGarr and the Politician's Wife* the discovery of a near-dead American yachtsman at a Wicklow marina leads to a somewhat pedestrian mystery involving the politician's wife of the title and gun smuggling between the IRA and their American contacts.

Apart from the main plot, there are a number of interesting details in this first novel of the series. The character of McGarr as it develops reveals a number of quirks, not all of which seem consistent with his position in the Gardaí. This can be seen when, for instance, he threatens an English steward at the marina with extradition for failing to comply with his orders, or his implicit support for the IRA. It does, however, present an interesting portrayal of Ireland in the 1970s, where the detective can still threaten a subordinate that he would find himself "tracking vagrant tinkers in Donegal",[8] or where the homophobic guards could still refer to homosexuals with terms such as "fairy" or "queer".[9]

---

7    Bartholomew Gill, *McGarr and the Politician's Wife* (New York: Avon, 1977), 5.
8    Ibid., 35.
9    Ibid., 124.

*McGarr and the Sienese Conspiracy* (1977), later retitled *The Death of an Irish Consul*, finds McGarr in Italy, investigating a series of murders connected with events in Northern Ireland and trying to prevent the death of the British ambassador. The novel reintroduces the London-based Irish private detective, Hugh Madigan, who had appeared in *McGarr and the Politician's Wife*. McGarr, who has introduced the "computer process"[10] to the Irish police, boasts of information he holds which has come from a contact, the brother of a fellow officer, who is Kerry commanding officer of the IRA, and threatens the British authorities with halting Irish cooperation on IRA intelligence if they refuse to cooperate. In *McGarr on the Cliffs of Moher* (1978), later repackaged as *The Death of an Irish Lass*, the detective investigates the murder of a young returned immigrant and her unborn baby on a lonely clifftop. Again the IRA and its American support group, Noraid, is involve, and again McGarr's ambiguous feelings toward the organisation are echoed. *McGarr at the Dublin Horse Show* (1979), also known as *The Death of an Irish Tradition*, and *McGarr and the PM of Belgrave Square* (1983) find the detective working on cases in his home city of Dublin, while in *McGarr and the Method of Descartes* (1984) he travels to Belfast to help thwart a murder plot against Loyalist leader Ian Paisley.

In *McGarr and the Legacy of a Woman Scorned* (1986) the policeman's wife Noreen is kidnapped while helping her husband on the murder case of an elderly horse breeder, while *The Death of a Joyce Scholar* (1989), nominated for an Edgar award and arguably the most accomplished work in the series, reveals numerous inter-textual links with Joyce's *Ulysses* as McGarr investigates the murder of Trinity professor Kevin Coyle during a Dublin Bloomsday celebration. *The Death of Love* (1992) sees McGarr, a first-time father at the age of 51, looking into the death of a banker against the backdrop of the economic crisis of the late 1980s. *Death on a Cold, Wild River* (1993) takes the now Chief Superintendent of the Serious Crimes Unit to rural Donegal and *Death of an Ardent Bibliophile* (1995) renews the literary themes explored in *The Death of a Joyce Scholar*, with the victim this time being an expert on the works of Jonathan Swift. The presence of McGarr's wife is humorously commented on by a reporter who, in the "voice

10    Bartholomew Gill, *McGarr and the Sienese Conspiracy* (New York: Avon, 1977), 79.

of a fishwife" asks him; "Do yeh always drag the wife along with yeh on a moorder investigation".[11] *The Death of an Irish Sea Wolf* (1996) is a routine murder mystery with Second World War overtones, while both *The Death of an Irish Tinker* (1997) and *The Death of an Irish Lover* (2000) are more memorable for the events surrounding the private lives of Hughie, Bernie and Rose. In *The Death of an Irish Sinner* (2001) McGarr's investigation into the Opus Dei and the death of a woman reputed to be a daughter of sect founder Escrivá is overshadowed by tragic events in his own family.

McGarr's last fictional outing, *Death in Dublin*, would be published in 2002, the year of the author's untimely death in a domestic accident. It is a melancholy novel, with a hauntingly valedictorian tone, in which McGarr sadly watches the police force he had formed part of for so long seeming to disintegrate under the weight of political patronage. Dublin, as Gill sees it, is awash with drugs, sex and illegal money, and the honourable guards of the past have been replaced by politically motivated mavericks. The McGarr novels were popular in Ireland, where Irish readers were given the unusual opportunity of reading about Irish police officers solving Irish crimes within an Irish context. It is not difficult to see how his work influenced the younger generation of Irish crime writers whose careers would begin in the mid-to-late 1990s and the first years of the twenty-first century. For Elizabeth Mannion, although Gill's work "problematizes consideration of transnationalism in Irish crime fiction, as it pertains to Irish American influences and settings" the McGarr series, nevertheless, like no other "looks out and in simultaneously".[12]

*Patrick McGinley* (b. 1937) has, since the publication of his first novel *Bogmail* (1978), "attracted appreciative critical attention – just not enough of it".[13] *Bogmail* is a fascinating work and stands as a fine example of the potential for Irish crime fiction, even in a decade, the 1970s, which was

11  Bartholomew Gill, *Death of an Ardent Bibliophile* (London: Macmillan, 1995), 46.
12  Elizabeth Mannion, "Before the Tiger Roared: Bartholomew Gill's Ireland" in *Guilt Rules All: Irish Mystery, Detective, and Crime Fiction*, ed Elizabeth Mannion and Brian Cliff (Syracuse, NY: Syracuse University Press, 2020), 38.
13  Thomas F. Shea, "Patrick McGinley's Appropriation of Cúchulainn: Revisions in *The Trick of the Ga Bolga*", *New Hibernia Review/ Iris Éireannach Nua* 5, no. 3 (Autumn 2001), 114.

not exactly renowned for either the proliferation or proficiency of writers working within the genre. Owing as much to Flann O'Brien as to Sherlock Holmes, the novel begins with Roarty, the local publican and a former priest, killing his barman with volume twenty-five of the *Encyclopaedia Britannica* after feeding him an omelette laced with poison mushrooms. The crime is apparently undetected in the small Donegal community, but a series of mysterious messages from a "bogmailer" threaten to reveal the crime. The identity of the "bogmailer" remains a mystery, and the suspects include an Englishman working for a mining company, the Catholic priest, a local Marxist, a lobsterman and a journalist. *Bogmail* is also notable for the figure of Sergeant McGink, who considers that a good police officer requires imagination, rather than logic, believing that a "born policeman has a criminal imagination".[14] The sergeant was, we are told, "two men in one", the first "who had a mind like a magpie, was a treasury of forensic knowledge" while the second "who drew conclusions, was an inept imbecile".[15] Although "it is Roarty rather than the local lawman who is the true "detective" of the piece",[16] McGinty's characterisation is excellent and McGink remains one of the most memorable of fictional Irish detectives ever produced.

*Bogmail* was criticised in McGinley's native Donegal, with the *Donegal Democrat* labelling it "a horrific concoction of filth" and "a shocking libel".[17] It was converted into a three-piece television drama by BBC Northern Ireland in 1991, with the title being changed to *Murder in Eden*, and the novel was reissued by New Island in 2017 to excellent reviews. Like *Bogmail*, the author's second novel, *Goosefoot* (1982), mixes absurd comedy with murder mystery in the story of a young country woman who goes to Dublin to work as a teacher and becomes embroiled with a number of men, including Bernard Baggotty, accused of his wife's murder, and the

---

14    Patrick McGinley, *Bogmail* (London: Flamingo, 1978), 61.
15    Ibid., 193.
16    David Roy, "Author Patrick McGinley on 'concoction of filth' that Disgusted Donegal", *The Irish News*, 27 July 2017, <https://www.irishnews.com/arts/2017/07/27/news/back-to-the-bog-patrick-mcginley-on-the-new-edition-of-his-debut-novel-bogmail-1092825/>, accessed 5 September 2017.
17    Ibid.

degenerate Detective McMyler. In *Fox Prints* (1983), Martin Reddin, a postgraduate student working on Joyce's *Finnegan's Wake*, is forced to leave Ireland. He takes employment as cook and butler in Foxgloves, a suburban mansion, where he keeps the company of an Englishman, a Welshman and a Scot. When a number of local women, including the Irishman's lover, are murdered, suspicion immediately falls on Reddin, who has changed his name to Charles Keating to avoid detection. The murders are all accompanied by some reference to foxes – one victim wears a fox fur, another reads *Foxe's Book of Martyrs* – and the killer sends a number of clues, squares of material cut from the victims' dresses.

*Foggage* (1983) returns to the world of Donegal farms and is a tragicomic tale of incest and redemption which highlights McGinley's skills as a storyteller and his mastery of dark humour. *The Trick of the Ga Bolga* (1985) is "an intriguingly allusive Irish novel" created by "appropriating and warping legends of the ancient Ulster cycle".[18] George Coote, an Englishman who has come to rural Donegal to avoid the horrors of the Second World War and start a potato farm, is caught in the middle of a meaningless feud between his two neighbours, Salmo and the Proker. During a heated dispute Coote accidentally kills the Proker and hides his body by sinking it with potatoes in the pockets. Salmo is initially blamed and the local constable Sergeant Blowick, more interested in solving the mystery of his stolen cap, arrests him. Coote becomes obsessed with the legend of the Ga Bolga, which he mistakenly believes is a sexual trick, and tries to provide alibis for the innocent Salmo, who nevertheless refuses to protest his innocence, believing himself to be guilty in thought, while at the same time occulting his own guilt. The novel plays with the intricacies of Irish mythology as it provides a comic but poignant portrait of an Englishman in the rural Ireland of the 1940s. The air of licentiousness and physical violence comes to a head with the jealous, shell-shocked McMackin returning from the war and Coote discovering that "Ireland is the last place one should seek refuge from the cruelty, anger, and mayhem associated with war".[19]

18   Shea, "Appropriation of Cúchulain", 114.
19   Ibid.

*The Red Men* (1987) is a parable-like narrative set once again in rural Donegal. Gulban Heron, hotel and shop-owner, gives each of his four sons a gift of ten thousand pounds, telling them that the one who after a year shows he has best used the money will become his heir. The quest is complicated by the sudden death of Gulban's favourite son, Jack, also the favourite to become heir. The three remaining red-headed brothers, the red men of the title, a playboy, an academic and a priest struggle to come to terms with their situation and "the Irish mood turns oddly Greek and doom-laden as the actors discover the truths of their own histories and na-tures".[20] Murder is important in *The Red Men*, but not central to the plot, as it is in *The Devil's Diary* (1988), in which Father Jerry McSharry returns to Ireland, physically and psychologically scarred after a long period of illness and existential doubt. He finds that a school friend, Art Brennan, has also returned to the village after making a fortune in America, and has spent time and money in attempts to modernise the area. The priest resents this intrusion on traditional rural life and berates his childhood friend, causing a rift – complicated by both men being attracted to the same woman – which would widen when Jerry's brother, Hugh, also returns to the village after a period overseas and buys a field which Brennan had sought to purchase. A number of circumstances, including a suspicious car accident, seem to point to the fact that Brennan is trying to harm the two brothers, and when the businessman is found dead, suspicion falls on Hugo. Jerry discovers a hand-written book which he believes to be his brother's diary and which gives an apparently fictional account which faithfully copies the events surrounding Brennan's death.

Hugo explains to his brother that the "diary" is a work of fiction based on dreams, and the revelation of incidents related to the priest's past help to cast doubt on the reliability of Jerry's reading of the text. Typically, a letter sent to explain all explains nothing, and textual truths, we learn, are subject to various degrees of interpretation. The Devil's Diary retains some of the author's characteristic humour, but the realistic setting and premise give this psychological thriller a sense of urgency and anxiety missing,

---

20    Walter Nash, "Father Bosco to Africa", *London Review of Books* 9, no. 3 (5 February 1987), 22.

perhaps, from McGinley's more parabolic or fabulous fictions. The influence of Flann O'Brien is still there, but the novel falls more clearly into the category of mainstream crime fiction than his earlier works. *The Last Soldier's Song* (1994) is a historical novel set in the time of the Irish revolutionary period, and would be his last work in nearly twenty years until McGinley published two surprising novels in the second decade of the twenty-first century.

The comic crime novels written by Dublin-born *Ruth Dudley-Edwards* (b. 1944) are light, but often biting satires, generally directed against the British Establishment and its institutions. Edwards, an English resident, claims that she "fell into crime writing by accident (an unexpected offer), intended to write straight detection but couldn't stop the farce and the jokes".[21] *Corridors of Death* (1981) introduces Superintendent Jim Milton and Robert Amiss, both of whom would feature in the writer's subsequent novels. Milton befriends Amiss, Private Secretary to the departmental head at Whitehall, Sir Nicholas Clark, who has been murdered with an abstract sculpture titled "Reconciliation". Confused by the apparently interminable bureaucracy in Whitehall, the Scotland Yard officer uses Amiss to help him understand the procedures and seek the killer or killers of Sir Nicholas and his secretary Gladys. In the process of the investigation they discover that Clark is not the well-liked patriarch they had originally been led to believe, but instead had been making multiple enemies, including his cheating wife, his gay son and most of his colleagues. Edwards uses the structure and many of the conventions of the Golden Age mystery for this satire, with diagrams and lists helping the unlikely team of career police officer and civil servant to discover the murderer. The use of an amateur detective by a modern police officer gives the work an extemporal, anachronistic feel, which adds to the overall comic nature of the book.

The same characters are reunited in *The Saint Valentine's Day Murders* (1984), where Amiss, seconded by his civil service department to a boring packaging department of the British Conservation Society, and Milton, are joined by a young graduate police officer, Ellis Pooley, a fan of murder

21 Ruth Dudley Edwards, "Crime fiction or Mystery", <https://www.ruthdudley edwards.co.uk/crime-fiction/>, accessed 16 March 2019.

mysteries, to resolve the deaths of employees and their families who have
been victims of the Saint Valentine's day murders of the title. The political incorrectness which would become Edwards' hallmark is evident
throughout the novel, with the disagreeable Melissa, a radical lesbian feminist, and the Irish clerical assistant Cathy, "who bears on her face signs of
the 800 years of sorrow and oppression of her race" bearing the brunt of
Edwards' satire.[22] *The School of English Murder* (1990) finds Robert Amiss
working in an Irish pub after having resigned his post in the civil service.
His police friends place him in a London language school in an (unofficial) undercover capacity to investigate a number of mysterious murders
where "Ahmed killed Ned at the behest of Sven and Cath, an as yet un-
identified Arab killed Ahmed, almost certainly at Sven's behest; and Rich
killed Cath".[23]

In *Clubbed to Death* (1992) Amiss is again working undercover as a
waiter at a staid gentleman's club in London's St James. Ellis Pooley believes
the club secretary has been murdered and wants Amiss to investigate from
within the institution. The gentlemen of the club are bigots who see it as
"a nice change to have somebody white and English-speaking looking for a
job".[24] Edwards playfully emphasises the members' hatred of the Irish, seen
as "unfortunate Micks",[25] "Hun lovers",[26] and "murdering bog-trotters".[27]
*Matricide at St Martha's* (1994) introduces Ida "Jack" Troutbeck, bursar at
St Martha's Women's College, Cambridge, where Robert Amiss has been
given a one-year visiting fellowship at his friend Troutbeck's behest. The
college has been left a sum of money by a rich former student and the disagreement divides the faculty into three distinct groups, who are named
Virgins, the conservative supporters of the Mistress, the radical feminist
Dykes and the Old Women, the ineffective male members of the staff.

---

22   Ruth Dudley Edwards, *The Saint Valentine's Day Murders*, 2nd edn (Scottsdale,
     AZ: Poisoned Pen Press, 2011), 14.
23   Ruth Dudley Edwards, *The School of English Murder* (London: Gollancz Crime,
     1990), 219.
24   Ruth Dudley Edwards, *Clubbed to Death* (London: Gollancz Crime, 1992), 26.
25   Ibid., 100.
26   Ibid., 115.
27   Ibid., 119.

The Virgins want to use the money for scholarships, the Dykes to build a centre for Gender and Ethnic Studies and the Old Women to furnish a wine cellar. The Mistress and a radical American feminist are murdered, and the amateur detective Amiss once again is faced with uncovering the killer, this time without the support of his friends in the police, but hampered by the bombastic police officer and religious fundamentalist Romford. This satire on the campus novel and on political correctness finds Robert undermined because of his "unrelieved white Anglo-Saxon maleness" and "his other twin disadvantages of heterosexuality and good health",[28] as the Dykes seek to create "a PC heaven in a dank corner of Cambridge".[29] Troutbeck reappears with Robert Amiss in *Ten Lords A-Leaping* (1995), set in the House of Lords where Troutbeck, who has been made a life peer, is to make her maiden speech on fox hunting. A number of peers are murdered, and the real killer manages for a time to cast suspicion onto anti-hunt activists until Robert, Pooley and Milton reveal the truth. The Troutbeck and Amiss series would continue throughout the 1990s and into the first decade of the new millennium.

One of the most interesting of the Irish crime writers who started to publish in the 1980s is *M. S. Power* (b. 1935). His first novel, *Hunt for the Autumn Clowns* (1983), tells the story of Pericles Stort, a backward adolescent in the rural west of Ireland who is responsible for the death of his grandfather. The boy's burgeoning sexuality becomes the object of attention from his schoolteacher, from the local Guard constable who is having an affair with the boy's mother, and from the local priest, banished to the rural parish for assumed misconduct and who dies trying to save Pericles. This often humorous, at times tragic, tale, was followed by the more conventional *Children of the North* trilogy, consisting of *The Killing of Yesterday's Children* (1985), *Lonely the Man without Heroes* (1986) and *A Darkness in the Eye* (1987). Set in the Northern Ireland of the Troubles, these novels introduce the figures of Arthur Apple, a diplomat who has been forced to leave the service and who is now living in retirement in Belfast after

28 Ruth Dudley Edwards, *Matricide at St Martha's* (London: HarperCollins, 1994), 15.
29 Ibid., 214.

an incident regarding a mystical experience in Mexico. In *The Killing of Yesterday's Children*, Apple (who constantly talks to two imaginary friends) is working in a betting shop, which is in fact a front for an IRA money laundering operation, supervised by republican assassin Martin Deely. When Martin fails in an attempt to kill British army Colonel Maddox, the RUC under Mr Asher hunt Deely down, aided by his former IRA colleagues who have disowned the gunman. Feeling sympathy for Deely, Apple tries to negotiate his freedom by kidnapping Asher, but their safe house is discovered by Reilly, Martin's erstwhile republican colleague, who kill him and, inadvertently provokes a fatal heart attack in Apple.

In *Lonely the Man without Heroes*, Asher and Seamus Reilly again join forces to solve a case in which a British army execution squad is apparently targeting innocent civilians in Belfast. As in the previous novel, the outstanding feature of this work is the mutual dependence and cooperation by the RUC and the IRA, with Asher and Reilly openly recognising that their similarities as Irishmen are greater than those between either and the British security forces. They declare that, above all, they are "both Irish"[30] and Asher's allegiance to his police force and the ethos under which it operates can only be subservient to his status as an Irishman:

> For all his hatred of the IRA, for all his deep-rooted if somewhat flimsy Protestantism, for all his allegiance to the Crown, Asher was first and foremost an Irishman, and there was something in his Irish blood that abhorred the pounding of British boots on Irish soil.[31]

This insistence is further emphasised in *A Darkness in the Eye*, where Asher and Reilly are described as being "totally Irish".[32] In this novel, set among the events surrounding the Brighton bombings, the IRA is split over its tactical future, with Reilly among those who support the calling of a ceasefire.

30   M. S. Power, *Lonely the Man without Heroes* (London: William Heinemann, 1986), 196.

31   Ibid., 83.

32   M. S. Power, *A Darkness in the Eye* (London: William Heinemann, 1987), 39.

*Bridie and the Silver Lady* (1988), the story of a young girl who, after suffering sexual abuse from her father, is urged to commit murder by a ghostly presence believed to be the human transmutation of an owl, marks a return to the rural gothic of *Hunt for the Autumn Clowns*. A similar tone is set in *Crucible of Fools* (1990), which tells the tragic tale of Dan Loftus who, after the loss of his child and subsequent suicide of his wife, is accused of murder and necrophilia and is hunted down by his implacable neighbours. Between these two works set in the west of Ireland, Power published *The Crucifixion of Septimus Roach* (1989), a murder mystery set in the Haiti of "Baby Doc" Duvalier. Power returned to the Northern Ireland of the Troubles for *Come the Executioner* (1991), where the murder of a British army officer in Belfast is attributed to the IRA, while the RUC, the British government and the British army collude to conceal the truth – that Captain Peter Larski has in fact been killed by the army. The plot is typical of thrillers of the period, and is ultimately pessimistic with regards to the validity of the RUC as a legitimate and impartial police force. The fact that the situation can only be partially resolved by outsiders – an American journalist and an English police officer echoes the negative viewpoint of the period. Indeed, the only Northern Irish figure who appears to tell the truth is the IRA commander, anxious that his group not be blamed for the death of the army officer.

*The Stalker's Apprentice* (1993) is an accomplished work in which a London publisher's assistant, Marcus Walwyn, is given a manuscript that outlines a series of murders and seemingly supplies instructions which convert it into a textbook for murder. Walwyn and the police involved in investigating the case, Birt and Wilson, reappear in the sequel to the novel, *Dealing with Kranze* (1996), where they enlist the aid of the killer, released from prison on technical grounds, to help hunt down the psychopath who had allegedly provided the manuscript in the earlier novel. Between these two works, Power published *A Sheltering Silence* (1994), a murder mystery set in Ifreann in the rural west of Ireland. A young villager with mental disabilities, Christy Codd, is chosen as the scapegoat for the murder of a young girl whose body is discovered by the river bank. Lots are drawn to decide which man from the community is to kill the suspect, and the task is given to the narrator's father, who later kills himself when a stranger,

Johnsey, discovered to be the murdered girl's half-brother, arrives asking questions about the killing. Johnsey's investigations, much more thorough than those of the guards, discover the involvement of the village priest and serve to exonerate the innocent Christy.

Cork-born *T. P. O'Mahony* (b. 1939), commentator on religious affairs for the *Irish Press*, published two novels, the second of which, *The Vatican Caper* (1981), is a thriller set in the future of 1988 and chronicles the murder of the first Irish Pope. The investigation led by Irish journalist Michael John Carmody discovers a number of secrets regarding the Pope, including a secret marriage and the opposition of a group of Irish priests and Vatican officials who aim to help republican groups create a united Ireland through a coup involving the Irish Liberation Front. Although light in tone and ultimately conservative in scope and intent, *The Vatican Caper* reveals a new frankness when dealing with the sexuality of the clergy and the implied collusion between elements of the Catholic Church and terrorist groups.

Despite being in the middle of what Ross calls the "near forty- year hiatus" in Irish crime writing, the writers who published in the 1970s and 1980s managed to make a significant contribution to the genre in Ireland. Although Bartholomew Gill was an American, his use of an intelligent, if at times contradictory, Irish police officer effectively paved the way for future Irish crime fiction. Patrick McGinty made a fine contribution to the more metaphysical crime writing at which so many Irish authors excel, while Ruth Dudley Edwards's iconoclastic humour allowed a refreshing if exaggerated insight into the extremes of the idiosyncrasies of members of the establishment, be they Irish or English. That these writers coincided with the number of authors writing international spy thrillers points to a period in which, far from being in paralysis, Irish crime writing was pointing the way to a promising future.

# CHAPTER 15

# "It was the virus of my country's illness that felled him." Northern Ireland

Writing in 1976, James MacKillop noted that in the seven years since the beginning of the Troubles in 1969, sixteen novels had been published on the subject.[1] In 1989, Bill Rolston was able to state that, in the twenty years since 1969, over two hundred novels focussed on the Northern Irish Troubles had already appeared.[2] Aaron Kelly, in 2005, revealed that the production of Troubles-related thrillers had reached four hundred.[3] All of these critics complained that many of the early novels had been written by outsiders, often journalists who, during their stint covering the conflict, decided to take advantage by producing generic thrillers which, although ostensibly using the Northern Irish situation, could often have been written about any violent political conflict taking place in any part of the world. These were generally thrillers which "exploit the Ulster agony as another way of reaching a defined reader market".[4] These generally saw violence as deriving from the republicans, depicted as psychopaths, professionals or idealists, ignored the activities of loyalists, and regarded the British army as "a buffer between the warring tribes".[5] As such, these novels served to "faithfully replicate dominant British explanations of the aetiology of the Northern 'troubles'".[6] Kelly argues that, at its most mechanistic, the thriller "is a form which attempts to suggest that there

---

1   James MacKillop, "Ulster Violence in Fiction" in *Conflict in Ireland*, ed. E. Sullivan et al. (Gainesville, FL: Florida University Press, 1976), 134.
2   Bill Rolston, "Mothers, Whores and Villains", *Race and Class* 31, no. 1 (1989), 41.
3   Aaron Kelly, *The Thriller and Northern Ireland Since 1969: Utterly Resigned Terror* (Aldershot: Ashgate, 2005), 1.
4   MacKillop, "Ulster Violence", 136.
5   Rolston, "Mothers, Whores", 41.
6   Ibid., 42.

are no classes, no gender, no community or women's groups, no human agency or collective projects of emancipation".[7] But he also recognises that a thriller can likewise be "multicoded" and "a monumental form of social complexity" which "can house a reactionary façade of ideological defence or withdrawal" while also containing "a utopian architecture of social construction and spatialization".[8]

We have already examined some of the Troubles thrillers produced by Jack Higgins, a long-time resident in Belfast, or Dubliner M. S. Power's *Children of the North* trilogy, and later we will look at some of the Troubles thrillers written during the 1990s by Irish authors. There were, however, several writers who wrote interesting works that predated or covered the first years of the conflict, presenting many varied viewpoints and perspectives. These included Northern Protestants like Maurice Leitch, Glenn Patterson or David Park, Northern Catholics such as John Morrow, Benedict Kiely or Danny Morrison, or Southerners like Terence De Vere White, Jennifer Johnston or John Broderick. These writers did not write generic thrillers, but rather novels which captured the essential horrors of the conflict, informed by a literary tradition which included the narratives of predecessors such as Frank O'Connor, Seán O'Faoláin and Liam O'Flaherty, who had narrated an earlier conflict.

Despite this, however, it is perhaps necessary to first consider the importance of *Frederick Lawrence Green*, an English-born author who, after marrying an Irish woman, lived in Belfast from the mid-1930s. His *Odd Man Out* (1945), while owing much to Liam O'Flaherty's *The Informer*, provided what could almost be seen as a blueprint for fiction coming from and concerning Northern Ireland. The novel is set in Belfast, and although the city is never named, references to the Falls and Shankill leave little doubt as to its setting. Similarly, the IRA also remains unnamed, although there is little doubt as to the identity of the revolutionary Organisation to which Johnny McQueen belongs. McQueen is wounded after a failed armed raid aimed at filling the coffers of the Organisation, and much of the novel is taken up by his comrades searching the claustrophobic streets

---

7    Kelly, *The Thriller*, 4.
8    Ibid., 5.

of Belfast in search of their companion. The characters are close to those who would become archetypes in the Troubles fiction from the 1970s onwards. These include Teresa, the evil, self-serving traitor, who sells the fugitives to the "peelers", the Protestant women and their initially reluctant husbands who help the Catholic outlaws, Agnes, the virginal innocent, the unrelenting nameless Inspector, Shell, who with his empty cage searches for his escaped budgerigar, a wonderful metaphor for the situation in Belfast, and, of course, Father Tom, the seemingly helpful priest who betrays the escapees. *Odd Man Out* was converted into a successful film, directed by Carol Reid and starring James Mason which, like Green's novel, succeeded in creating an image of the northern city which would permeate the popular imagination for years after its release.

The events depicted in *Odd Man Out* are, presumably, a fictional representation of those carried out during the IRA's Northern Campaign, which started in September 1942 and ended in December of the same year, and which saw gunfights, raids and hostage situations across Northern Ireland and into the Republic. The measures taken by both British and Irish governments contributed towards a lull in armed republican activity, which would last until the IRA's Border Campaign, from December 1956 until February 1962. Although notable more for its repercussions in popular song (especially Sean Costelloe's "Sean South of Garryowen") than in narrative fiction, at least one novel dealt with fictional events within this campaign. *John Broderick*, a native of Athlone, published *The Fugitives* (1962), a thriller in which Paddy Fallon is on the run from the authorities in his rural Southern hometown after returning from London, where he has been involved in the "execution" of a British politician. Helped by his sister, Lily, Paddy hides out in the bogs, and it is in his descriptions of the harsh scenery in which the fugitive seeks refuge that Broderick's writing is at its best. The novel also introduces some interesting characters, such as the young Guard who "looked like an overgrown schoolboy dressed up as a policeman".[9] Hugh Ward, the high-ranking IRA official who is responsible for assuring Paddy's compliance, could serve as a model for the cold, aesthetic stereotype of the republican ideologue who would appear in much

9    John Broderick, *The Fugitives* (London: Weidenfeld & Nicolson, 1962), 84.

later Troubles narratives. Hugh – to whom Lily is initially attracted – is openly homosexual and, in turn, attracted to Paddy, and would appear in various guises in works by writers such as Jack Higgins or, memorably, in the guise of Skeffington, a "Padraig Pearse clone" in Bernard McLaverty's *Cal* (1983).[10]

The period between the end of the Border Campaign and the start of the modern Troubles in 1969 is also somewhat under-represented in fictional terms. One exception, however, is *Maurice Leitch*, an early example of the "liberal" Protestant writer who, along with later figures such as Glenn Patterson and David Park, would play such an important role in the dissemination of Northern Irish fiction. Leitch's first novel, *The Liberty Lad* (1965), paints a fascinating picture of the territory in the mid-1960s, where Frank Glass, a shy young schoolteacher relates his experiences amid the tense atmosphere of a small mill town, Kildargan, where, in hindsight, it appears that something terrible is about to happen. The religious intolerance bubbles under the surface, and the divide between the two communities is exemplified by the railway line, which "skirts the energetic centre of population and separates also Protestants from Catholics".[11] *The Liberty Lad* deals with topics like homosexuality and political corruption, marking it a revolutionary debut in a land in which such themes had been taboo, a place where people "hadn't changed since their ancestors arrived from Ayrshire and the other depressed Scottish shires three centuries ago, not to better themselves, as it turned out, but to mark time, strugglingly".[12]

The oppressive nature of pre-Troubles Northern Ireland is also apparent in *Poor Lazarus* (1969) which, set in 1967, follows a film producer's attempts to record the day-to-day life of Albert Yarr, one of the few Protestants living in Ballyboe, leading to the mental deterioration of the helplessly unstable protagonist. *Silver's City* (1981) is one of the great novels to appear from the first decade of the Troubles, in which Scottish mercenary Ned Galloway is charged with engineering the escape from a guarded hospital room of "Silver" Steele, a member of the Protestant old Guard who has

10    Bernard McLaverty, *Cal* (London: Jonathan Cape, 1983), 119.
11    Maurice Leitch, *The Liberty Lad*, 2nd edn (London: Panther, 1968), 104).
12    Ibid., 15.

spent the last year in prison after being one of the first loyalist terrorists to be imprisoned. Converted into a hero among his community, Silver's time in prison has led him to reflect on his actions and his political vision. *Silver's City* is also notable for the depiction of Belfast at the heart of the Troubles, resembling, in the words of Stephanie Schwerter, "a necropolis in which peace and survival are excluded".[13]

*The Smoke King* (1999) is a fascinating crime thriller set in a small Northern Irish market town during the Second World War, where Willie Washington, a black American GI, is accused of the murder of a local white woman. The case is investigated by Lawlor, a Southern Catholic police officer who had moved to Northern Ireland to join the RUC on the disbandment of the RIC. Lawlor, whose wife has left him, is seen as a traitor by fellow Catholics, but is also mistrusted by the local Protestants who are suspicious of his true sympathies. Leitch cleverly draws contrasts and comparisons between religious and racial prejudice in a work whose underlying tragedy comments not only on the historical situation of Northern Ireland during the Second World War but also on the prejudices, ignorance and lack of understanding which contributed to the outbreak of violence in the late 1960s and which still haunted the province when the novel was written.

Leitch has continued to publish throughout the first decades of the new century, and his works are as varied in subject matter as they are in design. His latest novel, for example, *Gone to Earth* (2019) tells, like the Spanish film *The Endless Trench* (*La trinchera infinita*, 2019), the story of a former left-wing mayor forced to hide in his own house after Franco's victory in the Spanish Civil War. Leitch's victim, like his counterpart in the film, lives for years in a state of self-imposed imprisonment, and his condition, "frozen in a twenty-year-old block of ice" draws inevitable comparisons with the political situation in Northern Ireland.[14]

*Peter Leslie's The Extremists* (1970) is one of the first novels to make fictional use of the post-1969 Troubles. A British army officer, Lieutenant Giles Fleming, takes on the role of detective in an attempt to find the killer

---

13   Stephanie Schwerter, "Peacefire: Belfast Between Reality and Fiction", *The Canadian Journal of Irish Studies* 33, no. 2 (2007), 19.
14   Maurice Leitch, *Gone to Earth* (Belfast: Turnpike, 2019), 28.

of his friend Tony Clifford, shot by a single sniper bullet. Although his colonel does not want Fleming to be "messing around playing detective", the lieutenant makes contact with forces from both sides of the religious divide.[15] He uses his contacts to evaluate both sides, reasoning that the "patriotism of the Orangemen is perverted by narrowmindedness – by bloody ignorance, if you like", while "although the Republicans are far more intelligent, their intelligence is warped by bitterness and a refusal to face the facts".[16] *The Extremists* introduces several topics which would become common features in Troubles thrillers, including the use of double agents, name changes, and sex and conspiracy theories; it was published in London by the New English Library, a publishing house well known for its exploitation of topical themes.

Terence De Vere White's *The Distance and the Dark* (1973) provides an interesting look at the Troubles from a Southern perspective. When Everard Harvey's son is killed, suspicion falls on Gallagher, a militant in the terrorist organisation Gallowglass, a small republican splinter group. Although Harvey is convinced of Gallagher's guilt, he soon realises that the terrorist is protected by politicians, and McCarthy, a part-time FCA soldier who tells Harvey he believes that the explosives used in the killing had been stolen from an army depot, is killed by a car bomb alongside his baby son and the child's nurse. *The Distance and the Dark* is by no means a typical Troubles thriller, but its quiet intensity evokes the human tragedy caused by the conflict. De Vere White's subtle use of the disintegration of Harvey's assumed moral certainties in parallel with the collapse of his marriage provides a telling commentary on the crisis and its effect in the South.

Another Southern novelist, *Jennifer Johnston*, would also evoke the Troubles in her works. Although set during the First World War, *How Many Miles to Babylon?* (1975) provides an oblique commentary on the situation in Northern Ireland in the early years of the conflict, and the tragic death of the Protestant Alexander and his Catholic friend Jerry for refusing to obey mindless orders echoes the inhumanity of the contemporary Troubles. Similarly, *The Old Jest* uses events of the past, this time in

15    Peter Leslie, *The Extremists* (London: New English Library, 1970), 8.
16    Ibid., 64.

the early revolutionary period of the 1920s, to address current issues, while both *Shadows on Our Skin* (1977) and *The Railway Station Man* (1984) are set in the North during the Troubles. In the former, brothers Joe and Brendan Logan fall in love with Kathleen, a teacher from Dublin living in Northern Ireland. Brendan, the elder, has just returned from London, where he has been involved in the republican movement, unwittingly causes Kathleen, whose fiancée is a British soldier serving in Germany, to be betrayed and, after being tarred and feathered by republicans, she returns to her Dublin home. In *The Railway Station Man*, a schoolteacher – Helen's husband, and father ofher son Jack  has been "accidentally" killed while visiting the father of a pupil, an officer in the RUC. While Helen starts a relationship with Roger, a British war veteran who has come to live in an old railway station house in Donegal, Jack comes under the influence of Manus, a local youth involved in the IRA. When they bring explosives to the area, both Jack and Roger are killed, along with two terrorists, in a fortuitous blast. In *The Illusionist* (1995), the unsympathetic and unlikeable illusionist of the title is also fortuitously killed by an IRA bomb, this time in London.

By the late 1970s, several writers were using the Northern Irish Troubles as a starting point for interesting narratives, often incorporating noir themes, sensibilities and plotlines. *A Hole in the Head* (1977), by the subversive modernist *Frances Stuart*, follows Barnaby Shane, a writer under medical treatment for psychological problems, whose only remaining friend is Arnold Grundy, leader of the BAM, the Belbury Association of Militiamen. Belbury is Belfast, and his contacts, along with his "facility for entering into conflicting viewpoints" and an "aptitude for sharing extreme positions and attitudes" lead to his being chosen as a mediator to negotiate the end of a hostage situation involving a government minister and Grundy's two children. In *John Morrow's The Confessions of Proinsias O'Toole* (1977), the eponymous hero participates in ludicrous plots aimed at ending the Troubles. One of these would be supporting a far-right, racist English politician in the hope that, if he were elected, he would withdraw troops from Northern Ireland so that they could be redeployed controlling the immigrant population in the English West Midlands. Similarly, Proinsias supports Operation Starkey, "a plan for the 'resettlement' in Ireland of the dissident coloured population and its expeditious replacement by the displaced Irish".[17] The farcical narrative conceals a bated criticism of the situation in Northern Ireland where the tensions between the communities are deeply ingrained, and where "on both sides, the townees hate the culchies worse than they do each other, and the culchies hate everything that's not from their own townland".[18]

*Brian Moore*, after his early period as a writer of pulp detective fiction, had, by the 1970s, become one of Northern Ireland's most respected novelists, and in *The Doctor's Wife* (1976), he evokes the Troubles for the first time in his fiction. Sheila Redden, a Belfast resident, who has an affair with Tom, a young American, in Paris, is sought out by her brother Owen and her husband Kevin who, like perverse detectives, attempt to hunt her down and return her to Belfast. The search, which results in marital rape, is interspersed by Sheila's efforts to reach a degree of freedom that she has been denied within the twin constrictions of her marriage and the situation in Northern Ireland. Initially, Sheila feels that she is "a deserter from home" as she remembers a café bomb explosion in the Queen's Arcade in Belfast.[19] Although she is a lapsed Catholic, she knows that she has to maintain the pretence of abiding by a religion in which she no longer has faith, because "to declare that you were no longer a Catholic was to run the risk of being thought a turncoat".[20] *Colour of Blood* (1987) again uses features of the crime novel, including a kidnapping and a failed assassination attempt, in a political thriller which was nominated for the Booker Prize.

In *Lies of Silence* (1990), Moore approaches the world of the "Troubles" in an even more direct way than that used in *The Doctor's Wife*. Dillon, a former poet who is now working as a hotel manager, is ordered to park his car outside the hotel where a bomb, placed by the IRA, would explode. Dillon's heroic phone call, which saves the life of the wife he was about to leave, places him and his lover Andrea in the sight of the paramilitaries and in London, when faced with whether to identify Kevin McDowell, IRA

17    John Morrow, *The Confessions of Proinsias O'Toole* (Belfast: The Blackstaff Press, 1977), 67.

18    Ibid., 52.

19    Brian Moore, *The Doctor's Wife* (1976, London: Flamingo, 1994), 42.

20    Ibid., 88.

volunteer and nephew of Father Connolly, Dillon is forced to come to a decision which could lead to tragic consequences. *Lies of Silence* is, of course, very different from the earlier thrillers. The moral burden that Dillon has to shoulder is far removed from the motivation behind the actions of the one-dimensional characters in his 1950s' pulp thrillers. The setting, particularly the city of Belfast, is also described in a manner which has little to do with the portrayal of Montreal, Paris, Palma or Barcelona in these earlier novels, although Patricia Craig complains that the novel lacks the atmosphere of Moore's earlier works.[21] While Dillon and his wife lived in a middle-class area of north Belfast where Protestants and Catholics lived in apparent harmony and "just wanted to get on with their lives without any interference from men in woollen masks".[22] The protagonist also recognises the existence of sectarian ghettoes which "were the true and lasting legacy of the British Province founded on inequality and sectarian hate".[23] Brian Moore's penultimate novel, *The Statement* (1995), again uses what Craig calls the "enhanced thriller form"[24] to investigate issues of morality, guilt and atonement, in this case in the story of a former French fascist militant who, with the collusion of government and Church has steadily avoided criminal and moral expiation for the crimes he has committed.

Both *Eugene McCabe's Victims: A Tale from Fermanagh* (1976) and Benedict Kiely's *Proxopera* (1977) take as their starting point a situation which is similar in some respects to that of Moore's *Lies of Silence*. In *Victims*, Colonel Armstrong, his wife and daughter, along with two family friends, a politician and a clergyman are held hostage by an IRA cell seeking the release of three comrades imprisoned in Long Kesh. The characters are largely stereotypical figures, however, like Jack Gallagher, the red-haired killer from Derry for whom "all females were for screwing in ditches or in cars",[25] or one of the Protestant captives who believes that the native Irish were "dangerous deadly children".[26] McCabe's *Death and Nightingales*

21  Patricia Craig, *Brian Moore: A Biography* (London: Bloomsbury, 2002), 248.
22  Brian Moore, *Lies of Silence* (London: Vintage, 1990), 69.
23  Ibid., 82.
24  Craig, *Brian Moore*, 249.
25  Eugene McCabe, *Victims: A Tale from Fermanagh* (London: Gollancz, 1976), 40.
26  Ibid., 77.

(1992) is a rare Northern Irish historical novel, in which Beth Winters, after the death of her Catholic mother, is badgered by the Protestant landowner she believes to be her father. She is attracted to Liam Ward, a local nationalist militant, who persuades her to steal from her father before escaping with him, but she discovers that Liam plans to betray and kill her and skilfully plans her revenge and, alone, gains her freedom. In *Benedict Kiely's Proxopera*, a Northern Irish everyman, Mr Binchy, is forced by the IRA to drive a proxy bomb concealed in a milk churn to the house of a judge, under the threat that, if he fails to carry out the abhorrent task, his family will be killed. Aaron Kelly notes how, in both *Victims* and *Proxopera*, the narratives "trace the intrusion of terror upon a putatively normal bourgeois private sphere".[27] In *Nothing Happens in Carmincross* (1986) Kiely returns to the conflict, as Mervyn Kavanagh, an Irish historian, arrives home from the USA where he lives and works, to attend the wedding of his niece. The bride-to-be's death in a bomb explosion before the wedding forces Mervyn to try to come to terms with the madness his homeland has become, but even his professional interest in the country's history does not allow him to comprehend the extent to which the events of the past have come to create a tragic present.

With *Lamb* (1980), *Bernard McLaverty* examines the actions of Michael Lamb, whose religious name is Brother Sebastian, a woodwork teacher in a Donegal industrial school. Indignant at the way the institution treats Owen, an epileptic pupil, Sebastian absconds with the troubled child to London, apparently unaware of the implications this evokes. *Cal* (1983) is one of the most popular – and most widely criticised – novels to come out of the Troubles period. Set in 1975, it tells the story of Cal, a young Catholic living with his father as the only Catholics on a Protestant council estate near Magherafelt. Cal had participated as the getaway driver in the killing of an RUC reservist the year before, and sees his guilt at the involvement in the incident as "a brand stamped in blood in the middle of his forehead

---

27  Aaron Kelly, "The Troubles with the Thriller: Northern Ireland, Political Violence and the Peace Process" in *The Edinburgh Companion to Twentieth-Century British and American War Literature*, ed. Adam Piette and Mark Rawlinson (Edinburgh: Edinburgh University Press), 512.

which would take him the rest of his life to purge".[28] Cal becomes obsessed with the murdered policeman's beautiful widow, Marcella, but the weight of his past actions ensure a tragic denouement. *Cal* successfully captures the tensions of the period, especially when Cal and her father are burned out of their home, but the boy's IRA confederates are implausible- one, Crilly, is a stupid bully, while the other, Skeffington, is a cold, calculating intellectual – and Cal's eventual masochistic acceptance of his own fate is ultimately unconvincing. For Elmer Kennedy-Andrews, Cal is condemned because of a rash action in his past, and as such is portrayed as an innocent, guilty of "youthful transgression, not heroic revolt".[29]

*Roy Bradford* (1920–98) was an eminent Unionist politician who served in both the Stormont Parliament and the Northern Ireland Assembly and as Mayor of North Down Borough. *The Last Ditch* (1981) is a political thriller based on the events of the Ulster Workers' Council strike of 1974. Desmond Carson, Minister of Home Affairs, is the foremost candidate for the post of Prime Minister at Stormont, but his growing obsession with Jo Scanlon, a Catholic girl, the immobilisation of Northern Ireland because of the strike, and an armed action by the IRA help to thwart his ambitions. The "last ditch" of the title is a reference to the famous response by William III to the Duke of Buckingham's observation that the country was lost, and echoes the frustration felt by Unionist supporters in the wake of Sunningdale, which is reflected in this pessimistic thriller.

In *Deirdre Madden's Hidden Symptoms* (1986), Theresa lives in the shadow of the death of her twin brother, Francis, who has been the victim of a sectarian murder. After her brother's death, she has been left, she feels, "at the mercy of her own memory and imagination".[30] Her friendship with fellow student Kathy and aspiring writer Robert McConville is conditioned by her grief, and she calls Robert a "spineless liberal" for his unwillingness to write about the Troubles. In *One by One in the Darkness* (1996), Madden examines the story of three sisters and the lasting effect on their lives of their

---

28   Bernard McLaverty, *Cal* (London: Jonathan Cape, 1983), 89.
29   Elmer Kennedy-Andrews, "The Novel and the Northern Troubles" in *The Cambridge Companion to the Irish Novel*, ed. John Wilson Foster (Cambridge: Cambridge University Press, 2006), 246.
30   Deirdre Madden, *Hidden Symptoms* (London: Faber & Faber, 1986), 33.

father's murder, shot in cold blood by masked men in their sitting room. Sally is a schoolteacher, Helen is a solicitor who works on the Falls Road and who specialises in terrorist cases, while Cate, who has recently returned from London, is a magazine journalist. The narrative contains constant references to the day-to-day violence of the Troubles, such as the brother of a school friend killed while planting a bomb, their father's brother's involvement in the IRA, or the Protestant painter who stops coming to their house out of fear of being shot. *Frances Molloy's No Mate for Magpie* (1985) also follows the life of a young woman during the conflict. Told in her own, inimitable Derry idiolect, Anne Elizabeth McGlone comes of age during the Troubles. Her father is interned, and she herself participates in the early civil rights marches of the late 1960s. The violence of the situations is given greater intensity as a result of Anne's language. When her father is arrested, we are told that "dozens of polismen and "B" specials rushed in an' pointed guns at us. All the wains began to cry".[31] The police brutality on the protest marches is also vivid and harrowing: "A polisman called us fuckin Fenian baatards an' toul us that he would smash our brains out if we didn't turn roun' an' ger through the arch".[32]

In *Give Them Stones* (1987), *Mary Beckett* also examines the effects of the Troubles from a woman's perspective. Tracing the life of her protagonist, Martha Murtagh, from before the breakout of the Second World War until the Troubles of the 1970s, Beckett's narrative follows the changing situation in Belfast as her fears shift from those about her imprisoned father and her brother, an IRA supporter, to her four sons who, unemployed and aimless, could easily fall victim to the situation. Martha's frustration at the injustice of life in Northern Ireland comes to a head when she is eventually burned out of her house by people supposedly from her own side. Throughout the novel Martha only finds solace in the books she reads, and the bread and scones she bakes and sells.

*Danny Morrison* was a republican activist who, after a spell of imprisonment in Long Kesh, became editor of Sinn Féin publication *Republican News*, which in 1979 would merge with *An Poblacht*. He went on to become

31    Frances Molloy, *No Mate for Magpie* (London: Virago, 1985), 26.
32    Ibid., 136.

Sinn Féin National Director of Publicity and, in 1985, published *West Belfast*, a novel he had been writing in secret.[33] Presumably autobiographical in many aspects, *West Belfast* follows John O'Neill as he comes of age in West Belfast during the early years of the Troubles. Working on ships travelling between Belfast and Canada, he starts to smuggle guns before joining the IRA. *The Wrong Man* (1997) is also largely autobiographical, following Raymond Massey, an IRA volunteer and, on his release after a seven-year sentence in Long Kesh, has become "a living monument to eight hundred years of unremitting resistance".[34]

Of those writing about the Troubles from a Protestant perspective, *Glenn Patterson*, like Maurice Leitch and David Park, has produced some fascinating works, including fine examples of thrillers set in the period. Patterson's first two novels, *Burning Your Own* (1988) and *Fat Lad* (1992) are haunted by the presence of the conflict, with the former tracing the growth of sectarian violence in Belfast through the relationship between two ten-year-old boys, the Protestant Mal and the Catholic Francie. From the petrol bombing of the Unity Flats in the Lower Falls area to Mal's father's reluctant participation in vigilante activities, *Burning Your Own* chronicles the inevitable tragedy of the epoch, reflected in the destiny of the two boys as they grow up during the Troubles and gradually become "socialised into the contradictions of adulthood and the dull, inflexible certainties of sectarian identity".[35] In *Fat Lad* Drew's return to Belfast brings back memories of his father's humiliation in front of Ulster Defence Association (UDA) pickets during the Ulster Workers' Council strike in 1974 but also highlights the continuing state of crisis in the city, with war-weary residents identifying the type of bomb and the place in which it has been detonated just by listening to the blast, and where daily life is accompanied by the constant menacing drone of army helicopters hovering over

33    John Hedges, "Danny Morrison's West Belfast, A Story of a Community in Struggle", *An Poblacht*, 1 June 2015, <https://www.anphoblacht.com/contents/25032>, accessed 3 January 2019.

34    Danny Morrison, *The Wrong Man* (Cork: Mercier Press, 1997), Kindle chap. 12, accessed 2 December 2019.

35    Gerry Smyth, *The Novel and the Nation: Studies in New Irish Fiction* (London: Pluto Press, 1999), 127.

Belfast. Tragedy too, hovers over the pages of the novel, with the memory of the brutal murder of Drew's friend Hugh, shot in the back of the head I cold blood in the centre of London.

*Black Night at Big Thunder Mountain* (1995) is a refreshing comic thriller, reminiscent to some extent of Colin Bateman's works in the same genre. Sam, a demented American who has been brought up in a hippy commune, seeks to hijack the construction of the Euro-Disney complex near Paris. As an embittered ex-Disney worker, he aims to replace the iconic Mickey Mouse with Mort, Walt Disney's original prototype cartoon creature. He kidnaps Ilse, a former German porn star, and Raymond, a Northern Irish construction worker who had previously been imprisoned for alleged participation in an attempted loyalist killing. The novel follows the captivity of Ilse and Raymond and Sam's threat to blow them up inside the Big Thunder Mountain, an attraction at the theme park. The humour is constant and full of Northern Irish irony and self-depreciation. Ilse tries to comfort the injured Raymond by whistling to him the only Irish song she knows, the rebel ballad Kevin Barry, and Raymond has a badly drawn Union Jack tattooed on his arm, which has faded to green. The car bomb, he suggests, is a Northern Irish invention which, alongside joyriding "was one of Northern Ireland's few contributions to its defining cultural obsession, the automobile".[36] *The International* (1999) is set in a central Belfast hotel on the day before the first Northern Ireland Civil Rights Association meeting was held there in January 1967.

Both of *Robert McLiam Wilson's* novels, *Ripley Bogle* (1989) and *Eureka Street* (1996), are works which, despite their iconoclastic nature, arguably do more to project the horrors of the Northern Irish conflict than any run-of-the-mill thriller. The former details the life of the eponymous Bogle, a down-and-out former Cambridge student living the life of a tramp in London, blaming Belfast for the Troubles and Ireland for his life.[37] Ripley's comical cynicism – he mocks the "disparate aims to strike an irrevocable blow to the British War Machine by blowing up Marks and Spencer's every

---

36    Glenn Patterson, *Black Night at Big Thunder Mountain* (London: Chatto & Windus, 1995), 55.
37    Robert McLiam Wilson, *Ripley Bogle* (London: André Deutsch, 1989), 326.

Saturday afternoon" – is tempered by his tragic memories of the death of a soldier under sniper fire or the murder of his father by the IRA for saving a young girl who was being tarred and feathered.[38] *Eureka Street* is equally full of comic pathos, a carefully constructed strategy which removes the edge only slightly from the horrific violent undercurrents which permeate the work. Jake Jackson is a "repo-man", a lapsed Catholic whose repossession crew "were willingly ecumenical" and who "raided Protestant estates with all the élan and grace with which [they] raided Catholic ones".[39] The novel charts Jake's relationship with his family, with his Protestant friend, the unlikely entrepreneur Chuckie Lurgan, and with Sarah Ellis, his English journalist girlfriend who, tired of the Troubles, has returned to London. At the centre of *Eureka Street*, however, lies violence. The peace train which is halted by a bomb, the murder of a prize-winning American diplomat on his arrival in Northern Ireland and, most shockingly, the Fountain Place bomb which erupts into the centre of the narrative with a power and forcefulness unparalleled in writing on the Troubles. The pages in which Wilson gives his description of the carnage are amongst the most memorable to be encountered anywhere.

David Park's *Oranges from Spain* (1990) is an accomplished collection of short stories which deal with aspects of the Troubles, generally seen from the perspectives of, alternately, young Protestant and Catholic protagonists. In "Killing a Brit" the death of a British soldier is viewed with "casual indifference", while in "The Apprentice", a young man starts a career as "bagman" for the IRA – that is, someone who carries concealed weapons to a designated location.[40] In "Searching the Shadows", a mother tries to save her son from a punishment shooting as he is accused of joy-riding by local paramilitaries while, in ironic contrast, other young joy-riders are shot by police in "The Pleasure Dome". The best stories in the collection are "The Fishing Trip", in which the son of a murdered RUC officer remembers his father's death, and the title story, "Oranges from Spain", narrated by a boy who works in a shop whose owner is killed in a mindless revenge killing,

---

38    Ibid., 44.
39    Robert McLiam Wilson, *Eureka Street* (London: Secker & Warburg, 1996), 63.
40    David Park, *Oranges from Spain* (London: Jonathan Cape, 1990), 20.

becoming "a casualty of convenience, a victim of retribution, propitiation of a different god".[41] Park's first novel, *The Healing* (1992), also features a young protagonist whose father is a victim of The Troubles. After witnessing his father's death in a sectarian shooting, Samuel moves to Belfast with his mother, where an ageing religious fanatic sees himself as being able to provide the child's salvation. In *The Rye Man* (1994) John Cameron returns as headmaster to the school in which he studied as a child. Mourning the baby he and his wife have just lost, Cameron tries to take up the cause of Jaqueline, a pupil with learning difficulties, who he believes is being abused by her father. When the girl disappears, he becomes an ad hoc detective in a search for her, which is also a search for meaning in his own barren life. In *Stone Kingdoms* (1996) Noemi, who has been working as a teacher at an interdenominational school in Belfast takes up work at a refugee camp in Africa. Although her intention is to escape the conflict, her experiences mirror those of Northern Ireland and she discovers that it is not an easy task to escape the past.

The quality and quantity of works which came out of Northern Ireland during such a dark historical period is highly significant. Far from the popular Troubles thrillers, often written by foreigners with little or no real empathy or feeling for the country or its situation, Irish writers, from North and South, and from both sides of the ideological divide, produced a corpus of work to which a short study such as this can do little justice. The Peace Process which followed the IRA ceasefire of the mid-1990s would be accompanied by the beginning of a new boom in Northern Irish crime writing. New writers, such as Brian McGilloway, Claire McGowan, Stuart Neville, Anthony Quinn and others would produce an astonishing body of work which, given the changed circumstances in Northern Ireland, would take on the format of more classical crime fiction in which, however, the events of the immediate past would play a hugely significant role.

---

41    Ibid., 190.

# "The authority to dispose of anyone who stands in my way." The 1980s and Early 1990s

With reference to the 1980s, former Taoiseach Bertie Ahern noted in his 2009 autobiography that an "IMS survey showed that Dublin had a higher crime rate than any large US city".[1] The rising level of crime affected not only the capital, but the inner-city areas of other cities such as Limerick and Cork, and continued a pattern of growth that had been apparent since the 1940s as, in the half-century from the end of the Emergency in 1945 "the indictable crime rate in the Republic grew by a factor of almost fivefold".[2] Despite such a marked increase in crime, however, this was not reflected in a corresponding growth in crime fiction. While writers who had been active since the 1950s or 1960s such as John Welcome, Jack Higgins or Patricia Moyes, or in the 1970s such as Patrick McGinley, Bartholomew Gill or Ruth Dudley Edwards, continued to publish in the 1980s, the number of new writers to begin in this decade was relatively low. Mike Shelley would provide a false start, as it were, to comical Northern Irish private investigator narratives, throwing down a gauntlet which would be picked up a decade later by Colin Bateman. A famous English novelist would attempt to convince readers that he was an Irish crime writer, and Peter Cunningham, J. B. O'Neill and Carlo Gébler would begin long careers in the production of "literary" crime fiction. Only towards the end of the decade, however, with the introduction of John Brady's Matt Minogue series would we see an example of the Irish police-led novels which would become so prominent in the following decades.

1   Bertie Ahern, *The Autobiography* (London: Hutchinson, 2009), 80.
2   John D. Brewer, Bill Lockhart and Paula Rodgers, "Crime in Ireland 1945–95", *Proceedings of the British Academy* 98 (1999), 166.

Quite understandably, the private detective could be seen as being little more than a professional informer, someone who, with a position perilously close to that of a police officer, was privy to secret information – information that could potentially be used against common interests. As such, it is not difficult to understand why there is little in the way of private detective literature from Ireland before the 1990s, and why the Galway writer Ken Bruen claimed that: "There are no private eyes in Ireland. The Irish wouldn't wear it. The concept brushes perilously close to the hated "informer". You can get away with almost anything except "telling".[3] The case of *Mike Shelley* is, it would appear, the exception which proves the rule. At a time when no one in Northern Ireland appeared to contemplate the writing of "ordinary" – that is, not Troubles-related – crime fiction, he produced a short novel with the fascinating title of *The Last Private Eye in Belfast* (1984). Published by the small Belfast publisher Domino, Shelley's first novel is a brave attempt at a humorous private detective novel in the underbelly of a city in which criminal activity, although largely over-shadowed by the political situation, is still rife. Bernard Holland, the book's unlikeable protagonist, is a former member of the British army who, after a spell working as a foreman on building sites in London has returned to Belfast where he runs three shady businesses, one of which is the Rapid Results Investigation Agency, the last of its kind in a city where such bureaus are looked upon with suspicion and where the role of private detection is also viewed as suspect. Although the work, according to Holland, is generally boring, it is somewhat "less so, perhaps, in a city like Belfast where you're asking questions of supersensitive people who possess more guns and explosives than you could shake a stick at".[4]

The plot is largely a parody of American pulp detective fiction, with a series of stock characters, including the untrustworthy foreigner Portuguese Joe, "sweaty, shifty and dangerous", the femme fatale Gloria "dark, accessible, and a woman with a past" and the cruel villain, the Professor "perhaps the most evil villain in the world".[5] The novel's action could take place

---

3    Ken Bruen, *The Guards* (Dublin: Brandon, 2001), 5.
4    Mike Shelley, *The Last Private Eye in Belfast* (Belfast: Domino, 1984), 73.
5    Ibid., 87.

anywhere, with few specific references to the particularity of Northern Ireland, although the RUC officer, Sergeant Murkley, is portrayed as being hopelessly and stereotypically inefficient, and Major Peppar, a British intelligence officer is claimed to possess "the authority to dispose of anyone who stands in my way".[6] There are occasional references to soldiers on the streets of the city, but little else to recreate the tensions of Belfast in the 1980s.

Shelley published two subsequent novels the same year with the same imprint, but neither used the character of Bernard Holland. Indeed, both *The Terror of Her Ways* (1984) and *Madame Edie's Chamber of Horrors* (1984) are set in London and feature another private detective, Barney Huggins, a master of disguise and, like Holland, hopelessly corrupt. Again stock characters abound, with a call girl who is suspected of hoarding Nazi gold, and a collection of alcoholics, misfits in a London underworld which differs little from that of Belfast in the first novel. It is tempting, of course, to speculate as to why Shelley transfers his action from Belfast to London in his two later works because, arguably, the attraction of his debut work lies largely in the minimal specificity given to Northern Ireland in *The Last Private Eye in Belfast*, while with the London setting both *The Terror of Her Ways* and *Madame Eddie's Chamber of Horrors* come across as relatively poor examples of cosmopolitan comic crime pulp.

According to information gleaned from the dust jacket of the original books, and the website when these were reissued in both print and electronic format some thirty years after their initial publication, the four novels featuring the bisexual private investigator Duffy were written by *Dan Kavanagh*, who was born in County Sligo in 1946:

> Having devoted his adolescence to truancy, venery and petty theft, he left home at seventeen and signed on as a deckhand on a Liberian tanker. After jumping ship at Montevideo, he roamed across the Americas taking a variety of jobs: he was a steer-wrestler, a waiter-on-roller-skates at a drive-in eatery in Tucson, and a bouncer in a gay bar in San Francisco. He is currently working in London at jobs he declines to specify, and lives in North Islington.[7]

---

6    Ibid., 99.
7    "Dan Cavanagh", <http://www.dankavanagh.com/>, accessed 18 October 2016.

CHAPTER 16

The biography obviously points towards a pseudonym, and a hint is provided at the foot of the "author's" homepage which states "If you like Dan Kavanagh, try Julian Barnes". Kavanagh is, indeed, the somewhat unexpected *nom de plume* of the English novelist Barnes, winner of the Booker Prize, and not conventionally associated with crime fiction. The three "Dan Kavanagh" novels and their anecdotal attribution of the authorship to a fictitious writer from Sligo can, perhaps, be seen as a premonition regarding the subsequent rise of Irish crime writing.

*Peter Cunningham*, writing under his own name, or under one of his pseudonyms, *Peter Lauder*, *Peter Benjamin* or *Peter Wilben*, has written several thrillers, many of which are set in either the world of horse racing or that of high finance and politics. *Noble Lord* (1986), published under the name of Peter Lauder, starts on Antigua, where Sergeant Winston Hope, a police officer on the Caribbean island sets out for New York where his brother-in-law, Ernest Wilson, a petty thief, has been murdered. Suspecting mafia or drug-related causes, Hope eventually discovers that Wilson has been killed in an attempt to recuperate a briefcase he has stolen which contains IRA plans to assassinate the queen on Derby Day at Epsom. Hope's timely intervention saves the monarch from the terrorists who have infiltrated the horse's training team. *The Snow Bees* (1988) was originally published under the author's own name but was republished as *White Line* under the Peter Wilben pseudonym in 2013. The novel introduces Joe Grace, a former commando who, accepting a job to manage a vineyard in southern France, discovers that, apart from losing money, the business is also serving as cover for the international drugs trade carried out by a group led by Marcellino Epalza Adarraga, a larger-than-life Basque-Colombian with links to ETA, the Basque separatist movement.

Both *The Bear's Requiem* (1989) and *Hostile Bid* (1991) are centred on the world of Wall Street. The former chronicles the rise and fall of trader Steve Ossorio who is duped by false Arab traders and ruined by the crash of the oil market, while the latter features another bankrupt trader, ninjas and mafias, and a plot to kill the Japanese Emperor. *Who Trespass Against Us* (1994) is narrated by Detective Superintendent Brian Kilkenny of the Gardaí. He is called in to find Adam Coleraine, a high-ranking civil servant who has disappeared along with a top-secret report on the IRA two months after the death of his daughter in an IRA bomb attack near Paddington Station. *Tapes of the River Delta* (1995) moves away from the genre fiction of Cunningham's earlier work with the tale of a powerful Irish family over the course of the twentieth century in the town of Monument, a fictional representation of the author's native Waterford. It does, however, contain healthy doses of political corruption, arms smuggling, suspicious deaths and a hint of incest. During the early years of the twenty-first century, Cunningham would continue to produce fiction set in Monument, while also turning his attention to the impact of the Celtic Tiger and participating in a collective crime project featuring a female Guard who becomes a nun.

*Vincent McDonnell's The Broken Commandment* (1988) starts with the narrator, Peter Farson, in prison for murder. As he relates the events that led him to his current situation, Farson reveals how two car accidents, one involving his wife and the other his lover, bring him to a point where, he believes, after rejecting a god, he has the chance to redeem himself by committing murder. McDonnell later published two crime novels for young readers, *Chill Factor* (2014) and *The Knock Airport Mystery* (2015). In the first, Dr Dennis Gunne, who has given up high-level genetic research to take on a general family practice, is kidnapped by Max Silverman, an American billionaire who has lost his son in an accident he attributes to Gunne's earlier research. The doctor's son Sean refuses to give credit to the police's belief that his father has been involved in supplying drugs to addicts and, with his friend Jackie, whose father, a former Guard, is now working as a security consultant, sets off to try and find Dr Gunne, hidden on a remote island off the Galway coast. In *The Knock Airport Mystery* Kevin overhears a plot to free Pug Banzinini, an American gangster being held in a Dublin prison, as he is being extradited back to the USA. Helped by his brother, sister and visiting English cousin, Kevin sets out to foil the escape attempt.

*Carlo Gébler*, eldest son of writers Ernest Gébler and Edna O'Brien, is a famed TV producer and writer whose literary output includes several novels in which crime plays a central role. In *Work and Play* (1987) Fergus Maguire, a young Irishman, is living in London where, blaming himself for his father's death, he tries to protect his Asian neighbours from the racist harassment they are faced with from right-wing racists. Maguire's eventual role as a police informer is seen as an ironic reflection of his determination to reform his life and take on a new sense of responsibility. Both *The Cure* (1994) and *How to Murder a Man* (1998) are set in nineteenth-century Ireland. In the former, the inability of Bridget Cleary, a countrywoman from Tipperary, to give birth to a child is attributed to the intervention of the fairies. Her husband Martin, for whom the fairies represented a real presence and to whom he attributes the disappearance of his mother, eventually kills Bridget in an attempt to rid her of the possession he believes her to be suffering. The story, told from a variety of viewpoints and centred around the evidence uncovered at Cleary's trial, reveals the widespread support offered to Martin by his family and neighbours and the ineffectiveness of a legal system which was only believed to be good for "summonses and dog licences".[8] *How to Murder a Man*, set against the background of the wars of the secret societies in nineteenth-century County Monaghan starts with the enticing opening line which states that "all histories are really murder stories".[9] When Thomas French is hired by a local landowner to reduce the debts owed by tenants, he suggests that, instead of having the debtors evicted, these be offered free passage to America so that new, productive tenants can be given the use of the land. French's apparently progressive ideas fall foul of the "Ribbonmen" who see in his plans a scheme to abolish tenant rights. Assisted by repentant "Ribbonman" Tim and his lover, the pregnant Kitty, French avoids the various attempts to murder him but is eventually unable to help Tim and Kitty who fall victims to the secret society. The cruelty and apparent lack of moral scruples attributed to them suggests that in *How to Murder a Man* Gébler is drawing crude but often realistic parallels between the secret societies of the nineteenth century and the paramilitaries of Northern Ireland in the 1990s. Much of the author's later work would reflect his experiences as writer-in-residence in a Northern Irish prison, where he worked from 1997 until 2015.

    *J. M. O'Neill* (1921–99) worked as a bank employee in Ireland, England, Nigeria and Ghana before becoming a publican, playwright and novelist in London. His first novel, *Open Cut* (1986), is set in the north London of Irish immigrant builders and violent beatings, police informers and

8    Carlo Gébler, *The Cure* (London: Hamish Hamilton, 1994), 243.
9    Carlo Gébler, *How to Murder a Man* (London: Little, Brown, 1998), 1.

precarious work in a city which is starting to become cosmopolitan with "the strange transfusion of Carib and Greek and Paki into dry cracking arteries", and where Nally, an Irish gangster, controls all illicit activity.[10] *Duffy is Dead* (1987) reveals the tension between the police and Irish workers in London, with the death of Duffy, who is "untouched by the merest blemish of work, a contented foster child of the state" providing an unlikely source of humour, as Robert Emmet Calnan attempts to gather the money for his friend's funeral.[11] The casual racism seen in *Open Cut* is intensified here, especially among the police, who suspect Calnan because of his first and middle names and try to plant a gun on him to be able to convict him as "provocative, political, undesirable".[12] *Canon Bang Bang* (1989) is also set in London, and features a defrocked priest, Father Herlihy, who inherits Dory's Jetty on the Thames in a lucrative area eyed for development. When the Church hears of the inheritance it sends another priest, Father Jim Kilmartin, to attempt to secure Herlihy's return to the flock and thus secure rights to the Jetty, a melting pot of London history and the history of Irish immigration.

In *Relligham, Undertaker* (1989), O'Neill uses a rural Irish setting for his tale of Detective Inspector Coleman who enlists the aid of the strange undertaker, apparently of Eastern European origin, to assist in his investigation into local deaths which appear to have started after Sommerville, the Protestant doctor, first met Ester Machen, the mysterious new neighbour. *Commissar Connell* (1992) is set in Africa in the 1950s when Lorimer, recently arrived from Belfast, accuses Connell, married to an African woman and with twelve children, of being a wanted terrorist in Northern Ireland and of encouraging revolutionaries in Africa. Connell, it appears, had killed two policemen in Belfast following the death of his father in 1922, but Lorimer had been the leader of a Protestant rape gang. The differences between the two men, from different sides of the religious divide, but also operating under two very different ethical codes, creates much of the tension in the work, which often reads like an allegory – one of Connell's sons,

10    J. B. O'Neil, *Open Cut* (London: Heinemann, 1986), 126.
11    J. B. O'Neill, *Duffy is Dead* (London: Heinemann, 1987), 11.
12    Ibid., 46.

an African activist, is on hunger strike while in prison for alleged terrorist connections while Lorimer is in favour of force-feeding.

For the first half of the 1990s, the country was very similar in most respects to the Ireland of the 1960s and 1970s. Unemployment was high, living conditions poor, and emigration was still the most feasible future for many young Irish people in search of a better life. Crime was in continual growth, reflecting the tendency of the previous twenty years, with inner-city gangs committing armed robbery on a regular basis and with a frightening increment in the use and sale of hard drugs in urban Ireland. The second half of the decade would see enormous changes. The Celtic Tiger, the great if transitory economic bonanza, would start in 1994 or 1995, depending on who provides the figures, while the murder of investigative reporter Veronica Guerin in June 1996 would lead to radical reforms in anti-criminal activity and, collaterally, a growing interest in the reading and production of crime narratives, be these journalistic or fictional. For the first half of the decade, crime fiction continued more or less along the lines of the previous decade, with many of the writers who had been active in the 1970s and 1980s continuing to produce works regularly.

Several writers touched on themes that would prove popular later on in the decade and into the new millennium. *Joe Joyce*, for example, would take on the question of police corruption, and Tom Phelan that of sexual abuse within the Church. Vincent Banville would introduce an early Dublin-based private investigator, while Rory McCormac would begin a successful crime series involving the world of a veterinary surgeon. The Dublin publisher Glendale would introduce a cheap but interesting crime series which did much to promote the popularity for narratives involving Irish crime being set in an Irish context, a field which would grow in popularity with the rise of the Celtic Tiger economy. Joe Joyce, a Dublin journalist who has also published a history of the Guinness family, published two crime novels *Off the Record* (1989) and *The Trigger Man* (1990), which were not followed up until more than twenty years later when independent Dublin publisher Liberties Press issued *Echoland* (2013) and its sequels. *Off the Record* is a fine example of late 1980s' Irish crime fiction, involving political and police corruption, financial swindles, blackmail and the peripheral involvement of both the IRA and the CIA. Seamus Ryle, a disenchanted journalist with marital problems, is following the case of the drowning of Maurice Clark, an up-and-coming politician, in Dublin harbour. The investigation leads to Ryle being given some documents which implicate the Irish government in secret negotiations towards NATO membership as a step towards the ending of partition. Unsure as to the veracity of these documents, which could be fakes used by the IRA to incriminate the Dail and provoke unrest in the Republic, Ryle uncovers a scam involving uranium, Clark's romantic involvement with a suspected IRA member and the blackmail to which he is subjected. *Off the Record* is an interesting early example of much of the fiction which would be developed over the following years, echoing the insecurity towards the forces of law and order and distrust of the political world and its selfish aims. Ryle, as the crusading journalist, foretells later characters, while Inspector Bill Devane, a positive Guard figure, stands out amongst his corrupt colleagues and sycophantic Chief Superintendent.

*The Trigger Man* is less ambitious in scope, but nevertheless a well-written and intense thriller featuring fugitive IRA volunteer Fergus Callan, who has been living illegally in Boston after being compromised on an active service operation in Ireland. Callan, who has no wish to become involved in the conflict once again, returns to Ireland to try to find out why an old comrade has disappeared out of a "residual sense of companionship".[13] On his return, Callan is pursued by the Gardaí, the IRA and British intelligence, discovering how his ex-partner, and mother of his child, has risen high in the ranks of the IRA after her years of imprisonment. Like *Off the Record*, *The Trigger Man* has, in Keerins, a Guard who is depicted in a positive light and who contrasts with his colleague Pursell, in the pay of British intelligence forces and whom Keerins has to remind that they are police officers, "not part of a dirty tricks outfit like your friend".[14]

*Dermot Bolger*, considered one of Ireland's leading novelists of the late twentieth and early twenty-first centuries, has approached the field of crime writing in his fictional output. *The Journey Home* (1990) gives a bleak vision of urban Ireland in the 1980s. Opening with Francis "Hano" Hanrahan and his friend, the teenage drug addict Cait, on the run after

---

13  Joe Joyce, *The Trigger Man* (London: Heinemann, 1990), 17.
14  Ibid., 115.

the murder of Hano's friend Shay, the novel explores the events leading up to their escape. The son of a family from rural Ireland, recently relocated to the city, Hano finds release from his dismal surroundings through his friendship with the older, and seemingly exotic, Shay. He is also given work, acting as a driver and bodyguard for local businessman and criminal Pascal Plunkett, brother of a high-ranking politician. When Shay is killed by Pascal's son Jason, Hano seeks revenge but the Garda, aware of the proximity of elections and the need to maintain cordial relations with the Plunkett clan, want to cover up the murder and, instead of investigating Jason, who is sent off to Europe by his father, prefer to raid the flat shared by Hano and the victim in an attempt to incriminate them. The final scenes, with Hano sexually abused by his boss and the fracas that occurs when Cait enters with a knife, ends in the comforting – if temporary – union of the two youngsters, with Hano rejecting the rest of society in favour of Cait, his "home" and his "only nation" (240).

*Father's Music* (1997) finds twenty-two-year-old Tracey Evans, daughter of an English mother and Irish father, going to Ireland to accompany her lover Luke Duggan, member of a leading Dublin criminal family, to the funeral of a family member who has been shot in a revenge killing. In Ireland, and relegated to a secondary position due to the presence of Luke's wife and family, Tracey is shocked at the state of Dublin she sees. The cranes and building which denote the approaching prosperity are offset by the world of drugs, gangs and police corruption she finds there and lead her to search for clues to the life of her estranged father and the answer that might help in her own mission of self-discovery. Tracey had been brought up in England by her English grandparents after the abandonment of her father, a traditional fiddler, and the death of her mother, and after a spell of travelling with tinker friends of her father's. Tracking down her paternal grandparents to rural Donegal, Tracey is able to prevent her grandfather from killing his terminally ill wife before Luke's death in a shooting arranged by his niece. Bolger would later return to the world of organised crime in *The Valparaiso Voyage* (2001).

One of the most notable advances in Irish crime writing was the significant, if brief, entry of the Dublin publisher Glendale into the field. Under the directorship of Thomas F. Turley and Brendan J. Tierney, this

Dublin-based outfit released several crime novels in the early 1990s, most of which dealt with the crime committed in Ireland. The series included works by H. J. Forrest, Vincent Caprani, Howard R. Simpson and Desmond Moore. *H. J. Forrest* is the pseudonym used by microbiologist Caroline Hussey, whose first novel *Publish or Perish* was published by Glendale in 1991. The apparent suicide of genetics professor Brian Barry is questioned by Inspector Mitchell, the Kerry-born Guard, who suspects that the academic has been murdered. This classic locked-room mystery – only Barry's colleagues had keys to the office in which he died – leads to a reduced number of suspects among academics and postgraduate students, and the author skillfully plays with many red herrings while a seemingly endless number of professional jealousies and resentments are revealed.

A second novel, *Murder by the Book* (1992), is again set against a university background. Tim Ronayne, a widowed botany professor rents the gate lodge of a Big House where he intends to write a mystery novel. The death of his aristocratic landlady's stepson and the apparent theft of her priceless brooch involves Tim in a real mystery which, with the help of Detective Inspector Connor Hogan, himself a keen amateur botanist, he solves in so far as the discovery of the murderer is concerned. The whereabouts of the brooch remains a mystery, in which the author invites her readers to participate by guessing its location using the clues provided in the text.

*Vincent Caprani's Murder Makes a Portrait* (1992), again in Glendale's crime series, is set on a windswept island off the west coast of Ireland. Goddard, a freelance photographer from Dublin, discovers the murdered body of Arthur Leon, an artist who after leaving the bright lights of London had since been a recluse on the island, annoying the locals with his "parties with the hippies".[15] As Goddard had struck up a friendship with Leon's estranged wife, the actress Gloria Fontana, he is immediately considered to be a suspect but, with the help of the private detective Medway, incognito on the island, and the similarly undercover Garda Ashling Kelly, Goddard discovers the truth about the ageing hippy. Leon, it appears, held connections to the world of forgery, and he had been using blackmail against members of the artistic and local communities. Goddard also uncovers the

15    Vincent Caprani, *Murder Makes a Portrait* (Dublin: Glendale, 1992), 31.

involvement of the rich Sefton family who, apart from helping Leon with his forgery scams, were also immersed in the pillaging of Sheela-na-gigs, grotesque stone carvings, seen by some as fertility symbols) and other items of national heritage. Although the setting is Irish, the atmosphere is that of a light international murder mystery. The apparently stereotypical figure of the local Guard Sean Muldowney, only weeks from retirement and more accustomed to dog licences, and fishing permits than to a murder investi-gation, is undermined when Goddard realises that "with all his homespun philosophy and damn proverbs he's no bloody fool".[16] The efficiency of the Guard is further proved when he uses his local knowledge and pieces of information gleaned from local gossip in order to find the truth, acknow-ledging that "the deepest mysteries lie in the hearts and minds of people".[17]

*Howard R. Simpson*, a reputed Californian writer, was a surprising non-Irish addition to the Glendale crime staple, which specialised in highlighting Irish crime writing. *Cogan's Case* (1992) features Roger Bastide, an officer in the homicide division of the Marseilles police who is seconded to Dublin to work with his Irish counterpart, Inspector Finbarr Cogan, and investigate the death of French fishermen in mysterious circumstances in Irish waters. Between them, the two officers uncover the machinations of a Breton crime syndicate which is working in collaboration with Patrick McMahon, a leading Dublin gangster in the movement and distribution of narcotics.

*Desmond Moore* was the author of two novels also published by Glendale. In the first of these, *Call Me Evil* (1992), Alan Firth, a writer and amateur investigator, receives news of the apparent death of his cousin Hugh, who has left him a letter revealing, among other details, secrets of industrial espionage, which seem a likely cause for his murder. Travelling to France, and enlisting the aid of a friendly hotel porter and his gendarme brother, Firth attempts to discover the truth behind his cousin's death. *Rogan* (1992) is set in an unnamed city in a similarly unnamed country which is under the domination of a secret criminal syndicate bearing the imaginative name of The Syndicate. The mysterious Rogan is called in to halt its corrupt practices and to expose its origins and organisational

16   Ibid., 48.
17   Ibid., 148.

structure, and its links with protection and drugs, while the Syndicate itself attempts to put an end to Rogan and to discover his true identity.

After publishing *An End to Flight*, a novel set in the Nigeria of the Biafra conflict, under the pen-name of Vincent Lawrence, *Vincent Banville's Death by Design* (1993) introduces the Dublin private detective John Blaine, who would feature in all three of the author's crime novels. Blaine's wife has left him and he is now "a merry drunk" who had been an insurance claims analyst before becoming a private investigator.[18] Modelled to a certain extent on the hard-boiled models of Raymond Chandler and Dashiell Hammet, Blaine is approached by Mrs Walsh-Overman, an Anglo-Irish heiress, to find her missing son Redmond, a kilt-wearing, Irish-speaking outsider who is presumed to have escaped to live with "a community of travelling people".[19] The search uncovers the corruption in the Walsh-Overman family and a series of murders of tramps connected to Redmond's brother and a perverse butler. In the tradition of hard-boiled fiction, Blaine is treated with hostility by the official forces of the law, and comments on the specific difficulties of private detection in Ireland, where the normal way of things was "to keep such things in the family circle or to send for the priest".[20]

The novel incorporates touches of humour – Blaine is contacted by his library to return a novel, *The Book of Evidence*, written by John Banville, Vincent's famous brother. It also provides an excellent portrayal of the Dublin of the early 1990s, a city still recovering from the slum clearance projects of the 1960s and 1970s and about to enter into a period of economic bonanza. Planners:

> were given carte blanche by the so-called custodians of Dublin with the result that no proper system of preservation was set up. Blocks of concrete and glass have been placed in the most inappropriate of settings, road widening has swallowed up some of the most exquisite of historic buildings, and big business, banks, insurance companies, supermarkets, condominiums, have chewed up the innards of the city and regurgitated them as freezeframe vomit that becomes ever more depressing.[21]

18   Vincent Banville, *Death by Design* (Harpenden: No Exit Press, 1993), 9.
19   Ibid., 42.
20   Ibid., 19.
21   Ibid., 64.

Blaine's Dublin is still a world of men-only pubs and of beggars and male prostitutes on O'Connell Street, but the new Dublin is emerging in the background, where "a pile driver was booming like a metronome and a long, thin, yellow crane pointed its finger into the sky and dribbled steel wires from its extension rod".[22]

*Death the Pale Rider* (1995) sees John Blaine investigating the murder of two gay men in a mystery which involves two connected series of photographs, one of which reveals several gay relations and the other crucial information regarding a re-zoning scam involving politicians and key members of the city's business community. Blaine seeks collaboration from the Guards, who resent his alleged interference, and from investigative reporters who fear the attacks being orchestrated against their fraternity by the burgeoning local gangster community. *Cannon Law* (2001), Banville's last crime thriller, finds the charmingly flawed Blaine investigating a double murder and the indiscretions of a member of the clergy, while looking after his baby daughter and conducting surveillance work on a funeral parlour. Banville would also contribute two novellas, *Sad Song* (2008) and *An Accident Waiting to Happen* – translated into Irish as *Timpiste Reidh le Tarlu* (2009) – to New Island's Open Door series for adult readers with literacy problems, as well as writing five novels for younger readers in the Hennessy series, starting with *Hennessy* (1990) and finishing with *Hennessy to the Recue* (1995).

*Julie Parsons*, an Irish resident born in New Zealand, has published several successful psychological suspense thrillers which started with *Mary, Mary* (1998) where a psychologist and single mother, Dr Margaret Mitchell, contacts the guards regarding the disappearance of her daughter. When the girl's body is found a week later bearing signs of rape and torture, Guard detective Michael McLoughlin is called in to investigate. McLoughlin, a once highly rated officer, who has lost much of his prestige through his troubles with alcohol and his problematic personal life, is attracted to Margaret, who uses her daughter's birth-father – whose identity has been kept secret as he is acting as the defence counsel in the case against his daughter's killer – in order to trick the murderer and bring about his death. *The Courtship*

22    Ibid., 79.

*Gift* (1999) begins when Anna Neale arrives home to discover her Dublin solicitor husband David lying dead on the floor. Although ostensibly his death has been caused by a bee sting, to which David is allergic, it is soon discovered that he has been murdered. Anna discovers some secrets pertaining to her husband's past, including his involvement in drug dealing and money laundering, but initially fails to suspect the motives of the debonair estate agent who has provided Anna with her husband's death as a courtship gift. Four further novels would appear in the first decade of the twenty-first century, all of which contained the same elements of mystery and suspense, of hidden secrets and revenge. Fittingly, perhaps, the final Parsons novel, *I Saw You* (2007), would be a sequel to her first work.

Although the boom in Irish crime writing would not start until the final years of the 1990s and the beginning of the 2000s, there were a number of factors which pointed towards a changing attitude to Irish crime fiction held by Irish readers. The creation of the Glendale imprint, although a short-lived phenomenon, revealed, it can be argued, a growing interest in Irish crime writing, and the continued success of Bartholomew Gill over this period suggested that readers were interested in the Irish police and in Irish crime. This was also underlined by the growing popularity of "true crime" accounts of leading Irish criminals of the period. Although this would reach its zenith in the second half of the decade, coinciding with the assassination of Veronica Guerin, the late 1980s and early 1990s would see multiple accounts of heists, gang battles and gangster biographies, both in the traditional outlet of the Sunday press and in the newly popular "true crime" paperbacks published by Irish publishers such as Gill & Macmillan or by British companies such as Pan.

# CHAPTER 17

# "A surly-looking cop lounging at the security desk." Northern Irish Crime Fiction in the 1990s

Northern Irish crime fiction has, of course, been largely shadowed by works relating to the Troubles, and before the 1990s it is difficult to find novels which deal with the same sort of criminal activity and its detection as in other territories, including the Republic of Ireland. If the informer in the South was considered to be the lowest form of human life, this status of total repudiation was magnified in the North, where the "tout" was considered – rightly, it would seem – to be a danger for the paramilitaries and their political leadership. The use of the informer had been a constant tactic used by the British administration in its dealings with the native population of Ireland, but its use extended greatly during the 1970s and 1980s. In 1981 the first "supergrass", Christopher Black, was arrested, providing evidence which led, in 1983, to the conviction and imprisonment of twenty-two members of the Provisional IRA. Although eighteen of these convictions were later overturned, the phenomenon of the "supergrass" was to continue throughout the following years, becoming as much a propaganda technique used in the British media – the word itself, "supergrass", was a widely popular headline used in the British tabloid press – as an (at times) effective tool against the paramilitaries. Importantly, and especially for the nationalist population, the fear of betrayal from members of their own continuity led to a rejection of any activity that could be construed as providing secret or otherwise inaccessible information to anyone outside that community, especially, of course, to members of the state apparatus.

If the figure of the private detective was widely rejected by the citizens of Northern Ireland, and his literary equivalent largely ignored by its writers, the esteem with which the police force, the RUC, was held, differed much from that of most other European police forces. The RUC had been created after partition and after the disbanding of the RIC, but since its inception had been broadly regarded as working on behalf of only one section of a divided community and was highly unpopular among the nationalist population, who saw its role as being the blatant promotion of unionist hegemony. The history of the RUC would seem to justify such fears. From its foundation in 1922, the force followed the traditions of the RIC, adopting a military model which distanced it from other police forces in the UK. Members were lodged in barracks and their uniforms had a markedly military appearance. They were kept "physically apart from the natives"[1] and shared characteristics with the police forces of then British colonies such as South Africa or India. According to one critic, the RUC was "an armed force with a primary role in protecting the established political order within a deeply divided state".[2] In Northern Ireland the police force was responsible for more than ordinary law enforcement duties, being charged with the role of protecting the fledgling state from armed attack from forces from both within and outside its borders in a territory in which "common" crime was largely overshadowed by the perceived threat of political subversion.[3]

From its beginning, the RUC was tainted with the suspicion of an overall sympathy towards one part of the divided community in Northern Ireland. The alleged Protestant sympathies shared by many members of both the rank and file and the command structure of the force led to claims from nationalists that the RUC was a sectarian force which was used as a weapon of discrimination and was only representative of the Protestant and unionist status quo. The demographic background of its officers was unrepresentative of the territory, and in the late 1960s, the number of Catholic officers stood at a mere 12 per cent, even though the initial declared intention, as voiced by the Campbell committee as early as 1923,

---

1    Mary Gethins, *Catholic Police Officers in Northern Ireland: Voices out of Silence* (Manchester: Manchester University Press, 2011), 5.

2    Dermot P. J. Walsh, "Police Cooperation Across the Irish Border: Familiarity Breeding Contempt for Transparency and Accountability", *Journal of Law and Society* 38, no. 2 (2011), 304.

3    Chris Ryder, *The RUC: A Force Under Fire*. Rev. edn. (London: Mandarin, 1997), 10.

that the force should have a one-third Catholic representation in its offi-cers,[4] in the entire history of the force, this figure never rose above 21 per cent of the total membership.[5] Policing in Northern Ireland, as such, was perceived by many as the use of majority power as a means of legitimising the dominant unionist ideology and reinforcing the norm of Protestant domination, while at the same time criminalising both explicitly and im-plicitly the political aspirations of the nationalist population. For Gethins, the prospect of the RUC providing a successful and popular police service was doomed from its inception, as "the very model of policing which they inherited in the political conditions of Northern Ireland in 1922 precluded the possibility of winning consent from the Catholic population".[6]

For many members of the Catholic minority in Northern Ireland, the negative image of the RUC was further enhanced by the awareness that a large number of RUC officers actively participated in prominent unionist groupings, most notoriously the Orange Lodge, and with charges of collusion with other official or non-official groups or agencies, from the B-Specials and Ulster Volunteers to paramilitary organisations such as the Ulster Defence Association (UDA) or the Ulster Volunteer Force, and the British army to British police agencies or information and in-telligence networks. Such fears were not altogether unfounded. In June 1922, just weeks after the establishment of the RUC, a letter was sent to the force's Chief Constable, asking if members could attend meetings or-ganised by the Orange Lodge, the Protestant fraternal order which had traditionally upheld the most radical unionist and anti-Catholic views in Ireland.[7] Although Chief Inspector Bates replied that officers could par-ticipate in functions organised by the Order as long as they did so in plain clothes, in January of the following year officers of the RUC set up their own branch of the fraternity, the Sir Robert Peel Memorial Loyal Orange Lodge, an action which left members of the community in little doubt as

4    Ibid., 60.
5    John Morrison, *The Ulster Cover-Up* (Lurgan, Co. Armagh: Ulster Society, 1993), 89.
6    Gethins, *Catholic Police*, 15.
7    Ryder, *The RUC*, 59.

to the loyalty and affiliations of a substantial number of the officers engaged by the new police force.

The RUC was rarely seen as a "normal" police force, and this is reflected in its portrayal in works of fiction. As seen previously, in the thrillers and other works centred on the Troubles, the presence of police officers is palpable, but their role is limited to one of repression or as victims of violence. Rarely, if ever, are they seen in carrying out routine police activity, and their involvement in the solving of crimes is generally limited to intelligence and special branch work, or activities similarly unrelated to the detection, solving and prosecution of crime. One significant exception to this rule is the case of *Nights in Armour* by *Blair McMahon*, the pseudonym of then serving RUC officer Sam Thompson. First published in 1993 by the small Lurgan-based imprint Ulster Society, owned by the future leader of the Democratic Unionist Party and First Minister of Northern Ireland, David Trimble, the novel was given an editorial overhaul and republished by Merrion in 2019. *Nights in Armour* provides an interesting portrait of the RUC at the height of the Troubles, set during the final days of Bobby Sands as his hunger strike draws towards its tragic conclusion and in the days immediately after his death. It follows the private and professional life of a group of young RUC officers, attempting to show their fears, prejudices, motivation and vices.

One of the most striking features of the work is the youth of its protagonists, mere boys dressed in the uncomfortable green uniform of the force. As Thompson comments, "the vast majority of patrol officers were in their teens or early twenties" and anyone aged thirty "would have been considered an old man".[8] The novel shows the police in their free time, drinking and playing Space Invaders, and at work. The fear and adrenaline they suffer is countered by the pleasure taken in beating suspects, the threat of disciplinary action overhanging their actions. The author of *West Belfast* and former republican press officer, Danny Morrison, praises the novel for its honesty. Despite, he says, the author's obvious ties to his own

8    Sam Thompson, "Lyra and I compared notes about our books. I lived to see my title in print, she did not", *Irish Times*, 14 May 2019, <https://www.irishtimes.com/culture/books/lyra-and-i-compared-notes-about-our-books-i-lived-to-see-my-title-in-print-she-did-not-1.3891068>, accessed 4 July 2019.

community, "to his credit those ties have not circumscribed or restricted his depiction of character and their prejudices".[9] For Morrison, the work reveals "the flawed, honest human being behind the gun and uniform; the crutch of masculinity, the broken marriages and relationships, the suicides, the alcohol-dependency, the rivalries, the guilt, the camaraderie".[10]

The heroes of *Nights in Armour* are certainly flawed. Constable Reid is under investigation for being overtly anti-Catholic, and Constable Clark cold-bloodedly kills a wounded terrorist in a church. A female officer is nick-named Diana Death on account of her morbid fascination with looking at and photographing the bodies of victims of the violence. These officers are in the RUC, as Clark's wife remonstrates, not out of any sense of duty or honour, but simply because they could not think of anything better to do.

*Eugene McEldowney*, a Belfast-born resident of Dublin, published four crime novels featuring Cecil Megarry, a superintendent in the RUC. The first novel in the series, *A Kind of Homecoming* (1994), introduces the troubled figure of Megarry, an alcoholic with a daughter suffering from an-orexia and whose wife has recently left him. His personal problems appear to be a reflection of the state of affairs in Northern Ireland at the time of the novel and, more specifically, the state of affairs within the RUC, where he encounters corruption at grassroots level, in the figure of the obnoxious Blair, and collusion at a higher level personified by the British army contact Prescott, who treated Cecil like a "colonial hick".[11] Megarry's investigation into a double murder, in which the two victims are of different religious backgrounds, seems to be thwarted from all levels, and he eventually dis-covers that both are somehow related to an earlier unsolved murder. His eventual realisation that the police and the paramilitaries are inextricably linked "like Siamese twins"[12] leads to the arrest of both Blair and Prescott, but also to Megarry's suspension from the force. *A Kind of Homecoming* highlights the extent of corruption and collusion the author perceives to exist within the RUC and his pessimistic portrayal of the force would

9   Danny Morrison, "Through RUC Eyes", <https://www.dannymorrison.com/thro ugh-ruc-eyes/>, accessed 2 December 2019.
10   Ibid.
11   Eugene McEldowney, *A Kind of Homecoming* (London: Mandarin, 1994), 159.
12   Ibid., 194.

be echoed in future novels written by Northern Irish writers in the final decade of the twentieth century. Although the crime is serious – the suggestion appears to be – even more serious is the involvement in that crime, both practically and ideologically, by those who are supposed to uphold law and order. The novel was praised by fellow-author Adrian McKinty, who considered it "a brave attempt to impose order on the disorder of a troublesome city" by providing Belfast with "a straightforward mystery novel with a sympathetic but dysfunctional detective".[13]

*A Stone of the Heart* (1995), not to be confused with the John Brady novel of the same name, sees Megarry reunited with his wife and reinstated in the RUC after his period of suspension. Here, his investigation of an apparently simple bank robbery is cleverly paralleled with the events which lead Sean Morgan, a crippled getaway driver for the IRA, into a kidnapping case in which his destiny would overlap with that of Megarry. As in *A Kind of Homecoming*, this second novel in the series reflects the character's criticism of the RUC, "a male club, seeing the problems of the world through middle-aged male eyes".[14] Despite the changes in the Constabulary, the introduction of new technology only reveals that the "police authorities care more for their costly computers than for the staff who had to use them".[15] The positive aspects to be gleaned from *A Stone in the Heart* include Megarry's surprising sympathy for the residents of the Falls Road who, he recognises, "have nothing but their hatred and their sense of pride"[16] and the mutual understanding which develops between Megarry, a Protestant police officer and Morgan, a Catholic IRA man, a sign, perhaps, of the prospects of a future of peace and tolerance. Patrick Magee praises McEldowney's "pragmatic outlook" as his detective is unconvinced by the attempts his superiors make to blame the murders on the

13    Adrian McKinty, "Odd Men Out" in *Down These Green Streets: Irish Crime Writing in the 21st Century*, ed. Declan Burke (Dublin: Liberties Press, 2011), 103.
14    Eugene McEldowney, *A Stone of the Heart* (London: Mandarin, 1995), 60.
15    Ibid., 131.
16    Ibid., 168.

IRA, noting how the author refuses to "adopt an absolutist position in his attitude to republican violence".[17]

The next two Megarry novels, perhaps reflecting the peace process, and certainly reflecting the author's move to the Republic, are both set in Dublin. In *The Sad Case of Harpo Higgins* (1996) Megarry, on holiday in the capital, is approached by an acquaintance in the Garda to help in the case of the murder of a young drug addict. Although he discovers that his Guard contact is involved in a cover-up under the patronage of a crooked businessman who offers Megarry work as security chief for his company, the RUC officer finds himself at home in Dublin, despite the reticence held by members of the Southern police force to his involvement in the case. Symbolically, Cecil, a Protestant, attends his first-ever Catholic mass in the city. The novel is also interesting for the Northerner's view of Dublin, particularly in his description of Ballymoss, a fictional recreation of the high-rise housing schemes of Ballymun, in which the Northern police officer detects "an air of poverty and desolation".[18] The initial positive impression created by the guards is mitigated by his discovery that corruption is also a feature of the Southern police, and despite attempts by high-level officers to curtail his investigations, he is able to help solve two murders and uncover the unethical officers.

In *Murder at Piper's Gut* (1997) Megarry has taken retirement in Howth but is frustrated by the lack of excitement afforded by his new status. Again he becomes involved in a case, and again meets with opposition from the local police. Whereas the criticism directed against the RUC was largely that of corruption, political impartiality and collusion, his disapproval of the guards is closely related to existing Southern stereotypes of the force. Thus Megarry is critical of the slovenly appearance of individual officers – "a surly-looking cop lounging at the security desk"[19] – and the perceived rural background of the police who with their "thick farmer's wrists"[20] all seemed to hail "from the

---

17    Patrick Magee, *Gangsters or Guerrillas? Representations of Irish Republicans in "Troubles Fiction"* (Belfast: Beyond the Pale, 2001), 191.

18    Eugene McEldowney, *The Sad Case of Harpo Higgins* (London: Heinemann, 1996), 25.

19    Eugene McEldowney, *Murder at Piper's Gut* (London: Heinemann, 1997), 25.

20    Ibid., 32.

sticks".[21] He is tempted to come out of retirement to help the local police when fishermen close to his home in Howth discover the head of a woman in their nets. Megarry's help is gratefully accepted by the Howth police, overwhelmed by the circumstances and the hysteria being raised in the normally quiet fishing village, but his intromission is challenged by a suspect who claims that he is using intimidation during his interrogation and that, while such a tactic may be common in the North, "we don't put up with this shit down here".[22]

The four Megarry novels are of great importance in the history of crime fiction from Northern Ireland, providing a rare example of a series featuring an RUC detective working on standard police procedures. The portrayal of a damaged but principled officer working in the RUC on the cusp of the peace agreement is unique in the genre, and the series anticipates the future with its particular but appealing depiction of cross-border collaboration. McEldowney, in the figure of Megarry, creates an interesting character, an upright officer working in a force which is depicted as being anything but ethical. The broken alcoholic of the first novel progresses over the four novels of the series, and his move to the Republic coincides with his moral and spiritual renewal, suggesting, perhaps that he precludes the "positive" police figures of PSNI (Police Service of Northern Ireland) officers who would start to appear in crime fiction of Northern Ireland at the beginning of the following decade.

Although the armed conflict continued throughout the 1990s, both republican and loyalist leaders appeared to be seeking a negotiated end to the conflict After high-profile incidents, such as the mortar attack on Downing Street in an attempt to kill British Prime Minister John Major and members of his cabinet, two ceasefires were declared, in 1994 and 1996. The second of these ended after the notorious Manchester and Canary Wharf bombings, which preceded the Good Friday Agreement of 1998. The decade was also interesting in terms of Northern Irish fiction, with authors such as Colin Bateman and Eoin McNamee producing their first works. A large number of thrillers were still being produced by non-Irish

---

21    Ibid., 136.
22    Ibid., 218.

writers, although the best of these lacked the unimaginative use of stereotypes, and works such as *Ordinary Decent Criminals* (1992) by American
*Lionel Shriver*, pen-name of Margaret Ann Shriver, who lived in Belfast for
twelve years during the period, or *The Psalm Killer* (1996) by Englishman
*Chris Petit*, added important nuances to the genre. Although Irish writers
such as Sarah Michaels, Richard Crawford and Shawn Clarke were still
producing thrillers reminiscent of those of the 1970s, the sophisticated
crime thrillers of McNamee would provide an example of how Northern
Ireland could provide a fruitful territory for serious, balanced and sophisticated narratives.

    *Sarah Michaels* (pseudonym of Michele A. McMullan), although ori-
ginally from a Catholic background, converted to Presbyterianism, and her
novel *Summary Justice* (1988) expresses the frustration of the Unionist community with what was believed to be the ineffectuality of the RUC in the
face of nationalist violence. In *Summary Justice*, Somerville, a rank and file
RUC officer, reacts to the killing of his wife and children in a bomb attack
by becoming a vigilante killer, intent on exacting his own revenge for the
death of his family. The most interesting feature in an otherwise formulaic
novel is that ultimately Somerville's rage is directed not against the IRA
who had been responsible for the attack, but against the other forces of
society – the intelligence services, the government, high ranking officers
of the RUC – whose treachery he believes to be as great or greater than
that of the terrorist enemy. This sense of grievance is often seen in terms of
the Protestant Northern Irish being let down by the cynical metropolitan
forces from London who, while purportedly supporting the Unionist dominance in the "Province" are believed to be undermining this dominance
in favour of concessions being granted to Catholic nationalists.

    In *Dieback* (1991), a radio transmission made from a derelict farmhouse
in rural Northern Ireland to a Libyan camp where international terrorists are
trained reveals complex infighting between the KGB and the Soviet military intelligence, the GRU, which revives the memory of a trained assassin
who had operated on the streets of Belfast some twenty years before and
reveals the existence of "sleeper" agents in the ranks of British intelligence
and the IRA, and of a plot to assassinate the Queen in Buckingham Palace
as a means of discrediting the GRU. Michaels' final novel, *The Heir* (1994),

delves deeper into the territory of the international thriller in the story of Elizabeth, the daughter of a Jewish diamond dealer from Amsterdam who, at the end of the Second World War, helps her husband, an Irish academic and agent for British intelligence, to smuggle a young boy, Peter, over to Ireland, before, on her husband's death, taking him to America. While Elizabeth seeks revenge on the Nazi officer responsible for the death of her family, she is unaware that Peter is the natural child of Hitler and Eva Braun, nor that he is to be trained to continue the plans of his birth father.

*Richard Crawford's* two published novels, *Fall When Hit* (1993) and *The Minstrel Boy* (1995), are interesting examples of Troubles era thrillers. In the former, Garret Kearns, a part-time Ulster Defence Force officer, is involved in a traffic incident which leads to a shoot-out and his subsequent arrest. When he discovers that he has unwittingly killed a British intelligence officer, Kearns finds himself involved in a situation where he is a party to knowledge concerning evidence of British negotiations with the IRA which could bring about the downfall of the Westminster government. In the words of Aaron Kelly "the text scrutinizes not only the filiative crisis of Unionism, but also the organic ideological bond with the British state".[23] The undermining of this ideological and political bond is further examined in *The Minstrel Boy*, in which the protagonist, Colin Rea, son of a loyalist militant is denied entrance into the RUC, precisely because of his father's history. Colin fails to understand what he believes to be the contradictions inherent in his rejection from the force, which he believes to be the guarantor of the rights and destiny of his people, the Protestant population of Northern Ireland, and takes the decision he had previously rejected, that of joining a paramilitary group. His involvement in a murder leads to his imprisonment – by the state he has tried, in his misguided way, to defend.

*Shaun Clarke* is the pseudonym which the Belfast-born writer W. A. Harbinson used to produce a series of military novels based on the exploits of the British Army Special Air Service (SAS). Among these are four which deal specifically with events in or concerning Northern Ireland. *Sniper Fire in Belfast* (1995) details the secret presence of SAS operatives in Ireland

---

23    Richard Crawford, *Fall When Hit* (London: Mandarin, 1993), 76.

and their illegal incursions into the Republic. Although the presence of the SAS was constantly denied, Clarke notes that they were "viewed by many as a secret army of assassins, not much better than the notorious Black and Tans of old".[24] *Death on Gibraltar: SAS Operation* (1994), like Vincent Flood's later *After Gibraltar* (2006), is a fictional reworking of the operation set up by the Thatcher government with the aim of killing three IRA volunteers in 1987, while *Underworld* (1997) foresees the degeneration of paramilitary groupings into criminal gangs following the peace process. Northern Ireland, one British operative states, "threatens to become the new Italy or Sicily, virtually controlled by the crime barons – all former paramilitaries – and we're going to have to do something about it before it gets completely out of hand".[25] SAS sergeant Michael Burton is sent to Belfast to perform "surgical cleansing" by removing "the biggest weeds" so that "the rest will wither and die on the vine".[26] Burton is described as "a decent man, a man of strong principles"; however, "like everyone involved in the Troubles, he'd had to stoop to some dirty tricks".[27] Burton's "dirty tricks" involved the killing of a young girl and her father in a previous tour of duty in Northern Ireland, something which would return to haunt him as he attempts to establish a relationship with a beautiful Catholic prostitute. Like *Underworld*, *Red Hand* (1999) is also set in the near future. In 1999 Pete Douglas, a former SAS officer, attempts to discover why high-profile figures from both sides of the religious and ideological divide are disappearing while the country tries to maintain its tentative hold on peace. Douglas is a Belfast man, and as a makeshift detective he investigates the city, in a work which "typifies the presentation of Belfast as a cartography of total criminality".[28]

24    Shaun Clarke, *Sniper Fire in Belfast* (1993, London: HarperCollins, 2016), Kindle, accessed 12 January 2019.

25    Shaun Clarke, *Underworld* (1997, London: W. A. Harbison, 2014), Kindle, accessed 12 January 2019.

26    Ibid.

27    Ibid.

28    Aaron Kelly, *The Thriller and Northern Ireland Since 1969: Utterly Resigned Terror* (Aldershot: Ashgate, 2005), 92.

*All Our Fault* (1991), the first novel by playwright *Daniel Mornin*, is
set in Belfast in 1969 (the fact being emphasised by references to the first
moon landing) at the beginning of the "Troubles". Liam Kelly is a Catholic
who has returned to Northern Ireland with his two children Katherine and
Liam after separating from his wife in London where he had been working.
One night, as the houses of Belfast Catholics are being burned down, Kelly
is attacked. He is looked after by a Protestant nurse who tends his wounds
but, not heeding her advice, he takes to the streets again. He is stopped by
a gang of Protestant youths who had been hunting for a Catholic and subjected to disturbing torture while his children walk the streets searching for
their father. The different attitudes of the members of the torture gang are
well developed through the dialogues and, when it looks as if the youths are
on the verge of killing their prey he is allowed to leave, thanks to the fact that
the leader of the gang remembers having played with Liam as a child. When,
however, Liam is released, the intervention of Katherine's friend, an armed
Catholic youth, results in tragedy. The ending of the novel is bleak and pessimistic as Liam once again waiting to board the ferry to England meets up
with Tommy, one of the gang, in a bar. Their salute and shared drink suggests
that a better future might someday be feasible but, in 1969 at least, this would
be impossible in Northern Ireland.

One of the most startling novels to come out of, and reflect, the period
of the Troubles in Northern Ireland is *Seamus Deane's Reading in the Dark*
(1996). Described by one critic as "a metaphysical detective story in which
the clues add up to an epiphany of entrapment", it traces events from the
mid-1940s until the summer of 1971, with an important flashback to the
original troubles in the early 1920s.[29] An almost-autobiographical coming-
of-age novel, *Reading in the Dark* "radically deconstructs the very notion
of genre itself" as the unnamed young protagonist sifts through the myriad
information to decipher clues about his family's past and the secrets which
remain unspoken.[30] The boy's almost unintentional quest is to ascertain

---

29    Dermot Kelly, "Joycean Epiphany in Seamus Deane's *Reading in the Dark*"
      in *Moments of Moment: Aspects of Literary Epiphany*, ed. Wim Tigges
      (Amsterdam: Rodopi, 1999), 435.
30    Danah Farquarson, "Resisting Genre and Type: Narrative Strategy and Instability
      in Danny Morrison's *The Wrong Man* and Seamus Deane's *Reading in the Dark*" in

the truth behind the events which took place in 1922 and which led to his uncle being branded an informer. As a background, Deane describes the almost casual routine brutality suffered by the citizens of Derry in the early years of the conflict.

The 1990s would also see some strange but interesting anomalies which, while transcending genre, offered an interesting glimpse at the events taking place. Such is the case of *Briege Duffaud's A Wreath Upon the Dead* (1993), which traces the difficulties off a Northern Irish writer who, while trying to write a historical novel based on Ulster's past, is forced to concede to the pressures of the present. Kitty, the protagonist of *Kate O'Riordan's Involved* (1995), a Southerner like the author, is forced to confront the situation in the North when she leaves her comfortable home to meet the working-class family of Danny in West Belfast. Her growing realisation of the family's involvement in the conflict leads to a tragic ending when Kitty, branded a tout and living in Canada, is killed by an IRA death squad.

*Patrick Quigley's Borderland* (1994) observes the conflict from the perspective of the farming communities just over the border in the Republic. Shane loses his mother and the family farm in a fire and moves with his father to the border farm of his uncle and cousin. The boy is obsessed with soldiers and arms, and during a play fight with his cousin near an old hill fort, Shane loses the sight of an eye. Bullied at school, he rescues a Protestant girl, Jocelyn (Joy) from a fight between pupils from his Catholic school and the children from the local Protestant school. Shane and Joy fall in love, but her rich father the Major opposes their friendship and the girl is sent away to England. Shane is badly beaten by Joy's brother Eric, and he does not meet her again until 1969 when, in the aftermath of the outbreak of violence in the North, Joy and her student friends are advocating radical solutions to the crisis. The timid student protests in the Southern town are met with brutal reprisals from the Gardaí, most especially by Guard Black John Duffy, the biggest bully when a pupil at Shane's school.

On leaving school, Shane is employed as a psychiatric nurse at a local hospital. He becomes actively involved in the marches, protesting against

---

*Writing Ulster: Northern Narratives*, ed. Bill Lazenbatt (Jordanstown: University of Ulster Press, 1999), 90.

the events in Northern Ireland, joins a Marxist group and purchases a gun. Joy's brother Eric is killed in a terror attack and Shane goes to visit her. He is shocked by how much the girl has changed, as she tells him she now wants to help her people in their struggle. She participates in an armed action to be carried out by Protestants from the North, and Shane is forced to drive the car carrying a bomb into the nearby border town. The results of the bomb attack change Shane dramatically, as the moral and psychological schizophrenia which has been hinted at throughout the novel are given physical status. *Borderland*, along with Terence De Vere White's *The Distance and the Dark*, provides a fine example of the early days of the Northern conflict as viewed through Southern eyes.

In *The Serpent's Tail* (1995), journalist *Martin Dillon* – whose *The Shankill Butchers: A Study in Mass Murder* (1989) would provide a key influence for Eoin McNamee – examines the "dirty war" being carried out by the British security forces in Northern Ireland in the early 1970s. Based on a true story, it follows two Belfast teenagers, Stephen Fitzpatrick and Michael McDonnell, who are used by the SAS and MI5 in an attempt "to draw the Provisional IRA and the Official IRA into a feud, and carry out sectarian killings to encourage a war between the IRA and the loyalists".[31] *The Serpent's Tail*, while exposing the complex web of intelligence and counter-intelligence which existed in Belfast at the time, also shows the difficulties faced by two ordinary youths who are unwittingly caught up in a war in which the main victims were innocent civilians like Stephen and Michael. The epilogue, set in the USA in 1994, and in which Stephen's wife, Bernadette, gives him news of the ceasefire, points towards a more hopeful future.

*Ian McDonald's Sacrifice of Fools* (1996) is set in the year 2004, and finds large parts of the planet – including Northern Ireland – colonised by the Shian, an intelligent alien race. The Troubles are over, and in post-conflict Belfast former loyalist paramilitary Andy Gillespie is employed as a go-between in one of the Welcome Centres where humans and Shian interact. Gillespie has learned Narha, the alien language, while serving time in Long Kesh. The island of Ireland is undergoing a period of uneasy

31    Martin Dillon, *The Serpent's Tail* (London: Fourth Estate, 1995), 13.

Joint Sovereignty, and despite the perceived threat of the alien presence, religious and sectarian issues persist. The new police force, anticipated by McDonald as the "NIPS" (Northern Ireland Police Servic), investigates the murder of a Shian family and Gillespie is called in as interpreter. Aided by a Catholic female police officer, Dunbar, Andy discovers the difficulties involved in examining a murder case which is not apparently related to sectarian issues. In Northern Ireland "we only have two tricks, the orange one and the green one", and "[o]ur crime has to be Unionist or Nationalist".[32] *Sacrifice of Fools* combines the genres of science fiction and murder mystery, but is most successful in its portrayal of post-conflict Belfast and the problems which persist, in spite of a potentially more lethal threat. As Stephanie Schwerter rightly commented, McDonald's use of the aliens conforms to a common Troubles narrative trope, that is, the introduction of an outsider or foreigner "as a medium through which Belfast is perceived and commented upon".[33]

*Ronan Bennett's* powerful literary thrillers, perhaps surprisingly given the author's background, are not all directly connected with the Troubles. As a youthful republican volunteer, Bennett was imprisoned without trial in the early 1970s, wrongly accused, as would later be revealed, of the murder of an RUC officer. Bennett's memory of the beatings and gas attacks he received while in prison are, however, reflected in his first novel, *The Second Prison* (1991). Kane, like the author himself, a young republican activist, is released from prison. Determined to avenge his apparent betrayal by Dec, the man who he believes has informed on his cell, Kane travels to kill his erstwhile comrade. Pursued in turn by the larger-than-life and horrifically brutal Special Branch officer, the aptly named Tempest, Kane is forced to come to terms with "the second prison" into which he has been released, the psychological incarceration to which former prisoners are subjected throughout the rest of their lives. Although it adheres to many of the common tropes of the genre, the real suspense and power of *The Second Prison* lies in the psychological portrayal of Kane as he faces his

32  Ian McDonald, *Sacrifice of Fools* (London: Cox & Wyman, 1996). Kindle position 735, accessed 14 December 2020.

33  Stephanie Schwerter, "Peacefire: Belfast Between Reality and Fiction", *The Canadian Journal of Irish Studies* 33, no.2. (2007), 19–27.

demons and tries to come to terms with his apparent liberty, which gives him anything but freedom.

*Overthrown by Strangers* (1992) is initially set in an unnamed but instantly recognisable Northern Ireland, where another republican activist, Sean Quinn, escapes from the British soldiers who nearly kill him and his best friend, Denis, who is intent on having an affair with Quinn's unfaithful wife. Running for both political and personal reasons, he arrives in Mexico after a spell in the USA. There, with a female lawyer, Judith, who is investigating her sister's disappearance, and Agustín, a Peruvian immigrant, he fights against the evil New Era Mission of Christ, a fundamentalist Christian sect which is using its new platform in Central America for non-religious ends. Although the second half of the novel lacks the promise of its opening chapters, *Overthrown by Strangers* is an interesting international thriller in which the author once again examines the guilt, despair and sense of betrayal of his protagonist. This sense of despair is central to *The Catastrophist* (1998), in which the Northern Irish historian and novelist James Gillespie goes to the Congo after his militant but fragile girlfriend, the Marxist Italian journalist Inès. Gillespie, who Inès accuses of not being a "real" Irishman, is caught up in the events which bring about the independence of the former Belgian colony under Patrice Lumumba and his followers, with one of whom Inès has become emotionally involved. While the events quickly unfold, with rebellion in the Southern province of Katanga and the openly hostile CIA involvement, Bennett's work examines the extent to which Gillespie's own personal failures reflect that of the events in the Congo and, arguably, concurrent events in his own homeland.

# CHAPTER 18

# "Technically a private investigator." Thrillers and the Diversity of Irish Crime Writing in the 1990s

Irish thrillers, whether dealing with situations which were Irish, international or both, saw great popular acceptance during the early 1990s, and writers such as Daniel Easterman, Glenn Meade, Victor O'Reilly, Con Cregan and Tom Phelan would begin their careers, as would Brian Gallagher with his police-based thrillers, and Rory McCormack with his novels featuring a veterinary surgeon as detective. Joseph O'Connor's early novels would also contain many elements of the crime and mystery novel, while Paul Carson would produce a successful Irish take on the medical detective narrative. The decade which heard the first roars of the Celtic Tiger would also see the publication of interesting political crime mysteries, such as the first incursion into the world of crime writing by Fine Gael politician Maurice Manning, and Neville Thompson's Northside novels, harsher at times than those of Roddy Doyle, apparently aim at creating a Dublin version of Irvine Welsh's Edinburgh.

Denis MacEoin is a Belfast academic specialising in Islamic Studies who has written supernatural mysteries under the name of *Jonathan Aycliffe* and several international thrillers using the pseudonym *Daniel Easterman*. The Aycliffe novels include *Naomi's Room* (1991), in which the murder of a child in the present reflect events which happened over a century earlier, *The Matrix* (1994) where a widowed academic takes solace in the search for eternal life and *The Silence of Ghosts* (2013) where the past crimes of a family which had been involved in the slave trade are visited on their descendants during the London Blitz. The Easterman thrillers are set mainly in the Middle East and make use of the author's extensive knowledge of the region's affairs, history and culture, often featuring archaeologists as protagonists. *The Last Assassin* (1984) is set in Iran immediately following the Islamic Revolution, while in *The Seventh Sanctuary* (1987), David

Rosen, an archaeologist who is compared to both a detective and an intelligence agent, discovers a plot by neo-Nazis using a hidden underground Jewish city which houses the Ark of the Covenant and which they intend to convert into the starting point for a Fourth Reich uniting German and Arab fanatics. *Brotherhood of the Tomb* (1989) features Patrick Canavan, an ex-CIA academic who uncovers a sect which claims to have found the tomb of the Holy Family along with important evidence that Christ did not, in fact, die on the cross, and a plot to install an anti-Islamic extremist as the new pope.

*The Ninth Buddha* (1988) follows the kidnapping of a British boy in the early 1920s. He is taken to a Buddhist monastery in Tibet where it is revealed that young William Wylam is the incarnation of the Buddha and future ruler of Mongolia, a fact which means that Bolsheviks and White Russians attempt to capture him to ensure future control of the territory. *Night of the Seventh Darkness* (1991) is set largely in contemporary New York and Haiti and features a tale of murders and voodoo as part of a high-level conspiracy, while *Name of the Beast* (1992) returns to the Middle East, where a fundamentalist regime led by an unlikely Spaniard has the intention of reconquering Al-Andalus as a Muslim caliphate in southern Spain, supported by far-right leaders from certain European countries who see this idea as a means of unloading unwanted Muslim immigrants. In *The Judas Testament* (1994) a professor discovers a scroll which purports to be the autobiography of Jesus and which a variety of forces seek to gain control of for political purposes.

Set in the Ireland of the near future, *Day of Wrath* (1995) sees American Christian fundamentalists from Waco kidnapping the members of the Muslim Leaders' Conference meeting in Dublin. The plan to rescue the leaders, led by Declan Carberry, head of the Garda Special Detective Unit involves an unlikely alliance featuring the IRA, radical Muslim groups, the Irish Special Branch, the Irish army and the British SAS. *K for Killer* (1997) is set in a fictional alternative America during the Second World War, where the USA, under President Lindbergh and with the Duke of Windsor as British ambassador, has taken a pro-Nazi stance. John Ridgeworth, half-British and half-American, is sent to assassinate the President who has legalised lynchings and given power to the Ku Klux Klan. In *Incarnation*

(1998) a young boy found in Northern India who claims to be the reincarnation of a British agent is interrogated about the secret knowledge he supposedly holds which contains secrets about Iraki and Chinese nuclear collaboration.

In *The Final Judgement* (1999) a young Israeli boy is kidnapped in Sardinia and his uncle, Yosef Abuhatseira, formerly of the Israeli special forces, attempts to rescue him, uncovering a plot to install neo-Nazi governments in Germany and Italy, where right-wing magistrates have been appointed to a case aiming to rebuke the memory of the Holocaust. *The Jaguar Mask* (2001) sees the return of Declan Carberry, the Guard who had appeared in *Day of Wrath*. Now working for Interpol in Lyon, Declan travels to Mexico to investigate a powerful sect backed by neo-fascists which is used to cover a logging company committing atrocities in the jungle near the spot where archaeologist Leo Mallory has found a lost Mayan city. *Midnight Comes at Noon* (2001) presents a near-apocalyptic situation when, in the near future, Turkey declares war on Greece, the Russian Federation is threatened by ultra-orthodox nationalists led by Cossack aristocrats, and the new American President, a Jewish liberal, is kidnapped and taken to Siberia along with his wife and Holly Crawford, daughter of Captain Jim Crawford of the USAF. Crawford sets out to rescue the President and his daughter, discovering the involvement of secret right-wing American interests in the kidnapping. *Maroc* (2003), set in Morocco and the UK during the Second World War and in the present, traces the past secrets of Nazis and Resistance in French Morocco, while in *The Sword* (2007) the murder of the wife and daughter of English history professor Jack Goodrich are seen to be related to his discovery of the sword of the title, the property of the descendant of the Prophet Mohammed, who awaits the return of the arm to be able to declare jihad on all non-believers. Another weapon is central to the premise of *Spear of Destiny* (2009) in which the spear is discovered by a group of British soldiers alongside a crown of thorns and a grail in Libya in 1942 at what is believed to be the tomb of Christ. Some sixty years later, following the mysterious death of the remaining soldiers, the nephew of one of these, an English police detective, realises that forces of the extreme right wish to locate the tomb, which they want to use to create a new Nazi revival.

*Victor O'Reilly*, an Irish-born American resident, has published three thrillers featuring Polling Fitzduane, former soldier in the Irish army and war photographer. In *Games of the Hangman* (1991), Fitzduane discovers an international conspiracy operating from an exclusive college on the island he owns off the west coast of Ireland. When he discovers a rich Swiss youth hanging from a tree in the school grounds, his investigations in Ireland and Switzerland lead to the discovery of a secret terrorist army. Fitzduane, who claims his family have lived in the same part of Ireland since the twelfth century, uses his contacts in the army, especially his friend Kilmara, head of the elite Irish Army Rangers who had seen action with Fitzduane in the Congo, to prevent the elusive Hangman of the title from carrying out his plans. In *Games of Vengeance* (1994), published for the American market as *Rules of the Hunt*, Fitzduane is pursued by Japanese disciples of the Hangman, who he had killed in the previous novel. The Japanese, led by the female hired killer Reiko Oshima and aided by members of a dissident Irish republican group, are planning, along with the North Koreans, Operation Tsunami, a nuclear weapon programme designed to put the West at risk and which Fitzduane, again accompanied by Kilmara, must thwart. The final novel in the series, *The Devil's Footprint* (1997), finds Fitzduane working for a congressional task force in the USA and forced to face Oshima again, as she leads a Japanese and Mexican coalition to create a super-weapon capable of inflicting huge damage on American soil.

Dublin-born *Glenn Meade* has published a series of successful international thrillers which commenced with *Brandenburg* (1994), chronicling the rise of the Fourth Reich after the great economic depression of 1994. Joe Volkmann, a British army officer working for the European security directive, investigates the attempts by neo-Nazis based in South America to take over Europe using a secret son of Hitler to lead the coup. *Snow Wolf* (1995) takes as its starting point an assassination attempt on Stalin in 1953 and centres on the investigation into this attempted killing by American journalist William Massey, the son of the CIA operative who had been sent to shoot Stalin. *The Sands of Sakkara* (1999), republished in 2016 as *The Cairo Code*, is a lengthy thriller set in Egypt during the Second World War, and repeats a formula which Meade would continue to use throughout the early years of the next century.

*Conor Cregan's* first novel, *Chrissie* (1992), is set against the background of the wasted generation of Irish graduates in the 1980s who were forced to seek employment overseas, given the negative economic climate they faced at home. Liam and Chrissie find work in southern Spain, teaching English in a language school where they meet Ian, a troubled English Malvinas veteran who has abused his ex-wife physically and sexually and who has attempted to kill himself. Liam and Ian fight over Chrissie, and Ian dies by his own hand in a strange duel of Russian roulette. The novel has elements of the thriller, with references to the beginnings of gangster Dublin appearing in the final pages,which culminate in Chrissie aborting Liam's child. *The Poison Stream* (1993) is a thriller in which Kate Keys, an investigator for the EEC, is sent by Brussels to look into claims about pollution being caused by MartinCorp, the company run by Ralph Martin, the richest man in Ireland. Tracking down her old friend Jack Clarke, currently working for Martin, Kate discovers the collusion between the businessman and the Taoiseach Frank Costello enabling both parties to evade existing legislation and increase the company's profits.

*With Extreme Prejudice* (1994) is a somewhat routine Troubles thriller, whose chief point of interest is the opposition between Tim McLennan, a unionist from Northern Ireland serving in the SAS, and Jack Cusack, the head of an IRA active service unit. *House of Fire* is an international thriller which takes place in the Balkan conflict of the early 1990s. A group of mercenaries, including Irishman Luke Ryan, are fighting for the Bosnians against the Serbs and their Russian allies. Ryan, the only idealist among his group, is constantly comparing the situation of the Bosnian Muslims with that of the Irish in their struggle against Britain. *Valkyrie* (1996) and *Ground Zero* (1998) are both set in the Second World War, and both feature the character of Claude Dansey, an agent in British intelligence. In *Valkyrie*, Haganah, the underground Jewish army, hire a German assassin using the codename of Valkyrie to kill Hitler. British intelligence, however, is afraid that if the German dictator is killed before allied troops are able to establish a strong presence in continental Europe, Hitler's death could lead to the Soviets taking power in Germany. The allies believe that with Hitler still alive an unconditional surrender might be achieved, and Dansey is entrusted with halting the assassination attempt. In *Ground Zero* the German army uses a special SS unit comprising of right-wing soldiers from the southern states of the USA, the Stonewall Legion who, under the confederate flag, had fought alongside the Spanish in the *División Azul*, to intercept a quantity of plutonium necessary for the fabrication of a German atomic weapon.

*First Strike* (1999) is set in 1949, moving between post-war Berlin and the Stalinist Soviet Union. The novel works from the premise that Stalin himself is, in fact, a foreign agent, who had been blackmailed over a rape he committed as a young man in London. The novel finds the CIA and the secret service attempting to work with a former member of the Tzarist secret police, currently interred in a gulag who, they believe, would be able to create havoc in Stalin's leadership of the country.

*Gareth O'Callaghan* has published three thrillers, the first of which, *Dare to Die* (1996), is set in the world of the Irish immigrant community in North London. On the ferry over to London before taking up a post as manager of a pub, Frank McCabe meets Jamie Carroll and, although they get on well, Jamie has a boyfriend, a London police officer, and they part without sharing contact details. In London, after hearing details of a murder by a tramp, Frank is drawn into a case which involves Jamie's police boyfriend – who uses his post as a cover for his drug dealing and who has murdered a fellow officer during a police raid – Jamie herself and a framed IRA suspect who has escaped from custody. *The Keeper* (1999) is set in the village of Sheep's Head on the Durrus Peninsula, where Jack Buckley, a former police sergeant, awakens after a night's drinking following the departure of his partner, Maggie, to find the drowned body of his best friend lying beside him. The novel develops into a tale of international terrorism and tax fraud as Buckley discovers how Maggie has been fooled by a Nazi war criminal controlling a German-owned company operating in Ireland.

Darren O'Shaughnessy, born in London and raised in Limerick, is best known as a successful writer of young adult fantasy novels, published under the pseudonym of *Darren Shan*. *Ayuamarca* (1999) was his first novel aimed at an adult reading public and, although originally signed with his real name, was re-issued in a revised version in 2008 under the Shan nom-de-plume. This revised version would also place the novel within the context of a trilogy which Shan was to entitle *The City*, with *Ayuamarca* being retitled *Procession of the Dead*, apparently a translation from the original in the Inca language. The work commences with Capac Raimi arriving in an unnamed City to work for his uncle Theo, a gangster who worked for "the Cardinal", the City's crime boss. When his uncle is killed, Capac is taken under the Cardinal's wing, while making his way in the world of crime in the City – a place with constant references to Inca culture in which the young gangster comes into contact with the mysterious Ayuamarcans who, he learns, are not real but in fact elaborate illusions which closely resemble human beings and who, along with the Cardinal, are used by the Villacs, a group of blind priests, as a means of controlling the City.

After the metaphysical quest undertaken by Capac in *Ayuamarca*, the second novel in the trilogy, *Hell's Horizon* (2000), while sharing the fantastic features of its predecessor, can be more clearly linked to the field of hard-boiled detective fiction. Running in a concurrent time period to that used in *Ayuamarca*, this second work finds Al Jeery, a black Guard at the Cardinal's Party Central, who is sent to investigate the murder of a woman who, it turns out, is his own girlfriend. This is the first of a series of murders which lead to Jeery confronting Paucar Wami, a mythical and seemingly invulnerable assassin with whom the detective discovers he has an unsuspected relationship.

After his debut work, *Cowboys and Indians* (1991), an acidic look at a young post-punk Irish immigrant in London, *Joseph O'Connor's* second novel *Desperadoes* (1994) contained elements of the thriller. An estranged Irish couple travel to Nicaragua to recover the body of their son, after hearing that he has been killed there. Like Eddie Virago in the first novel, Johnny Little is another refugee from the grey Ireland of the 1980s and early 1990s. The background of the war against the Contras and the world of drug smuggling gives atmosphere to a novel which is essentially concerned with interpersonal relationships, but whose surprise twist relates it in many ways to the genre of mystery. *The Salesman* (1998) provides an interesting take on the vigilante novel. Billy Sweeney, a middle-aged Dublin salesman, tries to take revenge on Donal Quinn, the man who has left his daughter Maeve in a coma following a robbery attempt at the shop where she worked. Sweeney kidnaps Quinn, but the robber escapes and reverses the process by imprisoning the disconsolate father. *Inishowen* (2000) is of particular interest in this study for the figure of Inspector Martin Aitken, a fine portrayal of a troubled police detective, who travels to the Inishowen peninsula in Donegal accompanying an American woman, Ellen Donnelly, in search of her birth mother, an elderly nun. Aitken has been demoted from Special Branch and is facing disciplinary action, which could lead to his expulsion from the guards. He is followed north by a gangster and, in Donegal, is taken prisoner and tortured by his former colleagues who are in collusion with the gangsters. At the novel's conclusion, Aitken hands evidence of police corruption over to a national newspaper for publication, reflecting the trend for whistle-blowing journalism that was so prominent in the second decade of the 1990s.

Brian Gallagher's first novel, *The Invincibles* (1993), is a historical crime novel set in the Dublin of the 1880s, and using as its main subject matter the real-life murders of Burke and Cavendish in Phoenix Park, a "dreadful and futile act" which would have important repercussions in Irish history.[1] In the early years of the new millennium Gallagher would publish a series of contemporary thrillers.

*Neville Thompson's* three novels are set in Dublin's Northside and make regular use of Dublin slang and dialect. *Jackie Love Johnser, OK?* (1997) Begins with the shooting of Johnser, a would-be gangster from Ballyfermot and continues to tell his story up to then through analepsis. Born into a large family, Johnser, at the age of five, had already decided that he wanted to grow up to become a robber. In love with Jackie, her initial refusal to have sex with him leads Johnser to become involved with Tara, the daughter of one of his underworld contacts, who he marries. When Johnser is imprisoned for a murder he did not commit, agreeing to take the sentence as a scapegoat for the real killer, he discovers that both Tara and Jackie are pregnant by him. Jackie marries the reliable, law-abiding Jeffrey, but still harbours feelings for Johnser who she sees as a working-class hero figure. While in prison, Johnser kills Sammy, one of the cohorts of IRA leader Frankie Fitz. On his release after eight years, Johnser finds out that Jeffrey has gambling debts and has been physically abusing Jackie. At this time,

---

1    Brian Gallagher, *The Invincibles* (Dublin: Town House, 1994), 236.

he is making a living from selling drugs at Dublin nightclubs, but Fitz and the IRA track him down and shoot him.

*Jackie Love Johnser, OK?* is a notable example of crime fiction from the early years of the Celtic Tiger period, revealing the world of Northside Dublin gangs and the manoeuvres of the paramilitaries as they attempt to infiltrate the booming drugs market in the city. *Two Birds/ One Stoned* (1999) starts where the previous novel both began and ended, with the killing of Johnser, and examines the lives of the two main female characters of the earlier novel after his death. Tara – who is a hairdresser addicted to heroin and married to the thief Stan, the man Johnser had saved from prison – and Jackie, who, after the violent treatment she has suffered at the hands of Jeffrey, has become an alcoholic, are reconciled at the end of the novel. *Have Ye No Homes to Go To?* (1999) is stylistically a more complex work which, through an ensemble narration shows the lives of eight characters, most of whom, like Simmo, the money-lender and debt collector, live on the margins of the law. The novel has memorable violent scenes such as the killing of Rasher with a crowbar and moments of pathos like the murder of Dolan by mistake in revenge for the suicide of Debbie.

*The Happy Pigs* (1999) is a police narrative told in the first person, set in London and written by *Lucy Harkness*, herself a former police officer. Louisa Barratt, London-born daughter of Irish parents, is working in the Child Protection Unit, a position she has been given because she is a woman in a police force in which sexism is rife, where she provides advice and counselling for rape victims. When Louisa herself is attacked in the street she fights back, leaving her assailant in an alley. When her new boss Fraser MacDonald fails to turn up at the police station the next day she realises exactly who her attacker was and what she has done.

*Rory McCormac* is the pen-name used by Maurice O'Scanaill, a veterinarian whose first three novels feature Dr Frank Sansom, a vet who runs his own locum business. In *Playing Dead* (1993), also published as *Snapshot*, Sansom finds himself the target for a criminal gang from the fictitious Hamrani Islands in the Indian Ocean after inadvertently photographing a dying stud-horse he has been forced to put down. Helped by investigative reporter Claire O'Sullivan, Frank tries to piece together the reasons for his unwitting involvement in the world of international horse racing, breeding and gambling syndicates. In *Outbreak* (1998) Sansom is surprised by certain inconsistencies while treating an outbreak of anthrax among horses in Ireland and, convinced that the cases are not coincidental, uncovers a blackmail plot designed to eventually prevent a particular horse from winning the Aga Khan Trophy in Dublin. The final Sansom thriller is *Malpractice* (2000), by which time the locum vet had "acquired a bit of a reputation as a sort of troubleshooter or crime buster".[2] As a result of this, he is contracted by Slattery and Partners, a veterinary practice which has been losing clients because of the mysterious death or injuries of animals under their care. While investigating the case, Frank also attempts to solve the mystery behind the death of his cousin Davy, a drug addict, in strange circumstances and starts to suspect a rogue drug company of being responsible for both Davy's death and the blackmailing of Slattery.

After his retirement, McCormac moved to Malta where he had lived for a time in the 1980s. There he published *A Moving Death* (2014), which introduces Inspector Leonard Cassar of the Maltese police. In this, his first outing, Cassar investigates the murder of a rich businesswoman from a leading island family. Although she has numerous enemies, the reason for her death remains unclear until Cassar and his team, who are forced to share their investigative efforts with a dog-poisoning epidemic which is shaking the island, scan for suspects amongst the business associates, lovers and family of the woman, all within the claustrophobic confines of Malta where, McCormac claims, everyone knows everybody else.

*Paul Carson* is the author of six medical thrillers which began with *Scalpel* (1997), in which the kidnapping of a businessman's newly born baby and the murder of colleagues by a doctor who has been diagnosed with Aids converge in the same Dublin hospital. The investigation is led by a female Guard, DS Kate Hamilton, who is forced to put up with the ill-will of certain male colleagues and the paternalist behaviour of associates like the pathologist Dunne who had been had "been brought up to treat women as ladies" and who is unsettled to have a female officer in charge of a murder investigation.[3] Kate had been a star recruit at the Garda Siochana training

---

2    Rory McCormac, *Malpractice* (London: Arrow, 2000), 70.
3    Paul Carson, *Scalpel* (London: Arrow, 1997), 73.

college at Templemore, but was now one of only three female detectives serving on the force. A single mother, both her father and her brother were also guards and she is described as being "your new generation woman, an independent spirit with her own opinions and certainly not intimidated at being one of the few women detectives on the force".[4] The novel is well plotted but is perhaps demeaned by an unsatisfactory ending in which Hamilton finds romance and decides to leave the Guards.

*Cold Steel* (1998) is also centred on a Dublin hospital where a series of patients have died from a rare blood condition. When a visiting American haematologist investigates, his daughter is murdered in a city park. The novel introduces some notable characters, such as the corrupt, populist politician John Regan, soon discovered to be in the pay of multinational pharmaceutical companies, the crime reporter and the Guard detective Jim Clarke who, by the end of the novel, has been forced to take a job as a security officer for a pharmaceutical corporation. International pharmaceutical concerns also feature strongly in *Final Duty* (2000), set in the USA, where Jack Hunt, an Irish doctor, takes on Zemdon Pharmaceuticals who have been carrying out secret medical experiments on children in American orphanages.

*Tom Phelan's In the Season of the Daisies* (1993) tells, within two time frames, the story of the murder of a young boy and the effects this has on his twin brother and on his community. The killing of Willie Doolin during an IRA operation in 1921 had involved some of the respectable citizens of the village, while others had aided in covering the events up. Seanie Doolin, driven mad after witnessing his twin's murder, recalls the events in 1948 on the eve of a visit to the village by De Valera. In *Iscariot* (1998), Frank Molloy, a former priest, returns to his village after the scandal which had seen him leave the priesthood. Disowned by his brother, Molloy meets up with his childhood friend Eddie Keegan, now the haughty parish priest who, Molloy discovers, is guarding a guilty secret. When he tries to find details about the death of Kim, a young girl for whose murder Keegan secretly blames himself, Molloy finds evidence of a far more complicated series of events involving double incest and gross police incompetence.

4    Ibid., 78.

*Betrayal* (1997) is a political thriller written by the Fine Gael Senator *Maurice Manning*, which features a fictional Taoiseach, Jack Mulcahy, at a point of crisis in his career. Faced with an attempted coup within his party, Mulcahy is also being blackmailed over a secret business deal involving the theft of Nazi paintings and a mysterious businessman of Austrian origins. *Betrayal* gives an insider's view of life in the Irish parliament in the 1990s, much in the way John Kelly had done back in the early 1960s.

*The Little Hammer* (2000) by *John Kelly* (born in 1965 and not to be confused with the politician and author of *The Naming of the Dead*) is a dark comedy featuring an artist who recalls a murder he had committed when, aged only nine, he had killed a paleontologist on a Donegal beach, using the man's own hammer. He is protected by his religious grandmother with whom he lives after the death of his mother – possibly murdered by his father. As an adult he travels to Prague with his female friend Billy Maguire who steals the statue of the Holy Infant of Prague, which he subsequently uses to help heal his grandmother's back. Lost between realism and the delusions of the protagonist, the narrative ends as it starts, with another death on the beach, apparently bearing out the narrator's observation that "murder ran in the family like big ears and crooked toes".[5]

*Michael Collins's* first novel, *The Life and Times of a Tea Boy* (1994), contains no crime as such, but details the descent into insanity of Ambrose Feeney a would-be architect whose job as a porter at a local hotel is exchanged for that of lighthouse keeper for the Ministry of Fisheries and eventually electric shock treatment in an asylum which the reader is invited to compare to the claustrophobia of provincial Ireland in the 1970s and 1980s. Although Feeney at times resembles one of Patrick McCabe's anti-heroes, his obsession with his mother and his doubt as to whether events can drive a person insane "or must there always be the propensity for madness?" reveal a disturbing character who seems to successfully reflect the national mood at that point in time.[6]

*Emerald Underground* (1998), the first of Collins's novels set in the USA, tells the story of Liam, an illegal Irish immigrant escaping conviction

5    John Kelly, *The Little Hammer* (London: Jonathan Cape, 2000), 147.
6    Michael Collins, *The Life and Times of a Tea Boy* (London: Phoenix, 1994), 76.

in his native Ireland, who joins up with a pregnant 16-year-old prostitute and seeks redemption through an athletics competition which will allow him to win a scholarship to an American college. A bleak, minimalist tale of the Irish in the America of the 1980s, *Emerald Underground*, like its predecessor, did little to allow the reader to expect the fine literary thrillers Collins would produce between 2000 and 2010. *The Keepers of Truth* (2000), nominated for the Booker Prize, is a first-person account set in "the killing fields of post-industrialism" and told by a disenchanted newspaper reporter.[7] Just as Ambrose in *The Life and Times of a Tea Boy* had wanted to be the new Beckett, the reporter Bill dreamt of writing serious articles on the economic and moral decay of the anonymous rust belt in which he lives, only to be limited to reporting on trivial local information for the ironically named *Truth* newspaper, until the murder of Old Man Lawton, one of the most unpopular characters in the town. The main suspect is Lawton's son Ronny, but Bill's investigation reveals secrets shielded by the claustrophobic, decadent community.

Dubliner *Philip Davison* produced, in the figure of Harry Fielding, one of the most charismatic and deviant heroes to ever appear in Irish spy and crime fiction. He first appears in *The Crooked Man* (1997), an "understrapper", a low-grade secret service agent or, as he later describes it, "a bob-a-job man for MI5".[8] In this first novel in the series, Fielding accidentally witnesses two different cases of gender violence. In the first, his Irish neighbour in London, Maureen, kills her abusive brother-in-law and is imprisoned, and in the second he watches while a senior cabinet minister commits murder. The understrapper is assigned to cover up the crime to avoid the politician having to take responsibility for his actions. With characteristics of both the private detective narrative and the spy thriller, *The Crooked Man* is most remarkable for the figure of Fielding and his wry first-person narrative. Although not exactly an international thriller, Fielding visits Dublin, where everybody seems to have a job on the side, "even the unemployed", and is sent to Bosnia at the end of the novel.[9] In

7   Michael Collins, *The Keepers of the Truth* (London: Phoenix, 2000), 205.
8   Philip Davison, *McKenzie's Friend* (London: Jonathan Cape, 2000), 37.
9   Philip Davison, *The Crooked Man* (London: Jonathan Cape, 1997), 126.

*McKenzie's Friend* (2000) Fielding, who wants to give up his post in the secret service, is approached by Alfie, an old friend and disgraced police officer. Alfie wants Fielding to help in a private investigation he has undertaken, to find a missing girl who had run away from an abusive husband. Fielding's idiosyncratic narrative takes us through him initiating an affair with Alfie's wife, killing the abusive spouse and, eventually, becoming involved in the murder of Alfie himself. The Harry Fielding novels toy cleverly with the norms and clichés of the thriller, giving a peculiarly individual character to the works. Although Harry is Irish "every other day", his distinctively quirky character and memorable narrative voice gives him a place within the Irish crime tradition, and places Davison alongside writers such as Flann O'Brien, Patrick McGinley and J. M. O'Neill, all of whom subvert the rules they apparently follow.

*Gemma O'Connor*, an English resident born in Dublin and brought up in Limerick and Cork, published six mystery novels during the 1990s and early 2000s. *Sins of Omission* (1995), set in Dublin and London, tells a complex tale of family secrets and loyalties. Grace Hartfield, an Irish book collector living in Oxford, discovers that the sister, Elaine, who she thought had died, had in fact lived until relatively recently, and that she had given birth to a daughter, Bid, who unwittingly became pregnant by her own father. The incest and suicides of both Bid and her father are placed within the context of Irish emigration to England and the family pressures on unmarried mothers for whom "Ireland was still Ireland".[10] *Falls the Shadow* (1996) is set with the backdrop of the Luftwaffe bombing of Dublin during the "Emergency", the Second World War. The mother of the narrator is killed in an apparent hit-and-run accident after witnessing the killing of a bullying landlord during the aftermath of the bombing. This historical murder mystery, in which the discovery of a secret eventually exonerates the main suspect, is particularly rich in its description of the Dublin of the 1940s and 1950s. *Farewell to the Flesh* (1998) is set in contemporary Dublin and Oxford. A re-zoning plan leads to the selling of a plot of land which had been the graveyard of a progressive Dublin convent. On exhuming the graves an extra, unmarked coffin is discovered and Tess Callaway, an

---

10    Gemma O'Connor, *Sins of Omission* (Dublin: Poolbeg, 1995), 431.

Oxford-based lawyer, finds that her life and that of her baby daughter are in danger as she tries to discover the identity of and secret behind the girl whose body is found in the coffin.

With *Time to Remember* (1998) O'Connor returns to the world of the historical thriller, set in the Alsace of 1945 and present-day Oxford. During the final days of the war a fifteen-year old boy witnesses the death of his childhood sweetheart by a German soldier, himself little more than a child. Some fifty years later the boy and the soldier come face to face in Oxford before apparently disappearing. The disillusioned young police officer Juliet Turbo, an orphan because of the Troubles in Northern Ireland, investigates the disappearance, which seems to lead to the involvement of the British intelligence services.

# CHAPTER 19

# "People loved reading about crime in Ireland." The Police and Private Detective Novel in the 1990s

John Connolly has stated that the police procedural novel was estab-lished only with some difficulty in Ireland because "the Irish police had yet to establish themselves in the mind of the populace".[1] Police detect-ives had, of course, been a staple of crime fiction for many years, the Irish contribution to this tendency being notable, with the figure of Freeman Wills Crofts widely considered to be an important predecessor of the hard-working and painstakingly efficient police officers found in the police procedural novel. While Ernest Mandel sees the first appearance of this new format in the late 1930s and early 1940s,[2] Heather Worthington places the publication of the earliest modern police procedural novels as taking place in the late 1940s or early 1950s.[3] While John Scaggs refers to Hillary Waugh's *Last Seen Wearing...* (1952) as the first police procedural novel,[4] both LeRoy Lad Panek and Lee Horsley cite the appearance of the first Ed McBain 87th Precinct novels of the mid-1950s as the starting point for the sub-genre. The former claims that before 1950 the police in crime fiction had generally "played a decidedly subordinate role", acting "as foils or representatives of the state clearing the boards at the end",[5]

---

1    John Connolly, "No Blacks, No Dogs, No Crime Writers: Ireland and the Mystery" in *Down These Green Streets: Irish Crime Writing in the 21st Century*, ed. Declan Burke (Dublin: Liberties Press, 2011), 48.

2    Ernest Mandel, *Delightful Murder: A Social History of the Crime Story* (Minneapolis, MN: Minnesota University Press, 1984), 53.

3    Heather Worthington, *Key Concepts in Crime Fiction* (London: Palgrave Macmillan, 2011), 68.

4    John Scaggs, *Crime Fiction* (London: Routledge, 2005), 87.

5    LeRoy Lad Panek, "Post-War American Police Fiction" in *The Cambridge Companion to Crime Fiction*, ed. Martin Priestman (Cambridge: Cambridge University Press, 2003), 155.

while Horsley credits McBain as being the first writer to consistently use an official team of investigators with an "emphasis on the collective rather than the individual effort".[6]

The police procedural, or simply "police novel" as some critics such as Peter Messent prefer, is, at its most basic level, a crime novel in which the police perform the primary detective function, but which also implies the suggestion of "an orderly sequence and certain narrative structure".[7] The police procedural novel, according to Julian Symons, should not be confused with earlier works which featured police detectives, because, while these "sometimes traced the course of a police investigation", they did so "rather superficially, and often from the lofty point of view of a Superintendent".[8] In the police procedural, "the eccentric solitary detective became part of a team, a professional organization to which each individual brings unique specialization and expertise".[9] The stress on the team is a fundamental one, as the modern police procedural theoretically represents a movement away from the individualism of the lone detective and towards the collective agency of a group of mutually dependent individuals. In practice, however, it can be seen that many writers of police procedurals, especially of those novels which form part of a series, actually rely on the individualism of one or more of their characters to provide a point of empathy for the readers. Early Irish police detectives, for example, from J. B. O'Neill's Tubridy to Bartholomew Gill's McGarr, dominate the proceedings in the novels in which they feature, and even in later police procedural series, such as those written by Brian McGilloway, Casey Hill or Alex Barclay – to provide examples focusing on police forces from the

6    Lee Horsley, *Twentieth-Century Crime Fiction* (Oxford: Oxford University Press, 2005), 100.
7    Peter Messent, "The Police Novel" in *A Companion to Crime Fiction*, ed. Charles J. Rzepka and Lee Horsley (Oxford: Wiley-Blackwell, 2010), 175.
8    Julian Symons, *Bloody Murder: From the Detective Story to the Crime Novel*, 2nd edn (Harmondsworth: Penguin, 1985), 193.
9    Jean Gregorek, "Fables of Foreclosure: Tana French's Police Procedurals of Recessionary Ireland" in *Class and Culture in Crime Fiction*, ed. Julie H. Kim (Jefferson, NC: McFarland & Company, 2014), 149.

Republic, from Northern Ireland and overseas respectively – often depend heavily on the specific characteristics of a particular officer.

In this respect, the hero of the police procedural often "has all the essentials of the hard-boiled detective" while still forming part of a team which is carrying out a job of work, albeit under unusually stressful conditions.[10] The detective in the police procedural, again like the hard-boiled private eye, is often situated on the margin of the society he or she defends.[11] Despite the routine nature of most police work, the hero of the police procedural is often a maverick who, despite being deeply committed to their mission, is often at odds with colleagues, superior officers or both. Despite the existence of extensive, specialised teams, police procedurals frequently focus on individuals, or pairs of officers, rather than on a truly collective grouping, and these novels are generally grouped in a series with "a number of novels connected in a chronological sequence by a recurring hero whose life story is as foregrounded as the stories of her or his investigations".[12] Indeed, the private life of this hero is often intrinsically linked to the case being investigated, with the overlapping of the personal and the professional being one of the defining features of many of these works.

Early Irish police procedurals, like most of their British and American counterparts, would focus almost entirely on individual male detectives, such as John Brady's Matt Minogue, Jim Lusby's Carl McCadden or, from Northern Ireland, Eugene McEldowney's Cecil Megarry. Although women police officers would appear, these would generally be in subservient roles, a situation which would last until the early years of the twenty-first century, when prominent female detectives would start to gain increasing importance. *John Brady* moved from his native Dublin to Canada after completing his studies at Trinity College in the mid-1970s. In *A Stone of the Heart* (1988) he introduced Sergeant Matt Minogue, who would feature in several novels between 1988 and 2010 becoming, if we exclude

10  LeRoy Lad Panek, *An Introduction to the Detective Story* (Bowling Green, OH: Bowling Green State University Popular Press, 1987), 175.

11  Scaggs, *Crime Fiction*, 90.

12  Karin Molander Danielsson, *The Dynamic Detective: Special Interest and Seriality in Contemporary Detective Series* (Uppsala: Diss. Acta Universitatis Upsaliensis, 2002), 11–12.

Bartholomew Gill's McGarr, the first modern Irish serial police detective. *A Stone of the Heart* is an accomplished debut and would introduce many of the themes and tropes found in later Celtic Tiger-era fiction and, in the figure of Minogue, a model for later police detectives. Although living and working in Dublin, Minogue is a native of Co. Clare and, despite his Dublin-born children berating "the vagaries of a bogman father", his country breeding provides him with a seemingly infinite supply of common sense and intuition which helps him in his mission.[13] In this first novel, the murder of a student at Dublin's Trinity College uncovers an apparent IRA plot which leads Minogue to the border with Northern Ireland and an armed encounter. Minogue returns in *Unholy Ground* (1989), in which a seemingly simple murder case is complicated by the involvement of the British secret service and Irish terrorists. The initial suspect, a traveller, is proved innocent by Minogue who, unlike a colleague who believes that tinkers "were shifty, dishonest, cunning",[14] realised that their pose of servility was simply "a foil to conceal the contempt it was bred from"[15] and that these itinerants "moved warily around such prickly institutions of the settled Irish as policemen and publicans".[16]

In *Kaddish in Dublin* (1990), the situation of chaos in Ireland which is reaching a state of "unnerving maturity"[17] is used by the Opus Dei to prepare to launch a coup, aimed at situating Gorman, a politician sympathetic to the Opus Dei cause, in power. Minogue is called upon to investigate two murders associated with the institution. Aside from this initial premise, however, the novel is notable for its portrayal of the Irish police, presenting a critical if balanced,, view of the Garda Síochána in one of the first police procedural works to show the Gardaí as a modern police force. Minogue's daughter Iesult calls the police "brutal, patriarchal rednecks", but we see police officers (and journalists) grappling to come to terms with newly introduced computers.[18] Brady uses the figure of Minogue to illustrate

13    John Brady, *Unholy Ground* (London: Arrow, 1989), 106.
14    Ibid., 122.
15    Ibid., 135.
16    Ibid., 137.
17    John Brady, *Kaddish in Dublin* (London: Arrow, 1990), 14.
18    Ibid., 8.

the progressive, liberal side of the force, comparing him to his superior and foil, Inspector Kilmartin. Like Minogue, Kilmartin is originally from the rural west of Ireland but, unlike Matt, he has failed to adapt to city life and retains several old-school police prejudices, such as misogyny and racism. Throughout the series, the contrast between the two officers provides a running dialectic addressing diverse aspects of Irish life and how these are perceived by the different policemen. *Kaddish in Dublin* openly criticises the political influence and control exerted over the Irish police and how, as a result, the Garda rank and file has been subject to the "dictatorial regime" which ruthlessly controlled "transfers and promotions, leaves and gratuities, discipline and training".[19] Such mismanagement, Brady suggests, contributed to the incongruous distribution of Gardaí, with officers from a closed, rural background being thrust into the cosmopolitan milieu of Dublin:

> Young Guards, countrymen, fresh from training, had been thrown into areas like Ringsend and had been backed up and directed by Gardai also overwhelmingly from the country. Over the years, those old hands had distilled their native dislike for Dubliners into a cynical and heavy-handed contempt.[20]

*All Souls* (1993) takes Brady back to his native Clare, where the re-opening of an old case of arson and murder reveals IRA involvement and police corruption, while also encroaching on the sergeant's personal life. In *The Good Life* (1994) Minogue investigates a murder in the Dublin of the period immediately before the advent of the Celtic Tiger, a city "pitted with office buildings so ugly that they absorbed light and space from the streets they had been driven into", streets awash with drugs, pornography and prostitution.[21] In *A Carra King* (2000) the murder of the son of an Irish-American millionaire uncovers the trafficking of historical Irish artefacts and reveals the collusion between the Irish police and the American authorities. Brady's novels in the early years of the new millennium would focus largely on criminal activity related to the economic boom, exploring themes of racism and attitudes towards immigrants in the Ireland of the

19    Ibid., 200.
20    Ibid., 36.
21    John Brady, *The Good Life* (New York: St. Martin's Press, 1994), 36.

Celtic Tiger and post-Tiger years. These books would also give more prominence to Minogue's young colleague, Tommy Malone, whose partner, reflecting a growing cosmopolitanism, is a native of Macau. Amongst these later works, Brady also makes a brief foray into European policing, with the introduction of *Inspektor* Felix Kimmel of the Austrian police in 2006. Kimmel, however, would only survive one novel.

Waterford-born *Jim Lusby*, whose first novel, *Snuff* (1992), was co-written with Myles Dungan, has since written five novels in the DI Carl McCadden series, as well as one stand-alone mystery and two thrillers written under the pseudonym of James Kennedy. *Snuff* is an entertaining debut, set in the world of Irish television and introducing Lynn, a female Guard on secondment to RTÉ, who is forced to investigate a series of murders of the television broadcaster's personnel, including a soap opera actress and a presenter. Lynn, in a failed marriage, sees how her personal life is affected by the case, which culminates in the kidnapping of her daughter and the discovery of the involvement of her estranged husband. *Making the Cut* (1995), the first DI Carl McCadden book, introduces this atypical Guard, criticised by his superiors for wearing t-shirt and jeans and for his unkempt, unshaven appearance, who lives alone in Waterford following his separation from his wife. The plot is curious, involving a greyhound keeper, an Iranian trade official and the illegal sale of an inheritance with the involvement of an art expert, a local businessman and a corrupt politician. The novel was developed into a television series by RTE under its original name, which was changed into *DDU: District Detective Unit* for its second season.

*Flashback* (1996) finds McCadden on "a black downer", pitted once again against his superiors, in a case which focusses on the world of entertainment, amateur dramatics, home movies, pub comedians and voyeurism, playing with the idea of seeing and being seen.[22] *Kneeling at the Altar* (1998), arguably the most satisfying of the McCadden mysteries, involves a suspected paedophile and the action of a group of vigilantes. DI McCadden saves the harmless eccentric John Ryle from a beating at the hands of a gang of vigilantes led by Joey Whittle, who believes Ryle has been

---

22    Jim Lusby, *Flashback* (London: Victor Gollancz, 1996), 8.

responsible for taking pornographic photos of his son, before discovering a scenario which had been sparked off by three Christian Brothers some years before. The title refers, apparently, to a colloquial definition of fellatio, and the novel broaches on the alleged abuses by Christian Brothers, which were topical in Ireland at the time. The figure of McCadden is developed more fully in this instalment of the series, as he is revealed to be observant, deductive and of quiet intelligence. We also learn that he has joined the Garda because his father had been a paratrooper in the British army and his brother a Guard. In contrast with his equanimity and open-mindedness, his superior Chief Superintendent Cody is seen as an antiquated figure who "admired the power of politicians" and "simultaneously respected and undervalued women".[23]

In *Crazy Man Michael* (2000), McCadden is the principal candidate to lead the new Murder Squad to be set up in Dublin. The Minister for Justice, however, is a "bantam man" who "was much in the news at the time", with a name which "kept cropping up at one or other of the judicial tribunals investigating corruption and graft and bribery and tax evasion among politicians", in spite of which, however, the "dirt would not stick".[24] This is the Ireland of the Celtic Tiger, with eco-warriors fighting a huge pharmaceutical company and drug dealers carving out their territory around Dublin's high-rise flats. McCadden is faced with a renegade ex-guard who turned to crime, disillusioned and with a sense of betrayal after eighteen years working for the state.

The two novels published under the *James Kennedy* nom-de-plume are readable, if somewhat pedestrian, international thrillers. In *Armed and Dangerous* (1996), a prison breakout leads to an escaped IRA man targeting the Queen of England and the British Royal Family in a complex plan which involves the flooding of London after destroying the Thames barrier. *Silent City* (1998) tells the story of a right-wing Catholic group which, through an English fascist plans to kill the first black American President on his visit to Ireland. Apart from the obvious pre-Obama interest, *Silent*

---

23    Jim Lusby, *Kneeling at the Altar* (London: Victor Gollancz, 1998), 156.
24    Jim Lusby, *Crazy Man Michael* (London: Victor Gollancz, 2000), 21.

*City* is an improvement on the earlier thriller, but lacks the originality and freshness of the McCadden novels.

*Sheila Barrett* only published one novel, but *A View to Die For* (1997) is an interesting murder mystery set in and around Dalkey, which features a female police officer. From a family of guards, Briege O'Neill helps her brother, himself a Guard, to bring up his daughter Talulla after her mother leaves them to return to America. Talulla joins the guards but is wounded in a bank raid, and the novel opens with her recovering from her injuries in the company of her aunt after her father's death. The novel is of particular interest for its vivid depiction of the early years of economic prosperity, as "the skies over Ireland tingled with numbers and conversations that bounced all the way to China, and the reedy growls of printers drowned the whispers of hands and pens".[25] This prosperity, however, is threatened by the "new era of young men with shotguns and sudden, intolerable needs", one of whom had shot Tallulah.[26] *A View to Die For* also introduces what is believed to be "Ireland's first serial killer" in a work which also provides an early example of ecological protest against construction in a protected woodland area, a protest which is supported by the guards.[27]

*Hugo Hamilton*, best known, perhaps, for his memoir *The Speckled People* (2003), produced two highly entertaining crime novels in the late 1990s. Neither *Headbanger* (1997) nor *Sad Bastard* (1998) can be considered to be a police procedurals, but both feature the rank and file Garda Pat Coyne, whose unorthodox attitudes toward policing provide an interesting look at Ireland in the early years of the Celtic Tiger economy. In *Headbanger*, Coyne is seen as a "crusader" who was "answering an inner mission to reform the society and clean up the city".[28] More like Leopold Bloom than Raymond Chandler, Coyne suffers his wife's infidelity while he single-handedly tries to clean up a country in which crime "was the nation's biggest growth industry".[29] He takes on the notorious Cunningham brothers, Dublin gangsters with celebrity status, but ends up losing both

25    Sheila Barrett, *A View to Die For* (Dublin: Poolbeg, 1997), 27.
26    Ibid.
27    Ibid., 185.
28    Hugo Hamilton, *Headbanger* (London: Vintage, 1997), 8.
29    Ibid., 34.

his wife and his job. In *Sad Bastard*, Coyne is separated from his wife, unemployed, and living with his son Jimmy, who, after a drunken misunderstanding, attracts the attention of both police and gangsters. *Sad Bastard* is interesting in that it represents one of the first works of the genre to pay attention to the question of illegal immigration which was starting to appear with some regularity in the national press. Coyne becomes inadvertently involved in a case in which immigrants are being brought into the country by fishing boats. The novel anticipates the generally liberal stance that will be apparent in crime novels published throughout the next decade, in that the immigrants are perceived to be innocent victims of adverse circumstances, along with the avarice and inhumanity of Irish criminals. In common with later works, the protagonist actively sympathises with the immigrants, as Coyne helps a young Romanian woman accused of shoplifting. Hamilton's East European characters are favourably compared with their Irish "hosts", and the novel makes repeated references to the similarities between the immigrants and the Irish. Thus the Russians who sing "Danny Boy" in the Anchor Bar are "as bad as the Irish" because they "can't go anywhere without starting a party", as they get drunk on plum brandy "enjoying themselves singing sad songs".[30] Inevitably, these similarities are used to compare the situation of these New Irish and the Irish emigrants forced to leave their homes in past times. As Coyne ponders, the new immigrants were "the Blasket Islanders coming home".[31]

Despite starting his writing career in the mid-1990s, it was not until the electronic book boom of the second decade of the twenty-first century that T. S. O'Rourke's books would reach a wider public. *Ganglands* (1996) is an early example of a Dublin gangster novel, in which Mike and Frank Costello, the latter recently released from Mountjoy Prison, are drawn into a world of drug dealing, theft and arms trafficking. Their entry into the world of crime, the author suggests, is an indirect result of the economic crisis of the 1980s in which their father, a builder from Bray, had lost his business and been forced to move to a council house on a rough estate where his sons had become mixed up with the wrong crowd. Working for

---

30   Hugo Hamilton, *Sad Bastard* (London: Vintage, 1998), 15.
31   Ibid., 59.

Sharky, a gang boss whose empire is beginning to be threatened by maverick paramilitaries offers the brothers control of the city's south side where they are followed by the guards Detective Phillips of the Serious Crime Squad and Detective Carroll of the Drug Squad. A Detective Carroll, whether the same as in the earlier novel or not is never specified, also appears in *Death Call* (1997), a police detective novel set in North London, where, with the help of his Jamaican colleague, Constable Samuel Grant, he sets out to hunt down a serial killer who is murdering prostitutes. Perhaps the most notable feature of this second novel is the portrayal of the initially tense working and personal relationship between the second-generation Irishman Carroll and the West Indian Grant, and the depiction of minor Irish characters such as the Tipperary-born Sergeant O'Meara. Carroll and Grant reappear in *Damned Nation* (1998) where they investigate two cases which, although apparently unconnected, turn out to be linked, the theft of dogs and the kidnapping of a child presumably by Satanists. The character of Carroll, hated by most of his colleagues, is dealt with in more detail in *Damned Nation*, in which the detective reminisces on his father and his Irish upbringing in Wembley.

    *John Galvin* wrote his two novels *Bog Warriors* (2000) and *The Mercury Man* (2002) when he was an actively serving officer in the Gardaí in Dingle, County Kerry. In *Bog Warriors*, set in the fictional western Irish village of Dunsheerin, a thinly disguised version of Dingle, Guard Jack Heggarty has returned to his native county after years of serving in Galway and Dublin. He is pleased to be back in a rural setting, and with a wife and two daughters he believed that there he would receive "a respect for the gardaí that is lacking in the cities".[32] The village is not, however, free from crime, and local gangster Michael Carroll calls the guards "bog warriors" who "couldn't detect their bollocks if they were stuck to the end of their noses", and it is to him an incensed villager turns when seeking revenge on John Burns, a local bully who has sexually abused several women and was now regularly beating his wife.[33] *Bog Warriors* is of particular interest because of its involvement with gender violence, and also because of its inside portrayal of

32    John Galvin, *Bog Warriors* (Dublin: Town House, 2000), 13.
33    Ibid., 155.

a village Guard. Hegarty's sexism – a rape victim was so "gamey" that "the only thing she didn't ride back in her early twenties was a Grand National winner" reeks depressingly of authenticity, as does the guard's struggle to come to terms with his desktop computer.[34]

*Ken Bruen* would obtain a reputation as one of the most interesting writers of Irish crime fiction in the early years of the twenty-first century with his Jack Taylor series, set in Bruen's native city of Galway. Before this, however, he had published a number of works which to a certain extent would anticipate, both stylistically and thematically, the novels which would feature the unorthodox former Guard turned private detective. Bruen's earliest works, short stories and novellas, were reprinted in the collection *A Fifth of Bruen* (2006). The collection reveals many of the stylistic and the-matic features of the writer's later work. *Tales of Morbidity* (1991) contains Bruen's first use of listing, a technique which would be present in all his major works. *Shades of Grace* (1993) uses the murder/revenge motif, while *Martyrs* (1994) contains a matricide and confession to a priest, and priests have a significant role in *Sherri and Other Stories* (1994). Vigilantes and violent revenge are central to *All the Old Songs and Nothing to Lose* (1994) while *The Time of Serena-May & Upon the Third Cross and Other Stories* (1994) features a child with Down Syndrome. All contain numerous quotes from and references to music, literature and film, in the immense homage to popular culture which would be a characteristic of all Bruen's work.

*Rilke on Black* (1996) is Bruen's first full-length novel, a stand-alone thriller telling of Ronald Baldwin, a black London businessman, a lover of the German poet Rilke, who is kidnapped by Nick, a former bouncer of Irish descent, Dex, his violent friend and Lisa, a drug addict. The novel introduces Detective Sergeant Brant of the Metropolitan Police, a character who would later be developed in the Roberts and Brant series which would start two years later. In *The Hackman Blues* (1997) the gay gangster Tony Brady and his former cell-mate Elias Rasheed "Reed" Mohammed ('Sydney Poitier had more street cred") run a lost property and repossession business in which they steal and then locate items.[35] They are approached by a rich

34 Ibid., 215.
35 Ken Bruen, *The Hackman Blues* (London: The Do-Not-Press, 1997), 17.

builder and "plastic paddy", Jack Dunphy, to locate his daughter Roz, who
has run off to Brixton to live with Leon, a black gangster.[36] When they find
Roz and take her from Leon, with the help of Irish *Big Issue* seller Ben, they
decide to kidnap the girl themselves and offer her to the highest bidder.

*Her Last Call to Louis MacNeice* (1998) is also set in London and features Dave Cooper, a bank robber and "criminally inclined yuppie", and
Cassie, a shoplifter, who he helps out.[37] Cooper, whose mother was from
Belfast and father from Glasgow, both "hard-line Presbyterians" who gave
their son "little as baggage save bitterness", runs a repossession business
with his Irish partner the Doc, and they are pitted against the police officers Noble and Quinn.[38] *London Boulevard* (2001) was filmed by William
Monahan starring Irish actor Colin Farrell in 2010. On his release from
prison, Mitchell is approached by his Irish friend Norton who offers him
a job as a loan enforcer working for gangster Tommy Logan, who also appears in *The McDead* (2000). Mitchell, however, wishes to put his criminal
life behind him, and gladly accepts work as a general handyman for rich,
ageing actress Lillian Palmer. Although deliberately recalling Billy Wilder's
*Sunset Boulevard*, Bruen's novel contains the mixture of humour and violence so typical of the author's work, and several memorable characters
including Jordan, Lillian's mysterious butler, Briony, Mitchell's sister and
Aisling, the Irish girl with whom he falls in love. These London novels are
entertaining, with a solid amount of black humour and a smattering of
social criticism. As stand-alone works, they hold their own, but it would
be as a series writer that Bruen would reach his full potential.

With *A White Arrest* (1998) Bruen introduced his London police officers Chief Inspector James Roberts and Detective Sergeant Tom Brant,
who had already made a brief appearance in *Rilke on Black*, in the first of the
police procedural series originally known as the *White Trilogy* but further
extended with four additional volumes. Roberts and Brant are corrupt and
unethical, and are at home in the sordid underworld of the South London
crooks they fight. In this first novel in the series, Brant, who refers to his

36    Ibid., 7.
37    Lee Horsley, *The Noir Thriller* (London: Palgrave Macmillan, 2001), 224.
38    Ken Bruen, *Her Last Call to Louis MacNeice* (London: The Do-Not-Press, 1998)

Irish background, searches for a serial killer known as The Umpire because of his obsession with cricket, who is murdering members of the England cricket team. In a parallel investigation, the two overworked officers also have to deal with a vigilante group targeting local drug dealers. In *Taming the Alien* (1999) Brant is attacked in his home by Roy Fenton, known as the "Alien", a hitman so called because he had murdered someone during the projection of the Ridley Scott film of that name. Following Fenton to Galway and then to the USA, Brant and another of the characters surviving from the previous novel, the now pregnant black WPC Falls are also trying to track down the Irish members of the Band-Aid couple Josie and Mick Belton, who Brant believes had been responsible for the murder of their colleague PC Cone. Meanwhile, Roberts is diagnosed with skin cancer, while WPC Falls loses her child. *The McDead* finds Brand and Roberts facing the false Irish gangster Tommy Logan who uses a hurling stick on his victims, while WPC Falls is used as bait in an attempt to trap the Clapham Rapist, a serial sexual predator who preys on Afro-Caribbean victims.

Bruen's mixture of humour and social critique, his encyclopaedic know-ledge of popular culture and his topical use of current political and social issues make him unique amongst Irish crime writers. His use of British, Irish and American settings is also without precedent among his peers, and while his greatest creation is, without doubt, the figure of Jack Taylor, "a tragic, lawless hero steeped in loss who damages himself almost as much as he hurts the evil characters",[39] he faces, Bruen's entire oeuvre commits to a series of issues in "writing which constantly strains at the edges of detective narration".[40] His work speaks out for minority and minoritised groups such as the homeless, travellers or tinkers, gays and lesbians, immigrants, alcoholics, and people with mental health issues. Having lost two "great wondrous friends to Aids", he swore he would "always have a gay character" in his books, and his own sad experience of the death of a daughter with

---

39   Andrew Kincaid, "Detecting Hope: Ken Bruen's Disenchnted P.I.", in *The Contemporary Irish Detective Novel*, ed. Elizabeth Mannion (London: Palgrave Macmillan, 2016), 61.

40   Paula Murphy, "'Murderous Mayhem': Ken Bruen and the New Ireland", *Clues: A Journal of Detection* 24, no. 2 (Winter 2006), 5.

Down Syndrome made this concern a recurrent topic in his novels.[41] Bruen shows the underbelly of life in post-Thatcher South London, in Bush-era and pre-Trump America and in Celtic Tiger and post-Tiger Ireland with a harsh humour which is unique and unmistakable.

Like Bruen, the similarly cosmopolitan Paul Charles would begin his career with works set in London but, also like the Galwegian, would turn to an Irish setting in the new millennium. Originally from Magherafelt, *Paul Charles* has published a number of crime novels since his debut *I Love the Sound of Breaking Glass* (1997). This introduced his Northern Irish, London-based detective Inspector Christy Kennedy, who would appear in nine novels, six of which were issued by the independent London publishers the Do-Not-Press, while of the final three two were published in Ireland by Brandon of Dingle and the ninth, in the USA by Dufour. Kennedy is a good-natured, tranquil police officer who is described in the first novel as "a gentle man with an Irish-sounding name who had an absolute passion for a good old cup of tea".[42] *I Love the Sound of Breaking Glass* also introduced Kennedy's assistant, Detective Sergeant James Irvine, a taciturn Scot, and the inspector's lover, the journalist ann rea (who spells her name in lower case letters). The novel makes use of Charles's knowledge of the music industry to examine the disappearance of a record company manager in a plot which brings Kennedy into contact with the chart-rigging and blackmail which would seem to be part of the industry. *Last Boat to Camden Town* (1998) is a prequel to *I Love the Sound of Breaking Glass* and the events it describes take place some six months before the action of the earlier work. Kennedy investigates the mysterious death of a successful young doctor who has been found in Regent's canal. Mid-way between a fully fledged police procedural and the classic whodunit, like its predecessor it relies on the equanimity and tact of its main character to give body to the novel.

*Fountain of Sorrow* (1998) and *The Ballad of Sean and Wilko* (2000) both involve crimes committed within the Irish and the musical community

---

41    Jaques Filippi, "'Zen' Bruen: The Dark Knight Resists", *The House of Crime and Mystery*, 2011, <http://houseofcrimeandmystery.blogspot.com/2012/08/intervie wdiscussion-with-ken-bruen.html>, accessed 18 April 2015.

42    Paul Charles, *I Love the Sound of Breaking Glass* (London: The Do-Not-Press, 1997), 157.

in London. The former introduces another Irish police officer, Sergeant Flynn, "whose forty-two years in London had not dulled his rich Ballymena tones",[43] while *The Hissing of the Silent Lonely Room* (2001) is also set within the world of music, as Kennedy discovers that the supposed suicide of Esther Bluewood, a renowned songwriter is, in fact, murder. While the first five novels had been set in the single space of London's Camden Town, *I've Heard the Banshee Sing* (2002) takes Christy Kennedy and his lover to Northern Ireland to investigate the murder of an old Northern Irish soldier in London. Kennedy is aware of the tensions of the post-Troubles North, where the kerbstones are still painted red, white and blue and the RUC are still policing the area, as the action takes place in 2000, before the creation of the Police Service of Northern Ireland (PSNI) in 2001. In the midst of the investigation ann rea is kidnapped, and Kennedy is introduced to Inspector Starrett of the Garda Síochána in Donegal, across the border in the Irish Republic. Starrett would later be rescued by Charles to feature in two novels set in Celtic Tiger Letterkenny.

From his London-based Kennedy novels to his later Northern Ireland fiction, Paul Charles maintains a well-developed sense of serenity throughout his works. His detectives are calm and thoughtful, the crimes they solve, although often vicious, never manage to break down the walls of taciturnity which are constructed around his characters. His novels can be categorised as "cosy", more because of the character of the detectives than for any other reason, and while it may be easy to write cosy crime fiction in the environs of Primrose Hill, it is certainly not easy to adapt the model to Northern Ireland.

The private detective has long been a popular figure in crime fiction, and the models from the brilliant if eccentric amateur like Sherlock Holmes, or the cynical private eye of hard-boiled fiction, are still common staples of the genre. As we have seen, and largely due to the social unpopularity of the figure of the informer within Irish culture, the private detective was rarely employed within Irish crime fiction. Those few private eyes generally appeared either in Irish works set in a non-Irish context – The UK, the USA – or, in the rare examples of home-grown Irish private investigators,

43  Paul Charles, *Fountain of Sorrow* (London: The Do-Not-Press, 1998), 25.

these were usually seen within a comedic framework. This situation would begin to change in the 1990s, when fictional Irish private detectives started to appear, although very often the investigator in the new crime novels which started to appear throughout the decade would be a journalist, a lawyer or someone likewise unrelated to official police detection, be this in the public or the private sphere.

*Maggie Gibson's* Grace de Rossa is, quite possibly, Ireland's first fictional female professional private investigator, and although she owes much to the comic private detectives mentioned above, the novels in which she features provide an interesting look at the Ireland of the 1990s in the time immediately before the impact of the Celtic Tiger began to be felt. De Rossa appears in three novels starting with *Grace, the Hooker, the Hard-Man and the Kid* (1995) in which Grace, a Guard who, after attempting to find a child killer amid a case of incest, is suspected by her fellow-police officers of having supplied information to gangsters. With the help of her friends Phoebe, a sex worker, and Mungo, the "hard-man" of the title, Grace, separated from her lawyer husband Andrew who has abandoned her for her best friend, leaves the police to set up her own detective agency, Sleuths Investigation and Security Specialists. *Grace, the Hooker, the Hard-Man and the Kid* contains several features which would become staples of the new Irish crime fiction of the period. Although the figure of the former police officer who becomes a private investigator is not exclusive to Irish crime writing, it would be used effectively by several authors, and seen, most notably perhaps, in the figure of Ken Bruen's Jack Taylor. The Fifteenth Amendment of the Constitution of Ireland, passed in 1995, permitted divorce in the country for the first time and its enactment would give work to both real and fictional private detectives.

In *The Longest Fraud* (1996) Grace is contracted by Tessa Peace to look into the alleged infidelity of her husband, Warren, a property developer. When Warren is found dead, and when suspected suicided becomes murder, Grace delves into the secrets of the victim's past and discovers the Long Firm Fraud, a pyramid-style project which had made him very particular enemies. Here, Warren's involvement in white-collar, financial crime can be seen as a sign of the changing times. In the second half of the decade, the illicit economic activity of politicians, bankers and captains of industry was becoming a source of growing concern, despite the apparent disregard of the political class. In 1997 Charlie McCreevy who, as a TD a decade earlier had boasted about evading betting tax, was appointed Minister of Finance, "the first time in the history of the state – this state and perhaps any other – in which a politician who encouraged the evasion of taxes" was given such a lofty position.[44] In *Deadly Serious* (1997), Grace's difficult private life is enlivened by her budding relationship with Luke, a member of the Gardaí but further complicated when, after helping Andrew's new wife to have her baby, her ex-husband attempts to renew their relationship. While trying to come to terms with her personal problems, Grace takes on a case when she is asked by ageing Ascendancy Hippy Poppy Dalglish-Stuart, mother of daughter Free and son Whispering Wind, to investigate the death of her sister Carenza, supposedly murdered by her husband, the respectable physician Dr Emmett O'Connell. Initially wary of Poppy, Grace's interest is aroused when Carenza's body is discovered. She realises, however, that although Emmet has secrets of his own, these do not include the murder of his wife, and her search for the culprit leads her back to Poppy's immediate circle.

In *The Flight of Lucy Spoon* (1999), the first of Gibson's novels not to feature Grace de Rossa, Lucy is an English woman who, trapped in a loveless marriage in Dublin, decides to leave her Irish husband. She meets Jodie McDeal, a young woman who has just had her car stolen, and offers her a lift as they set off on a perfect Thelma and Louise road movie. Jodie, however, has also separated from her partner, the powerful gangster Rogan Hogan, and she has stolen a valuable hoard of cocaine which she intends to use to make him give her the money she believes he owes her. Hogan sends his men after Jodie, and the chase is complicated when the hopelessly incompetent Corky and Bosco, who are planning to kidnap TV mogul Monty, steal Lucy's car. *The Flight of Lucy Spoon* combines features of screwball noir with others of chick-lit in a lively novel which also sees the involvement of Jake, a former lover of Lucy's who is working as a bus driver, and a gangster-eating crocodile. *Alice Little and the Big Girl's Blouse* (1999)

---

44   Gene Kerrigan and Pat Brennan, *This Great Little Nation: The A-Z of Irish Political Scandals* (Gill & Macmillan, 1999), 30.

finds Alice unemployed after being dismissed by a malicious employer. Her gay friend Conor, the "big girl's blouse" of the title, offers her work at his café, the Samovar, and further asks her to marry his boyfriend Hector, a Ukrainian immigrant under threat of deportation by a government which was "getting quite squiffy about illegals lately".[45] She agrees to do so in exchange for a part share in the business, but the Samovar has attracted the attention of local gangsters who try to exact protection rights. Conor and Alice contact a private detective to acquire listening devices with which they hope to trap the gangsters.

In *First Holy Chameleon* (2000), Cash Ryan is an unemployed actress who is working as a part-time secretary for Mort Higgins, private detective and former Guard, who is investigating the disappearance of several girls, for which he suspects a cult led by Rory Keogh, ex-member of the IRA. When Mort is discovered dead at his desk, with a gunshot wound to the temple, the police, especially Detective Sergeant Dan Doyle, consider it to be suicide, but neither Cash nor Mort's wife believe this to be the case. Helped by Cash's Jamaican-Irish friend Billie and Sister Jude, a motorcycle-loving nun and a gang Hell's Angels, Cash, recently evicted and whose boyfriend has just left her to join a Cistercian order, seeks out the truth behind Mort's death, unmasking an illegal adoption scheme from which members of the guards are also profiting. *Blah Blah Black Sheep* features Drew Looney, a journalist who, while covering a deportation uncovers a gang using immigrants as slave labour. Meanwhile, Georgina Fitz-Simons is being blackmailed by one of the gangsters, Broylan Grillo, who has threatened to reveal her cocaine habit. When Grillo dies in Georgina's bedroom Drew helps her to dispose of the body, aided by the friendly Guard Vinnie who is in love with Drew.

Journalist *Des Ekin* published two crime novels at the turn of the new millennium. The first of these, *Stone Heart* (1999), features Tara Ross, an investigative reporter who runs an on-line newspaper from her home in Clare. Tara becomes personally involved in a case when the mother of her boyfriend, Fergus, is savagely murdered and he is considered to be

---

45   Maggie Gibson, *Alice Little and the Big Girl's Blouse* (London: Victor Gollancz, 1999), 51.

the prime suspect. Tara believes in his innocence and, in her search for the truth travels to Dublin and Paris, from drug users' flats to bohemian garrets. The novel is notable for its surprise ending and the representation of the rural Guard, Sergeant Steve McNamara, suspicious of foreigners who, he believes, are "up to their necks in drug dealing and refugee smuggling".[46] McNamara, in turn, is referred to as a "bogman" and "bogtrotter" by Dublin drug dealers.[47]

Starting with *Revenge* (1999), *K. T. McCaffrey* has published a series of novel featuring Emma Boylan, an investigative reporter for a Dublin newspaper. *Revenge* presents a fascinating exposure of sexism and corruption in Ireland, as Emma explores the collusion between church and state in the story of Susan Furlong, a woman seeking revenge on the man who raped her, and on the temporal and spiritual authorities who have ruined her life. After giving birth, Susan's child was given up for adoption, and she was confined to a church-run mental institution. After killing the man who has raped her and who she believes to be her child's father, the rich businessman and controller of high-ranking police officers and politicians, JP Murray, Susan seeks the return of her daughter. Despite government recognition of abuse, little had been done in fifty years to amend the situation of victims or to atone for their suffering. Emma writes an article as a "damning indictment of the laws and law-makers who allowed such a state of affairs to continue for so long without seriously trying to do anything about it".[48] Her efforts, however, appear to have little impact on a male establishment which continues to believe that "every woman who did not respond positively to the male advance must necessarily be a lesbian".[49] The power of the Church, the complicity between police, politicians, big business and judges gives rise to the conclusion voiced by one of the characters, that Ireland is "a great little country. It's just a pity it's run by such a shower of fecking chancers".[50]

46  Des Ekin, *Stone Heart* (Dublin: The O'Brien Press, 1999), 75.
47  Ibid., 340.
48  K. T. McCaffrey, *Revenge* (Dublin: Marino, 1999), 265.
49  Ibid., 161.
50  Ibid., 401.

*Killing Time* (2000), the second Emma Boylan novel, sees the reporter investigating the death of a politician who has been murdered in the bed of his mistress. The identity of the killer is never in doubt, but the government, under Fionnuala Stafford, the first female Taoiseach, tries to cover up the case. Emma discovers a tale of sexual abuse involving key members of the Irish establishment and writes a report which, she believes, "will rock the state to its foundations".[51]

Dublin-born *Paul Kilduff* wrote four thrillers between 1999 and 2003, all based on the world of high finance and the stock markets. *Square Mile* (1999) takes its title from the novel's setting, the square mile which makes up London's financial district, the City. Anthony Carleton, an ambitious young investment banker is unwillingly drawn into the investigation surrounding the suspicious death of a director of his bank. As the story evolves, it becomes obvious that the murder of Jeremy Walker is directly related to the bank's new property fund, a multi-million-pound enterprise which has been used for illicit purposes. *The Dealer* (2000) is also set in the City, and involves a junior investigator in the Enforcement Department of the London Stock Exchange investigating the unscrupulous trading of an American ex-patriot equities dealer, Greg Schneider, suspected of insider trading. The investigation converges with that of Detective Inspector Ted Hammond who is working on the disappearance, later confirmed as murder, of Alexander Soames, the Finance Director of Providence Bank, involved in a high-level takeover deal in which Greg has interests. Like *Square Mile*, the plot is carefully constructed and fast-moving.

*Maureen Martella* has published three novels featuring Annie McHugh. In *Annie's New Life* (2000), the protagonist discovers, after the death of the people she had believed were her parents, that her birth certificate had been forged and that she had been adopted. Annie hires Dublin private detective Gerry Dunning, a George Clooney lookalike, to track down her birth mother. When she goes to confront her, this birth mother mistakes her for a job applicant, and Annie is contracted to work in her spacious house. After numerous misunderstandings and Cinderella-like scenes with her half-sisters, Annie is left the mansion on the old lady's

51    K. T. McCaffrey, *Killing Time* (Dublin: Marino, 2000).

death. Selling this to her siblings she uses the money to become a partner in Gerry's detective agency.

*Pauline McLynn*, a renowned comic actress perhaps best known for her role as Mrs Doyle, the housekeeper in the *Father Ted* series, published three novels blending crime, romance and comedy featuring private detective Leo Street between 2000 and 2002. Leo's work as a private investigator is far from glamorous. At the beginning of the first book in the series, *Something for the Weekend* (2000), she describes her job in the following terms:

> Most of my work is mundane – insurance claims, infidelities, fraud and sometimes a missing person. Jealousy, spite, greed and despair, that's my currency, so I don't usually meet people at their best, even if they have one. The cops deal with the glamorous side – murder, drug-dealing, terrorism and sometimes they wear a uniform. I take up whatever they don't, won't or can't do.[52]

Leo is sent to a Big House in County Kildare as undercover participant in a cookery course in order to investigate the marital infidelities of the wife of a rich Dublin businessman, in a novel which sees the detective meeting Ciara Gillespie, a young Goth who would become her sidekick in the next two Leo Street novels.

*Seamus Smyth* represents an interesting and unique case in Irish crime fiction. His first novel, *Quinn* (1999), published under the name of Seamus Smyth, was not followed up until the publication of *Blood for Blood* in 2016, this time attributed to J. M. Smyth. In *Quinn*, Smyth, a native of Belfast, introduces the protagonist, Gerd Quinn, a fascinatingly evil ex-IRA man relocated to Dublin and working for the main gangsters in the capital. Quinn's methods rely on the fact that, as there is only one state pathologist in Ireland, any murder which looks like an accident will not be considered worthy of investigation. Using this knowledge, he uses septic tanks to get rid of his victims' bodies. When his wife Sinead leaves him, Quinn plants narcotics on her so that she will be arrested and he will gain custody of his two sons. When Sinead hires a private investigator to follow her former husband, Quinn kills him in a septic tank.

---

52   Pauline McLynn, *Something for the Weekend* (London: Headline, 2000), 7–8.

With the profusion of police and private eye novels which appeared in the last decade of the twentieth century, the seeds for what would develop into the huge surge in in Irish crime fiction had been sown. The late 1990s, with the political, social and economic changes which were taking place on the island of Ireland during that period, opened up the market for a large number of new authors with ambition and talent. Some of these began their literary production during the last decade of the millennium, all of them were in some way influenced by the changes which had taken place in these years.

# CHAPTER 20

# "Killers who chop up their victims, that's all very American, or at the very least English. In Ireland it would only happen by accident, like most things." Towards the New Millennium

Apart from the large number of thrillers published during the 1990s, and the growing number of crime novels with an Irish setting, the decade also saw the first works of writers who would enjoy great success in the years after 2000. These include the Northern Irish writers Colin Bateman and Eoin McNamee, two very different writers but whose keen observation – from a position of humour in the case of Bateman and of journalistic faction in that of McNamee – cast a revealing glance at the present and past of Northern Ireland. The English Celtic scholar, Peter Beresford Ellis, using the pseudonym of Peter Tremayne, would set a standard for Irish historical fiction which both he and other writers would continue in the next decade, while John Connolly would publish his first two of his Charlie Parker novels, a series which would spawn numerous worldwide bestsellers. John Boyne, another writer who would sell millions of copies during the new millennium, also issued his first work, *The Thief of Time* which, like much of his later fiction, revealed a hybrid mixture of crime writing and other literary forms, in this case the historical fantasy novel.

Irish Crime fiction and comic writing are, perhaps, strange bedfellows, but the history of the genre has seen numerous attempts to present crime narratives in a comic mode. Black humour, parody and the deflating of stereotypes have always found a place in crime writing, and Irish crime writing is no exception. What is more surprising, perhaps, that in quantity and quality of comic crime writing, Northern Ireland has a distinct advantage over the Republic. Despite, or perhaps because of, the situation created by the Troubles, the amount of comic crime fiction produced in

Northern Ireland has been disproportionately high, and whether the authors come from a unionist (Colin Bateman) or nationalist (Garbhan Downey) background, or are "blow-ins" like Ian Sansom, the works are generally entertaining and very funny, while also adding perceptive observations on the conflict.

*Colin Bateman* arguably contributed more than anyone to the revival of Northern Irish crime fiction in the 1990s. His comic crime thrillers have reached wide audiences, not only within Ireland and Britain, but also in the worldwide market, with success in the USA and translation into numerous languages, as well as providing screenplays for popular feature films and television. Bateman, a former newspaper reporter, credits part of his success to the climate created towards the end of the Troubles, where "run-of-the-mill criminals are making a comeback, which is one reason why Northern Irish crime writing has been reborn".[1]

Bateman's first novel *Divorcing Jack* (1995) introduces the politically incorrect Belfast journalist Dan Starkey, "a hard drinker and confirmed Unionist"[2] who is given the job of escorting Charles Parker, an American journalist – who turns out to be an undercover CIA agent – in Belfast to cover the upcoming elections. After a fleeting, drunken extra-marital relationship with the young Margaret McBride, Dan's wife Patricia discovers the pair together and throws him out of their home. Margaret, who happens to be the daughter of a leading Republican politician, is killed while Dan is out collecting a pizza, and on his return he hears the dying girl's dying words, which he takes to be "divorce Jack". Dan then accidentally kills the girl's mother before becoming involved with several undesirable paramilitaries with names like Cow Pat Coogan, and Mad Dog Angus. Patricia is kidnapped and sleeps with her kidnapper but, at the end of the novel, the two unfaithful spouses are reunited in the family home, with Patricia pregnant by her terrorist captor.

The high-speed narrative provides Bateman's first comic critique of the apparently ridiculous extremes of life in the Northern Ireland of the

---

1    Colin Bateman, "Distance Lends Perspective", *Mystery Readers Journal* 24, no. 2
     (Summer 2008), 15.
2    Colin Bateman, *Divorcing Jack* (London: HarperCollins, 1995), 8.

1990s. The terrorists from both sides of the political divide are uniformly stupid, and the subject of collusion is broached with the revelation that Mad Dog is, in fact, an infiltrated British agent. The memorable characters include the Alliance Party candidate for First Minister of Northern Ireland, Mark Brinn, who had changed his name from O'Brinn by deed poll in order to conceal his Catholic origins, and the Catholic priest who, after open-heart surgery, received the transplant of a Protestant heart and was now rejected by his congregation. Although the plot is, following the conventions of "screwball" comedy as implausible as it is perverse, Bateman explores the themes which will dominate his later works. Although he satirises a wide variety of Northern Irish institutions, types and ideological tendencies, the most effective satire is that of the white, middle-class, unionist Ulsterman – someone like Dan Starkey or, indeed, Bateman himself. Aaron Kelly correctly identifies the sense of social and sexual inadequacy of the Northern Irish male as being central to an understanding of the author's comic thrillers, stressing the use of "the historical symbolism of the thriller to mediate not only the disruptions of urban space but also the provisional cartographic mode of a masculinity deprived of its traditional coordinates and securities".[3]

Bateman describes the novel as being "basically *The Thirty-Nine Steps* with one-liners".[4] Written in 1992 "when the worst of the Troubles were over", he says, if he had attempted it twenty years earlier he "can see how it would have been more radical".[5] The novel, written in his spare time between his newspaper work, and sent unsolicited to a major publishing house had, he claims, two possible purposes. Firstly "it was a rebellion against other books dealing with the North – the thrillers written by journalists who'd spent a few weeks here, who maybe got their facts right but didn't get the feel of the place".[6] Secondly, it was "also a reaction to my own background

---

3  Aaron Kelly, *The Thriller and Northern Ireland since 1969: Utterly Resigned Terror* (Aldershot: Ashgate, 2005), 81.
4  Colin Bateman, "The Troubles I've Seen" in *Down These Green Streets: Irish Crime Writing in the Twenty-First Century*, ed. Declan Burke (Dublin: Liberties Press, 2011), 176.
5  Ibid., 177.
6  Ibid.

as an Ulster Protestant and feeling that Ireland, or Northern Ireland, always meant Literary Ireland, it was about poets and playwrights and history, not about today or what former punk rockers were thinking".[7] Bateman defends his choice, claiming that the work is balanced in its representation of both communities and "if anything it was one of the first to have a Protestant as the leading character, and making him smart and funny and flawed was probably my way of sticking up for where I come from"[8]

*Cycle of Violence*, also published in 1995, features another young Belfast journalist, Miller, forced to use the cycle of the title after losing his driving licence. Miller is posted to the fictional village of Crossmaheart in the "bandit country" of South Armagh, where the only interests of the local people appear to be "fighting and rowing and collecting their unemployment cheques".[9] Miller's predecessor in the Crossmaheart newspaper, Jamie Milburn, has disappeared, and while attempting to find out the secret of his disappearance, Miller falls in love with Jamie's taciturn girlfriend Marie and uncovers a gang rape committed some years before involving a future priest, an IRA member and a newspaper editor, Miller's boss. The spiral of violence initiated unwittingly by Miller leads to many deaths due, he muses "to an unlikely combination of bad temper and unhappy coincidence".[10]

*Of Wee Sweetie Mice and Men* (1996) is partly set in New York, where Dan Starkey forms part of the entourage of Belfast boxer Bobby "Fat Boy" McMaster, assigned to work as press officer and biographer to the pugilist who is in New York for a St Patrick's Day showdown with heavyweight champion Mike Tyson. McMaster's wife is kidnapped in an attempt to force the boxer into declaring his support for a united Ireland at the fight, and Muslim militants take exception to his random remark that there were few black people in Northern Ireland. In America Starkey repeatedly ponders on his condition as a Protestant from Northern Ireland. He is disparaging when talking of his compatriots, like the bodyguard Stanley Matchit, a former member of the paramilitary Red Hand Commando who has "a penchant

7    Ibid.
8    Ibid.
9    Colin Bateman, *Cycle of Violence* (London: HarperCollins, 1995), 26.
10   Ibid., 208.

for hacking up innocent Catholics"[11] and who seems to represent "three hundred years of Protestant culture distilled in one man".[12] Questioned about any ambivalence he might have towards his national identity, Starkey declares that he is Northern Irish, not British nor Irish. For him, Northern Ireland is simply home. He couldn't, he says, "much be bothered fighting to make it one thing or the other, but if someone walked in and forced me into one thing or another, then I might get more protective about it".[13]

The North American setting is repeated in both *Empire State* (1997) and *Maid of the Mist* (1999). The former involves the survivor of a terrorist attack in Crossmaheart, Nathan Jones, who has emigrated and is working as a security guard in the Empire State Building. Jones uncovers a plot by a white supremacist to assassinate the President on a visit to the building. *Maid of the Mist* is set on the Canadian side of Niagara Falls where another Crossmaheart exile, police officer Frank Corrigan faces a convention of Drug Lords posing as florists. It is possible that, as Aaron Kelly states, Bateman's use of a transatlantic setting for these novels owes much to "the hegemonic and enticing gravitational pull of the international market"[14], and the North American works lack some of the vigour and spontaneity of the books with a Northern Irish setting.

*Turbulent Priests* (1999) returns to an Irish setting and, once again, features the hapless journalist Dan Starkey. The novel also reintroduces Father Flynn, the priest with a Protestant heart, now living on a remote island where the residents are enthralled by the apparent new Messiah, a girl named Christine. Christine, it would appear, was born in a discotheque called *The Stables* in Belfast after a Cliff Richard concert. Starkey, despite being "about as Catholic as Cromwell"[15] is charged by the Primate of All Ireland to investigate the phenomenon. Relocating with his wife Patricia and her child to the isolated, alcohol-free island, "a little paradise off the coast of frightened, bickering Ireland",[16] Dan is faced with a spate

---

11    Colin Bateman, *Of Wee Sweetie Mice and Men* (London: HarperCollins, 1996), 33.
12    Ibid., 51.
13    Ibid., 161.
14    Kelly, *Thriller and Northern Ireland*, 79.
15    Colin Bateman, *Turbulent Priests* (London: HarperCollins, 1999), 272.
16    Ibid., 48.

of killings, as it is revealed that the presence of poisonous radon on the island has been causing mass delusions. The novel provides a highly charged critique of religious fundamentalism on both sides of the sectarian divide, a theme which is further developed in *Shooting Sean* (2001), where Dan Starkey is sent to Dublin in the employ of the Irish film star, Sean O'Toole, who is directing a film based on an infamous IRA member, nicknamed "The Colonel". Sean and Dan are both from Belfast, but their experiences were divided "only by religion, a razor-wire-topped peace line and three hundred years of hatred".[17]

Bateman would continue to produce a stream of successful common novels, some of which featured Starkey, throughout the early years of the twenty-first century. The highlight of his later works would probably be the creation of another comic protagonist, The Mystery Man, who would feature in some of the better late novels. For the last few years the author has concentrated more on film production and script-writing, although a new Starkey adventure was shared online free of charge during the early days of the COVID crisis in spring of 2020.

It is impossible to overstate the importance of *Eoin McNamee's* contribution to the Northern Irish novel in recent years. Both stylistically and in terms of topic, McNamee has produced a series of works which have been characterised as "metaphysical espionage narratives",[18] which make use of "a Conrad-inflected noir aesthetic".[19] After the publication of two excellent novellas, *The Last of Deeds* (1989) and *Love in History* (1992), his first novel, *Resurrection Man* (1994), was a ground-breaking work which avoids the "sectarian simplicities and clichéd terrorists in balaclavas" and "creates a murky underworld where violence and subterfuge are sustained by 'a dark current of approval in the political sphere'".[20] Based on *The Shankill*

---

17    Colin Bateman, *Shooting Sean* (London: HarperCollins, 2001), 48.

18    Birte Heidemann, *Post-Agreement Northern Irish Literature* (London: Palgrave Macmillan, 2016), 84.

19    Thomas Rudman, "The Place You Don't Belong: Border-Crossings and Ambivalence in the Northern Irish Noir Thriller" in *Border Crossings: Nation and Imagination*, ed. Colin Younger (Newcastle: Cambridge Scholars Publishing, 2013), 253.

20    Eric Reimer, "Ulsterisation and the Troubles Thriller: Eoin McNamee's *Resurrection Man*", *Irish Studies Review* 20, no. 1 (2012), 66.

*Butchers: A Case Study of Mass Murder* (1989), a non-fiction study by Martin Dillon, *Resurrection Man* examines the terrifying murders committed by a loyalist gang under the leadership of Victor Kelly, based on the real-life murderer Hugh "Lenny" Murphy. Using some of the techniques of "faction", McNamee paints a harrowing portrait of apparently meaningless violence – much of which is directed against fellow Protestants – employing methods which carry "ritualistic, religious, aesthetic, and perhaps erotic charge".[21] After a period of imprisonment in Long Kesh, Victor takes to the streets of Belfast, carrying out his gangster fantasies on a murder spree which, while initially concentrating on Catholic victims, eventually comes to transcend its sectarian overtones. Kelly is a serial killer who, aided and abetted by a motley crew of violent nobodies spreads a wave of terror around the carefully delineated streets of Belfast.

McNamee's portrayal of Victor Kelly is a careful study of the psychological make-up of a mass murderer. He suggests that at least part of the killer's hatred towards Catholics stems from the stigma he has been forced to carry on account of his surname – both Kelly and Murphy have clear Catholic overtones – and the brief account of his childhood points to a future as a psychopath. He was born with a deformed head to a middle-aged mother, did not talk until the age of four, and was prone to sticking a compass into the face of classmates, simply to observe the effect. Kelly models himself on the gangsters seen in American films and he inspires terror and longs for the celebrity of his admired John Dillinger. McNamee's language is perfectly suited to the subject, and in the words of Elmer Kennedy-Andrews, it is "grounded in naturalism" but, at the same time, it "gestures towards mysticism".[22] He uses short, staccato sentences which suggest both urgency and a sense of inevitability, and the frequent use of the passive voice depersonalises events and implies the unavoidable and almost bureaucratic nature of them.

21  Edward J. Mallot, "'There's No Good Riot Footage Anymore': Waging Northern Ireland's Media War in Eoin McNamee's Resurrection Man", *New Hibernian Review/ Iris Éireannach Nua* 17, no. 3 (2013), 52.

22  Elmer Kennedy-Andrews, "The Novel and the Northern Troubles" in *The Cambridge Companion to the Irish Novel*, ed. John Wilson Foster (Cambridge: Cambridge University Press, 2006), 250.

The popularity of crime narratives which make use of a historical background has led to this sub-genre becoming the fastest growing category of crime fiction.[23] Ireland, where history is ubiquitously present, is no exception to this, and a number of writers have produced a fascinating body of work of historical fiction over the last few decades. Arguably the most influential figure in the world of the Irish historical murder mystery is Peter Beresford Ellis who, writing under the Peter Tremayne pseudonym, has published some thirty volumes featuring the seventh-century advocate and *religieuse*, Sister Fidelma. Born in Coventry, England, to an English mother and Irish journalist father, Ellis entered journalism as a trainee reporter for a Brighton newspaper before becoming, in 1970, deputy editor, on its foundation, of *The Irish Post*, a weekly publication whose target readership is the Irish population living in Britain. Despite some success in this paper, Ellis had also been publishing works on Irish, Scottish, Welsh and Cornish language and history, and in 1975 he decided to leave the deputy editorship to take up full-time writing. He became a highly regarded authority on Celtic studies and several of his publications have become acknowledged as key texts within this field.

As *Peter Tremayne*, he initiated his Sister Fidelma series in 1993 with the publication of a short story, "Murder in Repose", which appeared in *Great Irish Detective Stories*, edited by Peter Haining. As he states, the creation of Fidelma was fortuitous, as, after delivering a lecture on Celtic women in seventh-century Ireland at a Canadian college, a student, inspired by his reading of the English translation of Umberto Eco's *Nome della Rosa* (*The Name of the Rose*), suggested that "the idea of a female lawyer among the Celtic religious solving murder mysteries would make a great setting".[24] Some years later, when Peter Haining asked Tremayne if he had a short story to add to a collection, the author produced the first Fidelma story which, after changing the protagonist's name from Sister Buan on

23    Ray B. Browne, "Historical Crime and Detection." In *A Companion to Crime Fiction*, ed. Charles J. Rzepka and Lee Horsley (Oxford: Wiley-Blackwell, 2010), 223.
24    Edward J. Rielly, "Interview with Peter Tremayne" in *The Sister Fidelma Mysteries: Essays on the Historical Novels of Peter Tremayne*, ed. Edward J. Rielly and David Robert Wooten (Jefferson, NC: McFarland & Company, 2012), 212.

Haining's suggestion, "Murder in Repose" (1993) was born. Sister Fidelma is introduced near the beginning of the story:

> Sister Fidelma, tall, green-eyed, stood before the Brehon with hands folded demurely in front of her. Her robes and hood, from under which wisps of rebellious red hair stuck out, scarcely disguised her youthfulness nor her feminine attractiveness. The Brehon had placed her age in her mid-twenties. He noticed that her stance was one of controlled agitation, of someone used to movement and action in life. The habit of a religieuse did not suit her at all.[25]

Four Fidelma stories were published in 1993, and while Tremayne would continue to write and publish mysteries in the short story format, it was the publication of the first Sister Fidelma novel, *Absolution by Murder* (1994) which saw the character become popular. In this novel, set in 664 AD, Fidelma forms part of the delegation led by Abbess Étain of Kildare at the Synod of Whitby. Fidelma is a member of the Celtic Irish aristocracy, daughter of a former king of Manan (Munster) and sister to a future ruler. She is also an *anruth*, a high-ranking advocate in the Irish *Brehon* system of justice, a post which has required years of intense study. She is also a *religieuse* – Tremayne balks at the use of the word "nun" – who has taken religious orders at the behest of her cousin, Abbot Laisran, mainly as a means of being able to exercise the legal profession without undue hindrance.[26]

The setting and events of *Absolution by Murder* are important for an understanding of the themes and concerns which are central to an understanding of the whole series, as well as providing an early blueprint for Fidelma's methods and means of operating. The Synod had been called so that Oswy, king of Northumbria, could decide whether to accept the rulings of either of the Christian Churches attempting to control the spiritual affairs of the kingdom. At this convention a number of representatives debate the issues at stake, but the Synod is interrupted by the murder of Abbess Étain. Fidelma, as an *anruth*, a lawyer associated with the Celtic Church, is asked to investigate and, to compensate any potential bias,

25 Peter Tremayne, "Murder in Repose" in *Great Irish Detective Stories*, ed. Peter Haining (London: Souvenir, 1993), 338.
26 Rielly, "Interview", 211.

she is to be aided by a representative of the Roman Church, Eadulf, one of the Archbishop of Canterbury's party who has studied in Ireland and Rome. The two religious detectives are faced with more murders before the case can be resolved, mainly through Fidelma's "engaging mixture of imagination, reason, and methodical use of probing interviews", helped by Eadulf's intuition.[27]

The conflict between the Celtic and Roman Churches outlined in the narrative was one of enormous transcendence in western Europe in the seventh century. Celtic Christianity had been powerful but by the last half of the century the main concern was the threat of total dominance by the Church of Rome. Although ostensibly concerned with differences over theological issues and the form of liturgical practice, over the style of tonsure to be worn or the exact dating of Easter, the real dispute was over political power. As Eadruf concisely puts it, the final decision taken by the Northumbrian king to accept the Roman Church "was crouched in the language of theology" but, notwithstanding, "his decision was made in the hard reality of political concerns".[28] If the king had supported the Celtic Church, he would have offended the Roman Church. If, however, he supported Rome "then he would be accepted by the other kingdoms of the Angles and the Saxons and they will join forces to assert supremacy over this island of Britain and, perhaps one day, the lands beyond".[29]

Tremayne's sympathies lie, of course with the Celtic Church, seen throughout the series as a continuation of the old faith, the druidic creed which had given Ireland its social structure, its laws and its sense of purpose in the world. Fidelma, a pragmatic member of the Celtic Church, is still greatly influenced by many of the aspects of druidism and, one suspects, in other circumstances would as readily have embraced the old faith as Celtic Christianity. Her "calling is the law, not the faith", and she is "frequently

27    Edward J. Rielly, "Sister Fidelma: A Woman for All Seasons" in *The Sister Fidelma Mysteries: Essays on the Historical Novels of Peter Tremayne*, ed. Edward J. Rielly and David Robert Wooten (Jefferson, NC: McFarland & Company, 2012), 5.
28    Peter Tremayne, *Absolution by Murder* (London: Headline, 1994), 267.
29    Ibid.

sympathetic to the old faith".[30] The ascendancy of the Roman Church is perceived as a threat not only to Celtic Christianity, but also to the entire framework of Irish society. Fidelma, as a woman, is given a freedom in seventh-century Ireland that would not be available to her in other places in the world, and this freedom would not be tolerated by Rome. The Celtic Church gave women religeuse an equal role to that of their male counterparts, and "as a consequence of the Brehon Laws, Irish women had more rights and protection than women in the rest of Europe".[31] This Brehon system – the name comes from the Irish *breitheeamh*, "judge" – is "the oldest formal law system in Europe", and is believed to have been implemented by Ollamh Foddlah in around BC 714.[32] This system was renovated in 438 AD when it was decided that three-yearly reviews should be put into place in order to assure the continued relevance of the stipulations involved. The system was based on a series of rights, duties and privileges which were shared reciprocally throughout society. A stratified system of compensation allocated a price on each member of society, and this price was taken into account in the Brehon courts where compensation was awarded according to the price assigned to the parties concerned. The system was based, therefore, on compensation, and the victim and their family were considered to be the primary concern of Brehon Law. If, for instance, a cow was stolen, the main interest of the court was the reparation of the offended part in order that any loss might be recuperated to avoid material discomfort which might result from the crime. Such a system differed, obviously, from Roman Law, which was based on retaliation and the harsh punishment of the perpetrator rather than on the reimbursement

---

30  Anita M. Vickers, "Druids and Brehons: Fidelma and the Druidic Tradition" in *The Sister Fidelma Mysteries: Essays on the Historical Novels of Peter Tremayne*, ed. Edward J. Rielly and David Robert Wooten (Jefferson, NC: McFarland & Company, 2012), 95–96.

31  Christine Kinealy, "Hidden from History: Fidelma of Cashel and Lost Female Values" in *The Sister Fidelma Mysteries: Essays on the Historical Novels of Peter Tremayne*, ed. Edward J. Rielly and David Robert Wooten (Jefferson, NC: McFarland & Company, 2012), 51.

32  Patrick O'Keefe, "Fidelma of Cashel and the Brehon Code" in *The Sister Fidelma Mysteries: Essays on the Historical Novels of Peter Tremayne*, ed. Edward J. Rielly and David Robert Wooten (Jefferson, NC: McFarland & Company, 2012), 81.

of the victim's loss. The Brehon Law, in other words, placed its emphasis on the victim and family; the Roman system on the state which became "the aggrieved party".[33]

In subsequent books in the series the chemistry which seemed to exist between Fidelma and Eadulf continues to develop as the pair are brought together. In *Shroud for the Archbishop* (1995) they travel to Rome where Fidelma, by solving a series of murders, manages to avert "a terrible conflict between the Saxon kingdoms and Ireland".[34] In *Suffer Little Children* (1995) her brother becomes king at Cashel and in this and *The Subtle Serpent* (1996), *The Spider's Web* (1997) and subsequent novels, Fidelma and Eadulf are in Ireland and, as they become involved in more cases, their personal relationship develops. As celibacy did not exist then either in the Celtic or the Roman Church, their growing closeness is generally accepted, although the *anruth's* royal status means that for some of the Irish characters there is a potentially prohibitive difference in social class between Fidelma and the foreigner. In *Act of Mercy* (1999), she travels by ship to Santiago de Compostela and later to Armorica (Brittany) in what is partially an attempt to calmly assess her relationship with Eadulf. On her return, on hearing of Eadulf's arrest, she travels to Canterbury via Wales (*Our Lady of Darkness*, 2000), and then on to Eadulf's homeland of East Anglia (*Smoke in the Wind*, 2001).

*John Boyne's* first novel, *The Thief of Time* (2000), tells the story of the ageless protagonist, Mattieu Zéla. Zéla was born in France in 1743 but, at the age of 256, is awaiting the start of the new millennium in 1999 with the body of a healthy man in his fifties. Zéla's life has been long and eventful, and includes many memories, from the death of his parents and his involvement in the execution of his stepfather, to his escape to England and childhood as a petty thief on the streets of Dover, to his involvement, always on the fringes, in some of the important events of the two and a half centuries of his life. These include the French Revolution, the Great Exhibition, The Wall Street crash and the McCarthy witch-hunts. Although he has been married nineteen times and has had, as he tells us, nine hundred

33    Ibid.
34    Tremayne, *Absolution by Murder*, 333.

lovers, Mattieu's life is overshadowed by two relationships, each of which profoundly influences his behaviour and his way of looking at life. His first love is Dominique Souvet, a French girl who accompanies Zéla and his stepbrother Tomas in their adventures in England after leaving France. Dominique's ethical stance regarding a sum of money with which Mattieu has been entrusted in order to help a friend escape from prison causes Zéla to examine his own integrity, giving him a new perspective on life. The second important relationship is with nine generations of boys and young men, all named "Thomas", and all "nephews" and all descendants of Tomas, the stepbrother who had accompanied Mattieu when as a child himself he had left France. Despite his efforts he is unable to help any of these nephews, each of whom dies in his twenties. By the final stages of the novel he takes the decision to help the current Tommy, a soap-opera actor and heroin addict. It remains unstated, but the reader assumes that the years which have been granted to Mattieu are those that have been deducted from the lives of his dissolute kinsmen and, therefore, should he, as seems likely, succeed in saving this Tommy his own longevity will be curtailed and Mattieu will meet his death.

Dublin-born *John Connolly* published his first novel *Every Dead Thing* in 1999. This introduced Charlie Parker, at first a detective in the homicide division of the NYPD who becomes a private investigator on leaving the force after the horrendous death of his wife and daughter at the hands of the Travelling Man, the first of a long line of larger-than-life villains who share an increasingly prominent supernatural element. The Charlie Parker novels are set far from Connolly's native Ireland, in the USA, most especially in and around Portland, Maine, where the author spends part of every year. This American setting is important for the author, as a premeditated and conscious "way of escaping the expectations that come with being an Irish writer" and as "a means of escaping a very parochial literary viewpoint".[35] Despite this, however, something about Connolly's writing remains intensely Irish. Many of the themes and issues found in

35 "John Connolly – On His Influences, Self-Doubt and The Future Life of Charlie Parker", *Material Witness*, <https://materialwitness.typepad.com/material_witn ess/2014/06/interview-john-connolly-on-his-influences-self-doubt-and-the-fut ure-life-of-charlie-parker-.html>, accessed 7 June 2014.

the collection are highly topical and relevant when placed within an Irish context, and include recurring references to subjects such as religious intolerance, the institutionalisation of familial roles in such institutions as mental hospitals, orphanages, and old people's and maternity homes, the legal status of abortion and homosexuality, adoption and fostering of children, problems of domestic violence and the abuse of alcohol.

Connolly's novels rely heavily on the Irish gothic tradition with Parker himself, the troubled male protagonist, haunted by the ghosts of his wife and daughter, fighting against criminals who, as the writer himself says, "are darker than the average murderer or burglar".[36] The victims in the Parker series are usually women, or more particularly young girls, and the settings, from the vast wilderness of the northern forests of Maine to the gothic mansions and crumble-down shacks from New England to Louisiana, are more often than not the scene of dysfunctional families where incest and abuse form part of the process of coming of age.

*Every Dead Thing* begins with the murder of Susan Parker and her young daughter Jennifer, in which the victims are skinned and flayed and their faces removed. Blaming himself, his obsession with his work and his problem with alcohol, Parker leaves the NYPD and, after a time of aimless wandering, decides to accept private investigation assignments. The first of these cases involves the search for Catherine Demeter, the fiancée of the stepson of Isobel Barton, a wealthy New England heiress. The investigation takes Parker to New Orleans where, through a blind creole seer, *Tante Marie*, the ex-policeman establishes what he believes to be contact with his dead child and daughter. Accompanied by Louis and Angel, two diametrically opposed criminals who form a gay sentimental partnership, and the criminal psychologist Rachel Wolfe, with whom Parker is to develop a more than professional relationship, he sees in the disappearance of Catherine, and its link to a series of crimes committed in the Louisiana bayou in the past, a connection with the double murder of Susan and Jennifer. Tracking down their killer, The Travelling Man, Parker understands why the murder had seemed to possess such personal motivation.

36    Ibid.

The gothic atmosphere of *Every Dead Thing* is heightened by the scenes set in Louisiana, where the ruins of the Dane house remind local people of past events, and whose gardens are overgrown with "the limbs of the evergreens fanning the darkness and the empty jangling of a chain in the wreckage of the yard".[37]

*Every Dead Thing* also constitutes Connolly's first attempt to examine the concept of evil and, quoting from Edmund Burke, he believes that "the only thing necessary for the triumph of evil is for good men to do nothing".[38] The Travelling Man is the first of his criminals to show the pure evil he is convinced exists:

> We do not believe in evil any more, only evil acts, which can be explained away by the science of the mind. There is no evil and to believe in it is to fall prey to superstition, like checking beneath the bed at night or being afraid of the dark. But there are those for whom we have no easy answers, who do evil things because that is their nature, because they are evil.[39]

Indeed the debate on the existence of "pure evil" is central to an understanding of Connolly's works, and he ponders on whether there exist "some things that seemed to defy any conventional notion of what it meant to be human, of what it meant to exist in the world".[40] This attempt to define the nature of evil, the idea that characters can be evil just because that is their nature echoes, of course, earlier gothic models, and The Travelling Man, like future villains in the Charlie Parker novels, owes more than a little to the evil monk figure so typical of the gothic, such as his intellectual and social arrogance, for example, *Every Dead Thing* also introduces a number of features which would appear throughout the series. The Travelling Man is interested in medieval paintings, engravings and anatomical diagrams, and in true gothic style his referents include Spanish and Italian models from the Middle Ages. He is also obsessed with the apocryphal text *The Book of Enoch*, setting the tone for the scores of esoteric, apocryphal and quasi-religious texts which will abound in subsequent novels within the series.

37    John Connolly, *Every Dead Thing* (London: Hodder, 1999), 212.
38    *Material Witness.*
39    Connolly, *Every Dead*, 151.
40    Ibid., 137.

In *Dark Hollow* (2000) this evil is represented by the feared bogeyman Caleb Kyle, the character adopted by serial killer Caleb Brewster who, as a child had tortured animals before killing his mother and feeding her body to the hogs. The mood of *Dark Hollow* is almost that of an obscure fairy tale in which there appears "an old evil" which "has a way of permeating bloodlines and tainting those who played no part in its genesis: the young, the innocent, the vulnerable, the defenceless".[41] The novel also reveals more about Parker himself, and about his two unlikely helpers, the gay couple of Angel and Louis, a streetwise Italian thug and a dapper Afro-American crook. In the third novel in the series *The Killing Kind* (2001) Connolly starts to develop his theory of the "honeycomb world", which would prove to be a constant point of reference and which relates to a belief in the "interconnectedness of all things".[42] This "honeycomb world", however, "holds a hollow heart", but, despite its apparently empty core, it creates patterns of empathy which are central to the series and, indeed, to Parker's very existence.[43] Along with the evil he encounters in his search for reparation and comprehension of events, Parker encounters a number of empathetic characters, ranging from Rachel to a number of secondary but important figures who help to keep the detective on track, as it were.

As in all gothic fables, the past is of constant and recurring importance in the series. Parker is who he is because of the events of his past, and this past, like that of all the major characters in the books, is constantly present:

> The present is imperfectly layered on the past; it does not conform flawlessly at every point. Things fall and die and their decay creates new layers, thickening the surface crust and adding another thin membrane to cover what lies beneath, new worlds resting on the remains of the old. Day upon day, year upon year, century upon century, layers are added and the imperfections multiply. The past never truly dies. It is there waiting, just below the surface of the now. We stumble into it occasionally, all of us, through remembrance and recall.[44]

41   John Connolly, *Dark Hollow* (London: Hodder, 2000), 21.
42   John Connolly, *The Killing Kind* (London: Hodder, 2001), 3.
43   Ibid.
44   Ibid., 3–4.

One of the most interesting features to be found in the Charlie Parker series is the development of the supernatural elements found in the novels. In the early works, and especially in *Every Dead Thing*, the author makes use of the principle of hesitation – leaving the reader to wonder on the existence or not of supernatural elements in the works. Is Charlie Parker literally haunted by the ghosts of his wife and daughter or are the psychological scars caused by their death distorting his perception? How could *Tante Marie* communicate with the dead?

Connolly himself admits that there is an increasing importance given to the supernatural as the series progresses, and on the publication of *The Killing Kind* he stated:

> It's gradually becoming more and more explicit as the novels progress. I think *The White Road*, the fourth book, will take it one stage further. In the end, I don't write realist crime fiction. (In fact, I don't think crime fiction in general can be termed "realist". Too much manipulation of the realities of police work, private investigation, and detection, too much telescoping and compression of events and time, is required for it to really claim that it reflects reality. Instead, it acts like a kind of prism, simultaneously distorting reality and also making the constituent elements of a story or plot clearer to the reader.) I'm interested in using the structures of crime fiction as a springboard to explore other themes: empathy, morality, compassion, maybe even life after death. And I'm also interested in mixing genres, creating hybrids. Not everybody is going to like that, but it's still legitimate to try to do it.[45]

The early years of the twenty-first century would, of course, see an almost unbelievable rise in the popularity of Irish crime fiction. The Celtic Tiger and its rapid and traumatic decline would help stimulate a proliferation of talented writers who were to enjoy a growing national and international market which gave rise to the phenomenon of "Emerald Noir" and the worldwide esteem with which Irish crime fiction came to be held. As well as the writers who started their career in the 1990s, the first two decades of the 2000s would be dominated by Tana French, Adrian McKinty, Declan Hughes, Maeve Kerrigan, Brian McGilloway, Claire McGowan, Conor Brady, Arlene Hunt, Liz Nugent, Stuart Neville and John Banville, writing as Benjamin Black. A number of writers – usually

---

45   *Material Witness.*

from a journalistic background, such as Gene Kerrigan or Liz Allen who, in the 1990s had published "true crime" works – would, in the next decades, turn to crime fiction with some success. The story of Irish crime writing in the twenty-first century requires a further volume, a work which will explore the rise of "Emerald Noir".

# Bibliography

Addison, Henry Robert. *Recollections of an Irish Police Magistrate and Other Reminiscences of the South of Ireland*. London: Ward, Lock & Co., 1862.

Ahern, Bertie. *The Autobiography*. London: Hutchinson, 2009.

Alexander, Mrs. *False Scent*. London: F. V. White, 1889.

_____. *Her Dearest Foe*. New York: Henry Holt, 1876.

Allan, Janice M. "The Contemporary Response to Sensation Fiction". In *The Cambridge Companion to Sensation Fiction*, edited by Andrew Mangham, 85–98. Cambridge: Cambridge University Press, 2013.

Almeri, Thomas. *The Life of John Buncle, Esq., Containing Various Observations and Reflections, Made in Several Parts of the World; and Many Extraordinary Relations. Vol. 1*. London: J. Noon, 1756.

_____. *The Life of John Buncle, Esq., Containing Various Observations and Reflections, Made in Several Parts of the World; and Many Extraordinary Relations. Vol. 2*. London: J. Noon, 1766.

Amigoni, David. *Victorian Literature*. Edinburgh: Edinburgh University Press, 2011.

Ascari, Maurizio. *A Counter-History of Crime Fiction: Supernatural, Gothic, Sensational*. London: Palgrave Macmillan, 2007.

Auden, W. H. "The Guilty Vicarage". In *Detective Fiction: A Collection of Critical Essays. Twentieth Century Views*, edited by Robin W. Winks, 15–24 (Englewood Cliffs, NJ: Prentice-Hall, 1980).

Banville, John. *The Book of Evidence*. London: Martin Secker & Warburg, 1989.

Banville, Vincent. *Death by Design*. Harpenden: No Exit Press, 1993.

_____. *Death the Pale Rider*. Dublin: Poolbeg, 1995.

Bateman, Colin. *Cycle of Violence*. London: HarperCollins, 1995.

_____. "Distance Lends Perspective". *Mystery Readers Journal* 24, no. 2 (2008): 15.

_____. *Divorcing Jack*. London: HarperCollins, 1995.

_____. *Empire State*. London: HarperCollins, 1997.

_____. *Maid of the Mist*. London: HarperCollins, 1999.

_____. *Of Wee Sweetie Mice and Men*. London: *HarperCollins*, 1996.

_____. "The Troubles I've Seen". In *Down These Green Streets: Irish Crime Writing in the Twenty-First Century*, edited by Declan Burke. 174–182. Dublin: Liberties Press, 2011.

_____. *Turbulent Priests*. London: HarperCollins, 1999.

Begnal, Michael H. *Joseph Sheridan Le Fanu*. Cranbury, NJ: Associated University Presses, 1971.

Beller, Anne-Marie. "Sensation Fiction in the 1850s". In *The Cambridge Companion to Sensation Fiction*, edited by Andrew Mangham, 7–20. Cambridge: Cambridge University Press, 2013.

Bennett, Ronan. *The Catastrophist*. London: Bloomsbury, 2004.

_____. *Havoc, in its Third Year*. London: Bloomsbury, 2004.

_____. *Overthrown by Strangers*. London: Bloomsbury, 1992.

_____. *The Second Prison*. London: Hamish Hamilton, 1991.

_____. *Zugzwang*. London: Bloomsbury, 2007.

Bertens, Hans and Theo D'haen. *Contemporary American Crime Fiction*. New York: Palgrave, 2001.

Birmingham, George A. *The Adventures of Dr. Whitty*. London: Methuen, 1913.

_____. *General John Regan*. London: Methuen, 1913.

_____. *Gossamer*. New York: George H. Doran, 1915.

_____. *Hyacinth*. London: Edward Arnold, 1906.

_____. *The Hymn Tune Mystery*. London: Methuen, 1930.

_____. *The Inviolable Sanctuary aka Priscilla's Spies*. London: Nelson, 1912.

_____. *The Island Mystery*. London: Hodder & Stoughton, 1918.

_____. *Lady Bountiful*. London: Christophers, 1921.

_____. *Lalage's Lovers*. London: Methuen, 1911.

_____. *The Northern Iron*. Dublin: Maunsel, 1907.

_____. *The Red Hand of Ulster*. London: Smith Evans, 1912.

_____. *The Simpkins Plot*. London: Edward Arnold, 1911.

_____. *Spanish Gold*. London: Methuen, 1908.

_____. *Two Fools*. London: Methuen, 1934.

Blake, Nicholas. *The Beast Must Die*. London: Pan Books, 1938.

_____. *The Corpse in the Snowman*. New York: Harper Perennial, 1941.

_____. *The Deadly Joker*. London: Pan Books, 1963.

_____. *The Dreadful Hollow*. New York: Harper, 1953.

_____. *End of a Chapter*. London: J. M. Dent, 1957.

_____. *Head of a Traveller*. London: J. M. Dent, 1949.

_____. *Malice in Wonderland*. Leicester: F. A. Thorpe, 1940.

_____. *Minute for Murder*. New York: Harper Perennial, 1947.

_____. *The Morning after Death*. London: Pan Books, 1966.

_____. *A Penknife in My Heart*. London: Collins, 1958.

_____. *The Private Wound*. London: Collins, 1968.

_____. *A Question of Proof*. Boulder and Lyons: Rue Morgue Press, 1935.

_____. *The Sad Variety*. London: J. M. Dent, 1964.

_____. *The Smiler with the Knife*. London: Hogarth Press, 1939.

_____. *A Tangled Web*. London: Collins, 1956.

_____. *There's Trouble Brewing*. New York: Harper Perennial, 1937.

_____. *Thou Shell of Death*. London: Collins, 1936.

_____. *The Whisper in the Gloom*. New York: Harper, 1954.

_____. *The Widow's Cruise*. London: Hamlyn, 1959.

_____. *The Worm of Death*. New York: Harper, 1961.

Bloom, Clive. "Introduction: The Spy Thriller: A Genre under Cover?" In *Spy Thrillers: From Buchan to Carré*, edited by Clive Bloom, 1–11. London: Macmillan, 1990.

Bodkin, M. McDonnell. *The Capture of Paul Beck*. New York: Little, Brown, 1909.

_____. *Dora Myrl, the Lady Detective*. London: Chatto & Windus, 1900.

_____. *Guilty or Not Guilty?* Dublin: Talbot Press, 1929.

_____. *A Modern Robyn Hood*. London: Ward, Lock & Co., 1903.

_____. *Paul Beck, Detective*. Dublin: Talbot Press, 1919.

_____. *Paul Beck, the Rule of Thumb Detective*. London: C. Arthur Pearson, 1898.

_____. *Pigeon Blood Rubies*. London: Eveleigh Nash, 1915.

_____. *The Quests of Paul Beck*. London: T. Fisher Unwin, 1908.

_____. *A Stolen Life*. London: Ward, Lock & Co., 1898.

_____. *White Magic*. London: Chapman & Hall, 1897.

_____. *Young Beck*. London: T. Fisher Unwin, 1911.

Bolger, Dermot. *Father's Music*. London: Flamingo, 1997.

_____. *The Journey Home*. London: Viking, 1990.

Bowen, Elizabeth. "Mystery at the Lilacs". *Home and Country*, August 1938.

_____. *The Last September*. London: Vintage, 1929.

_____. *The Little Girls*. London: Penguin, 1963.

Boyle, Andrew. *The Riddle of Erskine Childers*. London: Hutchinson, 1977.

Boyne, John. *The Thief of Time*. London: Penguin, 2000.

Bradford, Roy. *The Last Ditch*. Belfast: The Blackstaff Press, 1981.

Brady, Conor. *Guardians of the Peace*. Dublin: Gill & Macmillan, 1974.

Brady, John. *Kaddish in Dublin*. London: Arrow, 1990.

_____. *The Good Life*. New York: St. Martin's Press, 1994.

_____. *All Souls*. London: Constable, 1993.

_____. *A Stone of the Heart*. London: Constable, 1988.

Brennan, Robert. *The Man Who Walked Like a Dancer*. London: Rich and Cowan, 1951.

Brewer, John D., Bill Lockhart and Paula Rodgers. "Crime in Ireland 1945–95". *Proceedings of the British Academy* 98 (1999): 161–186.

Broderick, John. *The Fugitives*. London: Weidenfeld & Nicolson, 1962.

Brown, Terence. "Two Post-Modern Novelists: Samuel Becket and Flann O'Brien". In *The Cambridge Companion to the Irish Novel*, edited by John Wilson Foster, 205–222. Cambridge: Cambridge University Press, 2006.

Browne, Nelson. *Sheridan Le Fanu*. London: Arthur Barker, 1951.

Browne, Ray B. "Historical Crime and Detection". In *A Companion to Crime Fiction*, edited by Charles J. Rzepka and Lee Horsley, 222–232. Oxford: Wiley-Blackwell, 2010.

Bruce, Jim. *Faithful Servant: A Memoir of Brian Cleeve*. Raleigh, NC: Lulu, 2007.

Bruen, Ken. *All the Old Songs and Nothing to Lose*. London: Minerva, 1994.

_____. *Funeral: Tales of Irish Morbidities*. Pittsburgh: P. Dorrance, 1991.

_____. *The Guards*. Dublin: Brandon, 2001.

_____. *The Hackman Blues*. London: The Do-Not-Press, 1997.

_____. *Her Last Call to Louis MacNeice*. London: Serpent's Tail, 1998.

_____. *Martyrs*. London: Minerva, 1994

_____. *The McDead*. London: The Do-Not-Press, 2000.

_____. *Rilke on Black*. London: Serpent's Tail, 1996.

_____. *Shades of Grace*. Upton-Upon-Severn: Images, 1993.

_____. *Sherri and Other Stories*. London: Adelphi, 1994.

_____. *Taming the Alien*. London: The Do-Not-Press, 1999.

_____. *The Time of Serena-May & Upon the Third Cross and Other Stories*. London: Adelphi, 1994.

_____. *A White Arrest*. London: The Do-Not-Press, 1998.

Butts, Dennis. "The Hunter and the Hunted: The Suspense Novels of John Buchan". In *Spy Thrillers*, edited by Clive Bloom, 44–58. London: Macmillan, 1990.

Caprani, Vincent. *Murder Paints a Portrait*. Dunlaoghaire: Glendale, 1992.

Carleton, William. *The Black Prophet: A Tale of the Irish Famine*. London: Simms and M'Intyre, 1847.

_____. *Fardorougha, The Miser*. 1838, Belfast: Appletree Press, 1993.

Carson, Paul. *Cold Steel*. London: Arrow, 1998.

_____. *Final Duty*. London: William Heinemann, 2000.

_____. *Scalpel*. London: Arrow, 1997.

Cawelti, John. *Adventure, Mystery, and Romance*. Chicago: Chicago University Press, 1976.

Cawelti, John and Bruce A. Rosenberg. *The Spy Story*. Chicago and London: Chicago University Press, 1987.

Chaigneau, William. *The History of Jack Connor. Second Edition*, 2 vols. (London: W. Johnston, 1753).

Chan, Winnie. "The Linked Excitements of L. T. Meade and ... in the *Strand Magazine*". In *Scribbling Women and the Short Story Form: Approaches by*

*American and British Women Writers*, edited by Ellen Burton Harrington, 60–73. New York: Peter Lang, 2008.

Chandler, F. W. *The Literature of Roguery*. Boston and New York: Mifflin & Co., 1907.

Chaussinand, Christelle. "Love and Love of One's Fatherland: Aspects of Patriotic 'Ex-Istences' in Sean O'Faolain's Short Story 'The Patriot'". *Journal of the Short Story in English*, 34 (2000): 139–151.

Childers, Erskine. *The Riddle of the Sands*. London: Wordsworth, 1903.

Clarke, Shaun. *Death on Gibraltar*. London: Bloomsbury, 1994.

_____. *Red Hand*. London: Hodder, 1998.

_____. *Sniper Fire in Belfast* (1993, London: HarperCollins, 2016), Kindle, accessed 12 January 2019.

_____. *Underworld* (1997, London: W. A. Harbison, 2014), Kindle, accessed 12 January 2019.

Cleeve, Brian. *Assignment to Vengeance*. London: Hammond, Hammond & Co., 1961.

_____. *Cry of Morning*. London: Michael Joseph, 1971.

_____. *Dark Blood Dark Terror*. London: Hammond, 1965.

_____. *Death of a Painted Lady*. London: Hammond, Hammond & Co., 1962.

_____. *Death of a Wicked Servant*. London: Hammond, Hammond & Co., 1963.

_____. *Exit from Prague*. London: Corgi, 1970.

_____. *The Judas Goat*. London: Hammond, 1966.

_____. *Violent Death of a Bitter Englishman*. New York: Random House, 1967.

_____. *Vote X for Treason*. London: William Collins, 1964.

_____. *You Must Never Go Back*. New York: Random House, 1968.

Cliff, Brian. *Irish Crime Fiction*. London: Palgrave Macmillan, 2018.

Collins, Michael. *Emerald Underground*. London: Phoenix House, 1998.

_____. *The Keepers of Truth*. London: Phoenix, 2000.

_____. *The Life and Times of a Tea Boy*. London: Phoenix, 1994.

Connolly, John. *Dark Hollow*. London: Hodder, 2000.

_____. *Every Dead Thing*. London: Hodder, 1999.

_____. "No Blacks, No Dogs, No Crime Writers: Ireland and the Mystery". In *Down These Green Streets: Irish Crime Writing in the 21st Century*, edited by Declan Burke, 39–57. Dublin: Liberties, 2011.

Conyers, Dorothea. *The Experiments of Ganymede Brown*. London: Hutchinson, 1917.

_____. *Grey Brother*. London: Hutchinson, 1927.

_____. *Hunting and Hunted*. London: Hutchinson, 1930.

_____. *Lady Elverton's Emeralds*. London: Hutchinson, 1909.

_____. *A Mixed Pack*. London: Methuen, 1915.

Craig, Patricia. *Brian Moore: A Biography*. London: Bloomsbury, 2002.

Craig, Patricia and Mary Cadogan. *The Lady Investigates: Women Detectives and Spies in Fiction*. London: Victor Gollancz, 1981.

Crawford, Richard. *Fall When Hit*. London: Mandarin, 1993.

_____. *The Minstrel Boy*. London: Mandarin, 1994.

Cregan, Conor. *Chrissie*. Dublin: Poolbeg, 1992.

_____. *First Strike*. London: Hodder & Stoughton, 1999.

_____. *Ground Zero*. London: Hodder & Stoughton, 1998.

_____. *House of Fire*. London: Hodder & Stoughton, 1995.

_____. *The Poison Stream*. Dublin: Poolbeg, 1993.

_____. *Valkyrie*. London: Hodder & Stoughton, 1996.

Crofts, Freeman Wills. *The 12.30 from Croydon*. London: Hodder & Stoughton, 1934.

_____. *The Affair at Little Wokeham*. London: Hodder & Stoughton, 1943.

_____. *Antidote to Venom*. London: Hodder & Stoughton, 1938.

_____. *Anything to Declare?* London: Hodder & Stoughton, 1957.

_____. *The Box Office Murders*. London: Collins, 1929.

_____. *The Cask*. London: Penguin, 1920.

_____. *Crime at Guildford*. London: Penguin, 1935.

_____. *Death of a Train*. London: Hodder & Stoughton, 1946.

_____. *Death on the Way*. London: Collins, 1932.

_____. *The End of Andrew Harrison*. London: Hodder & Stoughton, 1938.

_____. *Enemy Unseen*. London: Hodder & Stoughton, 1945.

_____. *Fatal Venture*. London: Hodder & Stoughton, 1939.

_____. *French Strikes Oil*. London: Hodder & Stoughton, 1952.

_____. *Golden Ashes*. London: Chivers Black Dagger Crime, 1940.

_____. *The Groote Park Murder*. Thirsk: House of Stratus, 1923.

_____. *The Hog's Back Mystery*. Thirsk. House of Stratus, 1933.

_____. *Inspector French and the Cheyne Mystery*. London: Penguin, 1926.

_____. *Inspector French and the Starvel Tragedy*. London: Collins, 1927.

_____. *Inspector French's Greatest Case*. Edinburgh: Collins, 1925.

_____. *James Tarrant, Adventurer*. London: Hodder & Stoughton, 1941.

_____. *The Losing Game*. Bath: Lythway Press, 1941.

_____. *The Loss of the Jane Vosper*. London: Penguin, 1936.

_____. *Man Overboard!* New York: Dodd, Mead & Co., 1936.

_____. *Many a Slip*. London: Hodder & Stoughton, 1955.

_____. *Murderers Make Mistakes*. London: Hodder & Stoughton, 1947.

_____. *Mystery in the Channel*. London: Penguin, 1931.

_____. *The Mystery of the Sleeping Car Express and Other Stories*. Bath: Chivers Black Dagger Crime, 1956.

_____. *Mystery on Southampton Water*. London: Hodder & Stoughton, 1934.

_____. *The Pit-Prop Syndicate*. London: Collins, 1922.

_____. *The Ponson Case*. New York: Dodd, Mead & Co., 1921.

_____. *The Sea Mystery*. London: Penguin, 1928.

_____. *Silence for the Murderer*. London: Hodder & Stoughton, 1949.

_____. *Sir John Magill's Last Journey*. London: Penguin, 1930.

_____. *Young Robin Brand Detective*. London: University of London Press, 1947.

Cromie, Robert. *The Crack of Doom*. London: Digby & Long, 1895.          ·

_____. *The Lost Liner*. Clough, Co. Down: Avarard, 1898.

_____. *The Romance of Poisons: Being Weird Episodes from Life*. London: Jarrold and Sons, 1903.

Cronin, John. *The Anglo-Irish Novel, Volume One: The Nineteenth Century*. Belfast: Appletree Press, 1980.

Cunningham, Peter. *The Bear's Requiem*. London: Michael Joseph, 1989.

_____. *Hostile Bid*. London: Michael Joseph, 1991.

_____. *Noble Lord*. New York: Stein & Day, 1986.

_____. *Tapes of the River Delta*. London: Arrow, 1995.

_____. *The Snow Bees*. London: Michael Joseph, 1988.

_____. *Who Trespass Against Us*. London: Century, 1994.

Curtis, Robert. *The Irish Police Officer. Comprising the Identification and Other Tales, Founded upon Remarkable Trials in Ireland*. London: Ward, Lock & Co., 1861.

Cusack, Mary Francis. *Who Fired the First Shot? Or Ned Rusheen: An Irish Story*. Dublin: M. H. Gill & Son, 1883.

Daly, Nicholas. "Fiction, Theatre and Early Cinema". In *The Cambridge Companion to Popular Fiction*, edited by David Glover and Scott McCracken, 33–49. Cambridge: Cambridge University Press, 2012.

Danielsson, Karin Molander. *The Dynamic Detective: Special Interest and Seriality in Contemporary Detective Series*. Uppsala: Diss Acta Universitatis Upsaliensis, 2002.

Davison, Philip. *The Crooked Man*. London: Jonathan Cape, 1997.

_____. *McKenzie's Friend*. London: Jonathan Cape, 2000.

Dawson, Janis. "'Write a little bit every day': L. T. Meade, Self-Representation, and the Professional Woman Writer". *Victorian Review* 35, no. 1 (2009): 132–152.

Day-Lewis, Cecil. *The Buried Day*. London: Chatto & Windus, 1960.

Day-Lewis, Sean. *C. Day-Lewis: An English Literary Life*. London: Weidenfeld & Nicolson, 1980.

Deane, Seamus. *Reading in the Dark*. London: Jonathan Cape, 1996.

_____. *A Short History of Irish Literature*. Notre Dame, IN: University of Notre Dame Press, 1986.

Dillon, Ellis. *Death at Crane's Court*. New York: Harper Perennial, 1953.

_____. *Death in the Quadrangle*. Boulder & Lyons: Rue Morgue Press, 1956.

_____. *Sent to His Account*. Boulder & Lyons: Rue Morgue Press, 1954.

Dillon, Martin. *The Serpent's Tail*. London: Fourth Estate, 1995.

Douglas, Aileen. "The Novel before 1800". In *The Cambridge Companion to the Irish Novel*, edited by John Wilson Foster, 22–38. Cambridge: Cambridge University Press, 2006.

Dowling, Richard. *A Baffling Quest*. London: Ward & Downey, 1891.

_____. *Catmur's Caves*. London: Adam & Charles Black, 1892.

_____. *The Duke's Sweetheart*. London: Ward & Downey, 1881.

_____. *The Fate of Luke Ormond*. London: Hurst & Blackett, 1905.

_____. *The Hidden Flame*. London: Tinsley Brothers, 1885.

_____. *An Isle of Surrey*. London: Ward & Downey, 1889.

_____. *The Last Call*. London: Tinsley Brothers, 1884.

_____. *Miracle Gold*. London: Richard Bent, 1888.

_____. *The Mystery of Killard*. Londoon: Tinsley Brothers, 1879.

_____. *Old Corcoran's Money*. London: Chatto & Windus, 1897.

_____. *A Sapphire Ring and Other Stories*. London: Tinsley Brothers, 1882.

_____. *Sweet Inisfail*. London: Tinsley Brothers, 1882.

_____. *Tempest*. London: Tinsley Brothers, 1885.

_____. *The Weird Sisters*. London: Tinsley Brothers, 1880.

_____. *Under St. Paul's*. London: British Library Historical Print Reproductions, 1885.

Duffaud, Briege. *A Wreath Upon the Dead*. Dublin: Poolbeg, 1993.

Dunne, John J. "The Case of the Broken Ring", *Ireland's Own*, 11 March 1973, 11.

Dunsany, Lord. *The Little Tales of Smethers and Other Stories*. London: Jarrolds, 1952.

Easterman, Daniel. *Brotherhood of the Tomb*. London: Grafton, 1989.

_____. *Day of Wrath*. London: HarperCollins, 1995.

_____. *The Final Judgement*. London: HarperCollins, 1999.

_____. *Incarnation*. London: HarperCollins, 1998.

_____. *K*. London: HarperCollins, 1997.

_____. *The Matrix*. London: HarperCollins, 1994.

_____. *Naomi's Room*. London: Constable & Robinson, 1991.

_____. *Name of the Beast*. London: Grafton, 1992.

_____. *Night of the Seventh Darkness*. London: Grafton, 1991.

_____. *The Ninth Buddha*. London: Grafton, 1998.

_____. *The Seventh Sanctuary*. London: Grafton, 1987.

Edgeworth, Maria. *Popular Tales*. London: J. Johnson, 1804.

Edwards, P. D. "Frances Cashel Hoey". In *Victorian Fiction Research Guides*, no. 8.

Edwards, Martin. *The Golden Age of Murder: The Mystery of the Writers Who Invented the Modern Detective Story*. London: HarperCollins, 2015.

Edwards, Ruth Dudley. *The Anglo-Irish Murders*. London: Collins, 2000.

_____. *Clubbed to Death*. London: Gollancz Crime, 1992.

_____. *Corridors of Death*. London: Gollancz Crime, 1981.

_____. *Matricide at St. Martha's*. London: HarperCollins, 1994.

_____. *Murder in a Cathedral*. London: HarperCollins, 1996.

_____. *Publish and Be Murdered*. London: HarperCollins, 1998.

_____. *The Saint Valentine's Day Murders*. 2nd edn. Scottsdale, AZ: Poisoned Pen, 2011.

_____. *The School of English Murder*. London: Gollancz Crime, 1990.

_____. *Ten Lords A-Leaping*. London: HarperCollins, 1995.

Ekin, Des. *Stone Heart*. Dublin: O'Brien Press, 1999.

Escarbelt, Bernard. "William Chaigneau's Jack Connor. A Literary Image of the Irish Peasant". In *Rural Ireland, Real Ireland*, edited by Jacqueline Genet, 51–57. Gerard's Cross: Colin Smythe, 1996.

Evans, Curtis. *Masters of the "Humdrum" Mystery: Cecil John Charles Street, Freeman Wills Crofts, Alfred Walter Stewart and the British Detective Novel, 1920–1961*. Jefferson, NC and London: McFarland & Company, 2012.

Farquarson, Danah. "Resisting Genre and Type: Narrative Strategy and Instability in Danny Morrison's *The Wrong Man* and Seamus Deane's *Reading in the Dark*". In *Writing Ulster: Northern Narratives*, edited by Bill Lazenbatt, 89–112. Jordanstown: University of Ulster Press, 1999.

Filippi, Jaques. "'Zen' Bruen: The Dark Knight Resists", The House of Crime and Mystery, 2011, <http://houseofcrimeandmystery.blogspot.com/2012/08/interviewdiscussion-with-ken-bruen.html>, accessed 18 April 2015.

Fitzgerald, Nigel. *Affairs of Death*. London: Collins, 1967.

_____. *Black Welcome*. New York: Macmillan, 1961.

_____. *The Candles Are All Out*. London: Collins, 1960.

_____. *The Day of the Adder*. London: Collins, 1963.

_____. *Ghost in the Making*. London: Collins, 1960.

_____. *The House is Falling*. London: Fontana, 1955.

_____. *Imagine a Man*. London: Fontana, 1956.

_____. *Midsummer Malice*. London: Fontana, 1953.

_____. *The Rosy Pastor*. London: Fontana, 1954.

_____. *The Student Body*. London: Collins, 1958.

_____. *Suffer a Witch*. London: Collins, 1958.

_____. *This Won't Hurt You*. New York: Macmillan, 1959.

Flint, Kate (ed.). *The Cambridge History of Victorian Literature*. Cambridge: Cambridge University Press, 2012.

Forrest, H. J. *Murder by the Book*. Dublin: Gill & Macmillan, 1992.

_____. *Publish or Perish*. Dunlaoghaire: Glendale, 1991.

Forshaw, Barry. *Crime Fiction: A Reader's Guide*. Harpenden: Oldcastle Books, 2019.

Foster, John Wilson. *The Cambridge Companion to the Irish Novel*. Cambridge: Cambridge University Press, 2006.

\_\_\_\_\_. *Irish Novels 1890–1940: New Bearings in Culture and Fiction*. Oxford: Oxford University Press, 2008.

Fuller, James Franklin. *John Orlebar, CLK*. London: Smith, Elder & Co., 1878.

Furniss, Harry. *Poverty Bay: A Nondescript Novel*. London: Chapman & Hall, 1905.

Gallagher, Brian. *Invincible*. Dublin: Town House, 1993.

Galvin, Jim. *Bog Warriors*. Dublin: Town House, 2000.

Gardiner, Marguerite, Lady Blessington. *Meredith*. London: Longman, Brown, Green, & Longmans, 1843.

Garrido Ardila, J. A. *The Picaresque Novel in Western Literature*. Cambridge, Cambridge University Press, 2015.

Gébler, Carlo. *The Cure*. London: Hamish Hamilton, 1994.

\_\_\_\_\_. *How to Murder a Man*. London: Little, Brown, 1998.

\_\_\_\_\_. *Work & Play*. London: Hamish Hamilton, 1987.

Gethins, Mary. *Catholic Police Officers in Northern Ireland: Voices out of Silence* Manchester: Manchester University Press, 2011.

Gibson, Maggie. *Alice Little and the Big Girl's Blouse*. London: Victor Gollancz, 1999.

\_\_\_\_\_. *Deadly Serious*. Dublin: Poolbeg, 1997.

\_\_\_\_\_. *First Holy Chameleon*. London: Victor Gollancz, 2000.

\_\_\_\_\_. *The Flight of Lucy Spoon*. London: Victor Gollancz, 1999.

\_\_\_\_\_. *The Longest Fraud*. Dublin: Poolbeg, 1996.

Gill, Bartholomew. *Death of an Ardent Bibliophile*. London: Macmillan, 1995.

\_\_\_\_\_. *Death on a Cold, Wild River*. London: Macmillan, 1993.

\_\_\_\_\_. *The Death of an Irish Consul*. New York: Avon, 1977.

\_\_\_\_\_. *The Death of an Irish Lass*. New York: Avon, 1978.

\_\_\_\_\_. *The Death of an Irish Lover*. New York: Avon, 2000.

\_\_\_\_\_. *The Death of an Irish Politician*. New York: Avon, 1977.

\_\_\_\_\_. *The Death of an Irish Sea Wolf*. London: Macmillan, 1996.

\_\_\_\_\_. *The Death of an Irish Tinker*. New York: Avon, 1997.

\_\_\_\_\_. *The Death of an Irish Tradition*. New York: Avon, 1979.

\_\_\_\_\_. *The Death of a Joyce Scholar*. New York: Avon, 1989.

\_\_\_\_\_. *The Death of Love*. London: Macmillan, 1992.

\_\_\_\_\_. *McGarr and the Legacy of a Woman Scorned*. New York: Viking, 1986.

\_\_\_\_\_. *McGarr and the Method of Descartes*. New York: Viking, 1984.

\_\_\_\_\_. *McGarr and the P.M. of Belgrave Square*. New York: Viking, 1983.

Glover, David. "Publishing, History, Genre". In *The Cambridge Companion to Popular Fiction*, edited by David Glover and Scott McCracken, 15–32. Cambridge: Cambridge University Press, 2012.

Gorman, Ed. et al. *Murder Most Irish*, New York: Barnes & Noble, 1996.

Grant, John. "'I Was Too Chickenhearted to Publish It': Seán O'Faoláin, Displacement and History Re-Written". *Estudios Irlandeses*, 12 (2017): 50–59.

Grecorek, Jean. "Fables of Foreclosure: Tana French's Police Procedurals of Recessionary Ireland". In *Class and Culture in Crime Fiction*, edited by Julie H. Kim, 149–174. Jefferson, NC: McFarland & Company, 2014.

Green F. L. *Odd Man Out*. London: Michael Joseph, 1945.

Grella, George. "The Formal Detective Novel". In *Detective Fiction: A Collection of Critical Essays*, edited by Robin W. Winks, 84–102. Englewood Cliffs, NJ: Prentice-Hall, 1980.

_____. "The Hard-Boiled Detective Novel". In *Detective Fiction: A Collection of Critical Essays. Twentieth Century Views*, edited by Robin W. Winks, 103–120. Englewood Cliffs, NJ: Prentice-Hall, 1980.

Griffin, Gerald. *The Collegians*. 1829, Belfast: Appletree Press, 1992.

Haining, Peter. *Great Irish Detective Stories*, London: Pan Books, 1993.

Hall, Wayne "A Tory Periodical in a Time of Famine: *The Dublin University Magazine*, 1845–1850". In *The Great Famine and the Irish Diaspora in America*, edited by Arthur Gribben, 48–65. Boston, MA: University of Massachusetts Press, 1999.

Halloran, Jennifer A. "The Ideology Behind *The Sorceress of the Strand*: Gender, Race and Criminal Witchcraft". *English Literature in Translation* 2 (2002): 176–194.

Hamilton, C. J. "Tracked by His Crime". *Ireland's Own* 1, nos. 1–9 (1902–3).

Hand, Derek. *A History of the Irish Novel*. Cambridge: Cambridge University Press, 2011.

Harkness, Bruce. "The Fiction of Elizabeth Bowen". *The English Journal* 44, no. 9 (1955): 499–506.

Harkness, Lucy. *The Happy Pigs*. Belfast: Blackstaff, 1999.

Haut W. *Neon Noir: Contemporary American Crime Fiction*. London: Serpent's Tail, 1999.

Haycraft, Howard. *The Art of the Mystery Story. A Collection of Critical Essays*. New York: Carrol & Graf, 1946.

_____. *Murder for Pleasure: The Life and Times of the Detective Story*. New York: Carroll & Graf, 1941.

Head, Richard. *The English Rogue*. London: Henry Marsh, 1665.

Hedges, John. "Danny Morrison's West Belfast, A Story of a Community in Struggle". *An Phoblacht*, <https://www.anphoblacht.com/contents/25032>, accessed 1 June 2015.

Heidemann, Birte. *Post-Agreement Northern Irish Literature*. London: Palgrave Macmillan, 2016.

Herron, Shaun. *The Hound and the Fox and the Harper*. London: Coronet, 1970.

_____. *Miro*. London: Coronet, 1969.

_____. *Through the Dark and Hairy Wood*. London: Coronet, 1972.

_____. *The Whore-Mother*. New York: M. Evans, 1973.

Higgins, Jack. *Angel of Death*. London: Harper, 1995.

_____ [Martin Fallon]. *The Bormann Testament [The Testament of Casper Schultz]*. New York: Berkley, 1962.

_____. *Brought in Dead*. London: John Long, 1967.

_____. *Cold Harbour*. London: Heinemann, 1990.

_____. *Comes the Dark Stranger*. London: John Long, 1962.

_____. *Confessional*. London: Collins, 1985.

_____. *The Cry of the Hunter*. London: Harper, 1960.

_____. *The Dark Side of the Island*. London: Harper, 1963.

_____. *Dark Side of the Street*. London: John Long, 1967.

_____. *Day of Judgment*. London: William Collins, 1978.

_____. *Day of Reckoning*. London: HarperCollins, 2000.

_____. *Drink with the Devil*. London: Harper, 1996.

_____. *The Eagle Has Flown*. London: Penguin, 1991.

_____. *The Eagle Has Landed*. London: Penguin, 1975.

_____. *East of Desolation*. London: Hodder & Stoughton, 1968.

_____. *Eye of the Storm*. London: Signet, 1992.

_____. *A Fine Night for Dying*. London: John Long, 1969.

_____. *Flight of Eagles*. London: Harper, 1998.

_____. *A Game for Heroes*. London: Hutchinson, 1979.

_____. *Hell is Always Today*. London: Mayflower, 1968.

_____. *Hell is Too Crowded*. London: Coronet, 1962.

_____. *In the Hour before Midnight*. New York: Berkley, 1969.

_____. *The Iron Tiger*. London: John Long, 1966.

_____. *The Keys of Hell*. London: Abelard-Sshuman, 1965.

_____. *The Khufra Run*. New York: Berkley, 1972.

_____. *The Last Place God Made*. London: Harper, 1971.

_____. *Night of the Fox*. London: Harper, 1986.

_____. *Night Judgement at Sinos*. London: Hodder & Stoughton, 1970.

_____. *On Dangerous Ground*. London: Harper, 1994.

_____. *Passage by Night*. London: Harper, 1964.

_____. *Pay the Devil*. London: Barrie & Rockcliffe, 1962.

_____. *A Prayer for the Dying*. London: Harper, 1973.

_____. *The President's Daughter*. New York: Berkley, 1997.

_____. *The Run to Moring (Bloody Passage)*. New York: Stein & Day, 1974.

_____. *Sad Wind from the Sea*. London: Harper, 1959.

_____. *The Savage Day*. New York: Open Road, 1972.

_____. *A Season in Hell*. London: Harper, 1989.

_____. *Sheba*. London: Harper, 1995.

_____. *Solo*. London: William Collins, 1980.

_____. *Storm Warning*. London: Collins, 1976.

_____. *The Thousand Faces of the Night*. London: Arrow, 1961.

_____. *Thunder Point*. London: Signet, 1993.

_____. *To Catch a King*. London: Arrow, 1980.

_____. *Toll for the Brave*. London: John Long, 1971.

_____. *The Valhalla Exchange*. New York: Stein & Day, 1976.

_____. *The Violent Enemy*. London: HarperCollins, 1966.

_____. *The White House Connection*. London: Michael Joseph, 1999.

_____. *The Wrath of God*. London: Macmillan, 1971.

Hoey, Frances Cashel. *All or Nothing*. London: Hurst and Blackett, 1879.

_____. *A House of Cards*. London: Tinsley Brothers, 1868.

Hogan, Robert. *Eimar O'Duffy*. Cranbury, NJ: Associated Universities Press, 1972.

Hollingworth, Brian. *Maria Edgeworth's Irish Writing: Language, History, Politics*. Houndmills: Macmillan, 1997.

Holton, Leonard. *A Corner of Paradise*. New York: St. Martin's Press, 1977.

_____. *Deliver us from Wolves*. New York: Dodd, Mead, 1963.

_____. *The Devil to Play*. New York: Dodd, Mead, 1974.

_____. *Flowers by Request*. New York: Dodd, Mead, 1963.

_____. *The Mirror of Hell*. New York: Dodd, Mead, 1972.

_____. *Out of the Depths*. New York: Dodd, Mead, 1966.

_____. *A Pact with Satan*. New York: Dodd, Mead, 1960.

_____. *A Problem in Angels*. New York: Dodd, Mead, 1970.

_____. *The Saint Maker*. New York: Dodd, Mead, 1959.

_____. *Secret of the Doubting Saint*. New York: Dodd, Mead, 1961.

_____. *A Touch of Jonah*. New York: Dodd, Mead, 1968.

Hone, Joseph. *The Flowers of the Forest*. London: Faber & Faber, 1980.

_____. *Goodbye Again*. Dublin: The Lilliput Press, 2011.

_____. *The Paris Trap*. London: Faber & Faber, 1977.

_____. *The Private Sector*. London: Faber & Faber, 1971.

_____. *The Sixth Directorate*. London: Faber & Faber, 1975.

_____. *The Valley of the Fox*. London: Faber & Faber, 1982.

Horsley, Lee. "From Sherlock Holmes to the Present". In *A Companion to Crime Fiction*, edited by Charles J. Rzepka and Lee Horsley, 28–42. Oxford: Wiley-Blackwell, 2010.

_____. *The Noir Thriller*. London: Palgrave Macmillan, 2001.

_____. *Twentieth-Century Crime Fiction*. Oxford: Oxford University Press, 2005.

Jeffares, A. Norman. *Macmillan History of Literature: Anglo-Irish Literature*. London: Gill & Macmillan, 1982.

Johnston, Jennifer. *Shadows on Our Skin*. London: Hamish Hamilton, 1977.

_____. *The Illusionist*. London: Sinclair-Stevenson, 1995.

\_\_\_\_\_. *The Railway Station Man*. London: Hamish Hamilton, 1984.

Johnstone, Charles. *The Adventures of Anthony Varnish*. London: William Lane, 1786.

Jones, Clara. "'Mystery at the Lilacs' (1938): Elizabeth Bowen's Thriller Serial for *Home and Country*". *Literature and History* 27, no. 1 (2018): 3–27.

Joshi, S. T. *Lord Dunsany: Master of the Anglo-Irish Imagination*. Westport, CT: Greenwood Press, 1995.

Joyce, Joe. *Off the Record*. London: Heinemann, 1989.

\_\_\_\_\_. *The Trigger Man*. London: Heinemann, 1990.

Kavanagh, Dan. *Duffy*. London: Jonathan Cape, 1980.

\_\_\_\_\_. *Fiddle City*. London: Jonathan Cape, 1981.

\_\_\_\_\_. *Going to the Dogs*. London: Jonathan Cape, 1987.

\_\_\_\_\_. *Putting the Boot In*. London: Jonathan Cape, 1984.

Kayman, Martin. A. *From Baker Street to Bow Street: Mystery, Detection and Narrative*. London: Macmillan, 1992.

Kearney, Selskar. *The False Finger Tip*. Dublin: Maunsel & Roberts, 1921.

Keating, H. R. F. *Crime & Mystery: The 100 Best Books*. New York: Carroll & Graff, 1987.

Keightley, Samuel Robert. *A Man of Millions*. London: Cassell, 1901.

Kelleher, Margaret. "Prose Writing and Drama in English, 1830–1890: From Catholic Emancipation to the Fall of Parnell". In *The Cambridge History of Irish Literature*, vol. 1, edited by Margaret Kelleher and Philip O'Leary, 449–499. Cambridge: Cambridge University Press, 2006.

Kelly, Aaron. "'Ordered Dreams': Ideology and Utopia in the 'Troubles' Thriller". *BELLS* 11 (2000): 141–147.

\_\_\_\_\_. "The Thriller and Northern Ireland since 1969: Utterly Resigned Terror". *New Hibernia Review/ Iris Éireannach Nua* 11, no. 2 (2007): 156–158.

\_\_\_\_\_. "The Troubles with the Thriller: Northern Ireland, Political Violence and the Peace Process". In *The Edinburgh Companion to Twentieth-century British War Literature*, edited by Adam Piette and Mark Rawlinson, 508–515. Edinburgh: Edinburgh University press.

Kelly, Dermot. "Joycean Epiphany in Seamus Deane's *Reading in the Dark*". In *Moments of Moment: Aspects of the Literary Epiphany*, edited by Wim Tigges, 435–444. Amsterdan: Rodopi, 1999.

Kelly, John. *The Little Hammer*. London: Jonathan Cape, 2000.

Kelly, John. *The Polling of the Dead*. Dublin: Moytura Press, 1993.

Kemp, Sandra. "But One Isn't Murdered: Elizabeth Bowen's *The Little Girls*". In *Twentieth-Century Suspense*, edited by Clive Bloom, 130–142. London: Palgrave Macmillan, 1990.

Kenyon, Michael. *May You Die in Ireland*. New York: William Morrow, 1965.

\_\_\_\_\_. *A Sorry State*. New York: David McKay Company, 1974.

_____. *The 10,000 Welcomes*. London: William Collins, 1970.

Kennedy-Andrews, Elmer. "The Novel and the Northern Troubles". In *The Cambridge Companion to the Irish Novel*, edited by John Wilson Foster, 238–258. Cambridge: Cambridge University Press, 2006.

Kiberd, Declan. *Irish Classics*. London: Granta, 2000.

Kiely, Benedict. *Nothing Happens in Carmincross*. Boston: David R. Godene, 1986.

_____. *Proxopera*. London: Methuen, 1977.

Kilduff, Paul. The Dealer. London: Hodder & Stoughton, 2000.

_____. *Square Mile*. London: Hodder & Stoughton, 1999.

Kilfeather, Siobhán. "The Gothic Novel". In *The Cambridge Companion to the Irish Novel*, edited by John Wilson Foster, 78–96. Cambridge: Cambridge University Press, 2006.

Killeen, Jareth. *The Emergence of Irish Gothic Fiction: History, Origins, Theories*. Edinburgh: Edinburgh University Press, 2014.

Kincaid, Andrew. "Detecting Hope: Ken Bruen's Disenchnted P.I.". In *The Contemporary Irish Detective Novel*, edited by Elizabeth Mannion, 57–71. London: Palgrave Macmillan, 2016,

Kinealy, Christine. "Hidden from History: Fidelma of Cashel and Lost Female Values". In *The Sister Fidelma Mysteries: Essays on the Historical Novels of Peter Tremayne*, edited by Edward J. Rielly and David Robert Wooten, 50–59. Jefferson, NC: McFarland & Company, 2012.

Klein, Kathleen Gregory. *The Woman Detective: Gender and Genre*. 2nd edn. Urbana: University of Illinois, 1995.

Knight, Stephen. *Form and Ideology in Crime Fiction*. London: Macmillan, 1980.

_____. "The Golden Age". In *The Cambridge Companion to Crime Fiction*, edited by Martin Priestman, 77–94. Cambridge: Cambridge University Press, 2003.

_____. *The Mysteries of the Cities: Urban Crime Fiction in the Nineteenth Century*. Mcfarland & Company, 2012.

Kontou, Tatiana. "Sensation Fiction, Spiritualism and the Supernatural". In *The Cambridge Companion to Sensation Fiction*, edited by Andrew Mangham, 141–153. Cambridge: Cambridge University Press, 2013.

Kreilkamp, Vera. *The Anglo-Irish Novel and the Big House*. Syracuse, NY: Syracuse University Press, 1998.

Lawless, Emily. *Hurrish*. Edinburgh: Blackwood, 1886.

Le Fanu, Joseph Thomas Sheridan. *All in the Dark*. London: R. Bentley & Sons, 1866.

_____. *Checkmate*. London: R. Bentley & Sons, 1871.

_____. *A Chronicle of Golden Friars*. London: R. Bentley & Sons, 1871.

_____. *The Cock and Anchor*. Dublin: William Curry, 1845.

_____. *The Evil Guest*. London: R. Bentley & Sons, 1895.

_____. *The Fortunes of Colonel Torlough O'Brien*. Dublin: James McGlashan, 1847.

_____. *Ghost Stories and Tales of Mystery*. Dublin: James McGlashan, 1851.

_____. *Guy Deverell*. London: R. Bentley & Sons, 1865.

_____. *Haunted Lives*. London: R. Bentley & Sons, 1868.

_____. *The House by the Churchyard*. London: Willian Tinley, 1863.

_____. *In a Glass Darkly*. London: R. Bentley & Sons, 1872.

_____. *A Lost Name*. London: R. Bentley & Sons, 1868.

_____. *Madame Crowl's Ghost and Other Stories*. London: Wordsworth, 1994.

_____. *The Prelude*. London: R. Bentley & Sons, 1865.

_____. *The Purcell Papers*. London: R. Bentley & Sons, 1880.

_____. *The Rose and the Key*. London: R. Bentley & Sons, 1871.

_____. *Spalatro*. Ignacio Hills Press, 1843. Kindle, accessed 24 June 2019.

_____. *The Tenants of Malory*. London: Tinsley Brothers, 1867.

_____. *Uncle Silas*. London: R. Bentley & Sons, 1864.

_____. *The Watcher and Other Weird Stories*. London: Downey, 1894.

_____. *Willing to Die*. London: R. Bentley & Sons, 1873.

_____. *Wylder's Hand*. London: R. Bentley & Sons, 1864.

_____. *The Wyvern Mystery*. London: R. Bentley & Sons, 1869.

Leitch, Maurice. *The Liberty Lad*. 2nd edn. London: Panther, 1968.

_____. *Poor Lazarus*. Belfast: The Blackstaff Press, 1987.

_____. *Silver's City*. London: Secker & Warburg, 1981.

_____. *The Smoke King*. London: Vintage, 1998.

Leslie, Peter. *The Extremists*. London: New English Library, 1970.

Lever, Charles. *Confessions of Con Cregan: An Irish Gil Blas*. London: W. S. Orr, 1849.

Lines, Joe. "Contesting Masculinities in Thomas Amory's *The Life of John Buncle, Esq.* (1756–66)". *Journal for Eighteenth-Century Studies* 41, no. 3 (2018): 447–463.

Lusby, Jim (as James Kennedy) *Armed and Dangerous*. London: Heinemann, 1996.

_____. *Crazy Man Michael*. London: Victor Gollancz, 2000.

_____. *Flashback*. London: Victor Gollancz, 1996.

_____. *Kneeling at the Altar*. London: Victor Gollancz, 1998.

_____. *Making the Cut*. London: Victor Gollancz, 1995.

_____. (as James Kennedy) *Silent City*. London: William Heinemann, 1998.

Mackay, William. *Pro Patria: The Autobiography of an Irish Conspirator*. London: Remington, 1883.

MacKillop, James. "Ulster Violence in Fiction". In *Conflict in Ireland*, edited by E. Sullivan et al., 131–153. Gainesville, FL: Florida University Press, 1976.

Madden, Deirdre. *Hidden Symptoms*. London: Faber & Faber, 1986.

_____. *One by One in the Darkness*. London: Faber & Faber, 1996.

Magee, Patrick. *Gangsters or Guerrillas? Representation of Irish Republicans in "Troubles Fiction"*. Belfast: Beyond the Pale, 2001.

Malia, Jennifer. "Liam O'Flaherty's Disillusionment with Irish Revolutionary Martydom in *The Informer* and *the Assassin*". *Pacific Coast Philology* 44, no. 2 (2009): 191–204.

Mallot, Edward. "'There's No Good Riot Footage Any More': Waging Northern Ireland's Media War in Eoin McNamee's *Resurrection Man*". *New Hibernia Review/ Iris Éireannach Nua* 17, no. 3 (2013): 34–55.

Mandel, Ernest. *Delightful Murder: A Social History of the Crime Story*. Minneapolis, MN: Minnesota University Press, 1984.

Manning, Maurice. *Betrayal*. Dublin: Blackwater Press, 1997.

Mannion, Elizabeth. "Before the Tiger Roared: Bartholomew Gill's Ireland". In *Guilt Rules All: Irish Mystery, Detective, and Crime Fiction*, edited by Elizabeth Mannion and Brian Cliff, 26–39. Syracuse, NY: Syracuse University Press, 2020.

_____. (ed.). *The Contemporary Irish Detective Novel*. London: Palgrave Macmillan, 2016.

Mannion, Elizabeth, and Brian Cliff. *Guilt Rules All: Irish Mystery, Detective, and Crime Fiction*. Syracuse, NY: Syracuse University Press, 2020.

Martella, Maureen. *Annie's New Life*. London: Arrow, 2000.

Matheson, Steve. *Maurice Walsh, Storyteller*. Dingle: Brandon, 1985.

McAvoy, Sandra. "The 'Wild Irish Girl' in Selected Novels of L. T. Meade". In *Adolescence in Irish History*, edited by Catherine Cox and Susannah Riordan, 63–81. Palgrave Macmillan, 2015.

McBride, Frances. *Death in the Cathedral*. Dublin: Dublin Catholic Truth Society, 1946.

McCabe, Eugene. *Deaths and Nightingales*. London: Viking, 1992.

_____. *Victims: A Tale from Fermanagh*. London: Gollancz, 1976.

McCaffrey, K. T. *Killing Time*. Dublin: Marino, 2000.

_____. *Revenge*. Dublin: Marino, 1999.

McCormac, Rory. *Malpractice*. London: Arrow, 2000.

_____. *Outbreak*. London: Arrow, 1998.

_____. *Playing Dead (Snapshot)* (1993). London: Arrow, 1996.

McCormack, W. J. "Irish Gothic and After (1820–1945)". In *The Field Day Anthology of Irish Writing: Volume II*, edited by Seamus Deane, 831–949. Derry: Field Day Publications, 1991.

_____. *Sheridan Le Fanu*. Oxford: Oxford University Press, 1980.

McDonald. *Sacrifice of Fools*. London: Cox & Wyman, 1996. Kindle, accessed 14 December 2020.

McDonnell, Vincent. *The Broken Commandment*. London: Penguin, 1988.

McEldowney, Eugene. *A Kind of Homecoming*. London: Mandarin, 1994.

_____. *Murder at Piper's Gut*. London: Heinemann, 1997.

_____. *The Sad Case of Harpo Higgins*. London: Heinemann, 1996.

_____. *A Stone of the Heart*. London: Mandarin, 1995.

McGinley, Patrick. *Bishop's Delight*. Dublin: New Island, 2016.

_____. *Bogmail*. London: Flamingo, 1978.

_____. *The Devil's Diary*. London: Jonathan Cape, 1988.

_____. *Foggage*. London: Weidenfeld & Nicolson, 1983.

_____. *Fox Prints*. London: Weidenfeld & Nicolson, 1983.

_____. *The Red Men*. London: Jonathan Cape, 1987.

_____. *The Trick of the Ga Bolga*. London: St. Martin's Press, 1985.

McKinty, Adrian. "Odd Men Out". In *Down These Green Streets: Irish Crime Writing in the 21st Century*, edited by Declan Burke, 96–105. Dublin: Liberties Press, 2011.

McLaverty, Bernard. *Cal*. London: Jonathan Cape, 1983.

_____. *Lamb*. London: Cape, 1980.

McLynn, Pauline. *Something for the Weekend*. London: Headline, 2000.

McMahon, Blair. *Nights in Armour*. Belfast: Ulster Society, 1993.

McNamee, Eoin. *Resurrection Man*. London: Picador, 1994.

McNiffe, Liam. *A History of the Garda Síochána: A Social History of the Force 1922–1952, with an Overview of the Years 1952–1997*. Dublin: Wolfhound Press, 1997.

Meade, Glenn. *Brandenburg*. London: Hodder & Stoughton, 1994.

_____. *The Sands of Sakkara*. London: Hodder & Stoughton, 1999.

_____. *Snow Wolf*. London: Hodder & Stoughton, 1995.

Meade, L. T. *An Adventuress*. London: Chatto & Windus, 1899.

_____. *The Blue Diamond*. London: Chatto & Windus, 1901.

_____. *The Brotherhood of the Seven Kings*. London: Ward, Lock & Co., 1899.

_____. *A Double Revenge*. London: Digby, Long, 1902.

_____. *Dr. Rumsey's Patient: A Very Strange Story*. New York: Hurst & Company, 1896.

_____. *The Gold Star Line*. London: Ward, Lock & Co., 1899.

_____. *The House of Black Magic*. London: F. V. White, 1912.

_____. *In an Iron Grip*. London: Chatto & Windus 1894.

_____. *The Lost Square*. London: Ward, Lock & Co., 1902.

_____. *A Master of Mysteries*. London: Ward, Lock & Co., 1898.

_____. *The Medicine Lady*. London: Cassell, 1893.

_____. *Micah Faraday: Adventurer*. London: Ward, Lock & Co., 1910.

_____. *The Necklace of Parmona*. London: Ward, Lock & Co., 1909.

_____. *On the Brink of a Chasm: A Record of Plot and Passion*. London: Chatto & Windus, 1898.

_____. *A Princess of the Gutter*. London: Wells Gardner, Darzon, 1895.

_____. *A Ring of Rubies*. London: A. D. Innes, 1892.

_____. *The Sanctuary Club*. London: Ward, Lock & Co., 1900.

_____. *Silenced*. London: Ward, Lock & Co., 1904.

_____. *The Siren*. London: F. V. White, 1898.

_____. *A Son of Ishmael*. London: F. V. White, 1896.

_____. *Stories from the Diary of a Doctor*. London: George Newnes, 1894.

_____. *Stories from the Diary of a Doctor (Second Series)*. London: Bliss, Sands and Foster, 1896.

_____. *The Voice of the Charmer*. London: Greening, 1910.

Meade, L. T. and Robert K. Douglas. *Under the Dragon Throne*. London: Gardner, Darton & Co., 1897.

Meade, L. T. and Robert Eustace. *The Detections of Miss Cusack*, edited by Douglas C. Greene and Jack Adrian, 1892. Shelbourne, Ontario: The Battered Silicon Dispatch Box, 1998.

_____. *The Oracle of Maddox Street*. London: Ward, Lock & Co., 1904.

_____. *The Sorceress of the Strand*. London: Ward, Lock & Co., 1903.

Meade, L. T. and Clifford Halifax. *A Race with the Sun*. London: Ward, Lock & Co., 1901

_____. *Where the Shoe Pinches*. London: W. R. Chambers, 1900.

Meier, William and Ian Campbell Ross. "Editor's Introduction: Irish Crime since 1921". *Éire-Ireland* 49, no. 1 & 2 (2014): 7–21.

Messent, Peter. "The Police Novel". In *A Companion to Crime Fiction*, edited by Charles J. Rzepka and Lee Horsley, 175–186. Oxford: Wiley-Blackwell, 2010.

Michaels, S. J. *Run for Cover*. New York: Harper & Row, 1988.

_____. *Dieback*. London: Macmillan, 1991.

_____. *The Heir*. London: Macmillan, 1994.

Miller, Elizabeth Carolyn. "'Shrewd Women of Business': Madame Rachel, Victorian consumerism, and L. T. Meade's *The Sorceress of the Strand*". *Victorian Literature and Culture* 34 (2006): 311–332.

Mitchell, Sandy. "Children's Reading and the Culture of Girlhood. The Case of L. T. Meade". *Victorian Popular Culture* 17 (1989): 53–63. *JSTOR*, <https://www.jstor.org/stable/25057845>, accessed accessed 19 May 2022.

Molloy, Frances. *No Mate for Magpie*. London: Virago, 1985.

Molloy, J. Fitzgerald. *An Excellent Knave*. London: Hutchinson, 1893.

Moore, Brian. *A Bullet for My Lady*. New York: Fawcett Gold Medal, 1955.

_____. *French for Murder*. New York: Fawcett Gold Medal, 1954.

_____. *Intent to Kill*. London: Eyre & Spottiswoode, 1956.

_____. *Lies of Silence*. London: Vintage, 1990.

_____. *Murder in Majorca*. London: Eyre & Spottiswoode, 1958.

_____. *The Doctor's Wife*. London: Flamingo, 1976.

_____. *The Executioners*. Toronto: Harlequin, 1951.

_____. *This Gun for Gloria*. New York: Fawcett Gold Medal, 1956.

_____. *Wreath for a Redhead*. Toronto: Harlequin, 1951.

Moore, Desmond. *Call Me Evil*. Dunlaoghaire: Glendale, 1992.

_____. *Rogan*. Dunlaoghaire: Glendale, 1992.

Moore, Thomas. *Memoirs of Captain Rock: The Irish Chieftain with Some Account of His Ancestors*, edited by Emer Nolan. Dublin: Field Day, 2008.

Mornin, Daniel. *All Our Fault*. London: Hutchinson, 1991.

Morris. J. A. "Elizabeth Bowen's Stories of Suspense". In *Twentieth-Century Suspense*, edited by Clive Bloom, 114–129. London: Palgrave Macmillan, 1990.

Morrison, Danny. *The Wrong Man*. Cork: Mercier Press, 1997. Kindle chap. 12, accessed 2 December 2019.

_____. *West Belfast*. Dingle: Mercier Press, 1989.

Morrison, John. *The Ulster Cover-Up*. Lurgan, Co. Armagh: Ulster Society, 1993.

Morrow, John. *The Confessions of Proinsias O'Toole* (Belfast: The Blackstaff Press, 1977).

Moseley, C. W. R. D. "Richard Head's *The English Rogue*: A Modern Mandeville?". In *The Yearbook of English Studies*, 102–107. Modern Humanities Research Association, 1971.

Moyes, Patricia. *Angel Death*. New York: Holt, Rinehart & Winston, 1980.

_____. *Black Girl, White Girl*. London: Diamond, 1989.

_____. *Black Widower*. New York: Holt, Rinehart & Winston, 1975.

_____. *The Curious Affaiur of the Third Dog*. New York: Holt, Rinehart & Winston, 1973.

_____. *Dead Men Don't Ski*. New York: Henry Holt, 1959.

_____. *Death and the Dutch Uncle*. New York: Holt, Rinehart & Winston, 1968.

_____. *Death on the Agenda*. New York: Henry Holt, 1962.

_____. *Falling Star*. New York: Henry Holt, 1964.

_____. *Helter Skelter*. London: Macdonald, 1968.

_____. *Johnny Under Ground*. London: Chivers Black Dagger Crime, 1965.

_____. *Many Deadly Returns*. New York: Holt, Rinehart & Winston, 1970.

_____. *Murder à la Mode*. New York: Henry Holt, 1963.

_____. *Murder Fantastical*. New York: Holt, Rinehart & Winston, 1967.

_____. *Night Ferry to Death*. London: Diamond, 1985.

_____. *Season of Snows and Sins*. New York: Holt, Rinehart & Winston, 1971.

_____. *A Six-Letter Word for Death*. New York: Holt, Rinehart & Winston, 1983.

_____. *The Sunken Sailor*. New York: Holt, Rinehart & Winston, 1961.

_____. *To Kill a Coconut*. New York: Holt, Rinehart & Winston, 1977.

_____. *Twice in a Blue Moon*. New York: Henry Holt, 1993.

_____. *Who is Simon Warwick?* New York: Holt, Rinehart & Winston, 1978.

Murphy, James H. *Irish Novelists and the Victorian Age*. Oxford: Oxford University Press, 2011.

Murphy, James. *Luke Talbot, or the Cliffs of the Mullawn-Mor*. Dublin: Sealy, Bryers & Walker, 1890.

_____. "Novelists, Publishers, and Readers, 1830–91". In *The Oxford History of the Irish Book. Volume 4. The Irish Book in English 1800–1891*, edited by James H. Murphy, 411–419. Oxford: Oxford University Press, 2011.

_____. *The Oxford History of the Irish Book. Volume IV: The Irish Book in English 1800–1891*. Oxford: Oxford University Press, 2011.

Neuberg, Victor E. *Popular Literature: A History and Guide*. Harmondsworth: Penguin, 1977.

Nic Íomhair, Caitlín. "'A land of shame, a land of murder and a land of strange, sacrificial women': Representations of Wealth, Gender and Race in Modern Irish Language Crime Fiction". In *Guilt Rules All: Mystery, Detective, and Crime Fiction*, edited by Brian Cliff & Elizabeth Mannion, 55–71 Syracuse, NY: Syracuse University Press, 2020.

Ó Báille, Ruaidhrí. *Dúnmharú ar an Dart*. Inverin, Co. Galway: Cló Iar-Chonnachta, 1989.

O'Brien, Flann. *The Third Policeman*. London: MacGibbon & Kee, 1967.

O'Brien, Fitz-James. *The Diamond Lens*. New York: Happy Hour Library, 1858.

O'Brien, James Howard. *Liam O'Flaherty*. Cranbury. NJ: Associate University Press, 1973.

O'Brine, Manning. *Corpse to Cairo*. London: Hammond, Hammond & Co., 1952.

_____. *Dagger before Me*. London: Hammond, Hammond & Co., 1957.

_____. *Deadly Interlude*. London: Hammond, Hammond & Co., 1954.

_____. *Dodos Don't Duck*. London: Hammond, Hammond & Co., 1953.

_____. *The Hungry Killer*. London: Hammond, Hammond & Co., 1956.

_____. *Killers Must Eat*. London: Hammond, Hammond & Co., 1951.

_____. *Mills*. London: Corgi, 1969.

_____. *Pale Moon Rising*. London: Futura, 1978.

_____. *Passport to Treason*. London: Hammond, Hammond & Co., 1955.

O'Callaghan, Gareth. *Dare to Die*. Dublin: Poolbeg, 1996.

_____. *The Keeper*. Dublin: Poolbeg, 1999.

O'Connor, Gemma. *Falls the Shadow*. Dublín: Poolbeg Press, 1996.

_____. *Farewell to the Flesh*. Dublín: Poolbeg Press, 1998.

_____. *Sins of Omission*. Dublín: Poolbeg Press, 1995.

_____. *Time to Remember*. London: Bantam, 1998.

O'Connor, Joseph. *Cowboys and Indians*. London: Flamingo, 1991.

_____. *Desperadoes*. London: Flamingo, 1994.

_____. *The Salesman*. London: Martin Secker & Warburg, 1998.

O'Duffy, Eimar. *The Bird Cage: A Mystery Novel*. New York: H. Kinsey, 1933.

_____. *Head of a Girl*. London: Geoffrey Bles, 1935.

_____. *The Secret Enemy*. London: Geoffrey Bles, 1932.

O'Flaherty, Liam. *The Assassin*. Dublin: Wolfhound Press, 1928.

_____. *The Black Soul*. London: Bloomsbury, 1924.

_____. *The House of Gold*. New York: Harcourt, Brace & Company, 1929.

_____. *The Informer*. San Diego: Harcourt, Brace & Company, 1925.

_____. *Mr. Gilhooley*. Dublin: Wolfhound Press, 1926.

_____. *The Puritan*. Dublin: Wolfhound Press, 1932.

_____. *Shame the Devil*. Dublin: Wolfhound Press, 1934.

O'Faoláin, Seán. "Give Us Back Bill Sikes". *The Spectator*, 15 February 1935.

O'Farrel, Padraic. *The Burning of Brinsley MacNamara*. Dublin: The Lilliput Press, 2013.

O'Keefe, Patrick. "Fidelma of Cashel and the Brehon Code". In *The Sister Fidelma Mysteries: Essays on the Historical Novels of Peter Tremayne*, edsited by Edward J. Rielly and David Robert Wooten, 80–87. Jefferson, NC: McFarland & Company, 2012.

O'Leary, Philip. *Gaelic Prose in the Irish Free State: 1922–1939*. University Park, PA: Penn State University Press, 1994.

O'Mahony, T. P. The Vatican Caper. Dublin: Ward River, 1981.

O'Meara, Kathleen. *The Bells of Sanctuary*. London: Burns & Oates, 1879.

_____. *Narka: A Novel*. London: R. Bentley & Sons, 1888.

O'Neill, Desmond. *Life Has No Price*. London: Victor Gollancz, 1959.

O'Neill, J. M. *Bennett and Company*. Dingle: Mount Eagle, 1998.

_____. *Canon Bang Bang*. London: Hodder & Stoughton, 1989.

_____. *Commissar Connell*. London: Hamish Hamilton, 1992.

_____. *Duffy is Dead*. London: Heinemann, 1987.

_____. *Open Cut*. London: Heinemann, 1986.

_____. *Rellighan, Undertaker*. Dingle: Brandon, 1989.

O'Reilly, Victor. *The Devil's Footprint*. New York: G. P. Putnam, 1997.

_____. *Games of the Hangman*. New York: Berkley, 1991.

_____. *Games of Vengeance [aka Rules of the Hunt]*. London: Headline, 1994.

O'Riordan, Kate. *Involved*. London: Flamingo, 1995.

O'Sullivan, J. B. *Backlash*. London: Ward, Lock & Co., 1960.

_____. *The Case of the Three Black Crows*. Dublin: Dublin Catholic Truth Society, 1945.

_____. *Casket of Death*. Dublin: Pillar, 1946.

_____. *The Castle of Death*. Dublin: Grafton, 1945.

_____. *Cherry in the Wineglass*. Dublin: Grafton, 1945.

_____. *Choke Chain*. London: Ward, Lock & Co., 1958.

_____. *Cold Chisel*. London: Ward, Lock & Co., 1960.

_____. *The Death Card*. Dublin: Pillar, 1945.

_____. *Death on Ice*. Dublin: Pillar, 1946.

_____. *The Death Seat*. London: Ward, Lock & Co., 1957.

_____. *Death Stalks the Stadium*. Dublin: Pillar, 1946.

_____. *Disordered Death*. London: Ward, Lock & Co., 1957.

_____. *Don't Hang Me Too High*. New York: Pocket Books, 1954.

_____. *Double Negative*. London: Ward, Lock & Co., 1962.

_____. *Gate Fever*. London: Ward, Lock & Co., 1959.

_____. *Guilt Edged*. London: Ward, Lock & Co., 1959.

_____. *Hue and Cry*. London: Ward, Lock & Co., 1961.

_____. *I Die Possessed*. London: Panther, 1952.

_____. *It Could Happen to You*. Dublin: Pillar, 1946.

_____. *The Long Spoon*. London: Ward, Lock & Co., 1956.

_____. *Lunge Wire*. London: Ward, Lock & Co., 1965.

_____. *Make My Coffin Big*. London: Ward, Lock & Co., 1964.

_____. *Murder Proof*. London: Ward, Lock & Co., 1968.

_____. *Nerve-Beat*. London: Werner Laurie, 1953.

_____. *Pick-Up*. London: Ward, Lock & Co., 1964.

_____. *Raid*. London: Ward, Lock & Co., 1958.

_____. *Someone Walked over My Grave*. London: Werner Laurie, 1954.

_____. *The Stuffed Man*. London: Werner Laurie, 1955.

_____. *There is One S.O.S.* London: Ward, Lock & Co., 1961.

O'Toole. Tina. "Empire Girls". *The Irish New Woman*, 43–66. London: Palgrave Macmillan, 2013.

Orr, Leah. "From Pícaro to Pirate: Afterlives of the Picaresque in Early Eighteenth-Century Fiction". In *The Afterlives of Eighteenth-Century Fiction*, edited by Daniel Cook and Nicholas Seager, 72–89. Cambridge: Cambridge University Press, 2015.

_____. "The English Rogue: Afterlives and Imitations, 1665–1741". *Journal for Eighteenth-Century Studies* 38, no. 3 (2015): 361–376.

Panek, LeRoy Lad. *After Sherlock Holmes: The Evolution of British and American Detective Stories 1891–1914*. Jefferson, NC: McFarland & Company, 2014.

_____. *Before Sherlock Holmes: How Magazines and Newspapers Invented the Detective Story*. Jefferson, NC: McFarland & Company, 2011.

_____. *An Introduction to the Detective Story*. Bowling Green, OH: Bowling Green State University Popular Press, 1987.

_____. *The Special Branch: The British Spy Novel, 1890–1980*. Bowling Green, OH: Bowling Green State University Popular Press, 1981.

Park, David. *The Healing*. London: Jonathan Cape, 1992.

_____. *Oranges from Spain*. London: Jonathan Cape, 1990.

_____. *Stone Kingdoms*. London: Phoenix House, 1996.

_____. *The Rye Man*. London: Jonathan Cape, 1994.

Parsons, Julie. *The Courtship Gift*. London: Pan Books, 1999.

_____. *Mary, Mary*. London: Pan Books, 1998.

Patterson, Glenn. *Black Night at Big Thunder Mountain*. London: Chatto & Windus, 1995.

_____. *Burning Your Own*. London: Chatto & Windus, 1995.

_____. *Fat Lad*. London: Chatto & Windus, 1992.

_____. *The International*. London: Anchor, 1999.

Penzoldt, Peter. "The Supernatural in Fiction". In *Reflections in a Glass Darkly: Essays on J. Sheridan Le Fanu*, edited by Gary William Crawford and Brian J. Showers, 108–126. New York: Hippocampus Press, 2011.

Pepper, Andrew. "The 'Hard-boiled' Genre". In *A Companion to Crime Fiction*, edited by Charles J. Rzepka and Lee Horsley, 140–151. Oxford: Wiley-Blackwell, 2010.

Petit, Chris. *The Psalm Killer*. London: Pan Books, 1996.

Phelan, Tom. *In the Season of the Daisies*. Dublin: The Lilliput Press, 1993.

_____. *Iscariot*. Dingle: Brandon, 1998.

Pick, J. B. *Neil M. Gunn*. Travistock: Northcote House, 2004.

Pim, Sheila. *A Brush with Death*. Boulder and Lyons: Rue Morgue Press, 1950.

_____. *Common or Garden Crime*. Boulder and Lyons: Rue Morgue Press, 1945.

_____. *Creeping Venom*. Boulder and Lyons: Rue Morgue Press, 1946.

_____. *A Hive of Suspects*. Boulder and Lyons: Rue Morgue Press, 1952.

Pittard, Christopher. "From Sensation to the *Strand*". In *A Companion to Crime Fiction*, edited by Charles J. Rzepka and Lee Horsley, 105–116. London: Palgrave Macmillan, 2011.

Power, M. S. *Bridie and the Silver Lady*. London: William Heinemann, 1988.

_____. *Come the Executioner*. London: Hamish Hamilton, 1991.

_____. *Crucible of Fools*. London: Hamish Hamilton, 1990.

_____. *The Crucifixion of Septimus Roach*. London: Bloomsbury, 1989.

_____. *A Darkness in the Eye*. London: William Heinemann, 1987.

_____. *Dealing with Kranze*. Edinburgh: Mainstream, 1996.

_____. *Hunt for the Autumn Clowns*. London: Chatto & Windus, 1984.

_____. *The Killing of Yesterday's Children*. London: Chatto & Windus, 1985.

_____. *Lonely the Man without Heroes*. London: William Heinemann, 1986.

_____. *Nathan Crosby's Fan*. London: Victor Gollancz, 1999.

_____. *A Sheltering Silence*. Edinburgh: Mainstream, 1994.

_____. *The Stalker's Apprentice*. Edinburgh: Mainstream, 1993.

_____. *Vengeance*. Edinburgh: Canongate, 2002.

Power, Victor. "The Room of the Murder". *Ireland's Own* 1, no. 10 (1902).

Price, Richard. *Neil M. Gunn: The Fabulous Matter of Fact*. Edinburgh: Edinburgh University Press, 1991.

Priestman, Martin (ed.). *The Cambridge Companion to Crime Fiction*. Cambridge: Cambridge University Press, 2003.

Pritchett, V. S. "An Irish Ghost". In *Reflections in a Glass Darkly: Essays on J. Sheridan Le Fanu*, edited by Gary William Crawford and Brian J. Showers, 127–131. New York: Hippocampus Press, 2011.

Pykett, Lyn. "The Newgate Novel and Sensation Fiction, 1830–1868". In *The Cambridge Companion to Crime Fiction*, edited by Martin Priestman, 19–39. Cambridge: Cambridge University Press, 2003.

Quigley, Patrick. *Borderland*. Dingle: Brandon, 1994.

Rankin, Deana. "Kinds of Irishness: Henry Burnell and Richard Head". In *A Companion to Irish Literature*, edited by Julia Wright, 108–124. Chichester: Wiley-Blackwell, 2010.

Redmond, Liam. *Death is So Kind*. New York: Devlin-Adair, 1959.

Reimer, Eric. "Ulsterisation and the Troubles thriller: Eoin McNamee's *Resurrection Man*". *Irish Studies Review* 20, no. 1 (2012): 65–76.

Rickard, Victor. *The Dark Stranger*. London: Hodder & Stoughton, 1930.

_____. *The Empty Villa*. London: Hodder & Stoughton, 1929.

_____. *A Fool's Errand*. London: Hodder & Stoughton, 1921.

_____. *George Geith of Fen Court*. London: Tinsley Brothers, 1864.

_____. *Murder by Night*. London: Jarrolds, 1936.

_____. *The Mystery of Vincent Dane*. London: Hodder & Stoughton, 1930.

_____. *Not Sufficient Evidence*. London: Constable, 1926.

_____. *Upstairs*. London: Constable, 1925.

Riddell, Charlotte. *George Geith of Fen Court*. London: Tinsley Brothers, 1864.

Rielly, Edward J. "Interview with Peter Tremayne". In *The Sister Fidelma Mysteries: Essays on the Historical Novels of Peter Tremayne*, edited by Edward J. Rielly and David Robert Wooten, 208–219. Jefferson, NC: McFarland & Company, 2012.

_____. "Sister Fidelma: A Woman for All Seasons". In *The Sister Fidelma Mysteries: Essays on the Historical Novels of Peter Tremayne*, edited by Edward J. Rielly and David Robert Wooten, 5–19. Jefferson, NC: McFarland & Company, 2012.

Rolston, Bill. "Mothers, Whores and Villains: Images of Women in Novels of the Northern Ireland Conflict". *Race and Class* 31, no. 1 (1989): 41–57.

Ross, Ian Campbell. "Introduction". In *Down These Green Streets: Irish Crime Writing in the Twenty-First Century*, edited by Declan Burke, 14–35. Dublin: Liberties Press, 2011.

_____. "Irish Crime Fiction". In *The Oxford Handbook of Modern Irish Fiction*, edited by Liam Harte, 353–369. Oxford: Oxford University Press, 2020.

_____. "An Irish Picaresque Novel: William Chaigneau's *The History of Jack Connor*". *Studies: An Irish Quarterly Review* 71, no. 283 (1982): 270–279.

Rowland, Susan. "The 'Classical' Model of the Golden Age". In *A Companion to Crime Fiction*, edited by Charles J. Rzepka and Lee Horsey, 117–127. London: Wiley and Blackwell, 2010.

_____. *From Agatha Christie to Ruth Rendell: British Women Writers in Detective and Crime Fiction*. New York: Palgrave Macmillan, 2004.

Rudman, Thomas. "'The Place You Don't Belong': Border-Crossings and Ambivalence in the Northern Irish Noir Thriller". In *Border Crossings: Nation and Imagination*, edited by Colin Younger, 249–269. Newcastle: Cambridge Scholars Publishing, 2013.

Russell, M. (as MR), "Sketches in Irish Biography. The Late Richard Dowling, the Novelist". *The Irish Monthly* 27, no. 30 (January 1899), 13.

Ryder, Chris. *The RUC: A Force Under Fire*. London: Mandarin. Rev. edn. 1997.

Sage, Victor. "Irish Gothic: C. R. Maturin and J. S. Le Fanu". In *A Companion to the Gothic*, edited by David Punter, 81–93. Oxford: Blackwell, 2000.

Sayers, Dorothy L. "The Omnibus of Crime". In *Detective Fiction: A Collection of Critical Essays. Twentieth Century Views*, edited by Robin W. Winks, 53–83. Englewood Cliffs, NJ: Prentice-Hall, 1980.

Scaggs, John. *Crime Fiction*. London: Routledge, 2005.

Schwerter, Stephanie. "Peacefire: Belfast between Reality and Fiction". *The Canadian Journal of Irish Studies* 33, no. 2 (2007): 19–27.

Seed, David. "The Adventure of Spying: Erskine Childer's *The Riddle of the Sands*". In *Spy Thrillers*, edited by Clive Bloom, 28–43. London: Macmillan, 1990.

_____. "Crime and the Spy Genre". In *A Companion to Crime Fiction*, edited by Charles J. Rzepka and Lee Horsley, 233–244. Oxford: Wiley-Blackwell, 2010.

Shan, Darren. *Ayuamarca [Procession of the Dead. The City: Book One]*. London: Harper Voyager, 1999.

_____. *Hell's Horizon. [The City: Book Two]*. London: Millennium, 2000.

Shea, Thomas F. "Patrick McGinley's Appropriation of Cúchulainn: Revisions in *The Trick of the Ga Bolga*". *New Hibernia Review/ Iris Éireannach Nua* 5, no. 3 (2001): 114–127.

Shelley, Mike. *The Last Private Eye in Belfast*. Belfast: Domino, 1984.

_____. *Madame Edie's Chamber of Horrors*. Belfast: Domino, 1984.

_____. *The Terror of Her Ways*. Belfast: Domino, 1984.

Shiel, M. P. *The Pale Ape and Other Pulses*. London: Werner Laurie, 1911.

Shriver, Lionel. *Ordinary Decent Criminals*. London: HarperCollins, 1889.

Simpson, Howard R. *Cogan's Case*. Dunlaoghaire: Glendale, 1992.

Smajic, Srdjan. *Ghost-Seers, Detectives and Spiritualists: Theories of Vision in Victorian Literature and Science*. Cambridge: Cambridge University Press, 2010.

Smyth, Gerry. *The Novel and the Nation: Studies in New Irish Fiction*. London: Pluto Press, 1999.

Smyth, Seamus *Quinn*. London: Hodder & Stoughton, 1999.

Somerville & Ross. *Further Experiences of an Irish RM*. London: Longmans, Green & Co., 1908.

_____. *In Mr Knox's Country*. London: Longmans, Green & Co., 1915.

_____. *An Irish Cousin*. London: R. Bentley & Sons, 1889.

_____. *Naboth's Vineyard*. London: Spencer Blackett, 1891.

_____. *Some Experiences of an Irish RM*. London: Longmans, Green & Co., 1899.

Spooner, Catherine. "Crime and the Gothic". In *A Companion to Crime Fiction*, edited by Charles J. Rzepka and Lee Horsley, 245–257. Chichester: Wiley-Blackwell, 2019.

Stanford, Peter. *C. Day-Lewis: A Life*. London: Continuum, 2007.

Stewart, Victoria. *Crime Writing in Interwar Britain*. Cambridge: Cambridge University Press, 2017.

Stoker, Bram. *Dracula*. London: A. Constable, 1897.

_____. *Dracula's Guest and Other Weird Stories*. London: George Routledge, 1914.

_____. *The Jewel of Seven Stars*. London: Heinemann, 1909.

_____. *The Lair of the White Worm*. London: Rider & Son, 1911.

_____. *Miss Betty*. London: C. Arthur Peterson, 1898.

_____. *The Mystery of the Sea*. London: Heinemann, 1902.

_____. *The Primrose Path*. Dublin: The Shamrock, 1875.

_____. *The Shoulder of Shasta*. London: A. Constable, 1895.

_____. *The Snake's Pass*. London: Sampson, Low, Marston, Searle & Rivingston, 1880.

_____. *The Watter's Mou*. London: A. Constable, 1895.

Strong, L. A. G. *All Fall Down*. New York: Doubleday, Doran & Company, 1944.

_____. *Deliverance*. London: Methuen, 1955.

_____. *The Garden*. London: Gollancz, 1932.

_____. *Murder Plays an Ugly Scene*. Garden City, NJ: Country Life Press, 1945.

_____. *Odd Man In*. London: Pitman, 1938.

_____. *Othello's Occupation*. London: Collins, 1945.

_____. *Slocombe Dies*. London: Collins, 1942.

_____. *Treason in the Egg*. London: Collins, 1958.

_____. *Which I Never*. New York: Macmillan, 1952.

Stuart, Francis. *A Hole in the Head*. New York: Longship Press, 1977.

Symons, Julian. *Bloody Murder: From the Detective Story to the Crime Novel*. 2nd edn. Harmondsworth: Penguin, 1985.

Talairach-Vielmas, Laurence. "Sensation Fiction and the Gothic". In *The Cambridge Companion to Sensation Fiction*, edited by Andrew Mangham, 21–33. Cambridge: Cambridge University Press, 2013.

Taylor, Brian. *The Life and Writings of James Owen Hanny (George A. Birmingham) 1865–1950*. Lewiston: The Edwin Mellen Press, 1995.

Thompson, Neville. *Have Ye No Homes to Go To?* Dublin: Poolbeg, 1999.

———. *Jackie Loves Johnser OK?* Dublin: Poolbeg, 1997.

———. *Two Birds/ One Stoned* Dublin: Poolbeg, 1999.

Tremayne, Peter. *Absolution by Murder*. London: Headline, 1994.

———. *Act of Mercy*. London: Headline, 1999.

———. *Hemlock at Vespers*. London: Headline, 2000.

———. *Our Lady of Darkness*. London: Headline, 2000.

———. *The Monk Who Vanished*. London: Headline, 1999.

———. *Shroud for the Archbishop*. London: Headline, 1995.

———. *The Spider's Web*. London: Headline, 1997.

———. *The Subtle Serpent*. London: Headline, 1996.

———. *Suffer Little Children*. London: Headline, 1995.

Vickers, Anita M. "Druids and Brehons: Fidelma and the Druidic Tradition". In *The Sister Fidelma Mysteries: Essays on the Historical Novels of Peter Tremayne*, edsted by Edward J. Rielly and David Robert Wooten, 98–107. Jefferson, NC: McFarland & Company, 2012.

Walsh, Dermot P. J. "Police Cooperation Across the Irish Border: Familiarity Breeding Contempt for Transparency and Accountability". *Journal of Law and Society* 38, no. 2 (2011): 301–330.

Walsh, Maurice. *Danger under the Moon*. Edinburgh: Chambers, 1956.

———. *The Hill is Mine*. Edinburgh: Chambers, 1940.

———. *The Man in Brown*. Edinburgh: Chambers, 1945.

———. *The Road to Nowhere*. Edinburgh: Chambers, 1934.

———. *Sour*. Dublin: Pillar International, 2015.

———. *The Spanish Lady*. Edinburgh: Chambers, 1943.

Welcome, John. *Bellary Bay*. London: Hamish Hamilton, 1979.

———. *A Call to Arms*. London: Hamish Hamilton, 1985.

———. *Go for Broke*. New York: Harper & Row, 1972.

———. *Grand National*. London: Hamish Hamilton, 1976.

———. *Hard to Handle*. London: Faber & Faber, 1964.

———. *Hell Is Where You Find It*. London: Faber & Faber, 1968.

———. *On the Stretch*. London: Faber & Faber, 1969.

———. *A Painted Devil*. London: Collins, 1988.

———. *Reasons of Hate*. London: Collins, 1990.

———. *Red Coats Galloping*. London: Constable, 1949.

———. *Royal Stakes*. London: Sinclair Stevenson, 1993.

———. *Run for Cover*. New York: Harper & Row, 1958.

———. *Stop at Nothing*. New York: Harper & Row, 1959.

———. *Wanted for Killing*. London: Faber & Faber, 1965.

White, Barbara. "'The Inferior Sort of the Kingdom of Ireland': Irishmen and Tyburn Tree". *Irish Studies Review* 6, no. 1 (1998): 17–26.

White, Terence De Vere. *The Distance and the Dark*. London: Victor Gollancz, 1973.

Wibberley, Leonard. *Beware of the Mouse*. New York: Van Rees, 1958.

_____. *The Mouse on the Moon*. New York: William Morrow, 1962.

_____. *The Mouse on Wall Street*. New York: William Morrow, 1969.

_____. *The Mouse that Roared*. New York: Four Walls Eight Windows, 1955.

_____. *The Mouse that Saved the West*. New York: William Morrow, 1981.

Wilde, Oscar. *Lord Arthur Saville's Crime and Other Stories*. London: James R. Osgood, McIlvaine & Co., 1891.

_____. *The Picture of Dorian Gray*. London: Ward, Lock & Co., 1891.

Wilson, Robert McLiam. *Eureka Street*. London: Secker & Warburg, 1996.

_____. *Ripley Bogle*. London: André Deutsch, 1989.

Winstanley, William. *The Lives of the Most Famous English Poets*. London: H. Clark for Samuel Manship, 1687.

Winton, Calhoun. "Richard Head and the Origins of the Picaresque in England". In *The Picaresque: A Symposium on the Rogue's Tale*, edited by Carmen Benito-Vessels and Michael O. Zappala, 79–98. Newark, NJ: University of Delaware Press, 1990.

Wolle, Francis. *Fitz-James O'Brien: A Literary Bohemian of the Eighteen-Fifties*. Boulder, CO: University of Colorado Press, 1944.

Woolf, Michael. "Ian Fleming's Enigmas and Variations". In *Spy Thrillers: From Buchan to Le Carré*, edited by Clive Bloom, 86–99. London: Macmillan, 1990.

Worthington, Heather. *Key Concepts in Crime Fiction*. London: Palgrave Macmillan, 2011.

_____. *The Rise of the Detective in Early Nineteenth-Century Popular Fiction*. London: Palgrave Macmillan, 2005.

## Online Bibliography

"A Sorrowful Lamentation on the Execution of Patrick Power who Suffered at the Front of Wexford Jail on the 4th of April for the Unnatural Murder of his Father", Broadside BPP 1001-273, <https://rbsc-prod.library.nd.edu/collecti ons/ead_xml/images/BPP_1001/BPP_1001-273.jpg>, accessed 23 March 2018.

"A Sorrowful Lamentation on the Hollywood Tragedy where Two Sisters Have Been Brutally Murdered", Broadside BPP 1001-274, <https://rbsc-prod.libr

ary.nd.edu/collections/ead_xml/images/BPP_1001/BPP_1001-274.jpg>, accessed 23 March 2018.

"About Ireland's Own". *Ireland's Own*, <https://www.irelandsown.ie/about/>, accessed 18 September 2016.

"Dan Kavanagh". 18 October 2016, <http://www.dankavanagh.com/>, accessed accessed 30 January 2017.

"John Connolly – On His Influences, Self-Doubt and The Future Life of Charlie
Parker", *Material Witness*, 7 June 2014, <https://materialwitness.typepad.
com/material_witness/2014/06/interview-john-connolly-on-his-influences-
self-doubt-and-the-future-life-of-charlie-parker-.html>, accessed 7 June 2014.

"The Sorrowful Lamentation of Andrew Carr Who was Executed on the 28 of July
at Richmond Jail for the Murder of Margret Murphy", Broadside BPP 1001-
272 c1, c2, c3, <https://rbsc-prod.library.nd.edu/collections/ead_xml/images/
BPP_1001/BPP_1001-272-c1.jpg>, accessed

Fowler, Cristopher. "Forgotten Authors No. 28: Matthew Phipps Shiel". *Independent*,
22 March 2009, <http://www.independent.co.uk/arts-entertainment/books/
features/forgotten-authors-no28-matthew-phipps-shiel-1648079.html>,
accessedaccessed 6 March 2013.

Hedges, John. "Danny Morrison's West Belfast, A Story of a Community in Struggle".
*An Phoblacht*, 1 June 2015, <https://www.anphoblacht.com/contents/25032>,
accessed 3 January 2019.

Mitchell, Sandy. "Children's Reading and the Culture of Girlhood: The Case of L.
T. Meade". *Victorian Popular Culture* 17 (1989): 53–63. *JSTOR*, <https://www.
jstor.org/stable/25057845>, accessed 19 May 2022.

Morrison, Danny. "Through RUC Eyes", <https://www.dannymorrison.com/thro
ugh-ruc-eyes/>, accessed 3 January 2019.

Nash, Walter. "Father Bosco to Africa". *London Review of Books* 9, no. 3 (1987),
<https://www.lrb.co.uk/the-paper/v09/n03/walter-nash/father-bosco-to-afr
ica>, accessed 19 May 2022.

Roy, David. "Author Patrick McGinley on 'concoction on filth' that Disgusted
Donegal". *The Irish News*, 27 July 2017, <https://www.irishnews.com/arts/
2017/07/27/news/back-to-the-bog-patrick-mcginley-on-the-new-edition-of-
his-debut-novel-bogmail-1092825/>, accessed 21 Novemberr 2015.

Simmons, William P. "The Pale Ape and Other Pulses by MP Shiel". *Infinity
Plus*, <http://www.independent.co.uk/arts-entertainment/books/features/
forgotten-authors-no28-matthew-phipps-shiel-1648079.html>, accessed 6
March 2013.

Thompson, Sam. "Lyra and I compared notes about our books. I lived
to see my title in print, she did not". *Irish Times*, 14 May 2019,
<https://www.irishtimes.com/culture/books/lyra-and-i-compa

red-notes-about-our-books-i-lived-to-see-my-title-in-print-she-did-not-1.3891
068>, accessed 4 July 2019.

# Index

# Reimagining Ireland

Series Editor: Dr Eamon Maher, Technological
University Dublin

The concepts of Ireland and 'Irishness' are in constant flux in the wake of an ever-increasing reappraisal of the notion of cultural and national specificity in a world assailed from all angles by the forces of globalisation and uniformity. Reimagining Ireland interrogates Ireland's past and present and suggests possibilities for the future by looking at Ireland's literature, culture and history and subjecting them to the most up-to-date critical appraisals associated with sociology, literary theory, historiography, political science and theology.

Some of the pertinent issues include, but are not confined to, Irish writing in English and Irish, Nationalism, Unionism, the Northern 'Troubles', the Peace Process, economic development in Ireland, the impact and decline of the Celtic Tiger, Irish spirituality, the rise and fall of organised religion, the visual arts, popular cultures, sport, Irish music and dance, emigration and the Irish diaspora, immigration and multiculturalism, marginalisation, globalisation, modernity/postmodernity and postcolonialism. The series publishes monographs, comparative studies, interdisciplinary projects, conference proceedings and edited books. Proposals should be sent either to Dr Eamon Maher at eamon.maher@ittdublin.ie or to ireland@peterlang.com.

www.ingramcontent.com/pod-product-compliance
Lightning Source LLC
Chambersburg PA
CBHW070930100726
47908CB00001B/160